Modern Warfare

From 1939 to the present day.

Modern Warfare

From 1939 to the present day.

Ashley Brown
With a foreword by Lord Chalfont

CRESCENT BOOKS

New York

Acknowledgments
The following extracts from previously published material are used
by permission:

'The Blitz', page 29 – from *Looking for Trouble* by Virginia Cowles,
Hamish Hamilton, 1941

'Destruction from the Sky', page 64 – United States Naval Institute,
1955

'The Battle for Jerusalem', page 253 – from *The Seventh Day* by
Henry Near, André Deutsch, 1970

'Bomb Alley', page 280 – from *I Counted Them All Out and I Counted
Them All Back* by Brian Hanrahan, BBC Publications, 1982

Maps and diagrams by Swanston Graphics, Gordon Beckett and
Paul Bryant

Photographs are used by kind permission of the following:
APN, Agence France Presse, Associated Press, BBC Hulton Picture
Library, Bibliotheque Nationale, Bibliothek fur Zeitgeschichte, Black
Star, Boeing, Bundesarchiv, Brigadier Calvert, Camera Press,
Central Press, Colorific!, Communist Party Library, Cubaphotos,
René Dazy, Carina Dvorak, ECPA, The Economist, Eshel Dramit,
Fairchild, Andreas Feininger/Library of Congress, Flament/Rapho,
Fox Photos, GPO, HRU, John Hillelson Agency, Hughes Aircraft
Company, Robert Hunt Library, Imperial War Museum, Irish Times,
Keystone Press Agency, Lockheed Missile, MARS, MOD, Musée de la
Guerre Vincennes, National Archives, Navy Department, Novosti,
Pacemaker, Photri, Popperfoto, Press Association, Press-Bild-
Zentrum, Rex Features, Rijksinstitut, Signal, Soldier Magazine,
Frank Spooner Pictures, P Styllis, Suddeutscher Verlag, Sunday
Times, Tallandier, Tass, The Times, John Topham Library, UPI,
US Air Force, US Army, US Coast Guard, US Marine Corps,
US National Archives, US Navy, Wiener Library.

This edition first published in Great Britain by
Orbis Publishing Limited, London 1985

1986 edition published by Crescent Books,
distributed by Crown Publishers, Inc.

Library of Congress Cataloging-in-Publication Data
Brown, Ashley.
   Modern warfare.
   Includes index.
   1. Military art and science—History—20th century.
2. Military history, Modern—20th century. I. Title.
U42.B75   1986   355′.02′0904   85-30858

h g f e d c b a

ISBN 0-517-61184-8
Printed in Yugoslavia by Mladinska knjiga

Contents

Foreword

It is often pointed out that, since 1939, there has been only one year – 1968 – in which a British serviceman was not killed in action. This reflects one of the most sombre manifestations of modern life: war. Throughout the world, a series of conflicts – some large, some small, some short-lived and some long-lasting – has replaced the general peace which was the environment of the diplomatic world in the nineteenth century. Apart from World War II itself, there have been, according to some criteria, over 400 recognizable wars since 1945. This is an age of violence and international conflict – in spite of the existence of bodies such as the United Nations whose efforts are ostensibly devoted to the maintenance of world peace.

It can, indeed, be persuasively argued that war is an ineluctable ingredient of the human condition. Force, of one kind or another, is the ultimate sanction in all human conflict, and it would be strange if this was not to apply in the field of international relations. Although much genuflexion is practised in the general direction of disarmament, world government and universal peace, it is doubtful whether any kind of ordered civilization could be maintained without the deterrent power of military force. This proposition is implicitly accepted in the Christian concept of the just war, an attempt to regulate conflict by prescribing rules as to the legitimate reasons for resort to force, and the subsequent limitation of its use. It is, therefore, unprofitable to concentrate the mind too much on the search for utopian recipes for eternal peace; much more is likely to be achieved by the attempts to establish what causes wars to start.

The causes of war are many and various: from ideological conflicts to national disputes over territory; from the nationalist aspirations of subject peoples to the personal ambitions of politicians; from racial or religious antagonism to commercial greed. The wars themselves have taken a variety of forms, from the urban terrorism of the IRA to the Arab-Israeli tank battles of the Sinai Desert; from the slow guerrilla warfare of the communists in Vietnam to the sudden conquest of a nation in a matter of days, as in the Soviet invasion of Afghanistan. This increasing complexity has been reflected in the proliferating range of weapons. On the one hand there are nuclear weapons which can destroy the whole world, and on the other, rubber bullets to keep casualties down in situations which demand the minimum use of force.

World War II was the first real example of total war. This involved not only the development of the weapons and equipment which are still in the standard inventory of conventional forces – tanks, fighters, bombers and aircraft carriers – but also the introduction of the weapons systems which came to dominate the strategic thinking of the postwar period – the rocket, the jet engine and, most important of all, the atomic bomb. Furthermore, in the widespread involvement of civilians in warfare, a development that was hinted at in 1914-18 but accepted as inevitable by all the combatant nations by 1945, World War II set the scene for the present perception of war, in which the line between civilian and soldier is always blurred and often non-existent.

The recurrent warfare of the past 45 years has seen an unprecedented development in weaponry of all kinds and the most intensive competition in arms that the world has ever seen. The two superpowers, the USA and the USSR, have built up stockpiles of ever more destructive weapons, and many of their clients and allies have followed suit. This has raised apocalyptic and often fanciful nightmares about the very survival of the human race; but it also has important ramifications in the conduct of war itself. These modern engines of war demand of the men and women who operate them greater technical skills and mental adaptability than ever before; yet the human race remains just as vulnerable, both physically and psychologically.

In 1939, when the German Army invaded Poland, most people still believed that war concerned exclusively the armed forces of nation states, armed, equipped and uniformed in easily recognizable ways, with the issue decided by the clash of armies, fleets and air forces. Nowadays, with the threat of nuclear weapons hanging over everyone, smouldering guerrilla wars affecting large areas of the world, 'conventional' warfare and international terrorism posing a new and devastating threat, the large-scale movement of armies across frontiers and the ponderous manoeuvring of corps and divisions is generally recognized as the least likely of contingencies.

In this study Ashley Brown has set out to chronicle developments in modern warfare from the point of view of a student of war born after the end of World War II. It is a formidable task, and he has undertaken it with a sober realism which provides a refreshing contrast to much of the contemporary writing on the subject, which is the literature of protest more often than of reason.

THE RT. HON.
THE LORD CHALFONT,
PC OBE MC

Part One
German Victories in Europe 1939-40

Events in the battlegrounds of Europe in 1939–40 ushered in a new era of warfare, and changed previous conceptions of what could or could not be achieved by modern armed forces. To a certain extent the victories of this period were gained as a result of the adoption of new weaponry, but at this early stage in the war even the weaponry was lightweight and primitive in comparison with that used in later years. What really made the difference was the application of new *ideas* to the modern technology, and these ideas were to define much of the warfare that followed.

This period of the war certainly had dramatic results. Nothing like it had been seen in Europe since the Napoleonic conquests of the early 19th century. On 1 September 1939,

Germany struck into Poland and, untroubled by the declaration of war by France and Great Britain on 3 September, crushed its eastern neighbour in a matter of weeks, with some assistance from the Soviet Army. Early in 1940, following the Winter War, the Soviet Union forced Finland to grant it large tracts of territory, and then, in April 1940, the Germans took over Denmark and Norway in a swift campaign.

The most momentous events were in May and June, however. For then the German armed forces invaded Holland, Belgium and France, winning a complete victory that brought all mainland western Europe, apart from Switzerland and the Iberian peninsula, under Hitler's control. Before the year was out, the scope of the fighting had extended

Below: Junkers Ju-87 Stukas set off on a sortie. In addition to the two 50kg (110lb) bombs under each wing, each aircraft was probably carrying one 500kg (1100lb) bomb beneath the fuselage. When opposed by an effective fighter force, the Stuka was vulnerable, but in the German offensive of 1939 in Poland, of 1940 in western Europe, and of 1941 in Russia, it was of central importance.

yet again, when the entry of Italy into the war as an ally of Germany led to fighting in Greece and North Africa, while sea battles raged in the Mediterranean.

In spite of the fact that these battles of the first year of the war indicated that a new age had dawned, there was little in terms of men and machinery that had changed since the bloody stalemates of World War I. The armies of the European states were still generally organized, and to a large extent armed, along the lines of the forces that had fought the gruesome battles of 1914–18. All European armies were still based upon the infantry division, for example. These divisions typically had a basis of three infantry regiments of about 3000 men each, plus supporting artillery. The German divisions were between 15,000 and 18,000 men strong with one artillery regiment; the French 17,000 strong with two artillery regiments; the British divisions had only 13,600 men, but compensated with three artillery regiments, while the Polish divisions were very poorly supplied with support weapons.

Smallarms too were relatively primitive. The average infantryman was armed with a rifle of the type used in World War I – the British Lee-Enfield, the French Lebel, the German Mauser – while immediate support weapons – heavy machine guns and mortars, regimental and divisional artillery – were also similar to those used in the earlier conflict.

THE WEAPONS REVOLUTION

Two weapons had been greatly developed since 1918, however – the tank and the aeroplane. A debate over the effectiveness of armoured vehicles had been raging for some years, and even after 1940, when the Germans had shown just how critical tanks could be in punching a hole in the enemy line and exploiting the gap, there was still argument in the British Army over their precise importance. The Germans were the only nation to maintain self-contained armoured formations in 1939. Their five Panzer divisions consisted of two motorized infantry regiments and two tank regiments, normally equipped with the PzKpfw I and PzKpfw II tanks that had only machine guns and 20mm cannon; the heavier PzKpfw III and PzKpfw IV models were just coming into service in 1939 and were far more numerous by the time of the campaigns of May 1940. Czech 38(t) models supplemented the heavier Panzers, and in practice there would be about 320 armoured vehicles per division.

Light though these tanks were compared with later monsters, their armour was proof against smallarms fire, and this was enough to give them the impetus they needed to achieve success. For the Allies were badly

provided with anti-tank weapons: the best British weapon was only a 2-pounder, and there were few enough of those. By 1944, a 17-pounder would be considered the sort of weapon needed to stop a German tank.

Perhaps most interesting about this period in warfare is that it showed just how the new ideas and approaches of men like the German tank general, Heinz Guderian, changed the conduct of war. For the weapons themselves were not the all-powerful leviathans that they were taken to be after the victory.

Above: British Vickers Mk II medium tanks on manoeuvres in the 1930s. Britain had pioneered the tank, but her armour was outclassed by that of Germany in 1940. Below: German artillery, some still horse-drawn, but with other pieces towed by motorized half-tracks.

German tanks were not much better than French or British; but they were used more effectively. It was imagination and initiative, the ability to think in a new way about how to use the materials available, that made all the difference. The military establishments of every country, including Germany, contained many who were sceptical about armoured and mechanized warfare; but when deployed effectively the tank and its supporting infantry gave the attackers a momentum and speed of reaction that could prove decisive.

DEFENSIVE OR OFFENSIVE?

In World War I, the power of the machine gun on the battlefield and the ability of a defending nation to bring up troops by rail (while the attacker was ploughing through a shattered area of countryside) had given the defensive both a tactical and strategic advantage. In 1939–40, however, under the command of men like Guderian, the tank not only gave the offensive a tactical advantage (even if it could easily be lost) but also enabled the attacker to keep on driving through to make a strategic breakthrough.

To units expecting to defend conventional front lines, such movement into rear areas was hard to deal with. The defence had to be quick to react, or flexible enough to accept such penetration and sit tight. Where the defenders did not act quickly to plug the breach (as along the Meuse River in 1940) or where they took up dispositions that were too strung out to prevent infiltration and isolation (the Italians in Egypt in 1940, for example), then the defence would be swiftly ruined, and panic could set in.

The tank was only part of the solution to the World War I stalemate, however. The other part lay in the air, in the ability of aircraft to act as the screen for the tank divisions – providing reconnaissance, close support and protection. In 1939, Germany ruled the air over Poland, and the campaigns in western Europe in the spring and early summer of 1940 were to see this superiority maintained. During the attack on the west in May 1940, the Luftwaffe deployed 3500 aircraft, compared with about 850 modern French planes, less than 60 Belgian and Dutch and only 400 British. Of this Allied total, a mere 800 were fighters capable of serious aerial combat.

In the context of this new mobile warfare, Luftwaffe superiority made two major contributions. First, there was the ability to deliver airborne troops onto key locations. In

Above: Heinz Guderian, perhaps the most important of the proponents of the new form of armoured warfare, pictured here during the advance into the Soviet Union in September 1941. Known affectionately as Schnell ('Speedy') Heinz to his troops, Guderian owed much of his influence in the pre-war period to the backing of Hitler. Important members of the high command were very suspicious of the new weapons and tactics, and without Hitler's support, it is doubtful whether the German armoured forces would have assumed the form that led to victory in 1939 and 1940.

Above: A Czech-built 38(t) tank leads an attack during the campaign in France in June 1940, while supporting infantry cautiously moves up through the cornfield. Although the 38(t) had only a 37mm gun as its main armament, it was a useful addition to the German Panzers, and the Wehrmacht was happy to take it into German service after the invasion of Czechoslovakia in 1939.

Holland, for example, the men of Major-General Karl Student's 7th Airborne Division cleared the way for the advance of the Eighteenth Army; and in Belgium the taking of the fortress of Eben Emael and the descent on the bridges across the Albert Canal were vital to the timetable of the advance.

More important, however, was the close support given to the mechanized and armoured units and the attacks on enemy communications. The Junkers Ju-87 Stuka divebomber proved deadly in its role as flying artillery, and the fighters that strafed columns of troops wreaked havoc in both Poland and France. The crucial breakthrough on the Meuse owed much to the non-stop bombing of French positions by Stukas on 10 May in support of the small bridgehead established by General Erwin Rommel's 7th Panzer Division; and French morale all over northern France was severely affected by the constant strafing behind the lines. In addition, the railway network in northeast France was made practically unusable by concerted aerial attacks from 12–17 May.

So the tank gave an army manoeuvrability on the battlefield and the possibility of strategic exploitation of a breakthrough, while the air force gave this breakthrough mobile and devastating support. But above all, the new weapons needed new direction to make them effective. They needed to be manned by alert, confident troops, and to be under the control of commanders who could seize the fleeting opportunities they would be offered, in the full knowledge of what their men and machines could or could not do. In this the German Army was very lucky: men like Heinz Guderian, Hermann Hoth, Erwin Rommel and Karl Student had a feel for the new form of warfare that was to cost the Allies dear.

It is perhaps somewhat ironic that a Frenchman, Captain Philippe de Hautecloque, who fought in the Western Desert under the alias Captain Leclerc, should come up with a perfect description of how to direct the new mobile warfare: 'Wherever possible, attack from an unexpected direction and at an unexpected time. The commander should be well to the fore in order to make prompt decisions. Manoeuvre in wide, sweeping outflanking movements. The battle should be brief, and if not decisive at one point, switched to another.' It was these tactics that were to inflict on France her greatest military humiliation, and lay at the core of the new warfare that came to be known by the description the Germans gave it: Lightning War, or Blitzkrieg.

THE POLISH CAMPAIGN

The first fighting of World War II took place when German troops crossed the Polish border on 1 September 1939, at 0445 hours, when there was still early morning mist along much of the front. The German campaign set the scene for the new era of warfare and introduced the world to a form of combat based on tanks and close air support that was to dominate the battlefield for the rest of the war.

The Germans committed 55 divisions to the initial invasion, although there were 63 involved in the final battles of the campaign. These forces were divided into two Army Groups. In the south, attacking from Silesia and Slovakia, was Army Group South commanded by Colonel-General Gerd von Rundstedt. This consisted of the Eighth Army (four infantry divisions and the SS motorized regiment 'Leibstandarte Adolf Hitler'), the Tenth Army (six infantry divisions, two motorized divisions, three light divisions and two Panzer divisions) and the Fourteenth Army (six infantry divisions, one mountain division, one light division, two Panzer divisions and the SS motorized regiment 'Germania'). The Tenth Army in the centre was to drive straight for Warsaw, while the Eighth Army pushed through to Łódź and the Fourteenth Army occupied enemy units around Kraków and Przemyśl.

In the north, based on either side of the 'Danzig corridor' was Army Group North. Commanded by Colonel-General Fedor von Bock, this was divided into two armies. The Third Army, in East Prussia, comprised eight infantry divisions and its main task was to attack Polish forces in the Danzig corridor before moving south towards the Vistula River. In the area west of the corridor, the Fourth Army, with six infantry divisions, two motorized divisions, and one Panzer division was to concentrate on the destruction of Polish forces in the corridor.

The German plans were quite plain – the directive to the army described how the intention was 'to disrupt, by a rapid invasion of Polish territory, the mobilization and concentration of the Polish Army, and to destroy the bulk of troops stationed to the west of the Vistula–Narew line by converging attacks from Silesia, Pomerania and East Prussia'.

To resist this, the Poles had, it is true, a large army – about 1,500,000 men including reserves – and had been given sound advice by their French allies on the best way of maintaining a defensive struggle; while the members of the Polish high command could have predicted where the German blow would fall. But their mobilization was late: by the time the attack went in, the front was still held by only 17 infantry divisions, three infantry brigades and six cavalry brigades. Thirteen divisions were still moving up to their concentration areas, while nine were in barracks, nearing the completion of their formation.

The Poles also manifested grave weaknesses in the organization and equipment of their forces. At the very highest level, there was a very poorly coordinated command structure between commander-in-chief

Above: A German PzKpfw IV, armed with a 75mm low-velocity gun. This was the only German tank to stay in continuous production throughout World War II. Below: Soldiers move into Danzig, covered by an armoured car. These men are members of a paramilitary unit, the SS-Heimwehr Danzig.

*Below and bottom:
Contrasting headgear
and contrasting
approaches to war. The
German tank crew in
their tankers' berets are
mounted on one of the
few PzKpfw IV tanks
to see service in
Poland. Armed with a
short-barrelled 75mm
gun, the PzKpfw IV
outclassed all Polish
armour. At the bottom
is the band of the 7th
Lubelski Lancers
wearing characteristic
Polish headgear, the
square-topped czapka.
Polish cavalry
formations had
prepared themselves as
well as they could for
modern warfare, but
their country's entire
military machine was
outdated. Bottom right:
German infantry
practising mortar drill.*

Edward Rydz-Smigly and his eight army commanders, while the fact that Poland placed so much reliance on its 11 autonomous cavalry brigades was a sign of backwardness in a war that would be won by armoured forces and aircraft – although it must be said that the cavalry were never intended for large-scale charges against machine guns and tanks and they acquitted themselves well in an almost impossible situation.

The main Polish weakness lay, however, not in the shortcomings of their armed forces, but in the very shape of the country. The frontiers that had to be defended against Germany were 2000km (1250 miles) long, and this did not even include the Danzig corridor, a finger of land completely indefensible against attacks from East Prussia or Pomerania. The Poles had rejected advice, strongly urged on them by the French, that any attempt to hold German forces along the existing frontiers was suicidal, and that the defences should be based along the line of the Rivers Niemen, Bobr, Narew, Vistula and San. The reason for rejecting this militarily very sound plan was that the Poles could not afford to lose the valuable industrial and

agricultural resources of the lands that would necessarily have to be abandoned.

Finally, to compound these geo-strategic weaknesses, the Poles had at their head a commander-in-chief who chose to make dispositions that doomed many of his best formations to instant defeat. Marshal Rydz-Smigly posted one fifth of his units to the indefensible Danzig corridor and around Poznań. When the Germans moved in, these men stood no chance, and were either captured or cut off.

FLYING ARTILLERY

The final element in all this imbalance of forces lay in the air. The Polish Air Force consisted of 842 aircraft, many obsolescent, and was pitted against what was certainly the supreme air force in the world. On the day that war broke out, the Luftwaffe totalled 4700 planes (including 550 Junkers Ju-52 transports). Two *Luftflotten* (I and IV) were committed to Poland; together they had almost 900 bombers and, in addition, for a campaign in which the enemy had little fighter cover worthy of the name, the Luftwaffe possessed a weapon that terrified and unnerved all that were subject to its attacks – the Junkers Ju-87 'Stuka'. Two hundred and nineteen of these divebombers took part in the Polish campaign, and their cooperation with infantry and armoured units, their ability to strike far behind the lines, shattering communications and breaking up formations moving up to, and pulling back from, the front, had great effect. Within days of the declaration of war, the Polish Air Force had been destroyed on the ground, and was in no condition to put up any resistance.

Under the cover of this flying artillery, the five German Panzer divisions were able to

The fall of Poland

LITHUANIA

Hel Peninsula

Danzig

EAST PRUSSIA

Vilna

POMERANIA
Army Group B (North)

Niemen

Third Army

Narew

Vistula

Poznań

Bzura

Warsaw

Gora Kalwaria

Brest-Litovsk

Łódź

POLAND

Bug

Eighth Army

SILESIA

Tenth Army
Army Group A (South)

San

Kraków

Przemyśl

Lvov

USSR

Fourteenth Army

→ main axes of German advance
→ main axes of Soviet advance

CZECHOSLOVAKIA

HUNGARY

ROMANIA

Below: The view from the nose of a Heinkel He-111. The He-111 was successful over Poland and France, but was less effective after 1940 because of its short range (1200km/750 miles) and limited bombload (2000kg/4400lb).

operate in almost complete security (in spite of a few brave missions flown by the Poles), forming the spearhead of the Blitzkrieg that inaugurated the new age. Although these Panzer divisions were very lightly armoured and equipped compared with their successors of later years, they manifested all the essentials of armoured warfare. Under commanders such as Generals Erich Hoepner, Hermann Hoth and, above all, Heinz Guderian, they showed just how the static warfare of World War I was a thing of the past.

German tactics were based on speed and adaptability; not merely the successful attack on positions by armoured vehicles, but the bypassing of obstacles and the advance into rear areas, leaving infantry and artillery to deal with troublesome strongpoints. To the Poles, such a method proved difficult to deal with – the more so when it was combined with constant bombardment from the air that weakened morale and cut communications with headquarters, leaving troops without a complete picture of the battle.

The first engagements of the campaign took place as Guderian's XIX Panzer Corps pushed across the Danzig corridor, from the west towards the Vistula, during the early morning of 1 September, trying to make contact with the forces of the German Third Army in East Prussia. They had accomplished this objective on 6 September, by which time Marshal Rydz-Smigly had already ordered the Polish armies to withdraw eastwards. Meanwhile, from the south, Army Group South had achieved similar successes, the Tenth Army managing to reach the Vistula by 10 September at Gora Kalwaria, while the Eighth and Fourteenth Armies swung round and cut off large Polish formations, taking Łódź and Przemyśl in the process. The large Polish forces around Poznań were isolated and German armoured units were racing towards Warsaw, which almost fell to a surprise attack by the 4th Panzer Division of the Tenth Army on 8 September.

The Polish forces, by now confused and in retreat on all fronts facing a rampant

Wehrmacht, did not collapse, however. In spite of the heavy odds against them, they staged remarkable recoveries, trying to break out of encirclements to fight another day. Two episodes in particular stand out. First, there was the battle of the Bzura River, during which the Polish forces that had been so foolishly concentrated near Poznań and in the Danzig corridor tried to fight their way through the German Eighth Army that was pushing up from the south.

This manoeuvre involved capturing crossings over the Bzura which the Poles managed to do, and then holding them against heavy German pressure. Although initial German attacks were beaten off, the German Eighth Army was soon reinforced by formations from the Tenth Army, diverted from its advance on Warsaw, and by 19 September 170,000 Polish troops had been forced to surrender. The second episode was in the south, where the Polish troops isolated by the taking of Przemyśl managed to fight their way across the San River, even capturing 20 artillery pieces and 180 German vehicles in the process.

THE FALL OF POLAND

These heroic Polish efforts could only delay the inevitable, however. As early as 9 September, Guderian's Panzer forces, which had proved so successful in the first stage of the campaign, had been transferred far to the east, and had crossed the Narew River, aiming at a complete envelopment of all Polish forces, even those to the east of Warsaw. By 15 September, Guderian's advance units had taken Brest-Litovsk, and were making contact with the Fourteenth Army troops who were pushing north after their own enormous sweep through the south of the country.

With Warsaw invested by German forces, and Panzer units pushing far to the east, the forces of the Soviet Union now took a hand. The secret protocols attached to the German-Soviet non-aggression pact of August had given the Russians a 'sphere of influence' in the territories east of the line formed by the Narew, Vistula and San Rivers. Stalin could not take the risk of seeing the settlement of defeated Poland being administered solely by Nazi Germany, and so on 17 September, with a trumped-up excuse about looking after the rights of its 'blood-brothers the Ukrainians and Belorussians' the Red Army stormed westwards towards Vilna, Brest-Litovsk and L'vov. This was the final straw. The Poles now had no chance of putting up even a last-ditch resistance in the southeast of the country, and so, on 18 September, Poland's formal resistance ended as the rulers of the country fled to Romania.

This did not end the campaign, for some Polish units fought on, and Warsaw itself did not surrender until 27 September, after a long bombardment from both aircraft and artillery. Not until 2 October were the final shots fired, in the Hel Peninsula north of Danzig, when the 4500 Polish defenders there surrendered. These last sparks of national pride could not affect the crushing nature of German victory, however, which had largely been achieved before any Soviet forces took a hand. The world was stunned by the revelation of the new might of the German armed forces, although western observers, with their stories of 'plucky little Poland', tended to play down the extent to which the battlefield had changed, seeing the recent campaign as a question of Goliath overwhelming David, and the defensive ideas of Britain and France were hardly shaken by events in the east.

The last rites over the dismembered nation that was once again, as in the 18th century, sliced apart and incorporated in more powerful neighbours, were the talks between the German Foreign Minister Joachim von Ribbentrop and the Soviet leader Josef Stalin in late September, when in exchange for German territorial gains in Poland greater than those agreed in the non-aggression pact of August, the Soviet Union was given Lithuania as part of its sphere of influence.

German losses in the campaign were given as 10,572 killed, 3400 missing and 30,322 wounded. Poland's precise losses are unknown, but 694,000 prisoners were taken by the Wehrmacht, and 217,000 by the Red Army. About 100,000 Poles managed to escape across the border to Romania, whence they were able to reach western Europe to carry on the fight.

Below: Escorted by German troops, Polish prisoners of war trudge off to captivity. Approximately 900,000 Poles were taken prisoner during the brief campaign that snuffed out their country's independence.

ATTACK ON WESTERN EUROPE

The speed of the German offensive that had shattered the Polish armies in a mere 18 days had given the Western Allies little chance to respond effectively. In any case, their plans for mobilization had hardly got under way by the time the Panzer formations were smashing their way to Warsaw. The British Expeditionary Force (BEF) did not start its deployment until the beginning of October, and the Poles had realized well before the outbreak of war that they would have to wait over a month before an effective French offensive could get under way. The French commander-in-chief, General Maurice Gamelin, did try an assault in the Saar region on 7 September, with 31 divisions (only nine of which actually saw action), but it was a fiasco, and was soon abandoned, hardly troubling the German defences.

After the victory in Poland, the German armies began to redeploy slowly towards the west, and the French turned their back on any form of offensive action. Indeed, they did not believe that any assault on the German defences in the west could take place before 1941. The problem for the Allies, therefore, was how to cope with a German attack. Along the Franco-German frontier there was, of course, the Maginot Line, the defences of which were thought to be capable of absorbing whatever was thrown at them. The real fear was of a repeat of the German Schlieffen Plan of 1914 – a gigantic sweep through the neutral countries of Belgium and Holland, moving on Paris through northern France.

This avenue of attack was indeed the way that the German high command was envisaging any move on France. On 29 October 1939, in response to prodding from Hitler, the commander-in-chief of the German Army, Colonel-General Walter von Brauchitsch, produced just such a plan, *'Fall Gelb'* ('Case Yellow').

There were some who opposed the basic concept of the plan: notably Generals Erich von Manstein and Gerd von Rundstedt, who proposed giving more weight to an advance through the hills and woods of the Ardennes, relying on armoured formations. In the event, 'Case Yellow' was never put into operation, because, despite Hitler's enthusiasm for an immediate assault, the weather during the late autumn and winter was never good enough, and the German high command itself, with memories of the mud and rain of the Western Front of World War I, contained many individuals only too prepared to argue for cancellation.

Left: French troops during the winter of 1939–40. This period of the 'Phoney War' (or drôle de guerre as the French called it) saw little offensive thinking on the Allied side; the Germans, however, made use of these months to lay the plans that would lead to the conquest of France. Below: Erich von Manstein (foreground), chief of staff to von Rundstedt's Army Group A. Manstein conceived the scheme of attacking through the Ardennes, at the weak hinge of the Allied line, rather than throwing all the weight of the German Army into an offensive through Holland and Belgium.

The winter of 1939–40 passed quietly, therefore – so quietly that the period was known as the 'Phoney War'. The combatants strengthened their civil defence procedures, for fear of bombing raids, and trained their men. The only decisive fighting of the period took place far to the northeast, in Finland. The Soviet Union had forced the Baltic states of Latvia, Lithuania and Estonia to conclude 'mutual defence agreements', including the provision of bases, after the Polish campaign. In October, the Soviet Union tried to force Finland to give up territory and bases, and although the Finns tried to negotiate a settlement, the Soviets were not disposed to lessen their demands, and mounted an attack on 30 November without a formal declaration of war.

THE WINTER WAR

Facing 19 Soviet divisions and five armoured brigades, Marshal Carl von Mannerheim, the Finnish commander, had only nine divisions; and only 100 tanks with which to confront 800 Soviet machines. The Finns, however, were defending in wooded, broken terrain which favoured individual expertise rather than mass attacks. They also had a technical skill in the use of equipment such as skis which the Russians could not match, and their defences in the Karelian isthmus, known as the 'Mannerheim Line', were well sited. The attacks of the Soviet Seventh Army against these defences were a failure. Even more catastrophic were the defeats inflicted on the Eighth Army around Lake Ladoga, and the offensive against central Finland also ended in disaster. By the end of

December, the Russians had suffered an estimated 27,000 dead.

After a pause in January 1940, a new Soviet offensive got under way, beginning on 1 February. With a new commander, General Semyon Timoshenko, an enormous force of 45 divisions was used. By 11 February the Mannerheim Line had been breached, and the Finns were constructing new positions. Soviet landings in the Gulf of Finland, however, and the weight of Soviet material, with artillery in particular much better coordinated than in the earlier campaign, eventually told. The Finns concluded a treaty with the Russians on 12 March, and the Soviet Union obtained all that it had wanted from the Winter War.

The British and French had been very much on the side of the Finns, as had most of

Above left: A Finnish sniper, camouflaged and well protected against the cold.
Above: Marshal Mannerheim. Born in 1867, Mannerheim took command of the Finnish forces in the war of independence against Soviet Russia in 1918. He came out of retirement in 1931 to help plan his country's frontier defences. In World War II he commanded the Finnish armed forces and became president in 1944. He died in 1951.

The Soviet invasion of Finland – 1940

FINLAND

LAKE LADOGA

KARELIAN ISTHMUS

border 13 March 1940

front line 1 Feb
Mannerheim Line
front line 13 March

main axes of
Soviet advance

Thirteenth Army
border 30 Nov 1939

Seventh Army

SOVIET UNION

GULF OF FINLAND

Leningrad

world opinion, and the attractions of sending a force to aid the Finns were reinforced by the thought of making a move into Scandinavia, from where Germany obtained two thirds of her iron ore. Indeed, as early as 29 September 1939, the First Lord of the Admiralty, Winston Churchill, had advocated mining the 'Leads' – the sheltered sea-route between the northern Norwegian coast and the offshore islands along which much of the iron ore travelled.

The Winter War was, therefore, seen as an opportunity to strike a blow against German industry, and by early March 1940 a force of over 50,000 men had been prepared for an expedition to Norway. Both the Norwegian and Swedish governments were thoroughly alarmed at the prospect of being dragged into the war, however, and refused permission for the force to use their territory, while the conclusion of the ceasefire between Finland and the Soviet Union on 12 March meant that the Anglo-French scheme had to be put off. The plan to mine the 'Leads', however, was still in being, and had actually begun to be put into action on the night of 7–8 April.

But by then it was too late to affect anything, for the Germans had already made the first moves of their attack on Norway.

ATTACK IN THE NORTH

The assault on Norway and Denmark – Operation *Weserübung* – had first been considered as an option by Hitler in January, but had been given more urgency after the capture of the German supply ship *Altmark* in Norwegian waters by a British destroyer on 16 February had revealed just how vulnerable Norway was to British sea power. Under General Nikolaus von Falkenhorst, a force of two mountain divisions and five infantry divisions was earmarked for Norway, while two infantry divisions would attack Denmark. They would be supported by the entire German Navy, and about 1000 warplanes and transports. The Norwegians became aware that an attack was imminent on 4 April, but had still not mobilized on 9 April, when the first troops landed, in five task forces, aiming to take the ports of Oslo, Kristiansand, Bergen, Trondheim and

Above: Vidkun Quisling, head of the Nasjonal Samling, *the Norwegian version of the Nazi Party. His name became synonymous with 'traitor' and he was executed in 1945.*

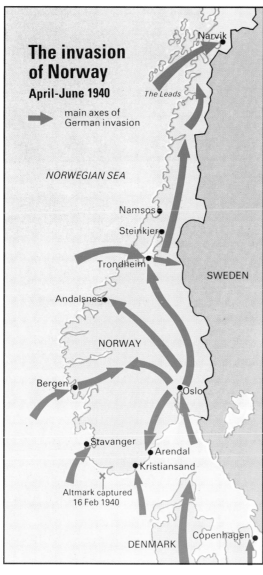

The invasion of Norway

April-June 1940

→ main axes of German invasion

Narvik

The Leads

NORWEGIAN SEA

Namsos

Steinkjer

Trondheim

SWEDEN

Andalsnes

NORWAY

Bergen

Oslo

Stavanger

Arendal

Kristiansand

Altmark captured
16 Feb 1940

Copenhagen

DENMARK

Narvik, while airborne units moved into the west-coast port of Stavanger.

The Danes capitulated on 9 April (they had little choice) but the Norwegians decided to resist, although their lack of preparation meant that they could do little to counter the initial landings. The Allied response was not well coordinated. The Royal Navy put various task forces to sea, and a destroyer flotilla moved against German destroyers in the northern port of Narvik. Two actions on 10 and 13 April destroyed 10 German vessels, and exposed General Eduard Dietl's mountain troops at Narvik to the threat of isolation. But the first troops that were landed to follow up this naval success achieved little.

In southern Norway, French and British troops landed near Trondheim hoping to retake the port, but they were unable to make much headway and were evacuated by sea on 1 May. Troops had been landed near Narvik at the same time, and by 7 May they had been reinforced by substantial French and British reserves. This force took Narvik itself on 28 May, and once again threatened Dietl's men

Opposite page, below: A German PzKpfw II in action. These agile tanks formed the backbone of the armoured divisions of the German Army in 1940. Their only disadvantage was the lightness of their 20mm main armament.

Below: A German sentry keeps watch over the 'Leads' (the sheltered sea route between the northern Norwegian coast and the offshore islands) after the German conquest of Norway.

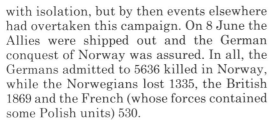

with isolation, but by then events elsewhere had overtaken this campaign. On 8 June the Allies were shipped out and the German conquest of Norway was assured. In all, the Germans admitted to 5636 killed in Norway, while the Norwegians lost 1335, the British 1869 and the French (whose forces contained some Polish units) 530.

THE GERMAN PLANS

It was the invasion of western Europe that had rendered Norway an irrelevant campaign. And the German offensive in the west that shattered the armies of Holland, Belgium and France, forced the BEF to evacuate the continent and put western Europe under German control showed beyond doubt that a new era in warfare had dawned. The collapse of Poland could perhaps be put down to the weakness of the Polish armed forces in comparison with those of Germany, but the defeat of the Allies in the west was indisputably the result of superior methods and organization, not mere numbers. The age-old military relationship between space and time was given a new twist in the application of the Blitzkrieg. Tanks, aircraft and mobile infantry and artillery cut through armies based on an older model.

The development of Germany's armoured forces owed much to Heinz Guderian, whose unswerving championing of formations in which tanks would be supported by their own artillery, infantry and engineer units attracted Adolf Hitler, in spite of the reservations of many of the members of the high command who believed, as did the most influential officers of the French and British Armies, that tanks were best used as close support for infantry, or for reconnaissance, and did not merit being used as the basis of large formations. Whereas the French only had four formations in which tanks were the

primary arm, and spread most of their heavy armour into 40 tank battalions, incapable of independent action, the Germans formed four more Panzer divisions in the winter of 1939, the Polish campaign having shown their value.

By the spring of 1940, the forces that faced each other on the Western Front were more or less equal in numbers. There were 138 German divisions, while the French deployed 100, the BEF 11, the Belgians 22 and the Dutch 10. In terms of armour, each side had about 4000 tanks. Only in the air did the Germans have a decisive numerical advantage. The superiority of the Wehrmacht

Above left: German mountain troops, complete with skis, on the march near Narvik. Mountain divisions were effective not only in Norway, but also in the Italian campaign, when they helped in defending positions around Monte Cassino. Above: French tankmen, distinctive in their leather clothing, take a rest on the hull of their Char B1 heavy tank.

Left: Dutch infantry man a mortar. Note the distinctive helmet, similar to that in use with the Romanian Army.

over the forces it attacked lay partly in the fact that the western nations were fighting under different high commands, and not until the German invasion itself were the Belgians and Dutch committed to fight on the Allied side; but, most importantly, the execution and planning of the German attack was such as to present their opponents with a form of war that they had only begun to comprehend when it had already succeeded.

Put most simply, the German plan was to move across Holland and Belgium, drawing the British and French forces into Belgium, and then to strike through Sedan, in the Ardennes, at the hinge of the Allied line along the Meuse River. From Sedan, the armoured units would drive to the Channel, isolating the northern Allied armies. These forces could then be destroyed by the German armies sweeping south through Belgium and Holland, before the German formations regrouped to push south to Paris.

Brilliantly successful though this plan was, it did not get accepted without a certain amount of opposition. The original scheme, as we have seen, was for a repeat of the World War I manoeuvre, the Schlieffen Plan, a giant sweep into Belgium and along the Channel coast. The chief of staff of Army Group A, General Erich von Manstein, had already sent several memoranda on the subject to the high command (which had ignored them) when Hitler heard of Manstein's proposal, and adopted it as his own. Manstein believed that an advance through Belgium alone would inevitably lead to stalemate, and

he could see no better approach than cutting into the rear of the Allied armies that would be sucked into the Low Countries by the initial attacks there. In mid-February, Hitler ordered the preparation of detailed plans of attack, and by May all was ready for the invasion.

The German armies were in three Army Groups. In the south, General Wilhelm von Leeb's Army Group C was to cover the Maginot Line, but its role was to be minor. In the north, von Bock's Army Group B, with three Panzer, one airborne and 27 infantry divisions, was to move through Holland and Belgium, using airborne landings to secure vital bridges. In the centre was von Rundstedt's Army Group A. This had seven Panzer divisions, five of them in a new formation, a *Panzergruppe*, and 36 infantry divisions. The armoured formations were to make the crucial breakthrough.

Facing this array were three French Army Groups, with the critical one being the First, under General Gaston Billotte, whose men would have to undertake the manoeuvre upon which Allied plans depended, the move into Belgium to link up with the Belgian Army along the line of the Dyle and the Meuse Rivers to shorten the Allied line. To the right of the First Army Group was the BEF, while on the Channel coast the Seventh Army had been instructed, in the belief that the Ardennes was impassable to large formations, to try to link up with the Dutch by advancing deep towards Breda, which it did.

Below left: Colonel Charles de Gaulle, who had been one of the great advocates of armoured warfare during the 1930s, an advocacy that had had little effect upon the French high command. After the fall of France, de Gaulle became head of the 'Fighting French' (later called 'Free French') who carried on the struggle, in spite of the existence of the Vichy regime in the south of the country that had signed an armistice with the Germans. Below: On 12 May, two days after the first German attacks, British troops (in the distinctive Bren Gun Carriers that were unique to the BEF) take up positions along a road in northern France while refugees from Belgium stream past. Soon the BEF too was pulling back, outflanked by the German push through the Ardennes and their drive to the Channel.

Below: German paratroops race into action after landing. Opposite page: German assault troops with weaponry for close-quarters combat.

THE INVASION OF THE LOW COUNTRIES

These Allied dispositions and plans were clearly vulnerable to Manstein's plan; and so it proved as the offensive moved into gear. The first attacks took place on 10 May, when airborne troops landed in Holland and Belgium and the main forces moved over the frontiers of these small neutral nations. The Dutch put up a brave fight, but were overwhelmed and capitulated on 14 May. The Belgians had to pull back but then managed to link up with the French and British forces

EBEN EMAEL

The line of the Albert Canal was one of the key points in the Allied defences in Belgium in 1940. At dawn on 10 May the line was held by the three regiments of the Belgian 7th Division. Their right flank was anchored by the fortress of Eben Emael, which was armed with two 120mm guns and sixteen 75mm guns, and considered impervious to direct attack, being encased in concrete with only the gun turrets protruding.

To attack this line, the Germans had decided on a daring plan using a new weapon. The key element in the scheme was to be the employ-ment of airborne troops – but not dropped by parachute. A special detachment of 424 men had been training with gliders for months, under Captain Walter Koch and Lieutenant Rudolf Witzig. The attack went in at dawn. The first gliders landed in the middle of the defences on the left bank of the canal, and the Germans were able to take advantage of the confusion caused by this new approach to cut the lines leading to demolition charges on two of the three main bridges.

On the fortress of Eben Emael itself, the key to the whole position, 11 gliders landed in the morning. Seventy-eight assault pioneers, equipped with 2.5 tonnes of explosive, began laying hollow charges against and inside the gun turrets and using portable flame-throwers through the gun slits and observation openings. The fortress garrison had no answer to this small group of men operating in the very heart of the enclosed defensive works, and within minutes much of the armament of the fort was out of action. The garrison, confined under cover, were helpless, and surrendered the next day, 11 May. The imaginative use of new technology had brought the Germans an unexpectedly rapid victory – and one that opened the road into Belgium.

that moved north to their aid, and within three days the new front was established.

The French Ninth and Second Armies had to hold the line of the Meuse from Namur to Sedan, and early on they had disturbing news from advance cavalry units that German armour was advancing in strength through the Ardennes. Some support units were moved up, but were unable to prevent a motorcycle battalion from Rommel's 7th Armoured Division establishing itself on the left bank of the river on 12 May. Although this was only a small bridgehead, held by infantry, the French battalion sent to cover the area hardly made any impression; there was little coordination when French tanks moved up in support, and under constant aerial bombardment from Stukas, the French allowed the bridgehead to expand, and tanks began to move across. Further south, too, near Sedan, Guderian's XIX Corps had moved across the river, and their immediate opponents, the reserve French 55th Division, broke, spreading panic in rear areas. By 14 May, 664 tanks of the 1st and 2nd Panzer Divisions were attacking the French rear.

The German invasion of France and the Low Countries
May 1940

main axes of German advance
Maginot Line

NORTH SEA
HOLLAND
12 May
Amsterdam
Rotterdam
10 May
Breda
Army Group B
evacuation of BEF from Dunkirk 26 May - 4 June
Ostend
Antwerp
10 May
Calais
Dunkirk
Schelde
Eben Emael
Aachen
GERMANY
Boulogne
Brussels
Liège
ENGLISH CHANNEL
27 May
Namur
Rhine
20 May
BELGIUM
Army Group A
Abbéville
Somme
18 May
Ardennes
10 May
Rouen 9 June
Oise
Aisne
Sedan 14 May
LUX
Serre
de Gaulle's counter-attack 17-19 May
Meuse
Paris 14 June
FRANCE
Army Group C

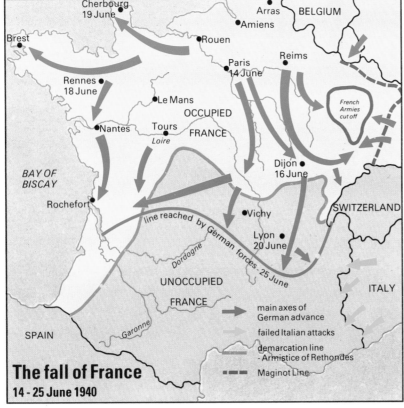

The fall of France
14 - 25 June 1940

Top: Weary Belgian troops pull back along the Louvain–Brussels road, 14 May 1940. The horse-drawn guns are of World War I vintage.

The two small bridgeheads first established by Rommel's and Guderian's men should have been attacked and reduced at once; but the French forces facing them consisted mainly of reserve divisions, woefully short of anti-aircraft guns and anti-tank weapons. In a sense, therefore, the weaknesses of the French Army were to blame for the beginning of the debacle. But the real German success came after this initial break in. For the speed, effectiveness and ferocity of the subsequent thrusts were what broke the Allies. Already, on 15 May, the Panzers had caught one of the few French armoured formations, the 1st Armoured Division, refuelling and had destroyed it. Pushing on at

great speed (Rommel, for example, flogged his men and machines through a night march on the 16th that took them 48km/30 miles westwards from the Franco-Belgian frontier at sunset to Le Cateau by dawn), they had reached the sea by 20 May, completing the isolation of the Allied forces in Belgium.

The problem of responding to this sudden, unexpected blow was compounded for the Allied high command by the difficulties of transport along roads open to the devastating attacks of German aircraft, and clogged with refugees (it is estimated that up to five million French people became refugees at some time during the fighting). Nor were the French sure of the direction of the attack. For some time it seemed that Paris might be the objective, rather than the Channel. Not until 16 May was the withdrawal of Allied troops from Belgium into northern France put under way. And in spite of some energetic attacks on the 'corridor' that the Panzers were carving out (by the newly organized French 4th Armoured Division under Colonel Charles de Gaulle on 17 and 19 May and by the BEF on 21 May near Arras), there was no way of plugging the gap.

THE FALL OF FRANCE

Caught between the remorseless advance of von Bock's Army Group B from the north (Belgium capitulated on 28 May), and the seemingly invincible Panzers in the south, the BEF was evacuated from Dunkirk, in Operation Dynamo. Between 26 May and 4 June, 338,000 men (including 110,000 French) were brought back to Britain. Miraculous though Dunkirk may have seemed, it set the seal on the German superiority – the way was

now open for the sweep south towards Paris.

The French commander-in-chief, General Maurice Gamelin, had been replaced by General Maxime Weygand on 19 May, and the new man set about organizing a new line of defences along the line of the Somme and the Aisne Rivers. He realized that the concept of a solid front line had to be abandoned, and so decided to use strongpoints as the basis of a flexible defence which would absorb the initial armoured thrusts and then strike back. The forces with which he hoped to put this plan into operation were lamentably small, however – the equivalent of no more than 44 divisions. When Panzer forces crossed the Somme on 5 June they met fierce resistance, and were unable to make swift headway; but on 9 June two armoured divisions moved over the Aisne, and the French forces had to pull back. Paris was left to the invaders and fell on 14 June, while by the 17th the four armies on the eastern frontier, holding the Maginot Line, were cut off. More than 400,000 troops had been rendered ineffective at a stroke.

As the armoured forces of the rampant Wehrmacht now swept triumphantly southward, plans for last-ditch French resistance in a 'National Redoubt' were proposed and abandoned. Benito Mussolini's Italy had declared war on 10 June, so now the French faced a threat in the south as well, although when the Italians did attack, on 20 June, they received a bloody nose and were stopped in their tracks. On 16 June, the French prime minister, Paul Reynaud, had been replaced by Marshal Philippe Pétain, a hero of World War I. He sued for an armistice, the terms of which were eventually agreed at Rethondes on 22 June. France was divided into an independent state in the south, with a much-reduced army, while the north and west was occupied by Germany.

The French had suffered most heavily in the campaigns of May and June, with over 90,000 dead. The Dutch lost almost 3000 killed, the Belgians 7500, and the BEF 3500. Germany lost about 40,000. But the victory had given Germany mastery of the west. Her only active opponent left was Great Britain; and Britain was so weakened by the recent military defeats that her army was unlikely to be able to resist if German troops could be moved across the Channel.

Above: The triumphant German entry into Paris.

Below: One of the forts built as an extension of the Maginot Line in order to deal with the threat from Italy. These fortifications proved their worth in 1940 when the Italian invasion of the south of France was repulsed.

BRITAIN HOLDS OUT

On 16 July 1940, Hitler sent out his famous Directive Number 16. This instructed the armed forces to prepare for the invasion of Great Britain (Operation Sea Lion), and the war now moved into a new phase. The German Army had proved itself supreme on the ground in Europe, but to move an invasion fleet across the Channel in the face of opposition from the Royal Navy and Royal Air Force the Germans would now have to exert a superiority at sea and in the air. The naval and air actions of this early part of the war may seem small when compared with the enormous fleets and air raids of the 1944–5 period, but they were decisive in determining the future shape of the conflict.

In 1939, Germany had ruled the air over Poland (although the small Polish Air Force and anti-aircraft fire had inflicted losses of 285 planes), and the campaign in the west during the spring and early summer of 1940 was to see this superiority maintained, expressing itself in various ways, all of which were of concern to the Allies.

First of all, there was the bombing of cities, the great fear of the 1930s. On 14 May, Rotterdam was bombed (by mistake, as it happened, as surrender terms had already been agreed). Allied propaganda made much of this action, claiming that 25,000 civilians had been killed, whereas only just over 800 had perished. But the popular conception of bomber fleets able to destroy a nation was reinforced by this propaganda. Then there was the ability of the Germans to deliver airborne troops onto key locations, as had been shown in Holland and Belgium. Finally,

and most important, was the close support given to the mechanized and armoured units, and the attacks on enemy communications, such as those by the Stukas in Poland and France.

Irrespective of these successes, however, the invasion of the British Isles set new problems for the German Luftwaffe. The original plans for the invasion were drawn up by Field Marshal von Brauchitsch (promoted since the victory in France), and envisaged a general landing all along the south coast of England, by a total of 41 divisions, to take place as soon after 25 August as possible. This force would certain-

Above: Winston Churchill, the incarnation of Britain's determination to resist in 1940. Up to this date, Churchill had had a chequered political career. He spent much of the 1930s in the wilderness, proclaiming the danger of Nazi ambitions to a political world that preferred to ignore him. In September 1939 he was First Lord of the Admiralty, and in May 1940 became prime minister after defeat in Norway had discredited the Chamberlain government. Churchill banished all thoughts of a negotiated peace with Germany, and set about preparing to repel the invasion which was expected at any moment.

Left: Scramble! Hurricane pilots make for their aircraft after the sighting of an enemy formation.

ly have been a match for the British armies, for as late as 17 September the commander of the Home Forces, General Alan Brooke, had only 29 divisions with which to organize defence against such an invasion. The British ground forces were also desperately short of equipment – on 8 June, they had only 54 2-pounder anti-tank guns available and by August there were still only 400 of the heavy Infantry and the faster Cruiser tanks. German invasion plans were, however, put back. Grand-Admiral Erich Raeder, who had started examining the possibility of invading Britain in the winter of 1939–40, said that the navy could not possibly transport the required force. A new scheme, in which only 27 divisions were to take part, with nine in the first wave, was discussed, and 21 September was decided upon as the invasion date. But even with novel new equipment (such as 128 submersible tanks) the critical issue was air superiority. To deal with this, Hitler's Directive Number 17 of 1 August ordered the Luftwaffe to smash the Royal Air Force as the preliminary to invasion.

The RAF had already shown that its aircraft were capable of taking on the

Luftwaffe. Over Dunkirk, for example, British fighters had downed 156 German planes, for the loss of just over 100 of their own aircraft. But the Luftwaffe had an enviable reputation. For the attack on Great Britain it deployed 2800 aircraft, in three air fleets, while the RAF had basically 650 fighter aircraft, in 52 squadrons (of which 29 were of Hawker Hurricanes and 19 of Supermarine Spitfires) to deploy in defence.

The British fighters were superior in aerial combat to the German Messerschmitt Bf-110 twin-engined fighter, and could run rings around the Junkers Ju-87 Stuka. But the Messerschmitt Bf-109 single-engined fighter had a better rate of climb than any British plane, and was faster than the Hurricane in level flight. The British planes were more manoeuvrable than the Bf-109, however, and although their armament of eight ·303in machine guns was less deadly than the two 20mm cannon carried by the Bf-109 (in addition to its two 7.92mm machine guns), the eight guns gave a wider cone of fire, and therefore more chance of scoring a hit.

Although they were outnumbered in aircraft, the British rate of production of fighters was steadily increasing – from 157 in January 1940 it had reached 496 in July. The real British weakness lay in trained pilots, of whom there were a mere 1341 in July. The aviators seconded from Coastal Command, and the Czech and Polish flyers who fought on the British side were thus vital to the outcome of the battle.

The Battle of Britain itself is normally divided into five phases. First there were the

Above: Soldiers carefully prop up an unexploded bomb in London during the Blitz, while waiting for a bomb-disposal team to arrive. Left: Some of the damage caused to the House of Commons by a German air raid on London.

The Battle of Britain

Luftflotte V (operating from Norway)

IRISH SEA

Fighter Command 13 Group

Fighter Command 12 Group

Stanmore FC HQ

Fighter Command 11 Group

Fighter Command 10 Group

ENGLISH CHANNEL

NORTH SEA

BELGIUM

Luftflotte II

Luftflotte III

FRANCE

- British towns and cities bombed by the Luftwaffe
- sector airfields
- fighter airfields
- - - Fighter Command Group boundaries
- - - Luftflotte boundaries
- Luftwaffe bomber bases
- Luftwaffe fighter bases
- cover of low-level radar 150m (500 ft)
- cover of high-level radar 4500m (15,000 ft)

Glasgow, Belfast, Newcastle, Sunderland, Middlesbrough, Liverpool, Manchester, Sheffield, Nottingham, Birmingham, Coventry, Norwich, Ipswich, Swansea, Cardiff, Bristol, Bath, London, Canterbury, Southampton, Portsmouth, Exeter, Plymouth, Calais, Amiens, Cherbourg, Paris, Rennes

German attacks on coastal shipping and south coast ports, from early July until early August 1940. Then, following Hitler's Directive 17, came a period of attacks on radar stations and forward fighter bases, trying to tempt the British into dog-fights that would gradually wear them down. This proved costly for the Germans, however, and so from 24 August they switched to attacks with escorted bombers on the main fighter bases. German losses were again heavier than those of the RAF, but the British were now losing planes and pilots at an unacceptable rate.

The RAF was saved by Hitler's decision to change the target of the attacks yet again. In retaliation for an RAF raid on Berlin, Hitler ordered the Luftwaffe to bomb London, and although at the time this seemed the crisis of the battle – in particular the series of air battles of 15 September in which the RAF claimed 185 kills (after the war this figure was reduced to 56) – in fact, the best German chance of victory had already slipped away when the non-stop attacks on the fighter

bases had been called off. On 14 and 15 September, RAF and Royal Navy raids destroyed a considerable number of the barges that were being prepared to bring the German troops across the English Channel, and on 17 September, Operation Sea Lion was suspended.

THE BLITZ

The final phase of the battle was a reduction in the number of German daylight raids, to be replaced by the night bombing of London and other British cities – a signal of acceptance that the attempt to destroy British aerial power had failed. By the end of October, the Luftwaffe had lost over 1700 planes, and the RAF about 1400.

In retrospect, the Battle of Britain seems simple to analyse. While Fighter Command stayed in being, it could provide the air cover that would enable the ships of the Royal Navy to smash any invasion fleet in the Channel; and so Air Chief-Marshal Sir Hugh Dowding and the commander of 11 Fighter Group, Air Vice-Marshal Keith Park, both of whom saw the continued survival of the fighter squadrons as their prime task, are rightly given the credit for British victory. During the summer and early autumn of 1940, however, things were not as clear as they are with hindsight. The prospect of German invasion appeared very real, and to many it seemed inconceivable that the country could be saved from invasion without a victory that would break German air power. Dowding and Park were deprived of their commands within weeks of the end of the daylight raids, even though their calculating strategy had saved the country.

Hitler had been unwilling, in the summer of 1940, to indulge in a bombing campaign against the British people; but from the autumn, a steady policy of civilian bombing was instituted. Known in Britain as the

'Blitz' this was designed to shatter morale and destroy war industries. It certainly caused great suffering and disruption to civilian life – the thousands sheltering every night in the London Underground and the shattered centres of many cities bore witness to this new development in the war. The worst single night of destruction was in Coventry on 14 November 1940, and the British government was worried after this raid that there might be widespread breakdown of public order in the city. In general, however, British morale held up well. The German bomber force was never able to deliver sufficient tonnage of bombs seriously to affect war production, and, as Hitler began withdrawing his air forces east in preparation for the attack on the Soviet Union in 1941, the night raids became less frequent.

The Battle of Britain and the Blitz had shown just what an air force could, and could not, achieve, and had shown the value of new technology such as radar. Perhaps the most interesting aspect of the aerial warfare of 1940 was that the fear of a bomber force destroying a nation's war-making capacity had proved exaggerated – the German bombers were neither large enough nor numerous enough to bring Britain to its knees. This was not perceived as a 'lesson', however, and many in the RAF still believed that they would be able to crush Germany by a bombing offensive over her cities.

Having failed to destroy Britain with his air force, Hitler was left with the possibility of blockade, using his navy to cut the lifelines of the island. When war broke out in 1939, Germany had a navy of only 130 vessels, as opposed to the 676 of the Western Allies. Of this German strength, 57 were U-boats, most of which were incapable of long-range operations. During the first year of the war, therefore, Allied naval superiority was confirmed, in spite of some German successes, such as the sinking of the battleship *Royal Oak* at Scapa Flow in October 1939, and the activities of six raiders disguised as merchantmen in the spring of 1940. The new

German magnetic mines were dealt with efficiently by 'degaussing' Allied ships; the pocket battleship *Graf Spee* was cornered and then had to be scuttled off Montevideo; the German fleet did not perform very effectively during the Norwegian campaign; and German torpedoes were of very poor quality (more than once British capital ships were hit by torpedoes which failed to explode). Indeed, in June 1940, the Germans had only one pocket battleship, four cruisers and 12 destroyers as a surface fleet ready for action, and by September, one year after the outbreak of hostilities, there were still only 57 U-boats of all types – exactly the same number as in September 1939.

This weakness at sea was soon to be remedied, however. For after the fall of France, the German Navy had the chance to use the Atlantic ports of her defeated foe. In July, the first submarine (U-30) began working out of Lorient, and the construction of big pens for the 'wolves of the deep' was put under way. The U-boats accounted for 285 Allied ships from July until December 1940, and the Battle of the Atlantic now took over from the Battle of Britain as the key to the continued survival of Great Britain.

Top: The German pocket battleship Graf Spee. *The chase and eventual scuttling of this vessel in December 1939 was the first dramatic incident of the war at sea.*

Above: The architect of British victory in the Battle of Britain, Air Chief-Marshal Sir Hugh Dowding.

THE BLITZ

In her book Looking for Trouble *Virginia Cowles describes being caught in an air-raid on London in 1940.* '. . . people were running for shelter in all directions, and buses and trucks were coming to a stop. Lines of tramcars stood empty. Soon there was an ominous silence and mine was practically the only car on the road.

'Two stranded soldiers waved to me and I stopped and gave them a lift. It was difficult driving in the semi-darkness and the quiet was oppressive. Suddenly, a few hundred yards ahead of us, we heard a sickening whistle and a deafening explosion. A bomb landed in the middle of a street and there was a shower of glass and debris from the houses on either side. The whistles blew and ARP workers and special police deputies were on the job almost immediately; it was too dark to see what damage had been done to the houses, but the street was covered with rubble.

'I then drove through the heart of the City which seemed as eerie and deserted as a graveyard. I stopped to ask the way of an ARP warden and he asked me to take two of his workers up to Piccadilly. The men hadn't had their clothes off for 48 hours. They had just come from a building where five people were dug out of the ruins. "Three women and two children," one of them told me grimly; then, almost under his breath: "The price is going to be high for the Germans when the war is over."'

THE MEDITERRANEAN THEATRE, 1940

Below: Weary Italian soldiers on the Albanian front. The Italian Army was not at all ready for the series of offensives that Mussolini required it to undertake in 1940. It was the troops themselves who suffered the consequences, in southern France, in northern Africa, and in Greece. Below right: Greek troops, members of the armies that threw back the attempted Italian invasion of October 1940 and went on to win the great victory of Koritsa in November.

The decision by Italy to enter World War II, on 10 June 1940, immediately widened the potential scope of the conflict, for the Italians not only had ambitions in the Balkans and southern France, they also had an African empire that bordered British and French possessions and opened up fresh areas of fighting. From the summer of 1940 until the ceasefire in Europe in 1945, the Mediterranean was to be one of the main theatres of the war and in the deserts of North Africa there were remarkable developments in mobile warfare.

Mussolini's motive for entering the war was essentially to grab some of the spoils before the Germans completely swamped France. But his attack into southern France was a complete fiasco. Although there were only about 185,000 French troops available in the southeast, to meet assaults from some 450,000 Italians, the Italian Army was not at all prepared to take the offensive, and had, indeed, been ordered originally to maintain a strict defensive. The French had built impressive frontier defences and, in any case,

the terrain in the Alpine areas of the border favoured them. The result was that the Italians made no headway, and had to be content with crumbs from the German table when the Italian–French armistice was signed on 24 June.

Italian reverses in southern France were as nothing, however, compared with the disasters that befell the Italian armies in Greece. Albania had been in Italian hands since spring 1939, and Mussolini had had his eyes on some further Balkan acquisitions for some time. His original intention had been to attack Yugoslavia, but Hitler told him in August 1939 that such an action must not be undertaken. In October, however, Hitler moved elements of a motorized division into Romania, at the 'request' of the government that had just seized power there, in order to guard the oil wells at Ploieşti from Allied sabotage. Mussolini was furious at the news, and determined to begin his own manoeuvres in the Balkans. On 15 October he told the army, which had just completed the demobilization of 600,000 men after the decision not to move against Yugoslavia, that it was to invade Greece.

On 28 October, Mussolini was able to boast to Hitler that his troops had attacked Greece – news that enraged the Führer. But even worse than the news of the attack itself was

The Mediterranean 1940-41

Italian-held territory

British counter-offensive Dec 1940 - Feb 1941

the fact that, as in southern France, the Italians made very little headway. Four divisions made the first advances into Greek territory, but although the Greeks were very badly equipped, and their total army, when fully mobilized, only numbered some 15 divisions, they put up a staunch resistance, and only on the right of the Italian line did the Axis troops make much headway. The Italians found that their air force was unable to slow the Greek build-up of forces along the frontier, while bad weather in the Adriatic delayed their own intention to bring divisions over from Italy. By 12 November there were 100 Greek battalions facing some 50 Italian, and the Greeks went over to the offensive.

This offensive led to the great victory at Koritsa late in November, where the Greek V Corps smashed the Italian Ninth Army, taking 2000 prisoners, and by the beginning of December the Greeks had pushed the enemy back into Albania. Now, however, their lack of modern equipment, particularly modern transport, began to tell, and in bad winter weather over very difficult mountain terrain the Greek advance was halted.

During the autumn of 1940, Hitler made repeated attempts to lure General Franco's Spain into the Axis camp, in order to assert supremacy over the Mediterranean and to deal Britain a mortal blow by taking the crucial naval base of Gibraltar. Franco, however, refused to be tempted by any of Hitler's

blandishments, while Mussolini's Greek adventure made the Spanish leader even less inclined to accede to the Axis. Then, in December, came yet another indication that the Axis was not going to enjoy an easy or even inevitable victory: the Italian forces in Libya suffered a grievous defeat.

The Italian Army in Libya had advanced across the border into Egypt on 13 September. Led by Marshal Rodolpho Graziani, it reached Sidi Barrani and there halted, building up supplies before moving on again. The Italians had crossed only 100km (60 miles) of the 500km (300 miles) of desert between the

Below: As smoke billows from burning fuel dumps, British troops prepare to make the final assault on Tobruk. The capture of this important port early in 1941 was only the prelude to the series of sieges and attacks that Tobruk was to endure over the next 18 months.

Right: After breaking through the Italian perimeter defences around Bardia and seizing a bridgehead across the anti-tank ditch, British infantry wait for bridging equipment and the arrival of tanks before pushing on to Bardia itself.

Libyan frontier and Alexandria, but had found the going hard, and had been unpleasantly surprised by the superior armoured vehicles of the British 7th Armoured Division, which had withdrawn in good order. During the autumn, the British government made efforts to reinforce their North African forces, and included 107 Hawker Hurricane and Bristol Blenheim aircraft in the new equipment sent.

The British forces in the Middle East, under General Sir Archibald Wavell, were far outnumbered by the Italian forces, but as the Italians showed no signs of trying to push forward from Sidi Barrani, it was decided to attack them there. Under Major-General Richard O'Connor a force 36,000 strong, consisting of the 7th Armoured Division and the 4th Indian Division, assaulted the strung-out Axis dispositions at Sidi Barrani on 9 December 1940. Before the Italians had time to react properly, the British attack had smashed into the heart of their positions, using as a spearhead 57 'Matilda' Infantry tanks, that were invulnerable to the weak Italian anti-tank guns. For the loss of a mere 624 men killed, wounded and missing, O'Connor's men took 38,000 prisoners and swept the Italians out of Egypt. As the Germans had shown in Poland and France, the tank could not only penetrate a front line; more importantly, it could lead the exploitation of this initial penetration.

THE FALL OF BARDIA

Although Wavell had intended the attack to be no more than a raid in strength, O'Connor used the momentum of his victory to push on deep into Libya. On 3 January Bardia fell, with the surrender of 45,000 Italian prisoners, and by early February, having cut across the 'bulge' of Cyrenaica and caught the Italians again at Beda Fomm, the British were established before El Agheila, a narrow defile which offered excellent defensive opportunities, and had simplified their supply problems by taking the deep-water port of Tobruk.

At sea also, the Royal Navy had managed to assert superiority over the Italian fleet, once again by showing itself equipped to make the most of new methods of warfare. The Italian declaration of war had posed a

Below: Italian soldiers who failed to escape from Bardia await transport to prison camps.

Left: The Italian battleship Vittorio Veneto *lets off a salvo. The Italian Navy contained some fine vessels, and the quality of its sailors was proven on many occasions, especially in small-craft actions; but in late 1940 and early 1941 the supremacy of the Royal Navy was decisively asserted at the battles of Taranto and Cape Matapan. The* Vittorio Veneto *herself was damaged by British aircraft during the Cape Matapan engagement.*

great problem for Royal Navy planners, for with the defeat of France the balance of power in the Mediterranean might easily have swung the way of the Axis. (Indeed, the British attack on French warships at Mers-el-Kébir on 3 July was largely occasioned by fears that the powerful French fleet would fall into German hands.) The Royal Navy showed its normal aggressive spirit: in actions on 9 and 13 July, off the Calabrian coast and off northwest Crete, the Italians suffered heavy losses. But in August the Italian fleet was augmented, and for a while outnumbered the Royal Navy in capital ships; moreover the Italians had the advantage that their vessels were centrally placed, whereas the British forces were split between the bases of Gibraltar and those of the eastern Mediterranean. On 11 November, however, in a daring night attack, 21 Fairey Swordfish torpedo-bombers attacked the Italian fleet at Taranto, crippling three battleships.

The importance of air power in naval warfare was further illustrated when, in January 1941, the British aircraft carrier *Illustrious* was badly damaged by bombing attacks from German planes sent by Hitler to help his floundering ally. This loss severely curtailed British operations for a time. In March, however, the use of new techniques helped give the Royal Navy the decisive victory at Cape Matapan that stopped the Italian fleet from nurturing any dreams of upsetting British supremacy.

On 27 March, a Short Sunderland flying-boat reported an Italian squadron in the Ionian Sea. At once Admiral Sir Andrew Cunningham, commander of the British Mediterranean Fleet, slipped out of Alexandria with three battleships, and, most important, the aircraft carrier *Formidable*. On 28 March the battleship *Vittorio Veneto*

at the head of the Italian squadron was damaged by a torpedo from a Swordfish, and during the night a heavy cruiser was badly damaged; the Italian ships' movements were being observed all the while by British aircraft. That night, two Italian heavy cruisers were blown apart by the British battleships, which had been able to follow their movements on radar in the darkness, while the Axis vessels were unaware of the danger.

So, in the Mediterranean theatre, as in northern Europe, the war had opened with success going to the side that could make best use of the new weapons. Not mere technology but the spirit and the men to exploit the potential of that technology had brought victory. Unfortunately for the British, however, their victories had not been decisive, and they were now to be faced with a foe whose grasp of the new methods of warfare was to make him revered even by his enemies; for on 24 March, four days before the battle of Cape Matapan, Rommel's Afrika Korps had begun their first offensive in North Africa.

Above: Admiral Sir Andrew Cunningham. His aggressive approach maintained British superiority in the Mediterranean.

Below: Checking the Lewis gun on a Fairey Swordfish torpedo-bomber.

Part Two
The Escalating Conflict

The German attack on the Soviet Union in June 1941 and the Japanese attack on the United States in December of that year broadened World War II into a truly global affair. The war having spread, new factors took over. In Europe during the first year of the war, the sheer excellence of the German Army had brought success. But when Operation Barbarossa failed to break the Soviet Union and Pearl Harbor merely galvanized the USA into action, military victory became dependent on far more than success on the battlefield. The resources of the USA and the USSR were so vast that these nations could afford to trade territory for the time in which to bring their strengths into play. Two factors then became crucial to the outcome of the war – the long-term industrial capacity of the various combatants and the relative strengths of the two alliances.

In the event, no nation could compete with the United States when it came to the sheer scale of industrial production. Seventeen million rifles, 315,000 artillery pieces, 87,000 tanks, 2,434,000 motor vehicles and 296,000 aircraft were produced for the US war effort – the Axis powers and Japan never remotely matched this output. In 1942, the USA built

Below: The awesome sight of US production lines in action – here fuselage sections for Boeing B-17 Flying Fortresses are being worked on. It was the sheer volume of US industrial production that proved to be the greatest weapon in the armoury of the Allies.

Above: Mrs Florence Edgar inspects a Merlin engine at the Rolls-Royce factory at Hillington, Glasgow. Women in responsible positions in industrial work made a great contribution towards the efforts of the World War II combatant nations to maximize production. This was especially critical in Great Britain, where human resources were quite limited in comparison with those of the USA and USSR.

Right: Prefabricated US merchant vessels take shape. Some of these 'Liberty Ships' were completed within four days, a rate of production that more than compensated for vessels lost to U-boats.

Soviet Union, for example, increased the size of its forces, in spite of the enormous losses of 1941, from 175 infantry divisions in June 1941 to 513 by the end of 1943. In 1942, the Red Army had 5900 artillery pieces at its disposal, but by the end of 1943 this had increased to 19,000, and all through this period the German armies on the Eastern Front were declining in numbers and effectiveness.

Sheer resources were not the whole story, however. An essential part of the process was getting the mass-produced weapons to the fronts, and trying to disrupt enemy production. In this respect, there were four main campaigns during the war: the German attempt to isolate Great Britain during the Battle of the Atlantic; the US attempt to isolate Japan from its raw materials by waging submarine warfare in the Pacific; the bombing offensive conducted by the Western Allies over Germany, and finally the US bombing offensive over Japan. It can be said that only one of these was totally successful, and that was the US assault on Japanese sea lanes. The Battle of the Atlantic was won by the Allies – largely due to the capacity of the USA to build ships at a rate far higher than the U-boats could sink them. Some of the prefabricated 'Liberty Ships' built to carry cargo were completed in four days, for example, and escort carriers were produced in such numbers that all convoys eventually had the air cover that enabled the Allies to start inflicting considerable losses on the U-boats themselves. The bombing offensives on both Germany and Japan did not break either nation's will to resist, although they clearly hampered production and caused great hardship.

48,000 aircraft, while the Germans managed 15,556. In 1943, Japan produced 7,800,000 tonnes of steel, while the USA produced 90,000,000 tonnes – over ten times as much.

Nor was this all, for the Germans, although they had the occupied European states to milk for labour and materials, found the Italians a dead weight on their war economy. Mussolini's fascist forces were by no means ready for war when he dragged them into the fray, and the Germans had to compensate accordingly. The USA did, of course, provide enormous amounts of material to the Soviets and the British, but their allies on their own were a match for Germany industrially. In 1942, for example, the Germans produced only 7200 tanks, whereas Great Britain finished 8611 armoured vehicles and the Soviet Union about 20,000.

Germany made great efforts to improve war production after 1942, under the energetic direction of Albert Speer as Minister of Armaments. Aircraft production, for example, rose to 40,600 in 1944 (from the 15,556 of 1942) and the increase was maintained in spite of all efforts by the Allied bomber forces to halt it. The quality, too, of the German equipment – tanks like the PzKpfw V Panther, aircraft like the jet-powered Messerschmitt Me-262 – was often far better than that of anything the Allies possessed. But this relative increase in German quantity and quality was soon dwarfed by the capabilities of the Allies. The

The US submarine fleets in the Pacific Ocean and the South Seas on the other hand had sunk what amounted to over half of Japanese merchant shipping by the end of the war. They took full advantage of the fact that raw materials from the Japanese empire had to be brought back to Japan for refining and then sent to the fronts; compounding this weakness, the Japanese proved unwilling to adopt an effective convoy system.

ALLIED COOPERATION

While the Allies built up a superiority in industrial power, they also managed to achieve a far greater degree of cooperation in the running of their alliance than the Axis powers ever reached. On the Allied side, Great Britain, the USA and the Soviet Union were the three greatest powers, and (apart from the states of the British Empire and Commonwealth) they were joined by the governments-in-exile of the European states conquered by the Germans. Eventually, 16 states became members of the alliance. On the other side, Germany, Italy and Japan had signed the Tripartite (Axis) Pact on 27 September 1940, but this did little more than state common ground, and there was little cooperation between Japan and her European co-signatories during the war. In Europe itself, the Germans could count on support from the satellite nations of eastern and central Europe – Hungary, Romania, Slovakia and Bulgaria – and set up puppet governments in the conquered territories. In spite of great efforts, however, Hitler was unable to persuade General Franco's Spain to join the Axis, and Turkey too remained neutral in the face of German blandishments.

Cooperation between the forces opposed to Germany in the first year of the war had been rather poor. There was very little chance, in any case, that Britain or France could have given Poland any direct help in the first few weeks of the war, but even after the conquest of Poland, the nations of western Europe were not able to function very well as a unit. Holland and Belgium, for example, realized that they were in great danger of invasion, but were unwilling to coordinate their war plans with those of Britain and France for fear of provoking a German reaction; and as late as April 1940, only one month before the great German offensive in the west, the Belgians again refused to allow Allied troops to move into their country. Nor were the British and the French particularly well knit. The French acceptance of an armistice and the creation of the Vichy regime raised problems automatically, and incidents like the bombardment of the French fleet at Mers-el-Kébir by the Royal Navy (July 1940), were an indication of the lack of mutual trust.

Early Allied differences were nothing like as great as those that beset the Axis, however. Mussolini's entry into the war was regarded by many in the German high command with barely disguised contempt, while the Italian assault on Greece late in 1940 was kept a close secret – and sent Hitler into a rage when he found out. On the other hand, Hitler did not think it necessary to inform his Italian ally of the impending attack on the Soviet Union in the spring of 1941. Such mutual secrecy was bad enough, but in the southern European theatre the two nations' forces had to work closely together, and the distrust and dislike became even more obvious in the planning of operations.

When Rommel was commander of the Afrika Korps, in North Africa, he was constantly falling foul of the Italian high com-

Above, left to right: Mussolini, Hitler and Count Ciano, Italian Foreign Minister and Mussolini's son-in-law. Ciano's diaries are a prime source of information on Italian policy during World War II.

Below: Churchill and Roosevelt at Casablanca in 1943, at the press conference during which Roosevelt announced that 'unconditional surrender' was to be the Allied goal.

mand, refusing to obey orders he disliked and initiating offensives without prior consultation. His letters are full of complaints about his allies, and bemoan their failure to provide him with the war material he needed. On the other side, the Italians were furious with the way they were treated by the Germans. Marshal Ugo Cavallero, Italian chief of staff from 1941 until January 1943, was one of the few Italian generals who made a serious effort to improve relations with Hitler's forces. For his pains, he was described by the Italian Foreign Minister, Count Galeazzo Ciano, as a 'perfect buffoon' and a 'servile lackey'.

While Rommel was berating his supposed allies for the low levels of his stocks of fuel, an event occurred which perhaps typifies the difference between the Allies and the Axis. Tobruk had fallen on 20 June 1942, while Churchill was in the USA. Roosevelt at once offered Churchill the latest batch of the newest US tank, the Sherman. Three hundred were sent to the Middle East immediately and although the engines, being carried in a separate vessel, were sunk off Bermuda, the US president made sure that they were replaced at once.

CONSULTATION AND CONFERENCES

Relations between the USA and Great Britain were in general, then, very good. Combined planning was effective, and the sound personal understanding between Roosevelt and Churchill an immeasurable boon. Apart from the regular discussions of the Joint Chiefs of Staff, issues were discussed and grand strategy planned at a number of conferences. Most important were those at Casablanca in January 1943, Cairo and Tehran in November–December 1943, at Quebec in September 1944, at Yalta in February 1945 and at Potsdam in July 1945.

Naturally, there were some disagreements. The British predilection for offensives in what the Americans saw as the secondary theatre of the Mediterranean was a constant source of discord, and the difficulties of commanding large multinational forces were well illustrated during the closing months of 1944, when the ambitions of the British Field Marshal Sir Bernard Law Montgomery to retain control over all ground forces in Europe were at variance with what the Americans saw as the proper command arrangement. But this episode never seriously threatened to divide the two allies.

Relations between the Western powers and the Soviet Union were inevitably more distant, and on occasion very strained. Stalin was implacable in his desire to see a second front opened as quickly as possible, and believed that British stalling and concen-

tration on the Mediterranean was politically motivated. In contrast to what happened on the Axis side, however, the Soviet Union was kept fully informed about the preparations for operations such as 'Torch' in northwest Africa (Churchill himself went to the Soviet Union to explain the operation to the Soviet leader). Later in the war there was certainly suspicion, especially on the British side, about Stalin's clear intention to establish Soviet hegemony over eastern and central Europe, but this did not make any difference to military cooperation – indeed, in autumn 1944 Churchill was extremely harsh with the Polish government-in-exile in London because of its unwillingness to accept some of Stalin's demands. The supplying of the Red Army via the land route (through Iran) or by the Arctic Convoys was carried on steadily during the war (in spite of Soviet unwillingness to acknowledge it publicly) and when the Americans and British wanted Soviet action to help ease pressure after the 'Battle of the Bulge' early in 1945, Stalin brought forward his winter offensive to 12 January.

At many minor levels – the relationship between the Western Allies and the Free French of Charles de Gaulle, the problems of dealing with Chiang Kai-shek in China, the prejudices of individuals (Admiral Ernest King, the head of the US Navy, barely tried to conceal his anti-British bias) – there were difficulties in the alliance against the nations of the Tripartite Pact. But, in general, it was a very successful arrangement and contributed substantially to final victory.

Below: Checking bags of beans and other foodstuffs bound for the Soviet Union. Allied exports to the Russians, both by sea in the Arctic Convoys and by land, principally through Persia (now Iran), were very important for the Soviet war economy. However, Soviet spokesmen were often reluctant to acknowledge this.

BARBAROSSA AND THE BATTLE FOR MOSCOW

The German attack on the Soviet Union of 22 June 1941 – Operation Barbarossa – took World War II into a vast new arena, and had consequences with which we are still living today. The sheer size of the battles on the Eastern Front, and especially the numbers of tanks and artillery pieces involved, made this by far the largest of the conflicts subsumed under the general heading of World War II, while the extremes of temperature, particularly the cold of the Russian winter, made this one of the most exacting theatres of the entire war.

What gave the fighting in the Eastern Front its most intense character, however, was that here were the two greatest totalitarian states, espousing radically different philosophies, locked in a combat to the death. The Soviet people suffered severely during the war: it is estimated that 20,000,000 of them (one in five of the pre-war population) perished as a direct result of the German attack, and many of these were victims of deliberate acts of terror against civilians.

All in all, the Eastern Front was the area of the war in which all the characteristics of the new forms of warfare – the tactics based upon manoeuvre and new machines, the importance of sheer quantity of weaponry, and the inexorable involvement of civilians in the fighting – were seen at their most ferocious.

Hitler had intended to take on the Soviet Union in the autumn of 1940, soon after the fall of France and before the Battle of Britain had even been joined – or so he led many of the key officers of the German high command to believe. The high command, however, having within a year organized two large campaigns in Poland and western Europe, felt that they could not commit themselves to such an enormous undertaking without far more preparation, and so the attack was postponed. The Führer's Directive Number 21 set Barbarossa for the following May, and envisaged three Army Groups striking into the Soviet Union.

Right: German paratroops on the island of Crete rest in the shade of a stone wall and snatch a quick meal. Below right: A German armoured column pushes ahead in Yugoslavia, past the wrecks of Yugoslav Army vehicles that have fallen victim to the 'flying artillery' of the Luftwaffe. Below: A PzKpfw III fords a river during Operation Barbarossa – the invasion of the Soviet Union in 1941. This campaign had been postponed by the need to intervene in the Balkans.

There seems little doubt as to Hitler's reasons for attacking the largest nation in Europe: he had always put the destruction of Bolshevism high on the list of his priorities, and the raw materials – of the Donets Basin and the Ukraine – were, in his opinion, an invaluable goal. Nor had his attitude towards the Soviet leadership been softened by the fact that, while making every attempt to stay on good terms with Germany, Stalin and his Foreign Minister Viachislav Molotov had never made any secret of their ambitions for a sphere of influence in Russia's traditional areas of expansion – Finland, Turkey and the Balkans, particularly Bulgaria. In 1940, the Soviet Union had taken over the Baltic states of Lithuania, Estonia and Latvia, and had demanded (and been accorded) substantial territorial gains from Romania.

Hitler's original intention, to attack in the autumn of 1940, having been thwarted by the arguments of his generals, his next scheme, to attack in May 1941, was thwarted by his ally, Mussolini. As we have seen, Mussolini had ignored Hitler's warnings not to meddle in the Balkans and had attempted to invade Greece late in 1940. This bloody repulse was followed by another failure in Libya and Egypt, where the British had made considerable gains, and Hitler was obliged to go to the aid of his ally. To deal with North Africa, the dispatch of Rommel and the Afrika Korps (a mere two divisions) was organized, and did not seriously affect the planning for Barbarossa, but the Balkan adventure proved a greater problem.

At first, there seemed little to trouble the

German planners. Bulgaria joined the Tri-partite Pact on 1 March 1941, and German troops entered the country, giving them direct access to the Greek border. On 25 March Yugoslavia also acceded to a German alliance, giving the Panzers a way round the Greek defensive systems that were built to face Bulgaria. Although Great Britain had started to send help to the Greeks (in the shape of three divisions) in March, it seemed unlikely that they would be able to stop a German conquest of the country. On 27 March, however, a coup in Belgrade took Yugoslavia out of the Axis camp. At once Hitler decided to attack the country, and to strike without delay was essential – for Yugoslavia deployed 900,000 men, and a mobilization would increase her strength by another 500,000. To organize this attack, 32 of the divisions designated for Barbarossa had to be moved, and the timing of the attack on the Soviet Union was changed from May to late June.

The assault on Yugoslavia and Greece was very successful; another vindication of Blitz-krieg warfare. Armoured formations spear-headed an advance into Yugoslavia from north and east, and within a matter of days the demoralized Yugoslav Army was bundled into defeat. On 6 April 1941 the Blitzkrieg began; on the 10th the tanks rolled into Belgrade, and on the 17th came formal surrender. Some 340,000 prisoners fell into German hands for the loss of only 151 German dead. It was a complete victory.

The Greeks were attacked at the same time as the Yugoslavs, although along a much smaller front which allowed less room for the encircling manoeuvres that had been so suc-

cessful elsewhere. And the fortresses of the 'Metaxas Line' (the fortifications facing the Bulgarian frontier) were well armed with anti-aircraft weapons, denying the German Stukas their usual free rein. Mobility and penetration again carried the day for the Germans, however. A Panzer division struck through southern Yugoslavia, outflanked the defences of the Metaxas Line and reached the sea at Salonika on 9 April. Only bad roads and some fierce but piecemeal resistance were now delaying the German drive south, and so the decision was taken to evacuate the three British divisions on 19 April. By 24 April, Greece had capitulated, having lost 15,700 dead and 218,000 troops captured. British losses had been 12,712, including 9000 captured. In Yugoslavia and Greece together, the Germans had lost only 1700 men.

THE LANDING ON CRETE

The next act in this phase of the war was the German landing on the island of Crete, where there were substantial numbers (over 40,000) of British troops. This was to be an airborne operation, using gliders and paratroops, backed up by seaborne troops when the fighting had got under way. Once again, the action, which began on 20 May, seemed a brilliant vindication of new ways of waging war. The Luftwaffe ruled the skies, and caused the Royal Navy such losses that it was unable to prevent the seaborne assault, while the battle for the island and the subsequent evacuation cost the British and Commonwealth forces 1800 dead and 12,000 prisoners. But the elite German airborne forces had also suffered heavily in the oper-

Above: The German forces reach the Aegean. The next step was the invasion of Crete, but this proved a tricky operation. The first wave of paratroops landed on 20 May 1941, around Máleme, Réthimnon and Heraklion. The Commonwealth forces on the island had been expecting them, however, and the fighting was bitter. The German commander at Máleme, General Meindl, was severely wounded and had to hand over command to a subordinate, while at Réthimnon the glider carrying the German commander crashed into the Aegean. What saved the Germans was the power of the Luftwaffe, which inflicted heavy losses on the Royal Navy.

ation with losses of 3700 killed and missing.

By the end of May, therefore, Hitler had once again achieved great military victories, and stood dominant in Europe, with his armies seemingly invincible. But the delay in launching Barbarossa may well have cost him success in what was to be the crowning campaign. Six weeks of good campaigning weather had been lost – and those six weeks were later to seem a fatal delay to the German commanders as their men struggled through the mud of October and then froze in November.

Stalin had been given plenty of warning that his country would be the next target of the German war machine. The actions of the Germans themselves in asserting their influence in the Balkans should have put him on his guard, plus the fact that a very reliable spy in Japan (Richard Sorge) and the so-called 'Lucy Ring' of agents in Switzerland had provided details of both the strength of the attack and its timing. On 18 June, a German communist soldier deserted from his unit and went over the Soviet frontier; when Stalin was told the news that this informant had brought in, he is reported to have ordered him to be shot. He also refused to allow Soviet commanders fully to mobilize their forces in case the Germans took it as a provocation. The megalomania of the Soviet leader thus put his forces in a vulnerable position when the blow fell on 22 June.

THE GERMAN OFFENSIVE

The German forces that undertook the attack were divided into three Army Groups, stretching from the Baltic to the Black Sea. In all, there were some 200 German and satellite divisions, with 120 in the front line. Army Group South, under Field Marshal von Rundstedt, consisted of 42 divisions, Army Group Centre, under Field Marshal von Bock, of 49 divisions, and Army Group North, under Field Marshal von Leeb, of 29 divisions. But compared to the 10 Panzer divisions of 1940, there were now 21 armoured formations, although to achieve such an expansion the number of tanks had

been reduced from over 250 to under 200 in each. There were also 12 Romanian divisions in the southern part of the front, while Hungary and Slovakia provided a few brigades each. The most powerful additional force, however, was that of Finland. Eager to recoup some of the losses of 1940, Marshal Mannerheim put 18 divisions into the field, although not in formal alliance with the Germans.

Against this, the Soviet forces had about 138 infantry and 40 armoured or motorized divisions in five military districts running the length of the frontier. But the frontier fortifications (many of which had been occupied in 1939 after the partition of Poland) were not good; there were often large gaps between strongpoints, and the Soviet forces were so strung out as to be unable to provide concerted resistance. When the at-

42

Right: Heinz Guderian in his command vehicle, keeping in contact with his advance units. Guderian was responsible for some of the most astonishing German victories of 1941. Below: German infantry slogging on across one of the many rivers of European Russia, as the advance slows down. Far right: A German PzKpfw III moves forward during the fighting for Bulchevo, a village near Moscow. By the time the winter frosts arrived, all the resources of the Red Army were poured into the desperate struggle to save the capital.

tack came, the forward units were overwhelmed, stranded helplessly without aid and often outnumbered by the opposing forces. Nor was the Soviet Air Force a match for the Luftwaffe. Although the Soviets had at least 4000 aircraft available, they were usually of poor quality, and their pilots were trained to fly in formations that rendered them terribly vulnerable to the experienced fighter pilots of the German air arm. Field Marshal Albert Kesselring, who commanded Luftflotte II in

support of Army Group Centre, described the fate of the Soviet pilots as the 'massacre of the innocents'.

It is hardly surprising, then, that after a short barrage, the first troops into the Soviet lines made rapid headway. By the end of the day, some of the Panzer units of Army Group Centre had covered 80km (50 miles), as had Manstein's LVI Panzer Corps in the north. Only in the south, where the defences were stronger (even Stalin realized that Hitler had always been obsessed with the conquest of the Ukraine) was the German success anything less than spectacular, and even here it was satisfying enough.

The German plan, as laid down by Hitler, was for the three Army Groups to advance to a line along the Leningrad–Smolensk–Kiev axis, and then, having destroyed the Soviet forces to the west of the Dniepr and Dvina line, Army Group Centre would link with Army Group North to take Leningrad, before moving on to take Moscow, and, pushing past the capital, would sever the main arteries of the country's north–south communications. This final blow would prevent the Soviet

forces making any large-scale manoeuvres, and would, in effect, decide the campaign. For, with their armies in ruins and no prospect of moving large bodies of men north–south, the Soviet troops would be in no position to resist any further German advances. The final line reached by the German armies would be the axis Astrakhan–the Volga–Gor'kiy–Kotlas–Archangel.

The high command had agreed to this plan with reluctance; in classic military fashion, they wished to stake all on the attainment of the key strategic objective, which must be Moscow as the key to the north–south communication network. But Hitler overruled them, and they allowed themselves to be persuaded, hoping that as circumstances took over and the first plans had to be modified they would be able to enforce their point of view.

The first three months of the campaign saw the Germans enjoy the most astonishing successes. Their method of driving deep into enemy positions, and then encircling large formations, seemed irresistible. The Soviet troops, it is true, were frequently uncoordinated and communications were poor; some of them (the troops from the Baltic states, for example) were also less than enthusiastic about the fight, and Stalin's insistence on holding ground that was already strategically lost cost many casualties. But the Soviet forces did not, in general, show any signs of collapse; and nor were they less well equipped than the Germans. The best Soviet tanks – the slow but heavily armoured KV-1 and the revolutionary T-34 – were a match for any German vehicle; and whereas the Germans had only 440 of their best tank, the PzKpfw IV, there were about 900 T-34s and 500 KV-1s available during the summer and autumn. The German tank commanders were surprised by such Soviet weaponry, which was far superior to their own.

EARLY BLITZKRIEG SUCCESSES

What gave the Germans their victories was their mastery of mobile warfare: their ability to maintain the impetus of their attacks, to probe for new weaknesses in the enemy line, and to retain the initiative. Even where there were very few armoured vehicles available, they kept up this constant offensive, encircling and outmanoeuvring the Soviet forces. Manstein took the Crimea (where he was transferred in October 1941) in a swift campaign from 29 October to 16 November, by using the tactics of Blitzkrieg, even though he had very few of the tanks on which it ostensibly rested. Where the armoured vehicles were present, the results were spectacular, with hundreds of thousands of prisoners being taken. The Germans claimed to have captured 310,000 at Smolensk in August and 665,000 at Kiev in September.

The great victory at Kiev, however, was not bought without another loss of time. Hitler had decided, by 12 August, that he would stick roughly to his original scheme. Smolensk had fallen by 8 August, and now the German high command, previously convinced that they would be able to get their way once the campaign was in full swing, found they were unable to move the Führer.

He decided that von Bock's Army Group Centre, which had reached its first objective (Smolensk) as laid down in the 18 December Directive, would halt; armoured forces would be sent south to help von Rundstedt's Army Group take Kiev, while Army Group North would be able to call on von Bock's formations as well. In spite of the furious objections of Guderian, who harangued Hitler on 23 August, there was to be no change of plan. The drive on Moscow was halted.

The decision had important consequences. For although the results were undoubtedly very gratifying, in that the Kiev pocket yielded its hundreds of thousands of prisoners and Army Group North advanced to within sight of Leningrad, the offensive in the centre did not get under way again until 2 October. When it did, Operation Typhoon (the drive to capture Moscow) scored some immediate victories as two giant armoured pincers from von Bock's Army Group reached out to encircle the capital – the Bryansk and Viaz'ma pockets produced 660,000 prisoners, and the Russians were as

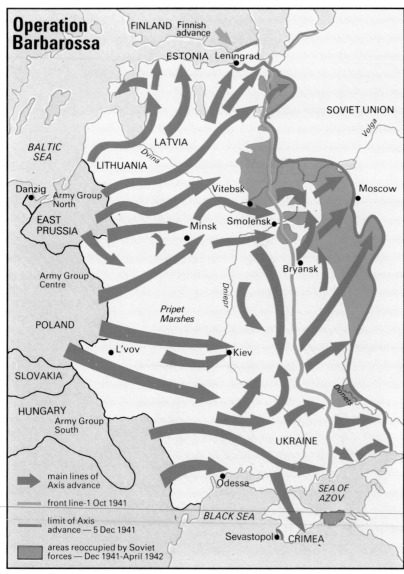

Operation Barbarossa

FINLAND Finnish advance

ESTONIA Leningrad

SOVIET UNION

BALTIC SEA

LATVIA

Dvina

LITHUANIA

Volga

Danzig

Army Group North

EAST PRUSSIA

Vitebsk

Minsk

Smolensk

Moscow

Bryansk

Army Group Centre

Dniepr

Pripet Marshes

POLAND

L'vov

Kiev

SLOVAKIA

Donets

HUNGARY

Army Group South

UKRAINE

Odessa

SEA OF AZOV

BLACK SEA

Sevastopol CRIMEA

main lines of Axis advance

front line-1 Oct 1941

limit of Axis advance — 5 Dec 1941

areas reoccupied by Soviet forces — Dec 1941-April 1942

nonplussed as before by German tactics. But by 20 October, the rains had come, and a sea of mud slowed the German motorized forces to a mere 32km (20 miles) a day on open roads without opposition. Just as important, the tanks were now in a state of mechanical exhaustion. They had all been driven at least 750km (450 miles). By 14 November there were only 50 usable armoured vehicles in Guderian's XXIV Panzer Corps, whereas in June there had been 350. Nor did the rains help the Luftwaffe, which found its airfields waterlogged and visibility poor.

The Soviet forces, meanwhile, were making enormous efforts in defence. On 10 October a new West Front under General Georgi Zhukov was set up to resist the drive on the capital. Some 500,000 civilians were conscripted to dig defences round the city, and had built 100km (60 miles) of anti-tank ditches and 8000km (5000 miles) of trenches by early December. Sorge, the spy whose advice Stalin had spurned in the spring, had informed the Soviet leadership in September that the Japanese did not intend to move against Manchuria in spite of Barbarossa, so Stalin felt confident in moving divisions from Siberia to the front. The Germans were surprised by the number of divisions that the Soviets kept pouring into the line, and realized too late that they had underestimated the ability of this enormous country to draw on its reserves of manpower. New units of tanks, including many T-34s, began appearing at the front, and took their toll of the German armour, however well the Wehrmacht fought.

The final straw for the German offensive came when the frost set in. The Panzer

counterstroke. Since October he had been preparing 50 divisions in the rear, and on 5 and 6 December, before the Germans had had time to prepare winter positions, they were hit by an estimated 718,000 Soviet troops and 720 tanks, in over 100 divisions. The ability to create this force, when the German high command believed they had shattered the Red Army, was an immense achievement. The Germans were forced back all along the front, often with severe losses of men and material.

NO WITHDRAWAL

It has been estimated that German casualties, from the beginning of Barbarossa to the end of 1941, were 830,000; of this number, 174,000 were dead, and 36,000 missing. The Soviet Union, on the other hand, had lost 2,800,000 prisoners alone between 22 June and 6 December. Even so, by the end of the year, Stalin could still put into the field 200 infantry divisions, 35 cavalry divisions and 40 armoured brigades, while still more formations were being organized in rear areas.

In December, the German high command had been reorganized: Hitler had relieved von Brauchitsch of his post as commander-in-chief and had assumed the position himself, while of the commanders of the Army Groups, von Bock and von Leeb had asked to be relieved of their posts, ostensibly for health reasons but to a large extent because they were unable to cope with the demands of the Führer, which seemed to them insane. Hitler refused them permission to draw their men back to more defensible positions, and insisted on holding as much ground as possible.

This policy almost had catastrophic consequences early in January 1942, for the Soviet armies renewed their offensive on the 9th, threatening to carve Army Group Centre to pieces, and also making holes in the front in the north near Leningrad and in the Donets Basin in the south. In the event, all these offensives were held by the sheer fighting quality of the German forces – effective counter-attacks and resolute defence, even when surrounded or cut off. And at this stage, the Red Army's commanders were not the experts they later became at keeping up constant waves of pressure until their opponents broke. By the time the spring thaw brought movement to a halt all along the front late in March, however, the German Army had suffered severely, with 240,000 casualties (65,000 of whom were killed or missing) as the price it had to pay for blunting the Soviet attacks since the beginning of January. The Russian adventure was already taking longer, and was far more costly, than Hitler and his generals had calculated.

Above left: Two German PzKpfw III tanks on the advance into the Soviet Union in 1941. Above: The bodies of men killed in the winter are uncovered by the spring thaw. Below: No sooner had the German offensive finally run out of steam early in December 1941 than the Red Army launched a devastating counter-attack that almost destroyed the Wehrmacht. Here, villagers welcome Red Army troops who have just forced the Germans out.

commanders had hoped that a few days' hard going would enable them to complete the encirclement of Moscow, but they found the cold the worst enemy of all. Not expecting a winter campaign, the machines were ill prepared. They lacked anti-freeze, and parts made of artificial rubber froze solid. For the men it was worse. No proper winter clothing had been issued, and in November 400 men per infantry regiment in the 112th Division were frostbite casualties. At this point the Soviet counter-attacks and prepared positions began to have their effect. The Germans could cope no longer; some infantry regiments were down to 400 men. By 4 December, the offensive towards Moscow had petered out.

As the German attack in the centre halted, and the offensives in the north and south also ran out of steam, Stalin unleashed a massive

PEARL HARBOR AND THE JAPANESE CONQUESTS

World War II was to become fully global in December 1941, when the Japanese Navy launched its attack on the US naval base at Pearl Harbor in the Hawaiian Islands. This attack extended the war to the Pacific, and brought in the world's most powerful nation. Now, the two countries that were to play the leading role in the postwar world – the USSR and the USA – had been forced into the fray by attacks from the expansionist warrior states of the Tripartite Pact.

Of course, the USA had been involved in the war for some time; not as a combatant, but as a friend and supplier of Great Britain. Indeed, the re-election of President Franklin Delano Roosevelt in November 1940 was a great relief to the British leader, Winston Churchill. For as early as November 1939, in the 'Cash and Carry' Bill, the US president had shown his willingness to help the Allies by allowing them to buy war material on unlimited credit. As the German armies won their great victories of 1940, the president became more determined that Britain should not go under. On 16 December, he declared that the USA should be the 'great arsenal of democracy' and on 8 March 1941, the Lend-Lease Act gave the British unprecedented access to US aid. The Americans made plain their distaste for the Axis on 16 June 1941 when German and Italian consulates in the USA were closed, but in discussions with the British earlier in the spring they were evasive about what they would do if Britain were directly attacked.

After the beginning of Operation Barbarossa, there was increasingly little doubt about the US attitude. On 12 August 1941, the 'Atlantic Charter' was signed by Churchill and Roosevelt. Among other statements, article six included the line 'after the destruction of Nazi tyranny . . .'. There were now also US bases in Iceland and Greenland, and the US Navy took over the protection of convoys between Newfoundland and Iceland. This provoked clashes with U-boats, one of which sank the US destroyer *Reuben James* off Iceland in October 1941.

How long the USA could have carried on in this state of semi-belligerence is difficult to say. In the event, however, the position was resolved when the Japanese decided to attack, and Germany declared war on the USA.

The reasons for the Japanese attack were a combination of expansionism and fear. Ever since the 1894–5 war with China, Japan had been a growing power. By the outbreak of World War I she had already asserted her hegemony over Korea; her partnership with

the Allies of that war had brought her many gains, and in the 1930s she had gradually begun to force another conflict with China, until by 1937 there was full-scale war. The Japanese took most of the cities on the Chinese eastern seaboard, and forced the government of Chiang Kai-shek to move the capital inland to Chungking. Although the total conquest of such a vast country proved beyond the capabilities of the Japanese Army in the short term, there were 27 divisions still fighting there in 1941. This expansionist policy was not directed merely at East Asia, however. Japan had few raw materials and looked greedily south to the great colonial empires of the Dutch in the East Indies, the British in Malaya and the French in Indochina, seeing there a springboard to becoming the leading power in Asia.

The defeat of France in 1940 left the French possessions in Indochina suddenly vulnerable to pressure, and as early as September 1940 Japanese troops had moved into Tonkin to close a route by which supplies had been reaching the Chinese forces of Chiang Kai-shek. A much greater step was taken in July 1941, when the Japanese were granted the right to place unlimited numbers of troops in Indochina. This at once put the Dutch East Indies and Malaya in a very vulnerable position.

The response of the Americans to Japanese aspirations was as firm as it had been to the Germans'. The USA, closely followed by Britain, Canada and the Dutch government-in-exile, put an embargo on oil exports to Japan. Oil was one of the staples of warfare, and although Japan had enough domestic stocks for two years, within a few months the embargo would seriously affect her military capacity. There were negotiations between Japan and the USA during the next few months, at first under Prime Minister Prince Fumimaro Konoye and then his successor, former Defence Minister General Hideki Tojo. The final talks, in November, saw deadlock, and the USA refused to remove the embargo.

'CLIMB MOUNT NIITAKA'

The fact that war was imminent was clear to all concerned, and on 27 November, the US Pacific Fleet was placed on the alert, while on 2 December the Japanese signalled 'Climb Mount Niitaka' to Vice-Admiral Chuichi Nagumo – the signal to attack Pearl Harbor.

The Japanese realized that in a long war they could not defeat the Americans. What they hoped was that in a lightning campaign they could establish themselves in a defensible perimeter, within which they would have all the raw materials they needed, and that they would be able to inflict sufficiently telling blows on the Americans to make it not

Left: The USS West Virginia *and the USS* New Jersey *ablaze after the Japanese attack on Pearl Harbor, as attempts are made to rescue survivors. The attack on Pearl Harbor had almost precisely the opposite effect to that intended by the Japanese high command. Rather than cowing the USA, it galvanized the American people into enthusiastic support for a war against all the Axis powers, and made Roosevelt's task of uniting the nation for war a comparatively simple one. Indeed, it has sometimes been argued that the US president deliberately provoked a Japanese attack in order to convince the US public that they had to enter World War II.*

TARGET AHEAD

On 7 December 1941, the Japanese pilot Nuzo Mori flew his torpedo-bomber into the attack at Pearl Harbor.
'I manoeuvred in order to make my line of approach absolutely right, knowing that the depth of water in the harbour was rarely more than 35 feet (11m). The slightest error in speed or altitude when firing might upset the mechanism of the torpedo and make it go to the bottom or break surface, undoing all my efforts either way.

'At the time, I was hardly aware of my actions. I acted like an automaton through force of habit which my long training had given me.

'The battleship appeared to leap suddenly into view across the front of my machine, looming huge, like a vast grey mountain. . . .

'All the while I completely forgot the enemy fire and the throbbing of my own engine, totally absorbed by my manoeuvre. At the right moment, I pulled with all my strength on the release lever. The machine jolted violently as shells hit the wings and fuselage. My head was flung back, and I felt as though I'd just hit an iron bar head-on. But I'd made it! The torpedo-launching was perfect! My plane still flew and responded to my control. The torpedo was going to score a direct hit. I suddenly became conscious of where I was and of the enemy fire.'

Right: Japanese Zero fighters on board the aircraft carrier Akagi prepare to take off to provide air cover for the bombers that will make the first strike on Pearl Harbor.

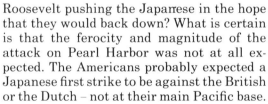

Below: As the crew abandon ship, the USS California settles into the mud at Pearl Harbor. The capsized hulk of her sister ship, USS Oklahoma, is visible on the far right of the picture.

worth their while to reduce this defensive screen. Admiral Isoroku Yamamoto, the commander of the navy, had said that he could guarantee victories for six months, but not necessarily any longer.

American motives for provoking the Japanese are more complex to unravel. Was the administration unaware of the risk of Japanese attack? Was it deliberately courting a Japanese strike so as to have the onus of declaring war put on its opponents? Or was Roosevelt pushing the Japanese in the hope that they would back down? What is certain is that the ferocity and magnitude of the attack on Pearl Harbor was not at all expected. The Americans probably expected a Japanese first strike to be against the British or the Dutch – not at their main Pacific base.

In January 1941, Yamamoto had instructed his planning staff to begin looking at the possibilities of an attack on the US fleet while it was at anchor. The Japanese may well have been influenced by the British strike on Taranto in November 1940, for they did not intend to engage the US vessels with their own warships. They would make a bombing and torpedo raid from their aircraft carriers. The Japanese Navy was the only force in the world that had a carrier fleet to equal its battleships: it had 10 of each. In the US Navy there was only one aircraft carrier for every three battleships. The aircraft carrier was the new capital ship, the basis of naval power. If anyone had been in doubt about that, then the attack on Pearl Harbor should certainly have convinced them.

The Japanese fleet that struck Pearl Harbor consisted of six aircraft carriers (*Akagi, Kaga, Hiryu, Soryu, Zuikaku* and *Shokaku*, carrying 423 planes), two battleships and two heavy cruisers. On Sunday 7

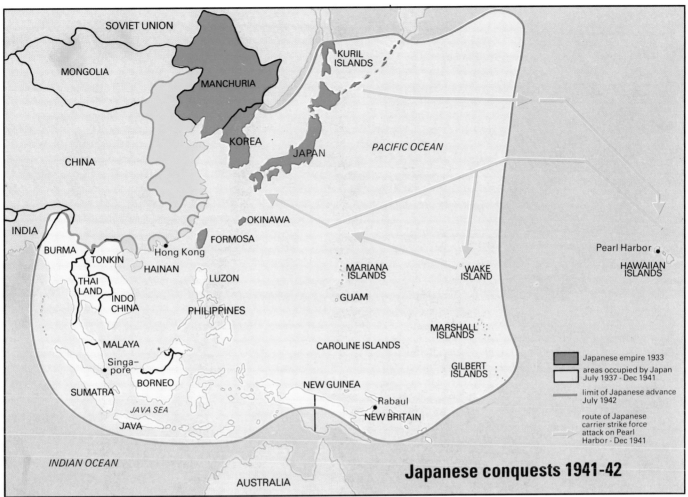

Japanese conquests 1941-42

Legend:
- Japanese empire 1933
- areas occupied by Japan July 1937 - Dec 1941
- limit of Japanese advance July 1942
- route of Japanese carrier strike force attack on Pearl Harbor - Dec 1941

December, at 0615 hours, Nagumo flew off the first wave of aircraft, under Commander Mitsuo Fuchida, which consisted of 40 torpedo-bombers (with specially adapted shallow running torpedoes), 51 divebombers, 50 high-level bombers and 43 fighters. The Americans had had some warning that an attack might be about to take place: apart from the general diplomatic situation, a destroyer had reported contact with a Japanese submarine at 0630 hours that morning, and radar operators had detected the approach of the Japanese aircraft at 0700 hours. Their report was, however, interpreted as a flight of B-17 Flying Fortresses that were due.

A SPECTACULAR ATTACK

Nagumo's planes struck a base where no attack was expected, where eight battleships were invitingly moored in pairs, and where visibility was clear. A second wave of aircraft set off at 0715, some 40 minutes before the first wave hit Pearl Harbor. The results were spectacular: five battleships were sunk, together with three cruisers and three destroyers, while 188 aircraft were destroyed. The Pacific Fleet was badly hurt – but not crippled, for its three aircraft carriers had not been in harbour. Their survival was the only disappointment for the Japanese.

If the Americans had underestimated the Japanese ability to carry out an effective first strike, so too had the British. Although the British commanders in the Far East were very worried about Japanese intentions, they still regarded them as inferiors when it came to making war. Brewster Buffalo fighters, that were obsolete in the European theatre, were considered by members of the British high command 'good enough for Singapore', while the capabilities of the Japanese Mitsubishi A6M Zero fighter were ignored. To defend Malaya the British had less than 150 aircraft available to take on over 700 Japanese.

British attempts to defend Malaya against the Japanese troops that had been assembling in Indochina met with disaster right from the beginning. The first catastrophe was the sinking of *Repulse* and *Prince of Wales*, a battlecruiser and battleship sent to the Far East to bolster the defences of Malaya. The aircraft carrier *Indomitable*, which was to have been an integral part of the squadron, ran aground on the way, and so the two vessels carried on without immediate air cover. Once in Singapore, they decided to set out to try to disrupt Japanese landings which had begun on 8 December in southern Thailand. Without the benefit of air cover, they were caught by Japanese planes in open

Above: Trying to salvage something from the wreckage just after the Japanese attack on Pearl Harbor. Here, the remains of the USS Cassin *and the USS* Downes *are examined. They were hit while in dry dock. Right: The talented and ruthless Japanese general Tomoyuki Yamashita. He believed that Japan should not attack the USA and Britain until her forces had been thoroughly modernized, but in 1942 seemed to disprove his theory when he conquered Malaya within 70 days of a declaration of war. Yamashita was retired to a training command after this success, but in 1945 directed a resourceful defence of the main Philippine island of Luzon against the Americans. He was executed as a war criminal in 1946.*

were within easy reach of the forces of the Rising Sun, swiftly fell before air and naval bombardment that the defenders could not match. The most heroic defence – as on Wake Island which held out until 23 December – could not resist this Japanese offensive. The real question was whether the Japanese land forces could match the success of their navy by winning victories on the ground in Malaya and the Philippines.

In the Philippines, General Douglas MacArthur commanded a force of some 31,000 men, 19,000 of them Americans. But he had only 300 aircraft at his disposal, against 750 Japanese. General Masaharu Homma's Fourteenth Army landed in the north of the main island of Luzon on 10 December 1941, and the Japanese forces quickly showed themselves able to expand their bridgehead. A second landing was planned further south, to trap MacArthur's troops, but rather than allow his forces to get caught the US general pulled his men back to the Bataan Peninsula, where they had prepared defences which, together with the fortress of Corregidor off its southern tip, commanded the entrance to Manila Bay. On 11 January 1942 the Japanese managed to break through the first line of defence, but the defenders merely pulled back once more. MacArthur himself was ordered to leave for Australia by Roosevelt, which he did with great reluctance in March. On 9 April the American and Filipino troops finally surrendered, and on 6 May the 1500 men in the fortress of Corregidor were forced to give up. The survivors of Bataan had to endure a forced march which killed a further 12,000 of them.

RETREAT TO SINGAPORE

The attack on Malaya was undertaken by the Japanese Twenty-fifth Army, under General Tomoyuki Yamashita. His troops carried out a flexible advance down the peninsula, having landed in the north. Lieutenant-General Arthur Percival commanded the British ground troops that were to stop this advance, but quickly found himself in extreme difficulty. The Japanese units fought expertly, and although the British forces slightly outnumbered those of the invader (by January, 88,000 British troops faced 70,000 Japanese) the defensive positions that were established were quickly bypassed or infiltrated by the mobile Japanese infantry. The British tried to block the main roads, but the Japanese proved able to move at will through terrain thought impassable to regular forces.

By 30 January, Percival had been forced to fall back on Singapore itself. The defences of the island base were not what they might have been, and on the night of 8–9 February the invaders crossed the Straits of Johore, took the reservoir that provided the island's

sea on 10 December and both were sunk, with the loss of over 800 lives. This was a reverse such as the Royal Navy had not experienced for many years, and it also asserted a superiority at sea that the Japanese were to put to good effect during the following months. They landed troops in Malaya, in the Philippines and in Thailand, and were then able to install themselves in Java and the rest of the Dutch East Indies.

Of the colonial possessions in the Far East, some were clearly indefensible against Japanese attack. One such was Hong Kong, isolated and vulnerable to the Japanese armies in China. General Takashi Sakai's Twenty-third Army stormed the defences of Kowloon on the night of 9–10 December, and on Christmas Day the 12,000 defenders surrendered. Islands such as Guam, too, which

Above: Under the Union Flag, British officers prepare to surrender Singapore to the Japanese. The fall of this stronghold on 15 February 1942 was described by Winston Churchill as the worst disaster in British military history. It was the culmination of a lightning campaign by the Japanese Twenty-fifth Army under Yamashita. Right: Japanese infantry double into the attack. In Malaya, Burma and the Philippines, the fluid assaults of Japanese infantry left their enemies floundering. Not until the US and Filipino forces in the Philippines had reached the lines of defences across the Bataan Peninsula could they check the tide of the Japanese advance, while the British forces in Burma were forced to undertake the longest retreat in their history, back to the Indian frontier.

under the command of the Dutch Rear-Admiral Karel Doorman, set out to meet utter defeat in the battle of the Java Sea. Five cruisers and six destroyers were lost, with Japanese aircraft monitoring the Allied fleet. By 10 March, Java had surrendered.

THE FINAL CAMPAIGN

The final land campaign in the Japanese offensive was the assault on Burma. This British colony was very lightly defended (its air defences were less than 40 aircraft) and the troops there were soon in difficulties against the men of Lieutenant-General Shojiro Iida's Fifteenth Army, some of which had moved in through Thailand. By the end of January there were only about two divisions to defend the enormous area into which the Japanese were advancing, and on 22 February, a disastrous crossing of the Sittang River resulted in the British forces becoming even more depleted. On 5 March, General Sir Harold Alexander took command of the British troops in Burma. His first objective was to hold the Yenangyaung oil-fields. In this he was to be aided by Chinese troops, but cooperation proved difficult. Yamashita's experienced forces soon pushed back the defences south of Mandalay; and as the Chinese withdrew northwards, Alexander once again had to pull back. By May, Mandalay had been abandoned and by the end of the month the British were back in India. The arrival of the monsoons then prevented any further large operations.

At sea, meanwhile, the Japanese fleet had established the defensive perimeter in the Pacific that was to be the buffer against US counters. The line of the Kuriles–the Marianas–Wake Island–the Marshalls the Gilberts–Rabaul (New Britain)–northern New Guinea had been attained, and naval units had even entered the Indian Ocean in April, forcing the British to consider moving their fleet to bases in East Africa, and opening up the prospect of a Japanese move across the Indian Ocean to link up with the Axis forces in North Africa. But Admiral Nobutake Kondo's squadron that had bombed Colombo in Ceylon, and had sunk the aircraft carrier HMS *Hermes* on 9 April, returned to the Pacific on the 12th – to the relief of the British Admiralty.

In six months, the Japanese had acquired a great empire, had humiliated their main rivals in the Far East and had shown again that warfare was changing. Their aircraft carriers had prevailed against more old-fashioned fleets, and their infantry had demonstrated superiority over the colonial armies. More important than all this, however, was that they had brought the USA into the war. Now the sheer scale of US industrial might would be the decisive factor.

water supply, and forced a surrender on the 15th – a shattering blow to British prestige.

In the East Indies, landings had been made on Borneo in December 1941. On 15 January 1942, the ABDA (American, British, Dutch, Australian) command was formed, under General Wavell, to try to stabilize the situation in the area. By now, the capabilities of the Japanese were well known, and the paucity of Allied defences gave rise to great concern. Indeed, the British were unenthusiastic at having one of their nationals at the head of a command that seemed doomed to defeat. Wavell could do little to delay the inevitable; Sumatra was invaded and on 25 February he moved his headquarters to Ceylon. Two days later, in an attempt to prevent two Japanese convoys from landing troops on the island, the naval forces in Java,

THE WESTERN DESERT TO JULY 1942

While the German assault on the Soviet Union and the Japanese offensives in the Pacific and Southeast Asia were taking the war into new arenas, the struggle in the Mediterranean was widening in scope, extending into East Africa and the Middle East, all the while growing in destructive power as the forces engaged grew larger and more expert.

The German decision to help the Italians in North Africa by sending two divisions under Erwin Rommel was to bring to the fore one of the most accomplished exponents of mobile warfare in World War II. Rommel's forces began to arrive in February 1941, and by March he had decided upon action. The Italian high command was only in favour of a small push forward, but gave consent to a move against the forward British positions at El Agheila. At dawn on 24 March, therefore, elements of the German 5th Light Division assaulted British outposts. The British had not been expecting an attack, and withdrew to Mersa Brega. Using the mobility of his troops, Rommel pushed on, outflanking the

Below: A motorcycle combination spearheads an advance by the 21st Panzer Division, the renamed 5th Light Division. Reconnaissance was an exacting task in the desert. The toll on men and machines was heavy, with the elements providing just as many problems as enemy action.

Top: Troops of the 4th Indian Division on the lookout, facing the key position of Halfaya, where they took part in the ill-starred 'Battleaxe' offensive of 1941. Above: A British patrol returns to base, threading its way through the perimeter wire around Tobruk.

Mersa Brega position, and on the night of 3–4 April advance patrols entered Benghazi. The Italian high command was horrified, but quickly found that they could not restrain the impetuous German general. Although he still had only one German formation (the 5th Light; the 15th Panzer Division was still not fully present), he thrust forward across the 'bulge' of Cyrenaica, taking Mechili.

The British commander, Sir Archibald Wavell, decided to make a stand at Tobruk, which was consigned to the 9th Australian Division under Major-General Leslie Morshead. Rommel's early attacks failed, and although he isolated Tobruk, moving the front line up to Sollum on the Egyptian frontier, he could not advance any further without over-straining his communications.

Wavell was urged to re-attack with all speed by the War Cabinet in London, which had at its disposal intelligence gleaned from the 'Enigma' intercepts of the Axis communications, and therefore knew how weak Rommel's force was during April and May, but Wavell had sound reasons for not wanting to undertake an offensive. Firstly, his command had become very widespread, and he had responsibility for an enormous area, over which his troops were scattered. Quite apart from the forces he had lost in Greece and Crete, there were three other areas where military activity was, or might soon be, taking place.

The most important of these was East Africa. Italian possessions there had been large, including Eritrea, Ethiopia and Italian Somaliland, and the Duke of Aosta who was in command of Italian forces there had used the 290,000 troops at his disposal to force Britain out of British Somaliland during the summer of 1940. Italian logistics were impossible, however; there were chronic shortages of both food and ammunition. The Duke was forced to stay on the defensive while Wavell organized an attack on him. From the Sudan, Lieutenant-General Sir William Platt and two Indian divisions moved into Eritrea in 1941, taking the mountain stronghold of Keren by the end of March. Meanwhile, from Kenya, Lieutenant-General Sir Alan Cunningham took Italian Somaliland and then moved up to Ethiopia, where the 1st South African Division captured Addis Ababa in February. Finally, in May 1941 the Duke of Aosta surrendered, although fighting continued in Galla-Sidamo province until November.

Wavell also had other responsibilities in the Middle East. In May 1941, a pro-German faction in Iraq, which had seized power in March, attacked the British base at Habbaniyah. Although troops were diverted from the Far East to deal with the threat, Wavell had to send a motorized division from Pal-

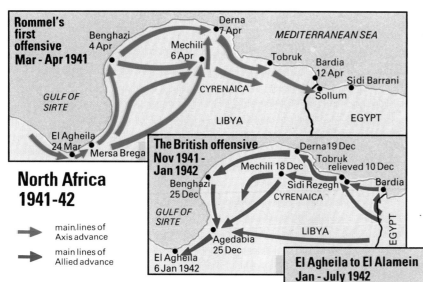

Rommel's first offensive Mar - Apr 1941

MEDITERRANEAN SEA

Derna 7 Apr
Benghazi 4 Apr
Mechili 6 Apr
Tobruk
Bardia 12 Apr
Sidi Barrani
Sollum
CYRENAICA
LIBYA
EGYPT
GULF OF SIRTE
El Agheila 24 Mar
Mersa Brega

North Africa 1941-42

→ main lines of Axis advance
→ main lines of Allied advance

The British offensive Nov 1941 - Jan 1942

Derna 19 Dec
Tobruk relieved 10 Dec
Mechili 18 Dec
Benghazi 25 Dec
Sidi Rezegh
Bardia
CYRENAICA
GULF OF SIRTE
LIBYA
EGYPT
Agedabia 25 Dec
El Agheila 6 Jan 1942

El Agheila to El Alamein Jan - July 1942

MEDITERRANEAN SEA
GULF OF BOMBA
Benghazi 29 Jan
1 Feb
Gazala
6 Feb
Tobruk falls 21 June
Mersa Matruh
Alexandria
Port Said
GULF OF SIRTE
Msus 25 Jan
El Alamein 1 July
Cairo
EGYPT
Suez Canal
El Agheila 21 Jan
LIBYA
Qattara Depression
Nile

and the Cruiser too lightly armoured (and mechanically unreliable) to offer much opposition to the German PzKpfw III, and were certainly no match for the PzKpfw IV. When an attack was reluctantly put under way in Operation Battleaxe on 15 June 1941, with the intention of relieving Tobruk, the results were as Wavell had predicted. The Germans lost only 338 men killed and missing, and 12 tanks, while one battalion of the 15th Panzer Division under ex-priest Wilhelm Bach blocked everything the British could throw at it. British losses were 380 dead and missing, but of the 180 tanks committed to the attack, 100 were lost.

estine. The troubles in Iraq were followed by difficulties with Syria, where the Vichy French were in control. After the fall of Crete, it appeared probable that a German attack on Cyprus would be the next move; and German aircraft were being allowed to refuel in Syria. To check this potential threat, an expeditionary force including the 7th Australian Division and a Free French brigade was ordered to take over the country. The fighting was very bitter (the Vichy French suffered some 6500 casualties); the assault began on 6 June and although Damascus was taken on 12 June, a ceasefire did not come into effect until 14 July.

All these considerations led the British commander to put off any attack on Rommel in the desert. But there were also other problems. Although he had received 135 Matilda Infantry tanks and 82 Cruiser tanks in May, Wavell was very aware of British technical inferiority: the Matilda was too slow

Below: A British Crusader tank passes a German PzKpfw IV in November 1941. The Crusader was no match for the PzKpfw IV in normal combat, as its 2-pounder gun was vastly inferior to the German tank's 75mm weapon.

The failure of Battleaxe cost Wavell his job. A new commander, whom Churchill hoped would be more aggressive, was moved to Egypt. This was General Sir Claude Auchinleck, formerly commander in India. He too soon found that Churchill's incessant demands for an attack in strength, to be code-named Operation Crusader, seemed to contain no appreciation of the need to build up the Allied forces to face the excellent tanks and superb soldiers of the Afrika Korps. Auchinleck managed, however, to gain himself some time by having Crusader delayed

from September to November, a delay that had little adverse effect, for the Axis supply lines to North Africa were at the time being seriously threatened by submarines, surface vessels and aircraft operating out of Malta. Rommel himself had been making plans for an attack to reduce Tobruk, freeing him for further offensive moves. In the event, Auchinleck's attack went in first, on 18 November.

Auchinleck's force, commanded by Lieutenant-General Sir Alan Cunningham, who had taken Addis Ababa, consisted of six strong divisions, in two corps (XIII and XXX) – the newly named Eighth Army. The British had a force of over 700 tanks, with 200 in reserve. The Germans had 174 tanks, and the Italians 146. The Axis combined force was the equivalent of 10 understrength divisions, and its core was the two German armoured formations, the 15th and the 21st Panzer Divisions (the latter being the renamed 5th Light Division).

The fighting during Crusader was confused. Cunningham's XXX Corps, that led the British attack, was badly mauled, especially at Sidi Rezegh on 22 November, and Rommel led a giant raiding party of 100 tanks into the British rear areas, believing that his opponents would fall back. Auchinleck, however, refused to let go. He relieved Cunningham, who wanted to withdraw, and put Major-General Neil Ritchie in control. Tobruk was relieved by the New Zealand Division, and although this was followed by more hard slogging as Rommel brought his armour back from the raid, the German commander re-

alized that he must withdraw because he could not rely on tank reinforcements before the end of December. There were acrimonious debates between the commander of the Afrika Korps and the Italians, but as usual Rommel got what he wanted, and pulled all his forces back to El Agheila, to get the breathing space for a new offensive. The unfortunate Italian 'Savona' Division was left on the frontier to cover the retreat.

GERMAN SUPERIORITY

Having advanced again over the Cyrenaican 'bulge' to confront the position of El Agheila, the formations of the Eighth Army had changed the fortunes of the Desert War once more. Auchinleck's firm stand during Crusader had matched Rommel's mastery of mobility and stranded the imaginative drive to the rear. But this success had not altered the basic disparity between the British and Commonwealth forces and the German units in the Afrika Korps. The German PzKpfw III and PzKpfw IV tanks were clearly better than anything that Auchinleck had under his command, while the British standard anti-tank gun, the 2-pounder, was no match for the 50mm gun carried by the PzKpfw III, and was easily outranged by the 75mm gun of the PzKpfw IV. The German '88' dual-purpose anti-aircraft and anti-tank gun was greatly feared by the British because it had much greater range than any British tank gun. Yet the British very often outnumbered their foe, and usually did so in armour.

What gave the Germans their superiority was the way they combined their weapons – the way that mobile infantry supported tanks; the way that tanks would force their way through a weak spot in defences, and

Left: Italian and Afrika Korps troops manhandle an artillery piece into position. In certain desert conditions, laying artillery was a very difficult business.

Below: Erwin Rommel (second from right), an inspiring leader of men, a natural master of mobile warfare and a commander respected by his enemies both for his abilities and his sense of honour. As a company commander in World War I, he had won Imperial Germany's highest military decoration for bravery, the 'Pour le mérite', at the battle of Caporetto. His handling of the 7th Panzer Division in France in 1940 was central to the German success of that year, and he proved well able to deal with the demands of desert warfare after his appointment to command German forces in North Africa in February 1941. Rommel's main weakness in the desert was an inability to liaise effectively with the Italian high command.

Above: German infantry among the Roman ruins at Apollonia, Albania. Below: Junkers Ju-52 transports bring in supplies for the Afrika Korps. The Ju-52 was a very successful design; almost 5000 were built in Germany, and apart from being used for freight movement, the Ju-52 was the main transporter of German paratroops.

would then be instantly screened by '88's which would pick off the enemy armour sent belatedly to plug the gap; the way that, whatever the situation, the German officers and men would always come to a rapid appraisal of the relative positions, and would act accordingly, in a thoroughly professional manner. This coordination of arms and professional approach contrasted with many of the British units, who were unable to match the expertise of their opponents.

This tactical superiority was soon highlighted again. Rommel had pulled back to El Agheila to give himself breathing space for another offensive; and he was able to start

planning it early in 1942. During this period the threat to his supply lines from Malta was partly lifted, and he was able to build up his stocks of tanks and especially oil. Events elsewhere in the war conspired to help him, too. The Japanese successes in the Far East weakened the British as three divisions (two Australian and the British 70th) were moved east, and the 18th Division was diverted to Singapore. The German commander noted certain weaknesses in the British forces facing him, and on 21 January he struck. The attack was not only a surprise for the British 1st Armoured Division, which was stationed in three separate areas and swept back before

Above: An Afrika Korps 88mm gun – a fearsome weapon, known as the '88' to British forces. Its armour-piercing shot could penetrate 226mm (almost 9in) of armour at ranges of up to 500m (540yd). This was enough to knock out any British tank. Below: A German PzKpfw IV pushes on to Gazala.

the units could support each other; it also came as a shock to the Italian high command. Ignoring orders to limit his incursion, Rommel destroyed many of the tanks of 1st Armoured Division, and then defeated the 4th Indian Division covering Benghazi. By 3 February he was back at the Gulf of Bomba, having taken 72 tanks and 1390 prisoners.

Here Rommel had to halt, to prepare himself for an attack on Tobruk, and to build up his supplies. Axis plans now took shape for a final offensive in the Mediterranean. The first target was to be Malta. When this island was taken, then Rommel's supply problem would be solved and he could advance on Egypt. But problems in training some of the units that would have to land on the island persuaded the German high command to reverse the priorities. Rommel was to be allowed to move first, in a limited offensive along the Egyptian frontier, and only then would Malta be attacked. Why it was imagined that Rommel could be controlled once he got the bit between his teeth is hard to say. But on 26 May, at dusk, Rommel moved out to attack the British again.

THE CAULDRON AT GAZALA

The British forces were positioned to the south of Gazala. They had a number of fortified 'boxes' and hoped to be able to contain any German moves, while Auchinleck was, as usual, being urged into an offensive by Churchill. When Rommel struck, the commander of the Eighth Army, Ritchie, had 994 tanks to the Axis 560. But the crucial figure was that only 167 of the new, relatively unwieldy but well-armed US Grant tanks were able to take on the 282 PzKpfw IIIs and PzKpfw IVs that were the German spearhead.

The battle of Gazala was one of the most extraordinary of the whole Desert War. While four Italian divisions pinned the Allied force down in a frontal attack, Rommel himself led the Afrika Korps and two Italian mobile divisions in a giant loop around the south of the British position. There was hard fighting for the southern end of the line, the Free French-held 'box' of Bir Hakeim, before Rommel swung north. He now seemed trapped, with his back to the minefields of the Allied front line and the whole of the British armour moving in to-

58

*Above: The British
Mediterranean Fleet at
sea. Aggressive use of
sea power was the key
to British success in
the Mediterranean
theatre. Below: British
artillery in action in
June 1942, just before
the fall of Tobruk.
Opposite page, top:
Weary German
infantry pull back on
the El Alamein front in
July 1942.*

wards him. His isolated position was aptly named 'the cauldron'. But in a confused series of skirmishes the armour of the Eighth Army was destroyed. By 14 June, the British were in retreat, and Tobruk fell on 21 June. Since 26 May, 45,000 prisoners had fallen into Axis hands and almost 1000 Allied tanks had been destroyed.

As the Germans pushed ahead, dragging the Italians with them, the Eighth Army was almost caught at Mersa Matruh, but Auchinleck, who had by now taken over more or less direct control, extricated his forces and pulled them back to the Alamein position, a comparatively narrow stretch of desert flanked by impassable marshes and quick-

sand (known as the Qattara Depression) to the south. Here Auchinleck prepared some light defences to meet the Afrika Korps.

Rommel had by now far exceeded his authority. He should not have attempted to reach the Alamein position; all attention now had to be focused on Malta. But Hitler could see the possibility of pushing on to the River Nile, smashing the British position in the Middle East, so he allowed the drive to continue. The German attacks at El Alamein began on 1 July, although Rommel was in a very vulnerable position. His supply lines were along 400km (250 miles) of road within easy range of Allied ground-attack planes, and he had not made good the losses of Gazala. On 1 July he had only 6400 men and 41 tanks at his disposal, and even by the 17th he had a mere 58 battleworthy machines. Auchinleck concentrated on attacking the Italian units in the Axis positions. Small local attacks gradually wore away the strength of the Italian forces, and the Germans could do little to restore the balance. Auchinleck's army, although it was nearer its bases, was exhausted too, however, and had suffered serious defeats in the previous two months. As the fighting died down after this first battle of El Alamein, each side had much to do.

Once again, as so often in this Desert War, much would depend on whether one side could build up its strength more quickly than the other. And in this the island of Malta was crucial. Indeed, the struggle for Malta was probably more decisive than any single action in defining the shape that the Desert War took. It was also the key to the naval war in the Mediterranean.

Malta is 100km (60 miles) from Sicily, and lay directly across the Axis supply lines to North Africa. On the other hand, its position left it terribly vulnerable to air attack from the Italian mainland. The major task of the Royal Navy in the Mediterranean was the preservation of Malta. From Egypt Admiral Sir Andrew Cunningham and from Gibraltar Admiral Sir James Somerville fought a ceaseless struggle to keep the island supplied and defensible. As early as December 1940, the Germans decided to move a *Fliegerkorps* to Italy to reduce Malta, and the island suffered severely in the ensuing months. At one point there were only eight Hurricanes left operational there. But in the spring of 1941, the German aircraft were needed to help in the invasion of Greece and to aid Rommel's attack in the desert, so there was less pressure. British destroyers, then cruisers and bomber aircraft were moved to the island. The three convoys sent to supply it during 1941 lost only one ship between them. With a submarine flotilla operating as well, Malta now became a thorn in the Axis side. In the second half of 1941, 189 Italian merchant vessels were sunk, and of the 94,000 tonnes of supplies sent to Rommel in September, 26,000 were sunk, including one quarter of the precious fuel for the armoured forces. These losses contributed greatly to Rommel's defeat in Operation Crusader.

MALTA HOLDS OUT

December 1941 saw a change in fortunes, however. Hitler ordered submarines to the Mediterranean, to offset British naval supremacy, and they had an immediate success when the aircraft carrier *Ark Royal* was sunk. On 18 December, Italian midget submarines put two battleships out of action in Alexandria harbour, and at the same time, a British cruiser squadron suffered severely while defending a convoy. In addition, Hitler had appointed Field-Marshal Albert Kesselring, a Luftwaffe officer, commander-in-chief of the southern theatre, and with more energetic direction, the Axis pressure on Malta began to show results. British surface vessels were no longer able to use the island, and its airfields were under constant attack.

In March 1942, 5000 sorties were flown against Malta; in April, 9500. By then, there were only 20 to 30 Allied fighters to face 600 Axis machines. Operation Hercules, the invasion of the island, designed to destroy for good its use to cut Axis supply routes, was planned for May. As we have seen, however, difficulties in organization led to its being put off until after Rommel's offensive, and once Rommel had got the bit between his teeth there was no stopping him. Hitler, who may have been influenced by the high casualties of the attack on Crete in May 1941,

seems to have been only too happy to see Rommel take the initiative, and so Hercules was postponed indefinitely.

The island was still under siege, however; two British convoys in June 1942 only delivered 33 per cent and 13 per cent respectively of the intended supplies. The one bright spot for the British was that the Italian Navy was now desperately short of diesel fuel, and the attacks on these two convoys had practically used up all its stocks. So as Auchinleck's troops slugged it out with the Axis forces on the El Alamein line, 100km (60 miles) from Alexandria, the fate of Malta too was in the balance.

Above: Claude Auchinleck, whose troops held the Germans in July 1942 at El Alamein. Below: HMS Kipling *on the Malta run.*

Part Three
Turn of the Tide

The technical developments in weaponry and tactics during World War II are rightly credited with having had a determining effect on the outcome of the war. Of great importance too were the relative strengths of the two alliances, and how each nation prepared itself for a fight to the death. It would be a mistake to assume, however, that because these general factors were of greater importance than before, World War II was less of a 'soldier's war' than earlier conflicts. Although the stubborn bravery of the troops who fought on the Western Front in World War I was less of a necessity in the newer context, the ordinary troops had to suffer as much as they had ever done, and, moreover, they had to do so in the context of a more extensive, more deadly battlefield that demanded higher technical skills. For the man in the front line, the fighting in World War II was as dangerous as in any previous conflict.

At no period was this shown more clearly than in the first few months of 1943. This was a time when the tide turned in all theatres; and in all of them the soldiers, seamen and airmen concerned had to fight in the most difficult conditions – from the street warfare in Stalingrad to the jungle fighting of Guadalcanal, and in extremes of temperature ranging from the blistering heat of the Western Desert to the freezing waters of the North Atlantic.

The Eastern Front was a theatre where men were mere pawns in a vast mechanized struggle, in which an enormous weight of armoured firepower often seemed the decisive weapon. Men might wait for some months, moving in the wake of other formations, trying to live off the land, hoping to survive in the bitter cold of the Russian winter, in which it might be fatal to take off one's boots, and then suddenly, as if by an arbitrary shake of a dice, the war would arrive.

The Romanian Fourth Army advanced eastwards in the wake of the German successes of the summer of 1942. In November, it found itself spread out, holding the line south of Stalingrad where the

German Sixth Army was engaged. On 20 November, the Soviet forces attacked the Romanians, and broke through them within a matter of hours. Unprepared for such an attack, and armed with 37mm anti-tank weapons that were quite unsuitable (the Romanian dictator, Marshal Ion Antonescu, had requested more modern 50mm guns, and Hitler had promised to supply them, but they were never delivered). The 1st, 2nd and 18th Romanian Divisions were practically wiped out by the Red Army in the first day of the attack. Thousands of men were killed, or wounded (which in the circumstances meant they would die fairly quickly) and those taken prisoner had little hope of long-term survival. The Romanian soldiers had not wanted to go to war, but once involved in the titanic struggle, they could not escape their fate.

For those more readily involved, the re-

Above: A German Panzergrenadier at Stalingrad, armed with an MG34 machine gun. The sufferings of the German and Soviet forces at Stalingrad are legendary, and yet the infantry of both sides sustained a savage hand-to-hand fight throughout.

Eastern Front. Tank warfare had an air of chivalry about it, and certainly the treatment of prisoners and the regard for the rules of war was higher in this theatre than in many others. But the consequences of a direct hit on a tank were very unpleasant. Some British tanks, such as the Crusader, were very lightly armoured, while others, such as the Sherman, were inclined to 'brew up' when hit. There was then very little chance for those inside to get out. They would be burned alive as the vehicle went up like a torch. The fighting at El Alamein in October and November 1942 was particularly bloody, and tank crews suffered very heavily: during the beginning of Operation Supercharge, the final Allied offensive that broke the Axis forces, the 9th Armoured Brigade, under General Bernard Freyberg, lost 70 out of 90 tanks, and a high percentage of their crews. The tanks were being hit by anti-tank guns at ranges as low as 30m (33yd), which left the crews with almost no hope of survival.

JUNGLE WARFARE

By comparison, however, war in the desert must have seemed quite acceptable to those Australian troops who had moved to New Guinea from the Middle East after the entry of Japan into the war. For the combination of a Japanese foe and the terrible climate of the southern Pacific made the fighting there horrific for those involved. A US commentator has described the problems that troops faced at night against the Japanese: 'The inexperienced Americans, bewildered by the weird noises and intense darkness of the jungle night were often terrified by their own imaginations. They mistook the slithering sound of land crabs for Japanese soldiers crawling to attack them, the phosphores-

Above: Men of the Romanian Mountain Corps, who fought with the German forces in the Soviet Union. Right: German troops on the Russian front in the winter of 1942. Such conditions tested soldiers' hardiness and morale to the limit.

sults were just as bitter. At Stalingrad itself, for example, the fighting in the ruins of the city was as grim as any there has ever been. Small combats at very close range, snipers picking off individuals, Molotov cocktails being used against tanks, and anti-tank rifles, which were of little use in open country, being used at close range – this kind of exhausting fighting went on for months. The commander of a German unit wrote: 'It was an appalling and exhausting battle at both ground level and underground in the ruins, the cellars, the drains of this large city. Man to man, hero to hero. Our tanks clambered over great piles of rubble, and plaster, their tracks screeching as they drove their way through ruined workshops, opening fire at point-blank range in narrow streets. . . .'

In the Western Desert, the fighting conditions could be just as bad, even though they did not tend to last for as long as on the

Right: A British Crusader Mark II tank, immobilized in the desert after shedding a track. Below: The corpses of Japanese soldiers, shattered ammunition boxes and other debris litter a beach near Gona, in New Guinea, after an assault by Australian and US troops.

cence of rotting logs for enemy signals, and the sick, dank smell of the jungle for poison gas. Fearing the nocturnal enemy who, it was said, would drag them from their foxholes with hooks and ropes, or at the least would knife or bayonet them while they slept, American troops fired wildly at the least sound.'

BATTLE FATIGUE

The Japanese themselves fared very badly in the jungles of the South Pacific. Their infantry were very heavily laden (carrying about 45kg – 100lb – of equipment) and as they were supposed to be happy to die for their emperor, they were not given the support and back-up services that could have saved them many hardships. The troops who managed to survive the retreat across the Kokoda trail in the autumn of 1943 were described thus: 'They had shaggy hair and beards. Their uniforms were soiled with blood and mud and sweat and torn to pieces. There were infantrymen without rifles, men walking on bare feet, men wearing blankets or straw rice-bags instead of uniforms, men reduced to skin and bone plodding along with the help of a stick, men gasping and crawling on the ground.'

This extreme combat fatigue was common in many areas. As a Soviet lieutenant noted: 'When one gets really cold one becomes indifferent to freezing to death or being shot. One has only one wish – to die as quickly as possible.' For the man in the front line in World War II, the options were the same as in all previous wars – continuing hardship, or death.

THE CORAL SEA TO GUADALCANAL

Above: Admiral Chester Nimitz, whose inspired command led to the US victories at Coral Sea and Midway. Below: TBD Devastator torpedo-bombers on the USS Enterprise at Midway.

The Pacific theatre was the last to become fully involved in World War II, but was the first to see an appreciable turn of the tide. The two naval battles of Coral Sea and Midway in May and June 1942 and the campaigns on New Guinea and Guadalcanal later that year were decisive checks to the Japanese.

Late in December 1941, the US Pacific Fleet was entrusted to Admiral Chester B. Nimitz, whose job, with a force much depleted after Pearl Harbor, was to hold the Japanese offensive and to prepare for the counter. This involved two main tasks: holding the line of Midway–Hawaii and retaining secure communications with Australia, which would have to be a major base for the counter-offensive. With his small forces (no battleships and only three aircraft carriers,

one of which was damaged in January 1942) Nimitz could do little against the perimeter that the Japanese had established as the limit of their first attacks. But should the Japanese attempt to expand out from this, he had an invaluable weapon in that cryptographers had broken the Japanese naval codes and so he was able to predict enemy movements. Meanwhile, he concentrated on establishing the line of bases that would give the USA an unshakeable connection with Australia.

For their part, the Japanese, although they had established their perimeter, were now realizing that US reaction was far stronger than they had expected, and that a rapid negotiated peace was unlikely. The question was, therefore, whether there was any action that could be taken while Japan was still superior in naval strength. There were various options open. One was to invade Australia, or at least to isolate it; another was to move in force against Hawaii and destroy the remains of the US Pacific Fleet.

In the event, it was decided that the iso-

DESTRUCTION FROM THE SKY

An eyewitness on board the aircraft carrier Akagi *describes the surprise aerial attack on the ship at the battle of Midway on 4 June 1942.*
'I looked up to see three enemy planes plummeting towards our ship. Some of our machine guns managed to fire a few frantic bursts at them, but it was too late. The plump silhouettes of the American Dauntless divebombers grew larger and then a number of black objects suddenly floated eerily from their wings. Bombs! Down they came straight towards me! I fell intuitively to the deck and crawled behind a command post mantlet.

'The terrifying scream of the divebombers reached me first, followed by the crashing explosion of a direct hit. There was a blinding flash and then a second explosion, much louder than the first. I was shaken by a weird blast of warm air. There was still another shock, but less severe, apparently a near-miss. Then followed a startling quiet as the barking of guns suddenly ceased. I got up and looked at the sky. The enemy planes were already gone from sight. . . .

'Looking about, I was horrified at the destruction that had been wrought in a matter of seconds. There was a huge hole in the flight deck just behind the amidships elevator. The elevator itself, twisted like molten glass, was drooping into the hangar. Deck plates reeled upwards in grotesque configurations. Planes stood tail-up, belching livid flame and jet-black smoke. Reluctant tears streamed down my cheeks as I watched the fires spread.'

lation of Australia (the Japanese Army, heavily engaged in China, could not commit the troops that would have been necessary to conquer it) was the better option. Forces were prepared to attack Port Moresby in southern New Guinea, and then to move onto the Solomons, New Caledonia, Fiji and Samoa. Admiral Yamamoto, the naval commander-in-chief, was not in favour of this plan; he wished to strike a final blow against the US fleet. On 18 April Lieutenant-Colonel James Doolittle led 16 B-25 Mitchell bombers off the aircraft carrier *Hornet* to drop a few tonnes of bombs on Tokyo. The shock was intense, and Yamamoto was given permission to go ahead with his plan to destroy the US fleet. Operation *Mo*, the assault on New Guinea and the Solomons, was not abandoned, however; Port Moresby was to be taken in May, while the shattering of the US fleet was scheduled for June.

THE CORAL SEA

By mid-April, Nimitz knew of the Japanese plans, and was able to place a force of two aircraft carriers (*Yorktown* and *Lexington*), eight heavy cruisers and 11 destroyers in the Coral Sea, under Rear-Admiral Frank Fletcher. From 4–8 May there were confused encounters: on neither side was intelligence or identification very accurate (at one point the Japanese concentrated their attacks on an oiler, believing it to be an aircraft carrier) and the Americans suffered the more heavily, losing the major carrier *Lexington* in exchange for knocking out the small carrier *Shoho* and damaging another. But the invasion fleet transports carrying the troops towards Port Moresby had turned back as soon as the US ships had begun their attacks, and the Japanese plan to destroy any US Navy vessels southeast of the Solomons, before they could reach the Coral Sea, had been foiled by the intelligence intercepts that had put the Allied vessels on the invasion route before the Japanese had set out.

Attention now shifted to the Central Pacific, for if Yamamoto's plan to destroy the US fleet could succeed, then the Coral Sea would have been a minor upset, requiring a mere adjustment to the timetable of Operation *Mo*. Yamamoto's forces were far larger than those of the US overall commander, Nimitz, and he planned a great drive, threatening both the Aleutians in the North Pacific and the island of Midway to the north of the Hawaiian chain. Vice-Admiral Chuichi Nagumo, with four aircraft carriers, would attack and take Midway, with help from Vice-Admiral Nobutake Kondo's support force of two battleships and four heavy cruisers if necessary. Meanwhile, attacks on the Aleutians and the bombardment of Dutch Harbor in Alaska would confuse the Americans. If Nimitz decided to move north against the Aleutian force, a fleet of four battleships and two cruisers would be waiting for him; while Yamamoto stationed a force of three battleships and one carrier under his direct control northwest of Midway as a reserve to complete the destruction of the US fleet wherever it chose to make its move. The Japanese admiral was convinced that the Pacific Fleet must come out to confront such a direct attack on its Central Pacific base. A line of submarines was placed between Midway and Pearl Harbor to observe the movements of the Americans.

Above: The last moments of USS Lexington *at the battle of the Coral Sea. Although the loss of the* Lexington *was a serious blow, the battle as a whole was a strategic victory for the Americans. Nimitz had deployed his forces at just the right point to disrupt attempted Japanese amphibious landings on the south coast of New Guinea, and so foiled the opening stages of the Japanese plan to cut US communications with Australia.*

MIDWAY: THE TURN OF THE TIDE

This conception was almost Napoleonic: scattered forces, luring the enemy into a battle in which the Japanese would be swiftly concentrated to deliver a knock-out blow. The problem was, however, that Nimitz was aware of Japanese intentions. The critical manoeuvre was his decision to place the available US capital ships – the three aircraft carriers *Enterprise*, *Hornet* and *Yorktown* – together with eight cruisers and 14 destroyers, under the overall command of Rear-Admiral Raymond Spruance, northeast of Midway. The US vessels set out in two task forces, on 28 and 30 May, and by the time the Japanese reconnaissance submarines took up their positions, the US warships had sailed.

The battle of Midway itself was partly determined by luck, and, like Coral Sea, it was one of the first naval engagements in which the rival surface vessels did not see each other, the battle being conducted principally by carrier- and land-based aircraft. It

confirmed, if confirmation were needed after the events of the previous six months, that the battleship was no longer the prime naval vessel. It had been replaced by the aircraft carrier.

On 3 June 1942, a Catalina reconnaissance plane spotted Nagumo's carrier task force steaming towards Midway, and on the following day the first wave of Japanese aircraft began battering the island. The aircraft stationed on Midway made a brave but fruitless attack on the Japanese fleet. In order to silence finally the air defences of the island, Nagumo decided to attack with a second wave of planes, including his torpedo-bombers, which had to be re-armed with bombs.

At 0728 hours, however, a Japanese seaplane suddenly saw Spruance's ships, sailing directly towards Nagumo's vessels. Nagumo decided to wait for the return of his Zero fighters from the attack on Midway to cover his divebombers and torpedo-bombers, which he then ordered to be re-armed once again in order to attack the enemy fleet, of whose existence he had been totally unaware.

Below: The four campaigns that reversed the tide of war in the Pacific. First, at Coral Sea in May 1942, Japanese attempts to land amphibious forces on the southern coast of New Guinea were foiled; secondly, the Japanese plan to destroy the US Pacific Fleet was utterly defeated at Midway in June. Then, late in the summer of 1942, Japanese overland attacks on Australian positions in New Guinea were forced back. Finally, from August onwards, US naval and ground forces were taking the initiative in the Solomons, on Guadalcanal.

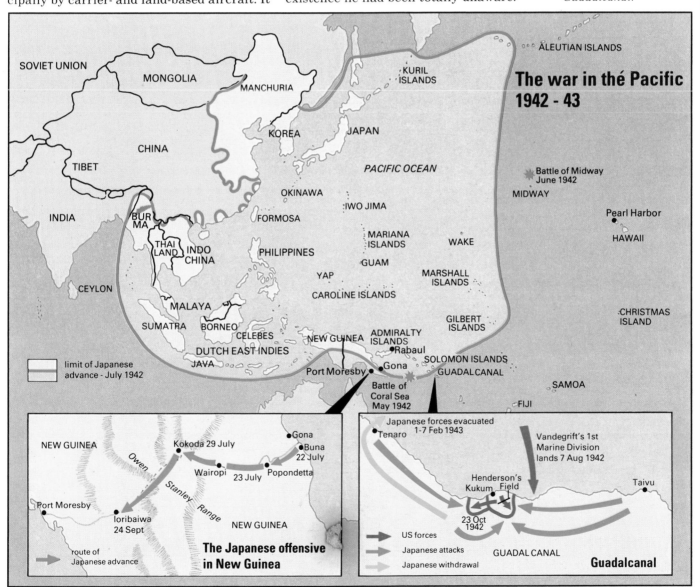

The US vessels had flown off their attacking force of divebombers, torpedo-bombers and escorting fighters between 0702 and 0838 hours. There was some confusion: *Hornet*'s divebombers and fighters never found the target, and the fighters designated to cover the torpedo-bombers of *Enterprise* and *Yorktown* were unable to prevent Japanese fighters and anti-aircraft fire destroying the formations. The torpedo-bombers of all three carriers were massacred, and by 1000 hours, the Japanese were winning the battle. Then, however, the divebombers from *Enterprise* and *Yorktown* arrived on the scene. With Japanese attention diverted, they carried out a series of strikes that were quite devastating. Within minutes, three of the Japanese carriers (*Akagi*, *Kaga* and *Soryu*) were put out of action. *Hiriyu* managed to send off planes that crippled *Yorktown*, but *Hiriyu* was itself put out of action by dusk.

Having lost four carriers in one day, Yamamoto felt unable to continue the battle; his battleships would be no opposition to the US carrier-borne aircraft so he pulled back. By striking at the crucial pivot of the Japanese fleet's manoeuvre, Nimitz had regained the initiative in the Pacific.

JUNGLE FIGHTING IN NEW GUINEA

The immediate consequence of the two sea battles of the Coral Sea and Midway was the successful prosecution of two land campaigns – those of Guadalcanal and New Guinea. In New Guinea, the Japanese had taken the offensive with ground troops after the abandonment of the naval-borne assault on Port Moresby. A force from Gona, on the north of the Papuan peninsula, moved across the Owen Stanley mountains (which were crossed only by tracks), taking Kokoda and

Above: The shattered wreck of the Japanese cruiser Mikuma. *She was one of the last Japanese victims of the battle of Midway. Retiring from the action, she collided with the cruiser* Mogami, *and although* Mogami *managed to limp to safety* Mikuma *was spotted by US aircraft. On the rear turret can be seen the remains of a US bomber that its pilot crashed onto the vessel.* Mikuma *finally sank on 6 June.*

Right: Rifles at the ready, a platoon of US troops fords a stream in the steamy jungle of an island in the Solomon chain.

Below: US troops in the jungle of New Guinea. Although the Allies suffered hardships in the tropical climate, the Japanese faced even worse problems because of their quite inadequate logistics system. The soldier in the foreground here is armed with an M1 carbine, a very popular weapon, being lighter than the standard M1 rifle and just as dependable.

reaching to within 50km (30 miles) of Port Moresby. This was an epic march, for Allied planes harassed the advancing infantry, who could bring few supplies or heavy support weapons with them. The strengths and weaknesses of the Japanese Army were shown in abundance: the incredible bravery and endurance of the men, coupled with an inefficient and unthinking attitude to logistics.

Between late August and early September, attempts to land another Japanese assault force at Milne Bay at the tip of the Papuan peninsula were repulsed (unknown to the Japanese the Australians had reinforced the garrison) and the nearer the attackers got to Port Moresby by land, the heavier grew the resistance of the Australian forces. Major-General Tomitaro Horii, in charge of the Japanese advance, was forced to order a halt to build up his strength on 20 September.

Unknown to Horii, the fatal blow had already been dealt to his plans. Earlier in September, the situation on Guadalcanal in the Solomons had become so serious that the Japanese high command had decided to concentrate its attentions there, and to return to the defensive in New Guinea. On the 24th, this intent was conveyed to Horii, who had to explain to his men that all their sacrifices had been in vain. The exhausted Japanese infantry dragged themselves back across the Owen Stanley range. Henceforth, there were no more Japanese offensives in New Guinea.

GUADALCANAL

Guadalcanal, which had caused the Japanese to withdraw from the attack on Port Moresby, is an island in the south of the Solomons chain. Its capture had been designed as one part of Operation *Mo*, the drive to cut Australia off from the USA. The Allied high command had received reports by June that an airfield was being established there,

and they decided to take it over, to lessen any threat to communications. On 7 August 1942, therefore, the US 1st Marine Division under Major-General Alexander Vandegrift landed there. Vandegrift's men had been hastily assembled for the operation and there was a certain amount of confusion, even though the landings were unopposed. Then, on the night of the 8th, Japanese naval units forced the US fleet covering the operation to withdraw, while on the same day Lieutenant-General Harukichi Hyakutake was ordered to drive the Americans off the island, and given 50,000 men based at Rabaul to accomplish the task.

The fighting on Guadalcanal was some of the most intense of the war and took place in atrocious conditions (malaria was endemic on the island, for example). Although they were badly organized at first, the Marines beat off the initial Japanese attacks, which were conducted by forces too small to drive the Americans back completely, and the Marines always managed to keep open the airstrip (called 'Henderson's Field' after a Marine pilot killed at Midway) that gave them air cover. On 9 October Hyakutake himself landed to take over operations. By now, the Japanese were slightly outnumbered by the Americans (20,000 as opposed to 23,000) but the issue was still in doubt while the fierce air and sea battles that raged in the 'Slot' (the area of water running northeast through the centre of the Solomons) were unresolved.

Gradually, superior US firepower won the day, and on the night of 7 February 1943, the final 13,000 Japanese troops were evacuated. The campaign had cost the Japanese almost 25,000 dead, including 2000 skilled pilots, over 600 aircraft and 24 naval vessels. The Americans had also lost 24 vessels, but only about 1600 men killed. Suicidal bravery had cost the Japanese very dearly.

STALINGRAD

When the rain and attendant mud brought all movement on the Eastern Front to a halt in March 1942, the soldiers of both sides were happy to receive some much-needed rest. But the rival political leaders – Hitler and Stalin – were making plans for further offensives that they hoped would bring final destruction to their enemy. The result was to be the massive campaign that led to the German catastrophe at Stalingrad.

Compared to the fighting on any other front, the war in Russia was a giant among dwarfs. At Guadalcanal, the Japanese lost 25,000 dead, but at Stalingrad the Germans lost 250,000. War seemed to be entering a new dimension, not merely because of the numbers and material involved (though these were certainly impressive enough) but because these numbers and this massive commitment of hardware produced decisive results. The mobilization of an entire nation like the USSR could provide sufficient momentum for it to be able to crush a smaller foe – even if that foe was as expert and battle-worthy as the German Wehrmacht.

On 5 April 1942, Hitler handed his generals Directive Number 41, which laid down the aims for the coming campaign in the Soviet Union. Briefly, these were to be a concerted attack across the Don and Donets Rivers by Army Group South, which would be split into Army Groups A and B. Stalingrad would be taken after the Soviet armies holding the Don Front had been disposed of, and then Army Group A would strike down into the Caucasus, whose valuable oil was much needed by the German war machine. Hitler was now formally commander-in-chief of the German armies, having replaced von Brauchitsch in December 1941, and little opposition was voiced to this plan.

The offensive was due to begin on 18 May, but before it could get under way the Soviet armies themselves attacked, on 12 May, aiming to take the communications centre of Khar'kov. This offensive was misconceived, and seems to have been due to Stalin's erroneous impression that the winter offensive had exhausted the German forces. Under

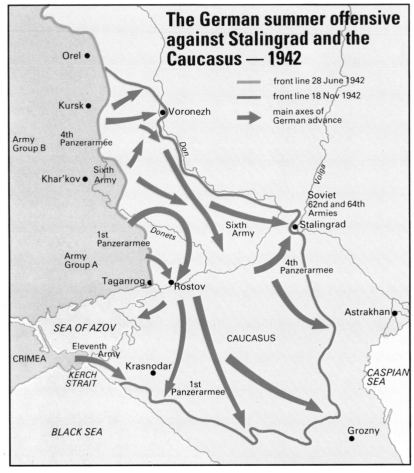

Bottom: A shell bursts in front of a PzKpfw IV as it shelters accompanying infantrymen in a maize field during the German advance through the foothills of the Caucasus.

Marshal Semyon Timoshenko the Soviet armies made some progress, enough to worry Field Marshal von Bock, the commander of Army Group South, but on the 17th an encircling move by Colonel-General Paul von Kleist's 1st Panzerarmee from the south and General Friedrich Paulus's Sixth Army from the north isolated the Soviet forces. By 28 May, 214,000 Red Army prisoners had been taken, and over 1200 armoured vehicles had been destroyed.

Stalin had been warned by his agents abroad that the Germans would attack in the south, and the fact that von Bock had assembled 73 divisions should have been an indicator that something was in the offing. The Soviet leader insisted, however, on believing that the German summer offensive would aim towards Moscow, and did not give his southern forces the reinforcements they needed. His almost wilful blindness and refusal to act on accurate intelligence contrasts strongly with the actions of other Allied commanders.

On 28 June the German offensive got under way. It all went as planned: Voronezh in the north of the sector was taken by Paulus's Sixth Army, and the Don–Donets corridor was opened. Von Bock wished to retain Colonel-General Hermann Hoth's 4th Panzerarmee in the north to block possible counters, and for this he was removed from his command by Hitler on 15 July and replaced by Colonel-General Maximilian von Weichs. In the Crimea, Manstein had ended the siege of Sevastopol by early July. The

Eleventh Army was now ready to join the drive into the Caucasus over the Kerch Strait.

Pushing down the Don–Donets corridor, Hoth's 4th Panzerarmee reached the confluence of the two rivers, and the city of Rostov fell on 23 July to the tanks of von Kleist's 1st Panzerarmee. The instruction to Hoth to move *towards* Rostov after he had

Above: Romanian cavalry halt for a brief rest during the summer advance into Russia in 1942. Below: German infantry advance on Sevastopol in casual marching order.

Above: Soviet infantry in a defensive position. They are armed with the standard DP light machine gun, with distinctive top-mounted drum magazine, and the Moisin-Nagant rifle, a design which had seen service in World War I. Below: A Red Army soldier with an anti-tank rifle, a weapon outmoded in general combat but useful in the street fighting for Stalingrad.

reached the confluence of the Don and Donets had appreciably affected the momentum of Army Group B, however, and Hitler made another error on 23 July, the day that Rostov fell. Instead of keeping to his 5 April directive, and pushing the two Army Groups on to Stalingrad, he decided to split the tasks of the two formations.

Army Group B was to hold the Don from Voronezh to Stalingrad (the latter city not yet taken, of course), push forces upstream from Stalingrad, and send an expedition to Astrakhan, on the Caspian. Army Group A was to abandon its move on Stalingrad from Rostov, and instead was to move directly into the Caucasus, pushing along the east coast of

the Black Sea and sending mobile forces towards Grozny. The net result was that although on 28 June the two Army Groups had covered 800km (500 miles) of front, they now had objectives which would present them with the task of holding 2200km (1400 miles), not counting 1600km (1000 miles) of sea coast. And to accomplish their tasks they actually now had smaller forces than previously. In his role as commander-in-chief Hitler made some dispositions between the various theatres that left the armies in southern Russia with only 57 divisions as opposed to the 68 of 28 June.

This failure to appreciate the realities of time and space had predictable conse-

quences. Paulus and his Sixth Army reached Stalingrad by early September, somewhat later than hoped because he had had to send some armoured forces to help Hoth's 4th Panzerarmee. And not all the Russian pockets on the west bank of the Don could be squeezed off by the satellite divisions, mainly Romanian, that were consigned to holding the line of the river. In the Caucasus, the troops of Field Marshal Wilhelm List's Army Group A were finding the going hard, too. Some of their forward Panzer units had to be supplied with petrol by camel, and List himself was dismissed on 9 September because of the slow progress. Indeed, the Chief of Staff of the German armies, Colonel-

General Franz Halder, was removed from his position on 24 September after trying to persuade Hitler that the situation was becoming serious.

THE GERMANS AT STALINGRAD

In Stalingrad, the Germans managed to reach some points at the banks of the Volga River on 20 September, but they could not break the resistance of the Soviet Sixty-second and Sixty-fourth Armies that held the city. In ferocious street fighting, especially in strongly built industrial buildings like the 'Red October' tractor factory, the Red Army refused to break. In house-to-house fighting

Above: A Soviet anti-tank gun in action in the ruins of Stalingrad.

Left: Soviet infantry creep cautiously forward in the ruins of Stalingrad, alert to the possibility of sniper fire.

Above: A Soviet assault team moves into the ruins of a factory during the bitter close-quarters fighting of the battle of Stalingrad. Below right: German soldiers advance through the fog and snow of the Russian winter. These troops (in contrast to the Red Army troops above, wearing snow boots and special clothing) are still in standard issue greatcoats, which gave little protection in sub-zero temperatures. During the fight for Stalingrad, the special winter uniforms that might have saved the men of the Sixth Army much suffering remained in depots well behind the front lines.

in the ruins of the shattered city German expertise in mobile warfare proved of no avail, and General Vasili Chuikov proved an inspiring commander of the Soviet forces. Every night ferries brought in Soviet reinforcements from across the Volga, and snipers took their toll of the hard-pressed German infantry. All the while, Stalin was making up for his earlier mistake by building up his reserves on the southern fronts. In the Caucasus, there were 90 formations opposed to 20 exhausted Axis divisions by 15 November, and around Stalingrad, a gigantic encirclement was being planned, under General Zhukov.

The Soviet intention was to hit the flanks of the Sixth Army, smashing through the understrength 4th Panzerarmee and Romanian Fourth Army to its south and the Romanian Third Army to the north-west. the attacks went in on the 19 November, and were instantly successful against weakened opposition. The field commanders were Colonel-General Andrei Eremenko, Lieutenant-General Konstantin Rokossovsky and General Nikolai Vatutin. They commanded over one million men, in 66 infantry divisions and four tank corps. Within a day, they threatened to cut Paulus's line of retreat.

Refusing requests to pull the Sixth Army out (as indeed he had refused such requests before the attacks had taken place) Hitler ordered Paulus to form a hedgehog, which would be supplied from the air. Reichsmarschall Hermann Göring, head of the Luftwaffe and Hitler's chosen successor, promised to supply 500 tonnes of supplies per day, although in the event only just over 90 tonnes a day arrived.

On 24 November, Manstein was ordered to form Army Group Don to retrieve the situation. He found that he commanded one

Hungarian Army, one Italian Army, the German Second Army (all on defensive duties), the weakened Gruppe Hoth which had suffered severely in the Soviet offensive, and he could expect the 6th Panzer Division from France and the weakened 23rd Panzer Division from the Caucasus. Manstein manoeuvred this *ad hoc* force expertly, however, and at one stage managed to push Hoth's men to within 50 km (30 miles) of linking up with Paulus. But the Russians

launched the second wave of their offensive on 16 December, and threatened Rostov.

Manstein was forced to deal with this new attack, and so the attempt to relieve Stalingrad was abandoned. Making the best use of his resources, Manstein held this new offensive too, desperately trying to avoid being cut off along the line of the Don River and yet trying to extricate the troops deep in the Caucasus. In spite of the fact that Eremenko's forces were on the left bank of the Don on 5 January 1943, while some elements of the 1st Panzerarmee were still 580km (350 miles) to the southeast, and in spite of another Soviet offensive on 13 January, along the Don near Voronezh, Manstein moved the 1st and 4th Panzerarmees over to the right bank of the Don at Rostov late in January.

THE FINAL COST

This success in saving Army Group A and Army Group Don from destruction was, however, poor compensation for the loss of the Sixth Army. On 30 January Paulus surrendered, and the last major formation gave in on 2 February. The Germans and their allies had lost 147,000 dead and 91,000 taken prisoner in this disaster.

Manstein still had much to do, even after he had extricated the armies threatened south of the Don. For the Soviet offensive of mid-January had threatened to sever his communications with Army Group Centre. Kursk had fallen into Russian hands and Khar'kov was abandoned by the Germans on 15 February. The Soviet forces had now overreached themselves, however. They had suffered severe losses in their advance, and had exposed their flanks to a counter that the Germans were not long in preparing. From

the north, Army Group Centre sent down I SS Panzer Corps, while from the south Manstein used the 4th Panzerarmee to cut off the Soviet salient. In the headlong Soviet retreat Khar'kov was retaken, and the Germans claimed 50,000 Soviet dead before the rain of March put a stop to active operations. This was a victory for Manstein; but nothing could obscure the fact that at Stalingrad the German Army had suffered an enormous defeat, from which it was never to recover.

Above: The Red Flag in the ruins of Stalingrad, soon after the final German surrender of 30 January. Below: Vasili Chuikov, whose direction of the Sixty-second and Sixty-fourth Armies in Stalingrad had helped to defeat the Germans.

EL ALAMEIN TO TUNISIA

By mid-July 1942 the German Afrika Korps commander, Erwin Rommel, had been halted along the line held by General Sir Claude Auchinleck's Eighth Army at El Alamein (see pp. 58–9). The Axis forces were exhausted by their offensive, and Auchinleck had worn them down even further in the first battle of El Alamein by concentrating his attacks on the Italian units.

Auchinleck was not to remain at his post to enjoy his success for long, however. Churchill had been determined to bring new blood to the Western Desert, and the Chief of the Imperial General Staff, General Sir Alan Brooke, broadly agreed with the prime minister that some changes had to be made in the high command in the Middle East. On 6 August, Auchinleck was sacked, and his place taken in a reorganized command structure by Sir Harold Alexander, who had already shown himself an effective leader during the long retreat of British forces from Burma in the spring of 1942. Under Alexander, the man picked to be the commander of the Eighth Army was Lieutenant-General Bernard Law Montgomery, after the original choice, General William ('Strafer') Gott, had died in an air crash.

There has been considerable discussion over the relative merits of Auchinleck and the new men. It seems clear that Auchinleck had decisively stopped Rommel's advance, and had a sound grasp of the desert battlefield; yet his choice of subordinates had sometimes been unfortunate. And irrespective of Auchinleck's merits or Montgomery's failings as a commander in the sphere of mobile warfare, Montgomery was the ideal commander to direct the deployment of the flow of war material that was shortly to give the Allied forces such an advantage in the theatre.

Montgomery's first task was to halt the last of Rommel's big desert offensives. Although the German commander realized that he was in a very vulnerable position and that the Allies now had considerable advantages, he was determined to attack before Allied strength became overwhelming. The ideal date would have been 26 August, under a full moon, but problems with re-supply meant that the offensive had to be put off until the 30th. The Eighth Army was well aware that a new German offensive was in the offing, and Auchinleck had prepared a set of positions using the geographic advantages that the Alamein position gave to the defence. Montgomery strengthened the defences in the time he had available, and made it absolutely clear to all involved that they were to sit tight, ignore any sudden German sweeps or penetrations, and take a full toll of enemy. He was not going to take the Germans on in mobile warfare.

STOPPING THE PANZERS

The result was that the Axis offensive fell upon well-sited defences and was stopped in its tracks. The battle of Alam Halfa, as the events were known, lasted a mere four days. Well dug-in British and Commonwealth troops on the Alam Halfa ridge to the south of the Alamein position repulsed Axis assaults which began on the night of 30–31 August, and Rommel's armour, caught in open desert by the Royal Air Force, suffered severely. The British commander deployed 712 tanks to the Axis 515, and in refusing to follow up the defensive success, Montgomery established a rigid pattern of fighting that suited the strengths of his army in artillery.

Top: Winston Churchill. It was his insistence on a shake-up in the command in the Middle East and Western Desert that led to the superb professional Lieutenant-General Bernard Law Montgomery (above) taking over the forces facing the Germans in North Africa in August 1942. Left: A curious British soldier examines the wreckage around one of the feared German '88' anti-tank guns destroyed during the battle of El Alamein. The better quality of much of the German equipment and the technical expertise of the German troops was defeated by the sound deployment of superior numbers of men and machines.

The success of Alam Halfa was reinforced by two other welcome pieces of news that summer. The first of these was the arrival of the 'Pedestal' convoy at Malta in August. The convoy was escorted by a large naval force, but even so, suffered severely in its passage from the Straits of Gibraltar to the beleaguered island; of the 14 merchant vessels only five got through, while of the escorting force, an aircraft carrier, a cruiser and a destroyer were sunk. Yet this was a success in strategic terms, if a disaster as a single episode. For the fuel and other supplies which did arrive enabled the torpedo-bombers and submarines on the island to carry on their task of attacking Axis communications between North Africa and Italy. The results were rapidly felt. In August alone, only 41 per cent of Axis fuel dispatched to North Africa arrived, and the shortage of petrol was a critical factor for Rommel's forces.

The second piece of good news for the Allies was the arrival of a convoy in Egypt from the USA. This contained 300 M4 Sherman tanks, new machines armed with a 75mm gun that were the equivalent of the German PzKpfw IV. The arrival of the Shermans gave Montgomery a material advantage that was to make the outcome of the Desert War inevitable.

Montgomery continued to build up his resources and refused to attack until he was satisfied that he had the troops and the weapons to complete the job of defeating Rommel. He finally sent in his forces on 23 October 1942, in Operation Lightfoot, the beginning of the second and better-known battle of El Alamein. The British had great material advantages; 195,000 men against the Axis 105,000 and 1029 tanks to the enemy's 496. The Axis troops had erected deep defensive positions, however, and the advantage of an open flank that the desert had always given the attacker was no longer so important.

Above: In training for El Alamein, a British officer leads his men forward. Preparation for the battle was very thorough. Montgomery, despite the urgings of Winston Churchill, refused to attack until he was completely ready, and the exact area in which the offensive was to take place was concealed from the Germans by an elaborate deception plan. Nevertheless, the fighting was extremely hard. The Axis positions were deep and well sited and the troops of the Afrika Korps were experienced and well led.

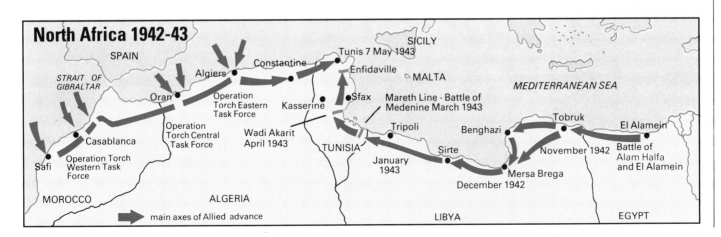

North Africa 1942-43

Above: Douglas Bostons of the Desert Air Force head out to hit at German communications. Allied command of the air, and the masterly way in which this was handled by Air Vice-Marshal Sir Arthur Tedder, magnified the logistic problems of the Axis forces in North Africa in late 1942. Below: A German tank crewman surrenders at El Alamein.

The British attacks began with an enormous barrage, but Montgomery's plan of gradually destroying the German units by fixing their infantry and 'crumbling' them was proved to be rather optimistic. The initial attacks made little progress, and only in the north where the Australian 9th Division was leading the way were there significant advances. Attempts to make armoured units push a way through failed, while the diversionary attacks in the south of the line were unable to push the Axis defences out of alignment. Eventually, on 2 November, Operation Supercharge, a redoubled push in the northern sector just south of the Australian positions, was launched. Although this too

was very costly and made little initial headway, the wear and tear was more than the Axis forces could take. Rommel was ordered to stand fast by Hitler on 3 November, but on the 4th the Führer relented and allowed the exhausted defenders to withdraw. El Alamein had cost the British and Commonwealth forces 4610 killed and missing, but the Axis had lost 50,000, including 30,000 prisoners.

OPERATION TORCH

Within a week of Rommel's withdrawal from the El Alamein line the Axis position in North Africa was suddenly rendered even more critical by Anglo-American landings in Morocco and Algeria – Operation Torch. The Americans had wanted to prepare for an assault on western Europe with all speed, as soon as they entered the war, but the British were able to persuade them that such an undertaking would be very risky, and that a landing in North Africa would be safer and would have sound strategic consequences. Not until July did the USA agree, however, and the final preparations were not put in hand until October.

In spite of an atmosphere of improvisation that surrounded the operation, Torch was very successful. Three task forces landed: the Western Task Force near Casablanca, Morocco, the Central Task Force near Oran in Algeria and the Eastern Task Force around Algiers itself. Resistance from the Vichy French ended quickly; Admiral Jean Darlan, Pétain's second-in-command, happened to be in Algiers and Pétain, the head of state of Vichy France, gave him authority to negotiate a settlement. A ceasefire came into force on 11 November, a mere 60 hours after the first landings, and at a cost of less than 700 American dead.

Torch had been the first amphibious operation of such a scale in the war, and taught the Allies valuable lessons. The assembly of the fleet of hundreds of vessels and the landing of 70,000 troops had not been accomplished without certain problems, but it immediately changed the situation in North Africa. For now the Axis troops there were faced with a war on two fronts. Rommel himself had no doubts that this must be seen as almost the end, but the Führer decided to hold out. Troops were rushed to Tunis and by the end of December there were 65,000 Axis troops in Tunisia, including the 10th Panzer Division, under General Jurgen von Arnim. The Allied forces found it difficult to advance rapidly through the 640km (400 miles) of difficult country between Algiers and Tunis and their operations were in any case slightly hampered by problems of command, especially where the French troops who were now fighting against the Axis were concerned. A

final problem was that the Luftwaffe in Tunisia was reinforced and managed to take its toll of the advancing Allied columns.

In contrast to the difficulties faced by the Allied troops in French North Africa, the forces of Montgomery covered hundreds of kilometres in the aftermath of El Alamein. On 20 November, only 16 days after the breakout, he had retaken Benghazi and by mid-December had reached the Mersa Brega position that had always marked the high-water mark of previous British offensives. He was not able to catch Rommel's armoured forces, however; the German general always stayed one jump ahead. Nor was Montgomery concerned to extend his forces too much in trying to trap the Germans. He did not want to risk falling into any trap – even though Rommel hardly had the resources to spring any surprises. In any case, Rommel could see only one strategy that held out any hope of success: to fall back on Tunisia, and abandon Libya. This he did, leaving Tripoli in January 1943 and setting up new defences on the old Mareth Line between Libya and Tunisia. This occasioned great disagreements between the Axis partners, as the Italians did not wish to abandon their Libyan possessions, but once again Rommel had his way.

Now that he had brought his men so far back, Rommel was able to operate between the two Allied armies, using the strategic advantages of interior lines. The Allies had reorganized their command structure by this

time. General Dwight D. Eisenhower, who had been in command of the Torch operation, was in supreme command of all the Allied forces in North Africa; under him General Alexander controlled 18th Army Group, that consisted of the Eighth Army under Montgomery and the First Army (the troops that had landed in Torch) under another British general, Lieutenant-General Kenneth Anderson.

It was at Anderson's units that Rommel struck first, concentrating his armoured forces (two Panzer divisions and an Italian armoured division) near Sfax and attacking the US II Corps. The offensive opened on 14 February 1943, and was initially successful. The Americans were not expecting it, and

Above: US infantry in training for the Operation Torch landings. Although much of the planning for Torch was done at short notice, the operation went very smoothly. Below: Keeping on the move in the pursuit of Rommel's retreating forces, a US-built Honey light tank of the Eighth Army passes an artillery listening post beside a knocked-out PzKpfw III.

Above: Operation Torch. Men of the Western Task Force disembark. Below: Eighth Army troops move into Tunis.

units of 10th Panzer Division moved through the Kasserine Pass. The attacks faltered, however, because of the poor condition of the Axis divisions, short of supplies and fuel, and (according to Rommel) because he was ordered to exploit this penetration in the wrong direction. Nevertheless, the engagements cost the US II Corps 7000 men (of whom 4000 were prisoners) and over 300 armoured vehicles. This was the first major battle in which US troops fought in the Mediterranean theatre.

Rommel's next move was to hit at the Eighth Army, which had moved up to positions opposite the Mareth Line. The British were this time expecting an attack and, as at Alam Halfa, had prepared a strong defence, including 810 artillery pieces. There were now some very effective anti-tank guns on the Allied side, including the new 17-pounder. The Axis attack, known as the battle of Medenine, was soon dealt with. For the loss of 52 tanks and 640 men, Rommel's forces managed to cause only 130 British casualties and destroyed only one tank.

VICTORY IN AFRICA

By 20 March, it was Montgomery's turn to take the offensive, and late that night, the battle of Mareth began. Although frontal attacks on the Mareth Line were unsuccessful, a flanking movement by two divisions made good progress, so this was turned into the main push. By 26 March, the Axis forces had been compelled to withdraw to the Wadi Akarit, from where they were driven back by a surprise attack on the night of 5 April. These two defeats cost the Axis 17,000 prisoners but the survivors established themselves along the Enfidaville position, an immensely strong natural barrier.

Meanwhile, the First Army had been steadily advancing towards Tunis, and by mid-April Alexander was sensing victory. Von Arnim was in charge of the 16 understrength Axis divisions of Army Group Africa (Rommel had left in March), while Alexander commanded 20 well-equipped divisions. Alexander's plan was for the Eighth Army to pin down the Axis forces on their front while the First Army took Tunis and Bizerta. These final battles in Tunisia were very hard-fought, in spite of the seeming hopelessness of the Axis position. The mountains and hills of the terrain gave the defenders a natural advantage of which they made excellent use. In particular, the Eighth Army found that its attack on the position at Enfidaville involved a kind of warfare to which it was unaccustomed, and the assault could not break through the German defences there. The First Army was more successful, however, and it managed to drive through to Tunis by 7 May. Some 238,000 prisoners were taken and very few members of the Axis forces in Africa escaped to fight again in Europe. The seven-month campaign to take Tunisia had cost the Allies 42,924 casualties, including 11,034 dead, but Africa was now cleared of the enemy.

THE BATTLE OF THE ATLANTIC

By late 1942, the decisive moment had been reached in most of the theatres of World War II. In the Pacific the battle of Midway had taken place in June; in Europe the fate of German forces at Stalingrad was sealed by the end of the year, while in North Africa the twin blows of El Alamein and Torch had effectively left the Axis fighting a rearguard action by December. In one crucial theatre, however, the decision was not reached until halfway through 1943. This theatre was as important as any other, for without victory there ultimate triumph for the Allies would have been at best uncertain.

This final theatre was the Atlantic Ocean, where the struggle to supply Britain and, from the autumn of 1941, to give the Soviet Union many essential materials was carried on with increasing intensity. The Battle of the Atlantic had no set front lines; and its fortunes swayed to and fro from 1939 until 1943. This was a war of attrition, where the fate of the individual, drowned in an icy sea as his merchantman sank, or gassed to death as a U-boat was destroyed by depth charges, was unpleasant indeed. Technical advances – radar, ASDIC, 'Huff Duff' and other inven-

tions – played a major part, as did the industrial capacity of the rival nations. For the ability to build submarines, merchant vessels and escort warships more quickly than they were being lost was of paramount importance.

Given the strategic importance of this theatre, it seems strange, with hindsight, that political leaders of both sides often appeared to give the forces involved in the Battle of the Atlantic a low priority when it came to the allocation of resources – for example, Britain's Bomber Command seemed more favoured than Coastal Command, despite the urgent need for long-range air cover for the convoys.

The German victory over France early in the war had given the U-boats under their commander Karl Dönitz valuable advantages in the form of the Atlantic seaboard bases of the defeated nation. The Germans were quick to exploit this opportunity, and sinkings of merchant vessels rose rapidly in the last six months of 1940. To reinforce this new offensive, there were bombing attacks on key British ports, especially those with shipbuilding yards, a campaign that reached its peak early in May 1941 when Liverpool was bombed for seven successive nights. Just when this series of operations was beginning to bite, however, the preparations for the attack on Soviet Russia led to a slackening of pressure. Nevertheless, by June 1941 the

Below: The depth-charge crew at work aboard an armed trawler. There was a desperate shortage of armed small craft and small escort vessels during the early years of the war, and many merchant vessels had to be converted to a military role. While this was the only short-term solution, in the long run more specialist vessels were used to eradicate the menace of the U-boat.

British position was not a comfortable one. Admiral Sir Percy Noble, whose role as Commander, Western Approaches, gave him control over convoy escort, had 248 destroyers and 99 corvettes at his disposal, but a considerable proportion were always being refitted. Aerial support was also meagre, as Coastal Command's Sunderland and Catalina flying-boats had a great many missions to carry out, and could not give effective air cover; and in July, there were 65 U-boats operational.

By the end of 1941 the Germans had sunk more vessels in the year than in 1940 (1299 ships displacing 4,398,018 tonnes as compared to 1059 ships displacing 4,397,772 tonnes in 1940) but the Allies were making advances that were very worrying for the U-boat commanders. The use of radar by Coastal Command aircraft and escort vessels meant that the favourite German tactic of attacking by night on the surface was becoming less effective, while US presence in bases in Iceland and Greenland from the summer of 1941 enabled the British to release vessels for service elsewhere. Nor was Dönitz's strategy helped by interference from Hitler, who posted submarines to the Mediterranean late in the year and also sent U-boats to Norwegian waters, which he considered the 'zone of destiny'. By the beginning of 1942, of the 91 operational U-boats, Dönitz only had 55 for use in the Atlantic.

Above: Manning the periscope of a U-boat. Below: U-boat supremo Admiral Karl Dönitz. Right above: The German cruiser Admiral Hipper *destroys an Allied merchant vessel. Right below: HMS* Hood *at anchor at Scapa Flow.*

Early in 1942, therefore, the issue was far from decided. The decision to declare war on the USA (in December 1941) gave the U-boat commanders a great opportunity to attack merchant shipping along the American east coast, and they took it with both hands. Admiral Ernest King, in charge of the US Navy, did not at first believe in the efficacy of the convoy system (although by April he was converted), and the USA had very few pilots trained in the specialized tasks of anti-submarine warfare. Using large 'milch-cow' submarines that carried fuel and ammunition to their fellows, Dönitz was therefore able to keep a fleet of submarines constantly at sea and take a grim toll of US shipping. General George Marshall, the chairman of the US Joint Chiefs of Staff, wrote to King in June: 'The losses by submarines off our Atlantic seaboard and in the Caribbean now threaten our entire war effort.'

Initially the Americans made the same mistake as the British had on occasion: they failed to realize that the U-boats could only be defeated in the vicinity of the convoys. There was little point in undertaking any offensive operations against them; it was like looking for a needle in a haystack. But if air cover from long-range aircraft and the fighters of escort carriers could be supplied, then attacking U-boats became vulnerable.

Further German successes in the attacks on the Allied sea lanes came in the early summer of 1942. The first convoys to the Soviet Union from Britain, the 'PQ' series, had escaped with relatively few losses, but Convoys PQ15 and 16 suffered severely, and Convoy PQ17 in June and July 1942 was a disaster. The Admiralty ordered it to split up because of the threat of German surface warships moving out to intercept it, and in the ensuing carnage, German aircraft and U-boats sank 19 of the 30 merchantmen that had

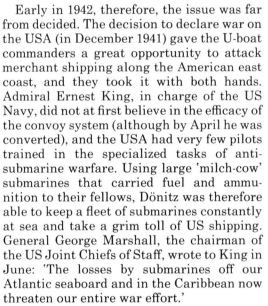

originally set out. In 1942 Allied losses in shipping were considerable, reaching a total of 1664 ships displacing 7,915,987 tonnes.

The threat presented by German surface vessels, which had occasioned the break-up of Convoy PQ17, was very real, and one that the Royal Navy had to take seriously. For a start, there were the disguised merchant raiders that had been operating since 1940. These ships were converted cargo boats with a series of different flags they could fly to persuade any neutral warships that they were genuine merchantmen. They carried concealed armament, and in the areas of the world where merchantmen did not travel in convoy – in the Indian Ocean, or the South Atlantic – they could wreak havoc on isolated vessels. The most important of these raiders were the *Thor*, *Pinguin* and *Atlantis*. Altogether German surface raiders accounted for nearly 434,000 tonnes of Allied shipping in the first half of 1941 alone.

GERMAN SUCCESSES

The most dangerous threat, however, came from the German surface warships, for if these should get out of their European ports, they could annihilate convoys in the North Atlantic. In February 1941, the British Admiralty had a nasty fright when the heavy cruiser *Admiral Hipper* caught a convoy between the Azores and Madeira, sinking seven merchant vessels in 90 minutes. Later in that month, the pocket battleships *Scharnhorst* and *Gneisenau* went on an Atlantic cruise that netted them 22 merchantmen. Then, in May 1941, the battleship *Bismarck*, accompanied by the heavy cruiser *Prinz*

Eugen, moved into the North Atlantic. The *Bismarck* was superbly armed, had very good armoured protection and her potential for threatening the sea lanes was enormous. British vessels made contact with the German squadron on 23 May, and on the following day, in a short action lasting less than 30 minutes, the British battlecruiser HMS *Hood* was sunk and the battleship HMS *Prince of Wales* was damaged. *Bismarck* herself had been hit, however, and within three days had been caught again. An air attack crippled her steering gear and she sank on 27 May, under intense bombardment.

The sinking of the *Bismarck* was by far the most important episode of the war against surface vessels. There were constant German attempts to embarrass the Royal Navy, such as the 'Channel Dash' of February 1942 when the *Scharnhorst, Gneisenau* and *Prinz Eugen* moved from Brest to ports in northern Europe, but the battleship *Tirpitz*, in spite of the threat that she posed, was never able to come out to catch any of the Arctic convoys. Her main success lay in tying down large numbers of British warships. Practically the last serious attempt by a major German surface warship to take the fight to the open sea was defeated in December 1943, when the *Scharnhorst* was sunk by HMS *Duke of York* in the battle of the North Cape. But by that time, the war for control of the sea lanes had been decided in the Allies' favour.

By this stage the Allies had also come to terms with the U-boat threat. At the beginning of 1943 there had been 212 operational U-boats taking a massive toll on Allied shipping. Their crews were skilled and experienced, and they were given a new advantage when the German codebreakers succeeded in deciphering many vital Allied messages, in-

cluding Admiralty communications about where the British thought U-boats were stationed. When the U-boats returned from their cruises, they took shelter beneath the enormous thickness of concrete over their submarine pens in the French ports of Bordeaux, Lorient and Brest. These pens were proof against the most massive Allied bombs of the period. Operating in ever-larger packs, the submarines had great successes early in 1943. During March, 102 merchant ships were sunk, and the 704,514 tonnes of shipping that were lost was about the figure that Dönitz was aiming for. He reckoned that around 700,000 tonnes a month sunk would mean victory.

There was debate in the Allied navies about whether these losses meant that the

Above: The Bismarck, *seen from the* Prinz Eugen *in the Baltic Sea. Superbly armed though it was, the* Bismarck *proved unable to take on the Royal Navy and was sunk in May 1941.*

Below: A Consolidated B-24 Liberator of the Royal Air Force escorts a convoy in the North Atlantic. The provision of such aircraft by the USA gave the Allies a decisive advantage in the Battle of the Atlantic.

convoy system was no longer working; and if not, what was to take its place? Fortunately, the tide turned in April. It was not merely that losses were fewer, but also that more U-boats were sunk in return. In March, one U-boat had been lost for every 6,000 tonnes sunk, but by July the ratio was down to one for every 10,000 tonnes. This was a situation that Dönitz could not sustain. German yards could not turn out submarines fast enough to compensate for the losses, and the loss of skilled crews was almost as disastrous.

NEW PRIORITIES

There were various reasons for the Allied success. An important one was technological superiority. Not only did radar in aircraft and escort vessels make the U-boats vulnerable on the surface at night, but the development of the echo device ASDIC meant that destroyers and frigates were also able to track them underwater. Then, too, a device known as 'Huff Duff' identified U-boats communicating with each other, as they had to if 'wolf pack' tactics were to work, and now convoys could avoid areas where the wolves were known to be gathering. The actual weapons being used once contact had been made were improving too. Rockets fitted to aircraft greatly increased their hitting power; new depth-charge launchers such as the 'Hedgehog' threw their bombs further and more accurately.

Most important, however, was that the Anglo-American conference at Casablanca had decided that the Battle of the Atlantic should have top priority. This led to a changing allocation of resources that had much to do with the turn of the tide. Whereas in February 1943 there were only 10 B-24 Liberator bombers operating with Coastal Command, and a mere 52 with the US Navy, by July the figures had risen to 37 and 209 respectively. Then there was the enormous US output of ships. The British had realized the usefulness of escort carriers in 1941, and had decided to build about six such vessels. But when the USA realized the importance of the craft, and turned the might of its resources to their production, the British effort was dwarfed. By July 1943 there were 29 US escort carriers in action, and one of these alone accounted for eight U-boats in that year. The same weight of production was applied to escort destroyers and gave the Allies far more punch than they had had in 1942. Finally, the provision of air bases and facilities in Brazil and (from October 1943) the Azores (granted by Portugal) gave Allied air cover much more effectiveness, and closed some of the gaps where the U-boats had been free of harassment.

Dönitz, who in January had taken over the entire German Navy from Grand-Admiral Erich Raeder, admitted in May 1943 that he was no longer capable of sustaining operations at the level of the earlier months of the year. By December 1943 there were only 168 U-boats operational, compared with 212 the previous January. During the year 237 U-boats had been lost: 148 destroyed by the Royal Navy and 75 by the Americans. Only 597 Allied ships displacing 3,271,810 tonnes had been sunk – about half the figure for the previous year. Up to the end of the war the Atlantic route would continue to be dangerous, but the sea lanes were not henceforth in danger of being cut. The build-up for D-Day and the subsequent conquest of northwest Europe would have been impossible without victory in the Battle of the Atlantic, while defeat might well have doomed Great Britain to starvation.

Below: Depth charges explode off the stern of a US escort vessel. Air power, mass construction of new escort ships, and technological innovations such as Huff Duff (a high-frequency direction-finding device) and 'Hedgehog' (a multi-barrelled mortar firing small depth charges) all contributed to the final defeat of the U-boats. By May 1945, 805 of the 1150 U-boats launched had been destroyed and 85 per cent of their crews had been killed or taken prisoner.

Part Four
Allied Offensives
1943-4

From the summer of 1943 to the autumn of 1944, the Allies took the offensive in all theatres of the war, and inflicted irreparable damage on the forces of the Axis powers. Italy was invaded, and Rome taken; Japan was forced back from the southwest Pacific and its carrier forces destroyed at the battle of the Philippine Sea. On the Eastern Front, the Germans were thrown back from Russian soil, and the Red Army moved into Poland and the Balkans; while in northwest Europe, an Anglo-American army landed in Normandy, and broke out of its bridgehead to liberate most of France.

Tank design had come on in rapid leaps since the beginning of the war. The original German Panzer divisions had included the PzKpfw I and PzKpfw II tanks that had been very lightly armoured and armed. By 1944 such weapons were obsolete, as were the British tanks that had been in use in 1941 – the slow Matilda, and the mechanically unreliable 'cruisers' such as the Crusader. The great leap forward in tank design came with the Soviet T-34, which first made its appearance in action during July 1941. This tank, with armour up to 66mm (2.5in) thick, a 76mm gun, a speed of 55km/h (33mph) and weighing 26 tonnes, outclassed the German opposition. The best German tank available in 1941, the PzKpfw IV, had only a short-barrelled 75mm gun that was markedly inferior to that of the T-34, and its maximum armour thickness was 50mm (2in).

The ultimate German answer to the T-34 was the PzKpfw V Panther, which was probably the best all-round tank produced during the war. At 43 tonnes, with a long 75mm gun, well-sloped armour with a maximum thickness of 120mm (4.7in) and a speed of 50km/h (30mph), it could handle itself in combat with any other armoured vehicle.

By the time the Panther had come into service, there had not only been a great advance in the design of armoured vehicles – there was also a diversification of models, to perform specific roles. Machines like the Panther and the T-34 formed the basis of tank forces, but there were particular tasks that

could be left to other, cheaper machines. The tank destroyer, for example, sacrificed armour thickness in favour of a heavy gun to knock out enemy tanks. The German *Jagdpanzer* models and the US M10 were effective in this role. Then again, for close support of infantry, in defensive or offensive roles, self-propelled artillery was very useful. Easier to manufacture than the tank, the self-propelled gun became a staple of both the German and Soviet armoured forces. On the

Above: The most influential tank of the war, the Soviet T-34. It surprised and worried the German tank commanders when it appeared in 1941. The response to the T-34 came in 1943 with the excellent PzKpfw V Panther (below), seen here in action.

German side, the StuG III (a 75mm gun mounted on a PzKpfw III chassis) became a standard weapon, while the Soviets countered with their SU models, the largest of which had a 152mm gun.

To take on better defences and to shore up defensive positions, tanks grew ever larger. Some, like the German PzKpfw VI Tiger, sacrificed important qualities because their weight made the operational range so short (the 88mm gun and 111mm/4.3in armour of the Tiger I made it an effective defensive weapon, but it could only function for 110km/ 65 miles before refuelling). By 1945, however, Soviet designers had overcome the problems and combined many of the elements necessary for armoured warfare in monstrous weapons systems. The Soviet IS-3 heavy tank, that came into service very late in the war, weighed 46 tonnes, had the heaviest tank gun of the war (122mm), mounted armour up to 200mm (8in) thick and could still manage 40km/h (25mph) with an operational range of 200km (120 miles). Armoured vehicle design had come a long way since the German PzKpfw II of 1940, with its 20mm gun and a weight of just 11 tonnes.

This development of weaponry was reflected in all spheres. In artillery, for example, new weapons, such as rocket launchers (the Soviet *Katyusha* and the German *Nebelwerfer*) came into use and self-propelled guns gave all armies more immediate access to artillery support. In smallarms, the proliferation of automatic weapons foreshadowed the assault rifles of the 1960s.

AIRCRAFT DEVELOPMENTS

In the air, four-engined bombers, night fighters, specialist ground-attack aircraft and new long-range fighters brought in possibilities that had not existed before. The Junkers Ju-87 dropping its bombload and machine-gunning columns of troops had been effective enough in 1940, but the British Hawker Typhoons and Soviet Ilyushin Il-2 Shturmoviks that the Allies deployed could do far more damage with rockets and heavy cannon (some Shturmoviks mounted a 37mm cannon). The performance of aircraft had improved enormously since 1940, and any nation that failed to keep up was in trouble. The Japanese, for example, made no great technical innovations to their carrier-borne aircraft after the victories of 1941, and found by 1944 that their machines were completely outclassed by US planes like the F6F Hellcat and the F4U Corsair.

The sheer technical strength of new weapons was not the only change, however. Just as important was the grouping of these new weapons in ever-larger formations. As early as the campaigns of 1941 and 1942, the German Army had begun, as a matter of course, to put its armoured formations together to form Panzer corps and Panzer armies, so that the corps took over from the division as the basic formation for German armoured forces. The Soviets did the same. Their 'tank armies', six by 1944, were the equivalent of the Panzer corps.

A similar evolution in weapons and their deployment was also taking place at sea in the Pacific theatre. The new US aircraft carriers were larger and better-protected than those of an earlier era (Essex-class carriers displaced 27,500 tonnes, whereas their predecessors, the Yorktown class, displaced around 19,300 tonnes), and the new

battleships had far more anti-aircraft armament than their precursors (a New Jersey-class vessel had only 32 anti-aircraft guns, whereas the later Missouri-class ships had 150). What lifted naval warfare in the Pacific to a new level, however, was the way that Nimitz combined his fleet into large segments, the crucial one being the fast carrier force. This consisted of a number of task forces, but was able to work as a single enormous fleet, deploying up to 17 aircraft carriers at some stages.

This kind of concentration of material, in its way similar to the way the Red Army concentrated artillery into whole corps to hammer a section of the German line to pieces, was the new method of making war. The German and Japanese armed forces had won their victories using fluid tactics and making the most of technical superiority in weaponry. The Allies made their great advances in 1943 and 1944 using a solid wall of steel to pound their enemies into defeat.

Above: The impressive bulk of a PzKpfw VI Tiger I. Although very useful in defensive positions, or when it managed to catch an enemy unit unprepared, the Tiger had several faults, notably its relatively short range. This made it less effective than its 88mm gun and heavy armour might suggest.

KURSK AND THE SOVIET OFFENSIVES OF 1944

Events on the Eastern Front during 1943 and 1944 were to prove momentous in their consequences. From the German attack on the Kursk salient in July 1943 to the Soviet drives that left the Red Army established in the suburbs of Warsaw and Budapest by Christmas 1944, they practically defined the direction that eastern and central Europe was to take after the war, with Soviet forces established over a vast area.

This period saw fighting on an immense scale, in a series of enormous offensives that ground the German Army down to a shadow of its former glory, and saw the application of massive amounts of firepower, taking coventional warfare to a hitherto unheard-of level. From the historical point of view the fighting is also interesting because of the differences in approach of the two sets of armies.

The German forces were, in general, far more expert at the combination of arms – tanks, anti-tank weapons, artillery and infantry – than the Russians, but the Red Army now contained massive formations, whole corps of artillery, for example, which were used to shatter the German units. The Red Army was also adept at many of the basic skills necessary for mobile warfare. The Germans were always surprised by the speed with which the Russians could cross river barriers

(the Russians had spent much effort in forming large pioneer formations: there were 17 pioneer brigades in 1942, and 55 by 1944) and the Red Army also benefited from its cavalry divisions. These were able to operate in the muddy conditions that regularly, in spring and autumn, slowed the mechanized units of both sides, and were also invaluable in crossing the vast areas of marsh in mainland Russia – the Pripet Marshes, or the low-lying parts of the Baltic coast. The comparison is made the more interesting by the fact that in many essentials both sides were equipping themselves with similar weapons.

Above: A German PzKpfw III emerges from the smoke of a grass fire during the opening stages of the battle of Kursk. PzKpfw IIIs were still an important part of the German tank force in 1943, although in comparison with up-gunned PzKpfw IVs or Soviet T-34s they were decidedly lightweight.

Left: German infantry look out towards the Soviet lines. They are manning an MG34 machine gun which has been set in the sustained fire role, to fire in a constant arc while the gunner remains under cover.

Kursk and the Soviet summer offensive
July – Dec 1943

front line –
7 July 1943

front line –
12 Dec 1943

Soviet advance

Operation Citadel – the
German attack on the
Kursk Salient

GERMANY | area shown on main map

U S S R

the northern sector of the line. An offensive in the north had begun on 12 January, and had even managed to open up a narrow corridor through which supplies could reach Leningrad (although the siege was not raised for another year). As a consequence of their exposed position in the north, the Germans moved forces back in February and March, straightening the line, before the spring thaw brought all mobile operations to a halt.

SUSPECT STRATEGY

Discussions over strategy for the summer were intense on the German side. There were two important salients in the front south of the Pripet Marshes: the Red Army held one in the Kursk sector, while the Germans had one through Orel. Manstein believed that the best approach would be to let the Soviet forces attack at Orel, and then to strike back, relying on German superiority of manoeuvre, but in a directive of April 1943, Hitler ordered that the German forces should themselves take the initiative, smashing into the Kursk salient in Operation Citadel. Guderian, now inspector-general of armoured forces, was very worried by the plans for Citadel, as were the generals who would have to direct the attacks. Manstein believed that success was possible, but only if the attacks went in without delay.

In the event, however, Citadel was delayed until 5 July, because of problems in equipping formations with the new Panther tank (which was, in any case, suffering mechanical teething troubles). In the interim the Red Army, which had been informed by its agents that the attack was imminent, was able to prepare a formidable defence. The German attacking forces consisted of 41 divisions (including 18 armoured or mechanized), with a total of 1800 tanks. In defence, the Soviets placed 3600 tanks and 6000 anti-tank weapons, and minefields used up 400,000 mines).

Such was the quality of Soviet intelligence

Below: A sight typical of the Red Army on the advance – infantry hitching rides on T-34/85 tanks. The T-34/85 was an up-gunned version of the original T-34 (as its name suggests, armed with an 85mm gun in place of the original 75mm weapon) and remained in service well after the end of World War II. In some parts of the world, T-34/85s were still in action during the 1970s.

The first months of 1943 had seen the Germans faced with complete catastrophe in the south, from which the fighting qualities of the divisions there and the skilled generalship of Field Marshal von Manstein had saved them, but only at the cost of abandoning much territory, and leaving the Sixth Army trapped in Stalingrad to its fate. January 1943 had also seen Soviet success in

Above: Waffen-SS troops take cover and prepare to deal with an attack. Above right: A Waffen-SS soldier attaches a rifle-grenade to the muzzle of his Mauser Kar 98, the carbine version of the standard infantry rifle. Below: Panther tanks on the retreat.

that they were able to disrupt the beginning of the offensive with a well-timed artillery barrage shortly before the German forces began their moves. The maximum penetration of the Soviet lines was only 16km (10 miles) in the north and 20km (12 miles) in the south, and although the German forces in the south, under Manstein, came close to breakthrough, the ability of the Russians to pour reinforcements into the threatened areas always plugged any gaps that opened. By 10

July, the battle had turned into a vast slogging match between the opposing tank forces, because poor visibility was making artillery and air support difficult. The Germans were forced to spend a lot of time finding a way through minefields and reducing dangerous strongpoints, and by 11 July the northern wing of the attack had ground completely to a halt. Classic Blitzkrieg had met its match in the form of an overwhelmingly well-equipped defensive system. On 13 July, Hitler called off the operation, and the last major German offensive on the Eastern Front came to an end.

A major reason for the German leader's decision to call off the attack at Kursk lay in the fact that the Red Army had, as early as 12 July, launched its own attack on the other salient, that of Orel. The Germans had, of course, strengthened their defences in the area, but were unable to resist the mass of artillery that shattered many of their units. Generals Vasiliy Sokolovsky and Markian Popov, commanding the West and Bryansk Fronts respectively, made sure that they could cut right through the Orel positions; the main attacking army, the Eleventh Guards Army, opened its barrage with 3000 guns and 400 rocket launchers.

Meanwhile, further south, Manstein was also facing attacks by overwhelming forces. He estimated that his 29 infantry and 13

armoured or motorized divisions were opposed by 109 infantry, and the equivalent of 17 armoured divisions. In spite of Hitler's initial refusal to let Manstein abandon the Donets Basin, in the end the situation became too desperate. The Panzer formations were dragged up and down the crumbling German line, desperately plugging holes; Khar'kov fell on 22 August, and from 7 September Manstein pulled his men back from the Donets Basin, trying to organize defensive positions in the Dniepr bend. Hardly had he done this, however, when the speed of the Soviet follow-up caught the Germans by surprise, and the Red Army established bridgeheads on the west bank of the Dniepr River.

THE RECAPTURE OF KIEV

Renewed Soviet offensives threatened to trap the Germans in a salient around Dniepopetrovsk, a threat from which a timely counter-attack relieved them in October. By now the Wehrmacht on the southern front was almost exhausted. The Soviets were able to change their direction of attack once again, breaking out of the bridgeheads over the Dniepr they had established above Kiev in early November. The ancient Ukrainian capital was recaptured by the Red Army by 6 November, but Soviet attempts to exploit this success further were blocked by Manstein again. He sent in the 4th Panzerarmee against the advancing Red Army, and regained the city of Zhitomir.

Manstein reckoned that this last counter-attack had netted 20,000 enemy dead, 600 tanks destroyed and 5000 prisoners. It was, however, poor compensation for the previous five months of fighting. Not only had there been reverses in the south for the Germans, but in the centre the Red Army had pushed on to take Smolensk and Bryansk, although

Above: A knocked-out German PzKpfw IV. In 1944, the PzKpfw IV was still the mainstay of many armoured units, but it had been modified considerably during the course of the war. This model has a long-barrelled 75mm gun and curved 'skirt armour' fitted around the turret to explode anti-tank shells before they can reach the main armour. Below: Red Army forces, part of a unit armed with PPSh sub-machine guns, liberate a Russian village.

attempts to reach further west than the line Vitebsk–Orsha–Zhlobin had been repulsed. Citadel had failed, the Wehrmacht had lost 104,000 men (half of them dead) since July, and now they could only expect a further offensive, the third of the great winter offensives of Stalin.

By 1944, the Red Army was not only enormous, it had also organized itself to cover the deficiencies that had previously restricted its operational effectiveness. There were 48 infantry armies between the Baltic and the Black Seas, divided into various 'fronts' – the equivalent of an army group. These fronts changed in name and composition during the advance west. In summer 1943 there was only one Belorussian Front, but after the victories of early 1944, two more were formed for the summer offensive. The Red Army had six tank armies, roughly the equivalent of a German Panzer corps, which acted as its spearhead, while the basic formation was still the rifle division, by 1944 a formation of about 9500 men.

Such divisions were kept in the front line until they were exhausted, and then they would be taken to the rear for a complete reorganization. A feature of the Soviet infantry was that large numbers of men were armed with sub-machine guns, usually the PPSh model. In many divisions, over 2000 men had such automatic smallarms. Guards divisions were units of better than average quality, and many of them were comparable to German formations. In general, however, the Soviet forces were not as expert as the Germans in the basic small change of modern warfare, in such areas as artillery range-finding, for example. The normal practice was for Soviet infantry support weapons to fire only at visible targets.

Above: Red Army infantry on the move on the northern front. In the low-lying and often marshy coastal areas to the north of the front line there was less spectacular movement than in the south and centre, but the fighting was often just as intense. The Red Army was locked in a desperate struggle to retain Leningrad from late 1941 onwards, while the Germans were just as determined to take this great prize. Indeed, Leningrad was not finally relieved until early in 1944.

It was to combat such deficiencies in the education of its troops that the Red Army had initiated the large artillery formations that were such a distinctive feature of Soviet forces. In these, expertise could be concentrated. The Red Army had also worked out the best method of using their numerical superiority to wear down the more skilful Wehrmacht. Just as Montgomery at El Alamein had used his numerical advantage to keep probing the Axis positions, in spite of many small reverses, until the Italians and Germans could no longer resist the progressive weakening of their line, so the Red Army commanders kept up an offensive at various points, switching direction and maintaining

a constant pressure that eventually found the gaps through which the more mobile formations could then race ahead. The Soviet cavalry divisions and pioneer formations were important in keeping up the momentum of advance, and the fact that the USA and Britain were also supplying enormous quantities of trucks (434,000 in all) contributed greatly to the increased effectiveness of Soviet offensives in 1944. The German Army was still largely dependent on horse-drawn transport, and its rear areas were subject to the debilitating attacks of Russian partisans, who claimed to have destroyed rails at 17,000 different places in the Orel and Bryansk areas alone between July and September 1943.

It was a well-organized Red Army, then, that launched itself at the Wehrmacht again in a renewed offensive in December 1943. The main advance was on the four Ukrainian fronts, with initial attacks going in towards Zhitomir, attempting to swing round to trap Manstein's Army Group South against the Black Sea. Hitler refused Manstein the opportunity to conduct a 'mobile' defence, and the Field Marshal had to do what he could with his hands tied. Pockets of German resistance at Kanev and Korsun were ordered to hold out by the Führer until they were conclusively trapped and destroyed. Nevertheless, the German forces still managed to check the Soviet advances, helped by the early onset of the spring rains. The Soviet offensives had been expensive, and in January and February 1944 the Ukrainian fronts had lost almost 4000 tanks between

Right: A young German soldier mans an MG42 machine gun. The MG42 was a very efficient weapon, first introduced into general service in 1942.

Manstein's Panzer divisions were down to about 30 tanks each, a mere fraction of their official strength of 150.

Having regrouped, the Red Army was soon ready to attack again against a weakened enemy. In March 1944, Marshal Zhukov led the 1st Belorussian Front in a sweep south-west, trying to cut off Army Group South from Army Group Centre. With 60 divisions and 1000 tanks, this offensive was only just held by the Germans; Manstein, who ordered the withdrawal that saved the bulk of his troops from being cut off, was dismissed for having disobeyed the Führer's orders. Almost as soon as this Soviet offensive ran out of steam another one started, this time against the Crimea. The German Seventeenth Army was cut off in the peninsula, and in whirlwind attacks in April the Red Army tore it to pieces, imprisoning or killing 31,700 Germans and 25,800 Romanians. While the major attack had been going in against Army Group South, the northern sector of the line had also seen German defeats. The German Army was pushed back from Leningrad to Lake Peipus, and no longer threatened the city.

A DENT IN THE ARMOUR

The Soviet spring offensives had, therefore, resulted in the reconquest of the Crimea and the Ukraine, while the siege of Leningrad had been permanently lifted. These offensives had also crippled the German Army. By 1944, its basic formations were being re-organized to cope with the smaller numbers of men available; the 1944 infantry division had a theoretical strength of only 12,772 men as opposed to 17,500 of the earlier formation, while the Panzer division was also reduced in size. These formations had, however, more punch than their predecessors, with an increased complement of self-propelled artillery, such as the *Wespe* with a 105mm gun, the *Hummel* with a 150mm weapon, and especially the StuG III with its 75mm weapon, that was turned out in great numbers and became a mainstay of the Wehrmacht on the Eastern Front. Yet even these reduced manpower figures exaggerated considerably the number of effectives. By the end of a few weeks' fighting, battalions that in theory contained 700 men were often down to 200. Nor was this the only problem. Hitler insisted upon creating large numbers of formations: in 1943 there were 226 infantry divisions in the German Army, and 240 in 1945. As Guderian complained, these formations were weak, invariably understrength and yet consumed transport and logistics out of all proportion to their fighting worth.

Remarkably, however, the German Army on the Eastern Front carried on the struggle without breaking to the very end. In spite of

Above: A knocked-out Soviet T-34 ablaze. The Wehrmacht was a formidable foe, even in retreat.

them – but the Soviets could afford these losses. And, perhaps ominously for the Wehrmacht, the numbers of prisoners taken was falling as the Red Army used its material superiority to save manpower. By March,

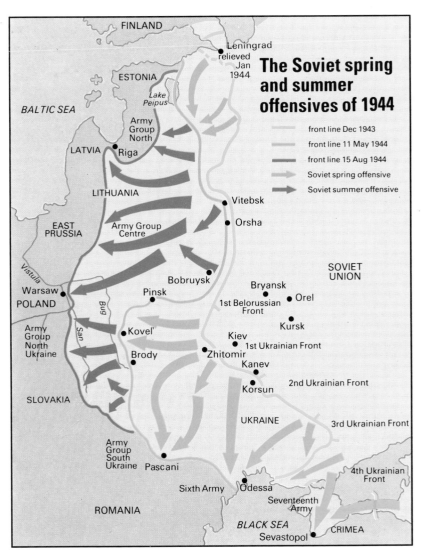

The Soviet spring and summer offensives of 1944

- front line Dec 1943
- front line 11 May 1944
- front line 15 Aug 1944
- Soviet spring offensive
- Soviet summer offensive

receiving the most ridiculous instructions from Hitler, the generals tried to plug the weakening line, and during 1943 were confident that they could, if they were permitted by the Führer, force a stalemate. But Hitler was incapable of formulating an effective answer to the Red Army's strategy. He believed in holding valueless ground, which meant that countless troops were cut off in 'pockets', and had no appreciation of the strengths of the enemy.

THE AIR WAR

The failure of German strength was not confined to the war on the ground. In the air, the Luftwaffe had put all its energies into supporting the attacks of the battle of Kursk, and since then had been unable to pose any challenge to Soviet aerial supremacy. Shortages of fuel and spare parts and the increasing numerical dominance of the Russians were making the heady summer days of 1941 seem far away for the German air crews. Soviet strategy for the air war did not include a sustained offensive on Germany itself; all the Soviet effort went into the creation of a ground-attack force capable of helping in the destruction of the German ground forces. As the summer offensive of 1944 opened, the Soviet Air Force had at its disposal 16,600 fighters, fighter-bombers and twin-engined bombers.

The optimism of the German commanders did not outlive the Soviet summer offensives of 1944. Before these, they had imagined that an effective defence could be established, and that a strategy based upon German advantages in mobile warfare could be formulated. But on 22 June an offensive opened that ruined any such hopes. Hitler had believed, against intelligence advice, that Stalin intended to strike in the southern sector again. In fact, the blow fell on Army Group Centre. Soviet forces comprising 166 infantry divisions with 5300 armoured vehicles in support attacked the 37 divisions of Field Marshal Ernst Busch that were in an enormous salient after the Soviet advances in the north and south the previous winter. Soviet success was instant, and was aided by Hitler's orders that German troops in the Vitebsk and Bobryusk pockets should stand and fight. In a series of giant sweeps, Rokossovsky's 1st Belorussian Front reached the Vistula, and the Warsaw suburb of Praga. This was accompanied by an offensive in the north that reached the Baltic near Riga on 1 August, cutting off the 30 divisions of the German Army Group North. Army Group Centre had suffered severely, losing over 250,000 dead or taken prisoner in June and July.

Nor was this all, for on 13 July new attacks started in the south, against the German Army Group North Ukraine. Under Marshal

Ivan Konev, the 1st Ukrainian Front smashed a way through the weakened Germans, who had been forced to give assistance to Army Group Centre, and drove from Kovel' to the River San. This enormous advance within such a short period (from some of their starting points, Rokossovsky's men and vehicles had covered 650km/400 miles in less than six weeks) inevitably slackened as the defences began to consolidate. Counter-

Above: A Red Army political commissar, suffering from a head wound, continues to direct his men. Below: Soviet troops push forward past a burning German Nashorn self-propelled anti-tank gun.

attacks across the Vistula stopped the momentum of Rokossovsky's forces, and the strategic reserves that would have been necessary to maintain his impetus were already earmarked for yet another offensive – this time into the Balkans.

There is little doubt that Stalin was not too concerned about the fate of the insurgents in the Warsaw Rising, those Polish underground fighters who rose against the Germans on 1 August in the expectation that the Red Army was about to liberate the Polish capital. He was fundamentally hostile to the government-in-exile that the insurgents represented, and although it would have been very difficult for Rokossovsky to renew his advance, this does not explain Stalin's refusal to allow US and British aircraft to use Soviet airfields to drop arms and supplies to the Poles. Already, the conflicts of the post-war world were taking shape. With no support from outside, the Poles were ruthlessly crushed by the Germans and Warsaw was destroyed. There were over 200,000 Polish casualties during the ten weeks of the fighting.

During the autumn of 1944, Rokossovsky made no more moves to advance through Poland, although there was an advance further north designed to cut off East Prussia. The first attack on East Prussia was undertaken in October, and was heavily defeated. The pressure in the north was now remorseless, however; the Soviet forces were gradually picking their way down the Baltic coast, and the fall of Prussia could not be long delayed. Finland had been forced out of the

war by September, releasing more troops for the main fronts.

In the south, meanwhile, Red Army gains were once more enormous, and were the main focus of attention in the autumn. On 20 August, the 2nd and 3rd Ukrainian Fronts, under Marshals Rodion Malinovsky and Fyodor Tolbukhin, struck into Romania. On 22 August the Romanians capitulated, and declared war on Germany on 25 August. This exposed the reconstituted German Sixth Army to disaster, and 105,000 prisoners were taken from the 16 divisions that were lost to the Germans. On 8 September Bulgaria, similarly attacked by Soviet forces, also declared war on Germany. Motoring through Romania and Bulgaria, the Red Army was able to move directly into Yugoslavia, and had taken Belgrade by 20 October. They linked up with the large partisan forces of Yugoslavia and Albania, and had secured the Balkans. The German Army Group E, stationed in Greece, made a long and successful retreat to Sarajevo, just avoiding being cut off, but by now battles were raging in the Hungarian plain. The Hungarians were prevented from defecting to the Soviet side by a German takeover, but by November Budapest was under siege.

These advances by the Red Army in the late summer and autumn of 1944 showed just how well it had learned to apply its material strength most effectively. It had made huge gains – Rokossovsky's 1st Belorussian Front had equalled anything that the Germans had achieved in their heyday. What is more, their gains were to be far more long-lasting than those of the 'Thousand-Year Reich'.

Left: Red Army troops in the streets of a Hungarian town. On 15 October 1944 Admiral Horthy, the Hungarian head of state, proclaimed an armistice with the Russians, but Hungarian Nazis and the German Army responded by taking over the country. Three Panzer divisions were sent to Hungary as reinforcements. Hitler refused to abandon Budapest, which he nominated a 'fortress', and so troops were diverted from the front in Prussia to help hold the Hungarian capital. This could only delay the inevitable, however. Budapest was under siege by December, and was, in effect, strategically lost by the beginning of 1945.

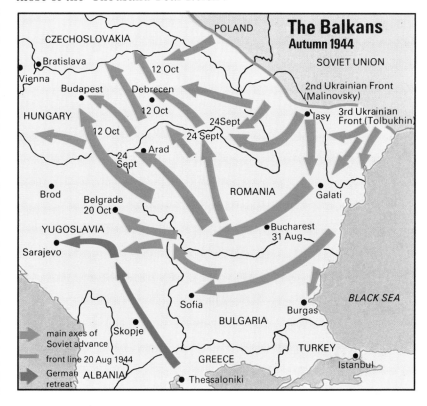

THE ADVANCE TO ROME

If the great Soviet successes of 1943 and 1944 had demonstrated the awesome power of decision of modern weaponry and modern tactics – in that enormous tracts of territory were crossed and taken – the battles fought in Sicily and Italy during the same period demonstrated another aspect: that even in the face of the most immense expenditure of ammunition and material, a well-positioned defence could still hold its own. It is, perhaps, a measure of the excellence of the German Army that it adapted itself to the grinding defensive positional warfare of the Italian peninsula equally as well as it had to the mobile campaigns in the Russian steppes or the Western Desert. And just as the fighting in the Soviet Union during the period had demonstrated the continuing importance of some traditional forms of transport, namely the horse, so the fighting in Italy showed that lightly equipped mountain troops and mules also had a place on a battlefield where the terrain was difficult.

The Allied decision to attack Sicily had been taken at the Casablanca Conference of January 1943. Although the US commanders still wanted to make an assault on northwest Europe as soon as possible, the British were able to persuade them of the benefits to be gained from taking the island that dominated the central Mediterranean – not least of these being that Italy might be persuaded to abandon her ally. The final details were worked out in the spring, after the fall of Tunisia, and the planning for Operation Husky was undertaken by the 15th Army Group, under Alexander with Eisenhower in overall command.

Husky was the largest amphibious operation of the war in terms of the area involved and the number of amphibious vehicles necessary, for 180,000 Allied troops were to be put ashore in the first phase of the operation. A fleet of 2590 ships was assembled, and included many vessels never used before,

Above: German paratroops watch the effects of an artillery bombardment. The stout resistance of the German forces in Sicily proved a foretaste of the power of the defensive in the rugged terrain of Italy. Below: Bringing supplies ashore at Salerno in September 1943. The Allied landings here met very strong resistance.

such as the Landing Craft Tank (LCT) and the amphibious DUKW (the name of which comes from US service designations). This scale of activity was a further sign of the immense logistic network necessary for modern warfare, for the planning and assembly of this vast armada was more important than the actions of any single divisional commander once the troops had been put ashore on 10 July 1943.

There were two armies involved. The US Seventh Army, under General George Patton, was put ashore in the Gulf of Gela, while the British Eighth Army under Montgomery landed south of Syracuse – a total frontage of 160km (100 miles). With complete air cover (over 4000 planes wiped the 550 Axis machines from the skies) the Allied troops made rapid initial progress. Syracuse fell to Montgomery on 12 July and Patton's men swiftly consolidated their bridgeheads. Then, however, resistance began to stiffen. The 230,000 men of the Italian Sixth Army were not the problem; but there were two Panzer divisions on the island and these were soon reinforced by paratroop regiments and a mechanized division. Montgomery's forces, designated as leading the way to the capture of Messina, soon stuck on the plains south of Catania. In the difficult terrain, the Germans proved impossible to shift by direct attack, and in the end were only driven back when Patton initiated a looping drive around the north coast. He took Palermo on 22 July, and his units reached Messina on 17 August.

Although Patton had seemed to show how bold sweeping moves were still the way to use modern weapons, in fact the most important harbinger of the style of warfare in the Italian campaign was the stubborn defence. Even when pushed back, the Germans had managed to extricate their forces across the Straits of Messina, and lived to fight another day. The Germans suffered 12,000 killed or taken prisoner, while there were 20,000 Allied casualties.

It was not until the end of August that the decision was taken to go for Italy rather than to remain in Sicily and move troops to Europe. Again, the Americans were more reluctant than the British, but now there was a very real possibility that Italy would desert the Axis if there was a landing in the south of the country. Indeed, on 3 September an armistice was signed as Eighth Army troops crossed the Straits of Messina and also landed near Taranto. These landings were barely opposed, but the most important invasion force (the US Fifth Army that landed at Salerno on 9 September, under General Mark Clark) certainly did run into difficulties.

Although the Italians had overthrown the fascist regime in July and had announced their withdrawal from the war on 8 September, German units swiftly took over the country (they had been preparing for such a contingency) and by 12 September, Mussolini had been rescued and reinstated,

Left: War correspondents are briefed near Anzio, soon after the landings there. Below: The long advance up the Italian peninsula. South of Rome, the Germans were able to build a series of defensive lines that delayed the fall of the Holy City until June 1944, and even after this Allied success, the German Field-Marshal Kesselring was able to fall back on the Gothic Line north of Florence in order to buy more time.

The Italian campaign 1943-44

➤ main axes of Allied advance
— Gothic Line

although by now he was no more than a puppet of the Germans. The German forces at Salerno fought hard to prevent the bridgehead from growing, and they threatened to throw the invaders back into the sea on more than one occasion. It was only the intensity of supporting naval bombardment that saved the Allied troops on the ground, and not until 20 September did the Germans pull back.

Hitler, advised by Rommel, had believed that Italy could not be defended south of Rome, but the commander-in-chief of the southern theatre, Field Marshal Albert Kesselring, was of a different opinion. He saw the geography of southern Italy as being ideal for defence, and was able to persuade Hitler to agree to the construction of various defensive lines. Kesselring was correct. The Allies advancing up the peninsula found that rapid movement was impossible in the autumn rains, and their reliance on mechanized transport may even have told against them during this period. Kesselring built three parallel defensive systems, the Barbara Line, the Bernhard Line and the Gustav Line. By the time operations ceased in the rains of December, the Allies had only just reached the Bernhard Line, and knew the problems involved in advancing further.

Winston Churchill believed that the answer to the natural obstacles was to use Allied sea power to land troops behind the lines, and to threaten Rome with capture and

Above: Sherman tanks of a Canadian regiment attached to an Indian division of the Eighth Army in Italy. Below: A watchful US machine-gun team.

the German armies with encirclement. On 22 January 1944, with his enthusiastic support, a two-pronged attack took place. The US Fifth Army launched an attack on the front, across the Garigliano and Rapido Rivers, hoping to break through into the Liri valley that runs north–south, while in Operation Shingle the US VI Corps was landed in the Anzio–Nettuno area, behind German lines. The plan foundered, however. The Fifth Army found the rivers impossible to cross in force, and at Anzio the drive off the beachhead was sluggish and the troops were pinned down in a slogging match to which, as at Salerno, the guns of the Allied naval forces made a powerful contribution.

MONTE CASSINO

The Eighth Army (on the east side of the Italian peninsula) now gave a corps to the Fifth Army, and Clark decided to use it to take the position around the town of Cassino to force a way through the German line. Unfortunately, the mountains of this sector were an immensely strong natural barrier. The corps designated to find a way through found its task impossible. Bombing the historic Benedictine monastery that dominated the area on 15 February and then the town itself on 15 March had little effect. Under the able direction of General Fridolin von Sengar und Etterlin, mountain troops and paratroops dug themselves in and prevented the Allies making any progress. Indeed, the bombing even helped the Germans by turning the houses of the town into impassable obstacles. In the week after the bombing of the town, the attacking forces suffered 2000

THE ADVANCE TO ROME | 97

Below: The breakthrough to Rome in spring 1944. In spite of the landings behind the German lines of Anzio in January, the Allied advance stalled along the defences around the town of Cassino. Not until mountain troops of the French Expeditionary Corps had outflanked Axis units were the Germans forced to withdraw. Bottom: Allied success – US troops march through Victor Emmanuel II Square in Rome.

casualties, and in the Fifth Army sector as a whole, Allied casualties were 52,000 killed and wounded from 16 January to the end of March.

The stalemate was eventually broken by Operation Diadem that began on 11 May. Twelve Allied divisions on the Fifth Army front attacked the six German divisions there, but even after an immense bombardment met with further checks before soldiers of a French Expeditionary Corps under General Alphonse Juin crossed supposedly impassable terrain to turn the German positions in the mountains. These men were colonial mountain troops, from North Africa, and their 4000 mules were an immense help in their advance.

To block the hole that was emerging in his front line, Kesselring was forced to move in some of the troops that had been surrounding the Anzio bridgehead, with the result that the Allied forces there were able to break out on 23 May. By then, Cassino had fallen to Polish troops on 18 May. Now the Allies' great advantage in numbers and air power came into play, and German movements, in retreat or in reinforcement, became hazardous. On 26 May alone, 665 vehicles of the German Fourteenth Army were destroyed by air attack. Clark made for Rome, rather than concentrating all his energies on cutting off the German armies that were still in the mountains, and the city fell on 5 June.

The pursuit of the German forces continued north, but with lessening urgency. The Normandy landings and the related descent on southern France (Operation Dragoon) were now claiming all attention and many resources. Kesselring was able to stabilize the line north of Florence, along the Gothic Line. Here, the autumn rains brought another stop to operations.

The Italian campaign had seen enormous technological might applied where it had great effect, as in the landings in Sicily, and in support of the bridgeheads of Salerno and Anzio, but it had also seen the continuing power of the defensive when skilled troops used advantageous terrain.

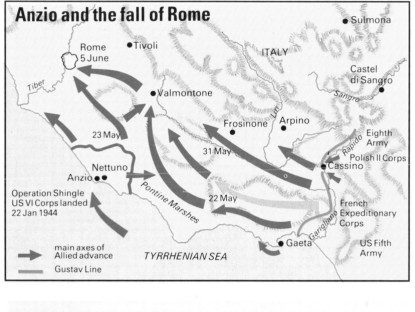

Anzio and the fall of Rome

ISLAND-HOPPING IN
THE PACIFIC

After the battles of the Coral Sea and Midway, and the successful campaigns on Guadalcanal and Papua New Guinea that came to a close early in 1943, the Americans could begin to take the offensive in the Pacific theatre. The sheer size of the areas to be fought over, and the importance of naval power, gave this part of the war a unique quality, quite unlike the campaigns in Europe, North Africa or mainland Asia. But as in the other theatres, new weapons, and especially the massing of these weapons in new fleets and formations, raised the level of warfare beyond anything that had previously been thought possible.

The American Joint Chiefs of Staff had originally intended to make their strategy one giant thrust through the Central Pacific, going due west from Pearl Harbor and mopping up Japanese bases in some of the island chains on the way, until Formosa was reached. Operations could then begin against the Japanese home islands which, cut off from the raw materials of Southeast Asia, would find it very difficult to resist Allied pressure. This plan was heartily endorsed by Admiral Nimitz, in charge of the Pacific Fleet, and by his superior Admiral King. General Douglas MacArthur, however, had other ideas. From his base in Australia, he wished to see a drive by the forces of his Southwest Pacific Area through New Guinea and up to the Philippines. He believed that the USA had a moral duty to make the liberation of these islands a priority, and that in practical terms they were a better base for the eventual attacks on Japan than Formosa.

The result was a compromise. It was decided that both MacArthur and Nimitz would initiate offensives, which would be aimed at the Philippines as an ultimate goal. In the event, the USA proved to have resources adequate for maintaining both axes of advance, and on occasion found that the twin drive had the additional advantage of splitting Japanese defensive capabilities. Although MacArthur always complained that his was a 'Cinderella' command (it was made clear that Nimitz would have first call on resources), the achievements of his forces were impressive.

The key to the Japanese position in the southwest Pacific was the base at Rabaul in New Britain, and it was clear that this would have to be dealt with before any further progress could be made. The problem was that to get to New Britain, the Allied forces would have to fight their way up the Solomons from Guadalcanal and along the north coast of New Guinea. This necessitated time and planning to build up the resources necessary. Nimitz, in the Central Pacific, had even more logistical problems to overcome in preparing his first series of attacks, in the Gilberts. There was, therefore, little chance of US offensive action until summer 1943.

In the meantime, the Japanese tried to disrupt US preparations, but with serious consequences for themselves. In March 1943, troopships carrying reinforcements from Rabaul to New Guinea were attacked by US and Australian aircraft, and in the battle of the Bismarck Sea eight transports and four destroyers were sunk. Reinforcement of the garrisons in New Guinea having failed, the Japanese then tried to defeat the US air

Below: US Navy heavy support for a landing in the Pacific. An enormous weight of firepower was required to destroy the Japanese island defences, but the US high command always favoured expending shells in an attempt to minimize loss of life among its forces.

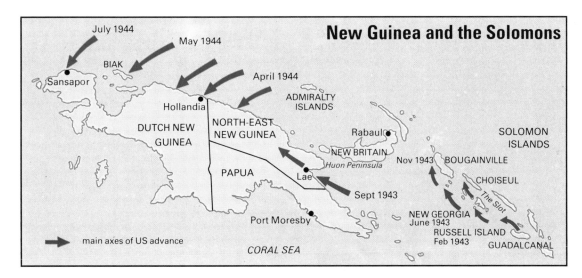

forces over the Solomons, but during air battles in the spring suffered heavier losses than their enemies. In April came another blow: Admiral Yamamoto, the commander of the Japanese Navy, was killed when US P-38 Lightning fighters shot down the aircraft in which he was travelling.

So all seemed auspicious for the beginning of the US offensive – except that the fighting was clearly going to be as hard as the US Army and Marines had ever known. The navy could put them onto islands, but once there they had a real battle on their hands, for the Japanese literally fought to the death. In May 1943, on the remote island of Attu in the Aleutian chain, a garrison of 2800 Japanese was attacked by the US forces of Nimitz. Of the entire garrison, only 28 prisoners were taken. This sort of last-ditch resistance by the Japanese was to be repeated time and again throughout the Pacific theatre.

The movement up the Solomon Islands chain was under the direct control of Vice-Admiral William Halsey, commanding the US Third Fleet. He was part of Nimitz's Central Pacific Command, but for this campaign was acting under the strategic direction of MacArthur. During June, the first landings were made on New Georgia and adjacent islands, and the fighting began in earnest. US progress on New Georgia was slow: the troops were unaccustomed to the jungle terrain and the fighting qualities of the Japanese soldiery made any advance hazardous. By the end of August, however, New Georgia had been cleared, and the next stage could begin.

Below: Amphibious tractors (known as 'amtracks' heading for the shores of the island of Tarawa in November 1943. Tarawa was a tough experience that taught the US Marines many lessons about the techniques of amphibious warfare. One of these lessons was that amtracks were a vital support weapon, for they gave the first wave of troops ashore essential protection against smallarms fire.

TERRIBLE TARAWA

The battle for Tarawa, a Japanese-held atoll in the Gilbert Islands (now Kiribati) was one of the bloodiest of the war, lasting nine days (20–28 November 1943). Although Tarawa cost the US Marines high casualties (3100 men killed or wounded), they learned valuable lessons from this desperate fight. First and foremost, they realized that the weight of bombardment needed to destroy well-sited fortifications was far higher than they had expected – for the Japanese on Tarawa had deployed eight medium artillery pieces that took a grim toll of the landing craft as they approached the beaches. Secondly, the Marines learned that communications between the first troops landed and the supporting fleet had to be vastly improved. On Tarawa, the junior officers in command on the beaches found that their radio links with the command post at sea were quite inadequate, so they were unable to call up accurate supporting fire. Thirdly, it had become clear that in the face of fanatical Japanese resistance the number of armoured support amphibious vehicles, 'amtracks', had to be greatly increased. The fruits of this experience were shown in the attacks on the Marshall Islands in January–February 1944, where it was decided to split the assaults into two separate stages, rather than attempt to spread resources in one series of landings on three atolls. As Admiral Turner noted – 'maybe we had too many men and too many ships for the job, but I prefer to do things that way. It saved a lot of lives.' This was the lesson of Tarawa – the lesson that was to be put into practice during the subsequent US amphibious operations in the Pacific War.

Below: A platoon of US Marines moves forward, with the strain of the fighting etched on their faces. Below right: Moving across the beach on Tarawa. Last-ditch Japanese snipers and the unwillingness of the Japanese soldiers to surrender made any movement on the island hazardous until it was cleared completely.

Feigning to prepare a landing on the southern shores of the island of Bougainville, the northernmost Solomons base which had a key Japanese garrison of 60,000 men, Halsey actually put troops ashore further north on the island at Empress Augusta Bay in November. The forces did not try to drive all the Japanese off the island; they were content to control an extended perimeter while naval vessels and aircraft made the Japanese airfields and heavy support weapons unusable. The result was that the Japanese forces, weakened by their attacks on the US bridgehead, and cut off from aid on Rabaul, lost any offensive power, although they kept large stretches of Bougainville.

This principle of cutting off Japanese garrisons and then leaving them to 'wither on the vine' was to be followed throughout the Pacific war. Halsey was now able to ignore any threat that Bougainville might once have posed. Rabaul itself had been bombed in raids from US carriers during November, and the naval units stationed there had been forced to seek refuge further north. The Japanese main base was now, therefore, impotent. Its garrison could do little without aerial and naval forces; and so rather than sustain heavy casualties by putting in a force of ground troops, the US commanders decided that they could afford to abandon this base to its own fate, and carry on their advance without physically seizing it.

MacArthur had, meanwhile, been adopt-

ing a similar approach in his drive across northern New Guinea. The terrain and the climate made this a difficult campaign for all concerned, but during the summer and early autumn of 1943 the Huon Peninsula was secured and the important centre of Lae taken on 16 September. While Australian troops moved across land, amphibious landings kept the Japanese on the defensive, and early in January 1944 MacArthur was able to occupy part of western New Britain and then, in February, the Admiralty Islands. The neutralization of Rabaul meant that ever more ambitious hops along the coast of New Guinea could be undertaken, and during the next six months the Allied troops established themselves at critical points, such as Hollandia, the island of Biak and at Sansapor late in July. Leaving the Australians to mop up the remnants of the Japanese Eighteenth Army, the Americans were now in a position to prepare to return to the Philippines.

Because of the great distances, it had taken MacArthur a whole year to move from Lae to the northwestern tip of New Guinea; and in the central Pacific, Nimitz also found that he needed time to ensure that his preparations were secure before he could begin his island-hopping approach from the east towards the Philippines. His first major offensive (apart from the retaking of the Aleutians in late spring 1943) was the assault on the Gilbert Islands in November 1943. Makin atoll was taken very easily, by army troops, but the Marines landed on the atoll of Tarawa found that the Japanese were well

dug in and determined not to surrender. The forces involved might seem small compared with those of the Eastern Front, but the fighting itself bears comparison with that of any of the war. Of the 4500 men in the Japanese garrison, only one officer and 17 men, plus 129 Korean labourers, survived, while of the 16,800 Americans landed, 3100 were casualties – over 18 per cent. Whereas on one level the Pacific war was large-scale sweeps over deserted ocean, at this end of the scale it was a grim close-quarters struggle in bunkers and foxholes, against a fanatical foe who was quite prepared to die. Flamethrowers and satchels of explosive charges were the currency of this bloody warfare.

CARRIER POWER

Yet the key to the Pacific war was not the hand-to-hand fight for foxholes on Tarawa. The war was won by the immense superiority of the US carrier forces. Vice-Admiral Raymond Spruance, in charge of Operation Galvanic, the attack on the Gilberts, controlled a fleet of 139 vessels. The ground forces consisted of two divisions: one army, one Marine. There was an Assault Force, under Rear-Admiral Richmond K. Turner, with seven battleships to provide the landing troops with close support; but the real strength of this fleet was in Task Force 81, under Rear-Admiral Charles Pownall. This consisted of five new fast battleships and eleven fast carriers – more than the entire total of carriers in the Japanese Navy during 1941.

This enormous concentration of naval aviation, with support from the battleships in case surface engagement was necessary, brought a new dimension to naval warfare. The Japanese had never expected to face such a force. They found that their defensive plans were hopelessly outmoded. Instead of being able to use their central position to

Above: The scene on the beach on Tarawa, 22 November 1943. The Japanese defences, and defenders, had performed very well, and the evidence of their effectiveness is plain – a knocked-out Sherman tank; an amtrack that was hit before it could take its occupants to a more sheltered area; and the bodies of dozens of US Marines.

Above: The battle of the Philippine Sea in June 1944. While Grumman F6F Hellcats stand idle, a Japanese aircraft plunges into the sea over an escort carrier. Below: The preliminary bombardment of Guam, 21 July 1944.

the 'Z' Plan of May 1943. But Truk itself was now very vulnerable. When the Marshall Islands were attacked by Spruance in January and February 1944, the US commander was able to detach a force of nine carriers and six battleships to raid Truk itself – before the fighting had even ceased in the Marshalls. This attack took the Japanese completely by surprise – for Truk was 1080km (650 miles) from the Marshalls. A total of 250 Japanese aircraft were destroyed and 35 ships (mainly auxiliaries) were sunk in this single blow.

SAIPAN, TINIAN AND GUAM

By January 1944, the carrier force had been renamed Fast Task Force 58, and was under Rear-Admiral Marc Mitscher. During 1944, its activities became increasingly aggressive and independent. Increasing numbers of the smaller, slower escort carriers gave the amphibious landings air cover while the great fleet carriers of the Essex and Independence classes could roam free to strike at will. The logistic effort needed to sustain these operations was, of course, immense. The Marshalls, for example, were some 5000km (3100 miles) from Pearl Harbor, and just as far from Australia. The capture of Majuro, Kwajalein and Eniwetok in the Marshalls in February 1944 would have been impossible but for the services of the 'Maintenance Fleet' as the supply services were known. It was the activities of this fleet that enabled the Americans to bypass Japanese strongholds with such ease.

Having taken the Gilberts and the Marshalls, Spruance's next target was the Marianas. Here, the islands of Saipan, Tinian and Guam were the chosen targets. The fighting was, as always, severe when the troops were put ashore. Of 29,000 defenders on Saipan, less than 1000 surrendered, and the mountainous terrain there posed new problems for the attackers. Nevertheless, the issue was not really in doubt, and Tinian and Guam too had fallen by 2 August 1944.

Fierce as the fighting on the ground was, the most important result of the attack on the Marianas was that it led to the annihilation of the Japanese naval air arm. When the attack began in June, the Japanese fleet, hitherto reduced to impotence for a year by the superiority of the US Navy, had been planning to attack in the seas north of New Guinea, where MacArthur had just moved against Biak Island. When the ships of Spruance's naval armada were known to be operating in the Marianas, however, the Japanese decided to move against them, and so the mobile fleet, with nine carriers and five battleships, moved into the Philippine Sea. Vice-Admiral Jisaburo Ozawa's force, however, was heavily outnumbered by

take a toll of US vessels as the US fleet gradually moved towards the nerve-centre of Japanese power, they found that their Imperial Navy was powerless to intervene against such an enormous force. The Americans, meanwhile, were able to isolate and carry out raids deep into Pacific areas the Japanese considered their own. The base of Truk, for example, was to have been a centre for naval counter-attacks around the Japanese defensive perimeter, according to

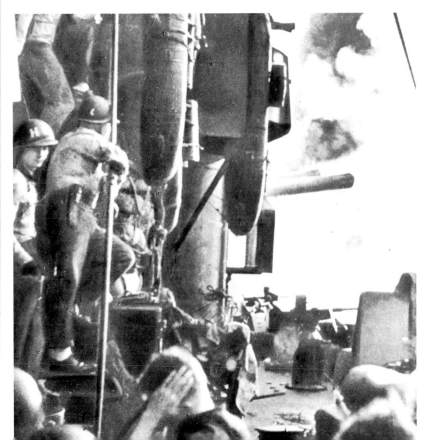

Spruance's 15 carriers and seven battleships, with a superiority of two to one in aircraft. Nor were the Japanese naval aviators any match for the US pilots on an individual basis. The US aircraft were superior by this time, and Japanese pilots were of lower quality, because of a shortage of good replacements for those lost earlier in the war and lack of combat experience in the previous year.

The battle of the Philippine Sea was dubbed 'The Great Marianas Turkey Shoot' by the US pilots who took part in it. During the two days of 19 and 20 June, over 300 Japanese aircraft and five aircraft carriers were destroyed. Underestimation of US capabilities, particularly the capabilities of the F6F Hellcat carrier-based fighter, and overestimation of the numbers of Japanese land-based aircraft available on Guam (they had been destroyed by the first US attacks) had contributed to the Japanese defeat, but by this stage of the war there was little that the Japanese could have done. In the face of Mitscher's Fast Task Force 58, the Imperial Navy was out-dated, out-classed and doomed.

Above: Mopping up on Guam. US forces move cautiously forward, accompanied by tanks, with everyone keeping an eye out for fanatical last-ditch Japanese defenders.

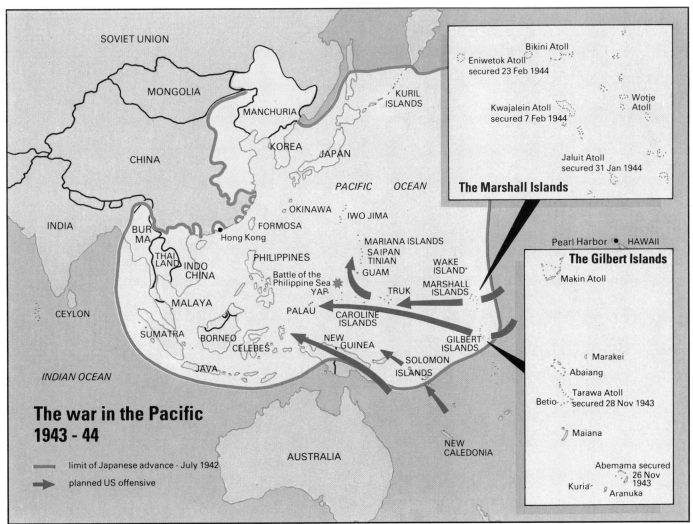

The war in the Pacific 1943 - 44

THE BOMBER OFFENSIVE
ON GERMANY

The bombing offensive on Germany and on industrial targets in occupied Europe was the Allies' attempt to assert their military superiority by ruining the German war industries, and thus strike directly at Germany itself. As such, it was a logical part of modern warfare, for the application of industrial might was clearly to be the critical factor in World War II. However, whereas massed formations on land and sea can be shown to have been vital to the outcome of the conflict, the arguments over the effectiveness of the intense bombing campaign continue to rage. There is no doubt that it caused severe problems for German industry, but it is equally clear that German production did not drop as a result of the raids. And the fact that the bombings used up a great deal of Allied resources – which might well have been allocated more profitably elsewhere – is a problem that has since engendered much discussion.

The idea that bombing on its own could bring a country to its knees had been common in the 1920s and 1930s, and was to a large extent still in vogue in the early 1940s in Great Britain, especially among such RAF senior officers as Sir Charles Portal (Chief of the Air Staff, 1940–45) and Sir Arthur Harris (C-in-C Bomber Command 1942–5). British belief in the power of bombing raids may well also have been strengthened by some of the events of the Blitz. Certainly, the government was worried about civil order in the wake of the bombing of Coventry on 14 November 1940. Early British bombing raids over Germany, however, were not very successful. The aircraft in use were twin-engined Handley Page Hampdens, Bristol Blenheims, Armstrong Whitworth Whitleys and Vickers Wellingtons, with neither the range nor the capacity to inflict much damage inside Germany itself. Daylight bombing was quickly abandoned because of the losses incurred, and yet night bombing was inaccurate, and reports of 1941, notably the Butt Report, showed that only about 33 per cent of all crews released their bombs within 8km (5 miles) of the target.

When Sir Arthur Harris took over Bomber Command on 22 February 1942, he saw it as his task to improve this state of affairs, and to put into operation the Area Bombing Directive of 14 February that set the morale and housing of German industrial workers as prime targets. He organized enormous raids designed to shatter large urban areas and demoralize the population rather than destroy a single target, and began massing his

control, or to be used in the night bombing programme. They preferred to try a more precise form of daylight bombing against selected industrial targets, and to this end the US aircraft, Boeing B-17 Flying Fortresses and Consolidated B-24 Liberators, had heavy defensive armament to enable them to operate in daylight.

The year 1943 saw the day and night bombing offensives getting into high gear, with constant raids on Germany, but results were mixed. There were some successes: the destruction of Hamburg in a fire-storm late in July, and the raid on Peenemünde in August that put back the German 'V'-weapon programme, but there were serious difficulties also. The US daylight bombing force had suffered some heavy blows, notably during the two raids on Schweinfurt in August and October, and RAF Bomber Command too

Above: Bombing up a Handley Page Hampden, one of Britain's best bombers of the first two years of World War II. It was soon superseded, however, by the larger bombers which came into service from 1942 onwards. Left: Staff Sergeant Lusic, a gunner with the US Eighth Army Air Force, wearing typical flight equipment. Far right: Captain Donald S. Gentile, with his North American P-51 Mustang 'Shangri-La'. He shot down 20 enemy aircraft during the course of the war. It was the advent of the P-51D, with its long-range fuel tanks, that gave the US heavy bombers the protection they needed to operate over Germany by day. Right: Bombing up a B-17F Flying Fortress. Powered by four Wright R-1820 Cyclone radial engines the B-17 could carry 7900kg (17,500lb) of bombs and was protected by 13 0.5in Browning machine guns.

aircraft in large formations. The first 'Thousand-bomber raid' was against Cologne on 30–31 May 1942. In August of that year, the Path Finder Force was set up to guide the bombing squadrons more accurately. New four-engined aircraft (Handley Page Halifaxes, Short Stirlings and Avro Lancasters) were moved into the fray, while radar devices, 'Gee' and then 'Oboe', came into use to direct the mass streams of aircraft. In a sense, the large bombing raids were a reflection of the fact that Britain could find no other way of striking directly at Germany, and yet had the resources to maintain some kind of constant campaign against the main enemy.

While the British programme was getting under way, the first US aircraft were arriving in the country, part of the Eighth Army Air Force under Lieutenant-General Ira Eaker. Neither Eaker nor his superior in Washington, General Henry Arnold, was willing to allow the Eighth to come under direct British

was finding that improved German air defences, a combination of Junkers Ju-88 and Messerschmitt Bf-110 night fighters plus large concentrations of anti-aircraft guns directed by radar, were taking a heavy toll. Nor was German industrial production being seriously cut; indeed, output of all war material went up dramatically between 1942 and 1944.

THE SHOWS GO ON

In October 1943, US losses in daylight raids had been running at 9.1 per cent, and in the first six months of 1944, losses of bombers remained high, but the introduction of the P-51D Mustang fighter, which had the range and the performance to escort the US bombers, had made the daylight raids much safer. The Fifteenth Army Air Force, flying from Italy, was able to attack the Romanian oil wells and refineries at Ploiesti, and a simultaneous series of raids on synthetic oil production in Germany paid dividends. In December 1944, of 226,600 tonnes of synthetic aviation fuel programmed in the Reich, only

Top: Lancasters on their way to bomb German cities by night. The Avro Lancaster was the best of the British heavy bombers. A typical machine would be powered by four Rolls-Royce Merlin XXII engines, carry 8200kg (18,000lb) of bombs, and have eight .303in Browning machine guns as defensive armament. Above: Air Chief-Marshal Sir Arthur 'Bomber' Harris, commander-in-chief of RAF Bomber Command. Right: The devastation caused by British bombers on the industrial centres of Germany was far worse than the effects of the Blitz on Britain.

26,400 were produced. In the build-up to D-Day, the heavy bombers pounded the communications system of France to good effect, and on occasion supported the ground troops directly – in the US breakout from St Lô, for example. And defence against the bombers was causing the Germans to direct resources away from the front lines. In 1942, anti-aircraft crews amounted to 439,000 men, whereas they had reached almost 900,000 in 1944, and over 30 per cent of artillery production was for anti-aircraft weapons destined for German industrial centres.

Nevertheless, by 1945 there were serious questions being asked in Allied circles about the real value of bombing raids, especially after the destruction of Dresden in February. The target had little military or industrial value, and the utter destruction of what had been an important cultural centre was regarded by many as a needless expenditure of effort. None of the explanations given for the attack on Dresden – to create a refugee problem, or to help the Russians by destroying a communications centre – was very convincing. The feeling remained that the massive bomber forces were being forced to look for targets to justify the enormous resources that they had commanded.

The dropping of the atomic bombs on Japan in August 1945 demonstrated beyond a shadow of a doubt that strategic bombing could be decisive, quite capable of winning a war on its own – provided, of course, that the other side did not have an equally potent weapon. But the arguments will continue to rage over whether the bombing of Germany was in fact as effective as everyone had hoped (and claimed) at the time. It is, perhaps, best to see the bombing offensive as just one way of converting resources into a means of striking at the enemy – albeit not necessarily the most effective method that could have been found.

Above: A Boeing B-17 Flying Fortress above Kassel. Below: Some of the 40,000 casualties caused by the raids on Hamburg in 1943.

D-DAY AND THE ALLIED BREAKOUT

The Allied landings in Normandy in June 1944 were the essential precondition for the defeat of German forces in the West, and they opened the way for the final defeat of Hitler's regime, for less than a year after D-Day the Allies were accepting the unconditional surrender of the Wehrmacht. 'Overlord', the code-name for the general operation surrounding the invasion of Europe, was the largest amphibious landing ever mounted (although there were more men landed in Sicily during Operation Husky, the naval and air involvement in Sicily was far smaller) and required a tremendous concentration of effort and resources to produce the final result.

British plans for crossing the Channel had been prepared as early as 1941, but only as a possible option should the German armies decide to withdraw from France. When the Americans entered the war, they were anxious to initiate cross-Channel operations as quickly as possible, but the British did their best to dissuade them from a possibly imprudent move, and after some discussion, the invasions of Sicily and then of Italy were the

first steps taken back into Europe's mainland. From March 1943, however, there was a planning staff at work in Britain on the problems of an invasion of France, under General Sir Frederick Morgan, who was known as COSSAC (Chief of Staff to the Supreme Allied Commander).

There was actually no Supreme Allied Commander appointed until early 1944, when the US General Dwight D. Eisenhower, who had been the successful commander of Allied armed forces in North Africa and Sicily was given the post. Under him were Generals

Above: The SHAEF team (Supreme Headquarters of the Allied Expeditionary Force) that directed the Normandy landings. From the left are: US General Omar Bradley; British Admiral Sir Bertram Ramsay (who controlled the naval forces); British Air Chief-Marshal Sir Arthur Tedder (Eisenhower's deputy); General Dwight D. Eisenhower himself; Lieutenant-General (soon to become Field Marshal) Sir Bernard Law Montgomery; British Air Chief-Marshal Sir Trafford Leigh-Mallory (head of the Allied air forces used for the invasion); and, on the far right, US General Walter Bedell Smith, Eisenhower's chief of staff. In spite of disagreements (notably over who was to have precise control over the land forces after the breakout from the Normandy beach-heads – a job Montgomery was unwilling to relinquish) this team in general worked very well together.

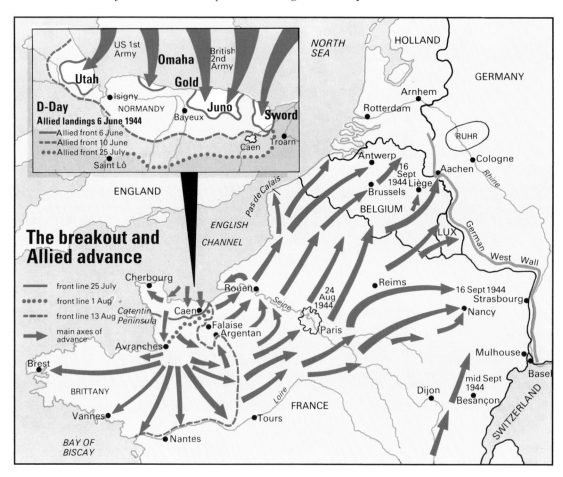

Omar Bradley and Sir Bernard Law Montgomery, in charge of the US and British ground forces respectively (Montgomery was also to have command of all the land forces during the crucial first few weeks of the battle for the bridgeheads). Admiral Sir Bertram Ramsay was placed in charge of naval forces and Air Chief-Marshal Sir Trafford Leigh-Mallory in control of the air forces. For his deputy supreme commander, Eisenhower chose Air Chief-Marshal Sir Arthur Tedder, whose abilities as a strategist and director of air power in the Mediterranean had been greatly admired, and whose grasp of the complexities and possibilites of modern warfare was to be very important to the Allied cause.

The original COSSAC plan had envisaged landing three divisions on a 40km (25-mile) front. Both Montgomery and Eisenhower believed this was too small, however, and to ensure an adequate build-up of support it was decided to go for a five-division landing, over about 65km (40 miles) of coast. The area chosen was Normandy, near the bottom of the Cotentin peninsula.

During spring 1944 there was intense preparation. German communications in France were attacked constantly from the air, although the attacks had to be carried out over a wide area so as not to alert the enemy to the likely invasion site; and a deception plan, designed to give the impression that the landings were to take place in the Pas de Calais, was put into action, with great success. An enormous invasion fleet of 5000 vessels was prepared, and the 154,000 Allied troops who would be landed by landing craft, parachute and glider were trained for their tasks. In the end, the major worry was the weather, which was so bad that, although set for 5 June, the invasion had to be postponed

Above: British glider-borne forces receive instruction. The job of the airborne forces on D-Day was to secure the flanks of the area where the seaborne landings were to take place. Due to unfavourable winds the airborne forces were not, however, as effective as had been hoped.

THE DIEPPE RAID

Even before D-Day, there had been various landings in German-occupied Europe, but these had always been extremely limited in scope and intent. There was a Commando raid on the Lofoten Islands in Norway in March 1941, followed by another on Vågsøy and Måløy in Norway the following December. Both of these were successful, as was the parachute drop by the 2nd Battalion, The Parachute Regiment, to capture and destroy a German 'Würzburg' radar installation at Bruneval near Le Havre on the French coast in February 1942. One month later, Commandos spearheaded an audacious scheme to sail an old explosive-laden destroyer, HMS

Campbeltown, into the French port of St Nazaire, in order to put out of action the only dry dock on the French west coast capable of accommodating the *Tirpitz*. This again was a success.

The most important descent on the coast of occupied Europe before D-Day was, however, a distinct reversal for the Allies, although valuable lessons were learned. For the Dieppe Raid of 19 August 1942 failed in all its main objectives. Canadian troops were to be landed at or near the town of Dieppe, while Commandos secured their flanks and destroyed German batteries. In the event, only on one flank were the Commandos able to fulfil their tasks; there was confusion and lack of coordination in the main assault on the beaches; and

the beaches proved far more of an obstacle than had been anticipated – only three tanks managed to get off the beach at Dieppe itself.

German response was rapid, and tough, and at 0900 hours, within hours of the landing, it was decided to pull the Canadians out (the original intention had been to hold the town for a day). The total Canadian losses were 24 officers and 3164 men. Even in the air, the Germans had worsted the Allies: the RAF lost 106 planes, the Luftwaffe lost 48. All in all Dieppe had been a sobering reminder of the difficulties of landing troops on a hostile shore, and the lessons were to be examined and absorbed by the staff who planned D-Day two years later.

*Right: The wounded
are shipped back from
the Dieppe Raid – the
experimental descent
on the coast of occupied
Europe in August 1942
that cost over 3500
casualties.*

for a day. Eisenhower had to take the decision as to whether to go ahead on the 6th on the basis of reports that the weather would improve; and he gave the order to set out at midnight on the night of 4–5 June.

THE NORMANDY LANDINGS

The Allied forces landed on five beaches – the US troops on those code-named 'Omaha' and 'Utah' to the west, and the Anglo-Canadian forces on 'Sword', 'Juno' and 'Gold' to the east. The flanks of the landing were covered by troops dropped by parachute or glider, although the bad weather had scattered many of these airborne units, and they did not have as much impact as had been hoped. The landings on four of the beaches went well, but the Americans put ashore at Omaha had severe problems in getting off the beach, and their casualties were heavy. On Utah there were only 210 dead and wounded; but at Omaha the defenders claimed 2500 US casualties. About 1000 Canadian casualties and 3000 British were suffered in securing a lodgement on the other three beaches.

D-Day was one of the greatest military operations of all time, not only because of the risk, effort and fighting involved, but also because it involved the precise coordination of so many elements. The combination of air power, naval strength and land operations saw the perfect utilization of technical and human skills to produce the desired result. Without any one of the elements, the landing would have been impossible; and yet each required the most sophisticated equipment, planning and individual ability in itself. From the months of bombing the French communications network to the terrific naval bombardment that not only shattered the beach defences but also broke up the most important German counter-attacks; from the

intelligence work that (via the French Resistance) gave the landing troops so much information to the deception plan that led the Germans to believe that the landing would take place elsewhere; from the training of parachute troops to the invention of a new breed of armoured vehicle (the 'funnies') to carry out specific tasks such as minesweeping or advancing against strongpoints on the shore; from the invention and utilization of landing craft that could put ashore the men and support weapons they would immediately need to the development of enormous floating harbours (Mulberries) and a fuel pipeline (PLUTO – Pipeline Under The Ocean) that ensured that support would continue over the weeks until a port could be captured; all this was war in a dimension that had never been seen before. A comparison of the German attempts to plan a landing in Britain in 1940 with the preparations for D-Day makes it clear just how far the science of war had progressed in the intervening four years.

Although the Germans had been expecting a landing, and the defences of the Atlantic coast had been greatly strengthened under Rommel, whose command of Army Group B, responsible for the Channel coast, had been marked by immense energy and drive, the German high command had not believed that Normandy would be the target, and neither had they thought that the weather was good enough for a massive cross-Channel operation. There was, therefore, comparatively little opposition to the first wave of troops. The major counter-attack was against the

*Below: A stepped gun
embrasure on the
'Atlantic Wall'.
Rommel had made
strenuous efforts to
improve the coastal
defences, and the Wall
was very much a
reality when the Allies
landed – as the US
troops at Omaha Beach
found to their cost.*

Above: Men of the 3rd Canadian Division disembark at Courseulles on Juno Beach, carrying the bicycles that they were to use for the advance inland.

British, on 7 and 8 June, by two SS Panzer divisions that had not been released for action until the afternoon of the 6th, because Hitler had been asleep and no one else dared give the authorization. These attacks were broken up by heavy gunfire from the invasion fleet, and by close-support aircraft that took a heavy toll of any German units moving by day.

From 7–12 June, therefore, the Allies were able to build up their forces in the bridge-head, and they began to push out to engage the German armies. But although the British and Americans had joined up on the 8th, they found the job of getting through the German units very difficult. The countryside on the US side, the so-called *bocage*, was a mass of hedges and narrow lanes that helped a resolute defence; and in the restricted front that the British were fighting near Caen the excellence of German tanks and anti-tank weapons gave Montgomery's men severe problems. Allied progress was much slower than had been expected and the armoured

units in particular found that they were fighting on terms of great inferiority when they came up against tanks such as the Tiger and the Panther. The German nickname for the standard Allied tank, the Sherman, was 'Tommy cooker', because of its tendency to 'brew up' when hit.

Montgomery always claimed that his basic strategy was to wear the Germans down and to pull their Panzer formations towards Caen, while the Americans under Bradley broke out in the west, around the village of St Lô. This is, in effect, what happened, and there seems little doubt that whatever his original intentions, such a strategy was forced on the British general by the failure of Commonwealth troops to secure the objectives they were set in a number of offensive operations. Having been badly mauled around Villers-Bocage on the 12th, Montgomery shifted the main thrust of his advance to the area around Caen, but Operation Epsom of 25 June and Operation Good-wood of 18 July both stopped far short of their

Below right: US troops break cover and dash across a road in Normandy, in an area that the Germans have only just abandoned (a knocked-out German Panther tank is in the right foreground). The US infantry found the fighting in this bocage *landscape of mixed woodland and pastureland very difficult. The endless lines of hedgerows inhibited free movement, and gave stubborn defenders every assistance.*

ostensible objectives. Nevertheless, they soaked up many German formations, so that when Bradley's men, having taken Cherbourg, moved through St Lô on 25 July in Operation Cobra, they faced a depleted German front. The US target was Avranches, at the base of the Cotentin Peninsula, and this was reached on 31 July.

SLAUGHTER AT FALAISE

Having broken through the initial defences in Cobra, the Americans then set out to exploit their success by swinging through into Brittany and pushing out into central France, spearheaded by units of the newly organized Third Army, under General George Patton. The German position was now precarious, but Hitler sealed the fate of many of his units by ordering a suicidal counter-attack. He aimed to cut through the US forces at Avranches and isolate their advancing armoured columns. But with the Anglo-Canadian forces pushing through from Caen and the Americans making a giant sweep round, the Germans risked being cut off along the line Argentan–Falaise. Although the Allied pincers never actually managed to close, partly because of a fear that bombing support might be difficult to control (there had already been some unfortunate incidents in which Allied aircraft had

bombed their own side), the Germans were badly mauled by artillery and fighter-bombers as they tried to pull back, and Army Group B, whose task was the defence of northwestern France, was in tatters.

The German position in France had been rendered doubly impossible by the invasion of the south of the country, Operation Dragoon, on 15 August, carried out by General Alexander Patch and the US Seventh Army. The landings on the French coast between St Tropez and Cannes obliged the weakened German Army Group G, under General Johannes von Blaskowitz, to retreat north up the Rhône valley, although units

Above: The liberation of Paris. A US soldier takes cover together with two members of the French Resistance as sniper fire continues from the few remaining Germans left in the city.

Left: British troops prepare for an assault near Cagny. The slow, slogging nature of the fighting in the British sector of Normandy is evidenced by the fact that the men have entrenching equipment at the ready. Note the 'new style' helmets, first introduced in 1944.

left behind in Marseilles and Toulon put up a fierce resistance. The advance of the Allied forces from the south was rapid in the extreme; by 26 August they had reached Grenoble, and were through Besançon and Dijon by mid-September.

Hitler had hoped to be able to maintain a bridgehead over the River Seine south of Paris, but as the German armies in western Europe had suffered over 290,000 casualties by 31 August and had lost enormous amounts of material they were in no position to resist the Allied surge. On 25 August, Paris was liberated by the Free French 2nd Armoured Division, and the tide of advance seemed to be flowing on relentlessly. Nor was the rapid advance over-costly: between the D-Day landings and the beginning of September, Allied casualties were only about 60,000. By 16 September, the armies under Eisenhower's command (he had arrived on the 1st of that month to assume overall control) had reached Nancy in the east, Liège in the northeast and Antwerp in the north.

Now, however, the advance began to run out of steam, not so much because of stiffening German resistance (the Wehrmacht had been so mauled as to present little active opposition) but because of lack of logistic support. Both Patton, in charge of the US Third Army, and Montgomery, commanding the British 21st Army Group, believed that if they had been given priority in terms of supplies, especially petrol and diesel fuel, then they could have won major strategic objectives. In August, Montgomery argued hard for a 40-division push in his sector that could sweep round to take the industrial area of the Ruhr, while in early September Patton urged that he be given the petrol he needed to strike through the thinly held West Wall and cross the Rhine.

Eisenhower has been criticized for not giving one of these subordinates his head, but, in fact, there seems little chance that either drive would have been logistically possible. Montgomery's 40 divisions would have been hard to find, given the amount of mopping up to be done along the Channel coast, while Patton's tanks, fulminate as their director might, were not deliberately starved of fuel. The D-Day landings had involved destroying the French rail and road network, and the retreating Germans had completed the process. The 'Red Ball Highway' bringing supplies from the beaches to the forward units just could not support the advance. As Rokossovsky had found in Poland in August, and as the US commanders in the Pacific theatre had always known, the Allied forces could not go further than their communications would support them. The battered Wehrmacht was able, therefore, to re-establish its defensive front in the west.

Above: General George S. Patton, the man who led the breakout from Normandy. Patton was a controversial figure, but a great armoured commander. Below: A US 57mm anti-tank gun in action at St Malo in Brittany. The resistance of the garrisons of the Channel ports was a severe problem for the Allies.

Part Five
The Allies Victorious

There can be no doubt that by the time the Allies stood poised for the final offensives against Germany and Japan in the closing months of World War II, the art of warfare had altered immeasurably since the conflict began in 1939. In no area was this more obvious than in the weapons used. They were bigger, more destructive and dwarfed anything produced in the prewar world. They were also to have a determining effect on the warfare that has occurred since 1945.

The atomic bomb that brought the war to an end was the most obvious example of this, but the jet-propelled aircraft and the V-2 rocket (the launching sites for which were captured before it could wreak havoc on London) were others. At sea, the Germans had designed U-boats, such as the Type XXI, which in their cigar-shaped hulls and their revolutionary 'schnorkel' system (which

enabled them to remain submerged for as long as they needed) were the basis of post-war models.

The mass of powerful weapons had led to a new approach to warfare. The successes of the Germans and Japanese in the early years of the war had been gained with relatively small forces which did not reflect total involvement of their populations in the war. By 1945, however, this had changed. The basic weapons of the early German and Japanese conquests – the tank, the fighter-bomber and (in the Japanese case) the aircraft carrier – were still the dominant weapons systems but now they were combined in far greater numbers, and the defending forces had learned how to subdue some of their potential. The battle of Kursk (July 1943), the problems faced by the Allied armies in their advance up the Italian peninsula, the successes of the

CODE-BREAKING

Code-breaking and intelligence have been important in many wars: the ability to read an enemy's orders, and especially orders that the enemy believe to be secret, can be a priceless advantage. In World War II, this was demonstrated as never before. All nations made strenuous efforts to understand the enciphered and encoded signals of their enemies, but the two greatest successes were enjoyed by the British and the Americans.

The Americans had managed to break the Japanese diplomatic codes even before the USA became embroiled in World War II, and, indeed, as early as July 1941 they were able to predict Japanese actions. Pearl Harbor might have been alerted to the imminence of Japanese attack had there been more effective channels for communicating the results of the code-

breaking to the commanders there. The most important results of code-breaking came in 1942, in the battles of the Coral Sea and Midway, when the US Admiral Nimitz was able to place his carriers where they could be most effective, and where they could take advantage of the Japanese dispositions. Perhaps the most striking single achievement of US code-breakers involved the Japanese commander-in-chief, Admiral Yamamoto. He arranged to visit Bougainville in the Solomons on 18 April 1943 but the US code-breakers found out. As his plane arrived, it was ambushed by 18 US P-38 Lightnings, and Yamamoto was killed as his aircraft went down. Such accurate and devastating code-breaking was obviously of great value.

Of even more importance, however, was the possession by the British of the 'Enigma' machines that the Germans used to encode

their secret messages. Two of these machines were given to Britain by the Poles in July 1939, and by November 1939 were decoding German signals. It was not until 1941, however, when further information and another machine were obtained from a captured weather vessel, that Enigma became of crucial importance. Then it became invaluable in the war at sea, and enabled the Allied commanders to see precisely what the strengths and weaknesses of the Germans were in all theatres. Even when the Germans realized that something was amiss, the British code-breakers retained the upper hand. A new cipher, 'Triton', adopted in February 1942, had been cracked by the end of the year, and the addition of a further refinement to the standard Enigma machine in March 1943 proved only a minor irritation to British experts – a group of men who were crucial to Allied success in the war.

US defensive forces in the 'Battle of the Bulge' (December 1944), and the difficulties that the Americans encountered in the Philippines and Okinawa (October 1944–June 1945) were all indicative of the ability of defending troops to blunt the assaults of more mobile attackers.

Thus it was that the two men who directed the great drive on Germany at the end of the war – Stalin in the Soviet Union and Eisenhower in northwest Europe – both came to the conclusion that an offensive at various points along a whole front might have greater long-term effects than one that concentrated on pouring through at a single point. Stalin in particular had worked to a fine art the strategy of pushing ahead in one sector, then suddenly changing the axis of the main thrust to catch the enemy off balance.

Quite apart from the changes on the battlefield, the new emphasis on large numbers of advanced weapons had altered the way in which warfare had to be directed. The traditional qualities of generalship – manoeuvre, the inspiration of troops, the timing of attack or counter-attack – were still, of course, very important. But there were other qualities that were now of equal moment. The correct allocation of resources, the analysis of national characteristics to get the best out of them, the coordination of forces in such operations as 'Overlord' (June 1944) – these were skills that it became essential to master. A general like William Slim of the British Fourteenth Army, who had to apply his resources not only to the task of dealing with an enemy whose basic fighting man displayed an awesome endurance and ferocity, but also to regain control of far-flung units with immaculate timing during the Imphal–Kohima battles in Burma (March–April 1944), had to exhibit skills far wider than those of earlier generals.

THE KAMIKAZE MIND

The Japanese and the Germans both suffered severely at this level of expertise, because their very governing systems tended to work against them. The Japanese emphasis on individual courage and down-grading of logistic requirements had fatal results. A warrior society, or at least, a society whose leaders aspired to be warriors and believed death preferable to retreat was no match for the managers of the US war effort. Kamikaze attacks, in which Japanese pilots attempted to destroy US naval vessels by crashing planes onto them, were not going to defeat fleets directed by men like Vice-Admiral Spruance – a leader whose meticulous attention to logistic detail and careful coordination of all his fighting and service networks was linked to an aggressiveness in action

that earned him the description of 'cold-blooded fighting fool' from one of his fellow admirals.

Similar limitations hampered Germany's conduct of the war. The promotion of some members of the Nazi Party to posts of considerable military importance – Göring and later Heinrich Himmler, for example, were given positions far outweighing their competence – had serious long-term results. The totalitarian system itself, with Hitler as the ruthless director of every detail, also worked against the Germans. The German generals had to deal with a string of orders that became steadily less in touch with reality as the war grew in scope. It is true that the infrastructure of Nazi Germany was better suited than that of Japan to sustaining a modern war, but the interference of Hitler at many levels of command, his meddling in weapons development and finally his descent into what can only be described as megalomania were powerful contributory factors to the German defeat.

Of course, the Allies too were beset with great problems in directing their war effort. The Soviet Union was ruled by a totalitarian dictator, who made enormous military errors in the first two years of Russian involvement, and caused his country untold suffering. Stalin was, however, able to learn from his mistakes, so that it is often argued that by 1945 he was the most effective warlord on the Allied side. British and US direction of the war also had its failings. But disagreements between the Anglo-American Chiefs of Staff, and their relations with the political leaders Churchill and Roosevelt were worlds apart from the Japanese beliefs in personal sacrifice and the German high command's relationship with Hitler.

This contrast between the Allies and their enemies was at its most acute early in 1945, just before the final offensives began. For no rational analysis of the situation would have given either Germany or Japan a chance of survival against the Allies. Yet both countries fought to the end, until they had been completely laid waste.

Above: The victory parade in Warsaw, October 1939. Hitler's early successes reinforced his control over the German Army.

Opposite page: General L. R. Groves, director of the Manhattan Project that developed the atomic bomb and so changed the face of modern warfare.

Below: Japanese fanaticism – a kamikaze *pilot photographed for posterity just before take-off.*

ARNHEM AND THE ARDENNES

The two most striking episodes of the campaign of autumn 1944 in northwest Europe were two failed offensives – Montgomery's attempt to drive through to northern Holland in Operation Market Garden, and Hitler's attack through the Ardennes that became known as the 'Battle of the Bulge'. Between them, these two failures seem to sum up the changes that had emerged in warfare since the German victories of the 1939–41 period. Mere penetration of an enemy's front was no longer enough. The experience and expertise of modern armies at dealing with a more fluid battlefield, and the need to concentrate far heavier quantities of material to destroy defenders who were armed with effective anti-tank weapons meant that both these operations were probably doomed to failure before they began. The component parts of the Blitzkrieg that the Germans had demonstrated in the early years of the war were still the most important elements on the battlefield – and, in the Ardennes in particular, the importance of air power was once again convincingly illustrated. But the approach of soldiers and their commanders and the increase in the weight and quantity of support weapons had brought a change in kind as well as a change in the scale of warfare.

General Eisenhower had assumed direct command of the Allied armies in northwest Europe on 1 September 1944, in spite of some opposition to this from the British, who wanted Montgomery, the previous commander of land forces, to continue in this role.

Above: One of the main dropping zones near Arnhem. Left: The interior of a Douglas C-47, known in Britain as the Dakota, with paratroops ready to jump. The soldiers carry their personal weapons, but their kit is packed in leg bags or worn under their smocks to prevent it catching in the parachute harness. The British 1st Airborne Division was an elite force, highly trained and well equipped, but it suffered heavily during the Arnhem operation.

Eisenhower's first task was to decide on the priorities in allocating resources, which were fast becoming his major problem. Whereas the Germans had a mere 30 understrength and badly mauled divisions available in the west, the Allies had over 60 by the middle of September in three Army Groups (the 21st under Montgomery, the 12th under Bradley and the 6th – the troops that had advanced north after Operation Dragoon – in the south under General Jacob Devers). Supplying these forces was a grave problem, for everything had to be brought from the beach-heads in Normandy or from the beaches in southern France. The Channel ports of Boulogne and Calais had not yet been cleared, and the rail network of France had been shattered by Allied bombing and German demolitions. The port of Antwerp had been taken on 4 September, but Montgomery's Army Group had made no moves to clear the Schelde estuary that dominated the approaches to the port – as it turned out, a serious oversight.

Montgomery was pressing for his Army Group to be given the task of conducting a major thrust into the Ruhr, the German industrial heartland, while Patton, with the US Third Army, was also demanding resources to try to smash through the Saar region. Eisenhower decided that the advance would continue on all fronts, but that Montgomery should have priority. The Allied commander-in-chief also sanctioned an ambitious scheme, Operation Market Garden, that Montgomery suggested to him. The idea was to drop three Anglo-American airborne divisions onto key crossing places on the Maas, Waal and Neder Rijn Rivers in Holland and then to rush the British XXX Corps, spearheaded by the Guards Armoured

Division, through the 100km (60 miles) of enemy-held territory to link up with them. XXX Corps could then push further north to the Zuider Zee, and the way would be opened for a giant sweep into north Germany.

Bradley was shocked when he heard of Montgomery's plan – partly because he thought that such a manoeuvre was completely out of character for the normally cautious and methodical British commander. Market Garden involved a great risk, for the armoured column would have to advance through low-lying country crossed by at least six major obstacles. Its advance would thus be slowed, and it would be vulnerable to anti-tank forces. In addition the northern paratroops, those dropped around the town of Arnhem, might find themselves exposed to a German counter before help arrived.

Above: The first drops during Operation Market Garden succeeded in catching the Germans by surprise, but not all of the paratroops had happy landings.

Below: A headquarters artillery group forms up soon after the landings near Arnhem.

On Sunday 17 September the operation got under way as airborne forces parachuted or were glider-lifted into zones north of Eindhoven, south of Nijmegen and northwest of Arnhem. At Eindhoven and Nijmegen, where US forces of the 101st and 82nd Airborne Divisions went in, the major objectives were soon captured, but at Arnhem things were very different. Two SS Panzer divisions (the 9th and 10th) were refitting near the town, and they soon made things very hot for the British 1st Airborne Division. The troops sent into Arnhem itself to capture the road bridge across the Neder Rijn, under Lieutenant-Colonel John Frost, were soon in difficulties, while the armoured troops and XXX Corps, having reached Nijmegen by 20 September, were counter-attacked by 10th Panzer when they tried to push further north. Of the 9000 British airborne troops, 2000 managed to pull back to the south bank of the Neder Rijn during the night of 25–6 September, to link up with the Allied armour, which itself was exposed to fire from its flanks and in a salient that might be cut at any moment.

Although Operation Market Garden had led to an Allied advance into some of the areas intended, the operation had basically failed in its objective – and at considerable cost. A major factor inhibiting the Allies had been the weather – only one fine day of the ten that the operation lasted had meant that the air support necessary was of poor quality. But the main reason for defeat was that the Germans, who were fortunate to have the two Panzer divisions in the vicinity of Arnhem,

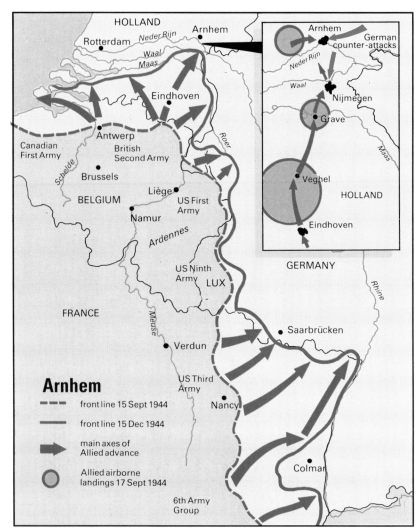

Arnhem

- - - - front line 15 Sept 1944

——— front line 15 Dec 1944

➤ main axes of Allied advance

⬤ Allied airborne landings 17 Sept 1944

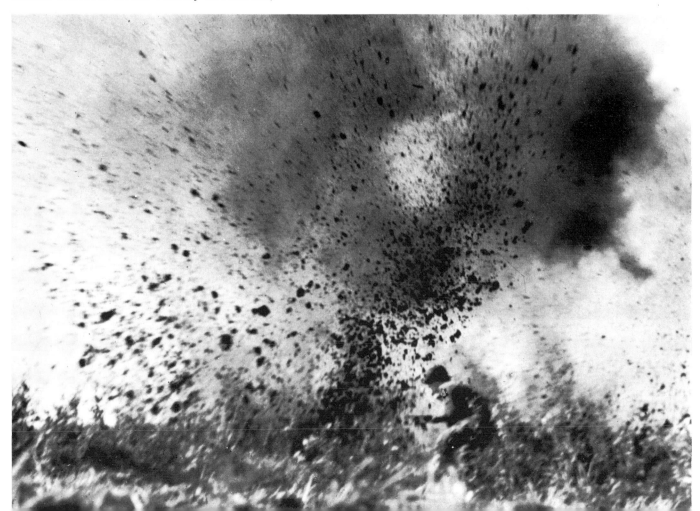

had been prepared to fight it out, and had not been thrown off balance by the airborne landings. They had accurately assessed the situation, and taken the steps necessary to deal with the incursion.

BUILD-UP TO THE BULGE

After Arnhem, it was clear that further advances would depend upon the provision of adequate supplies to all fronts, and so the clearing of the German forces on the banks of the Schelde estuary began, although it was mid-October before Montgomery gave overriding priority to this operation. Not until 8 November was the clearing finished (it involved the Canadian First Army in particularly heavy fighting that cost 12,800 casualties, and netted 40,000 German prisoners) and not until 28 November were the first ships using the harbour at Antwerp. Hardly surprisingly, Allied advances in the late autumn all along the front were far less impressive than those of the late summer. By mid-December in the south of the Allied line, the 6th Army Group was pressuring a considerable pocket of Germans west of the Rhine around Colmar; further north Patton's Third Army had moved up to the Saar, and was preparing to attack the West Wall in the region; and the US First and Ninth Armies (the latter a new formation that had come into service in November, holding ground between the US First and the British Second Army) had reached the line of the Roer River. Now, however, the Germans themselves

chose to attack, trying to catch the Allies off balance, and initiated what was known as the 'Battle of the Bulge'.

The Battle of the Bulge was an attack through the wooded hills of the Ardennes, designed to cross the Meuse River between Namur and Liège and push on to Antwerp. This manoeuvre, if successful, would have cut off the British 21st Army Group, and the bulk of the US 12th Army Group. It might also have created dissension within the Allied side, and even have led to panic. The plan was very much Hitler's own. His generals, Field Marshal Gerd von Rundstedt in overall command and Field Marshal Walther Model commanding Army Group B, felt that the plan was far too ambitious and would end in disaster.

Above: A German photograph of one of the bridges at Arnhem.

Left: British paratroops search for snipers in a shell-damaged house in Oosterbeek. Far left: US paratroops run for cover as they come under German artillery fire.

Above: An officer from Kampfgruppe 'Peiper' poses in his command car by a signpost. Jochen Peiper's units ranged deep into the valley of the River Amblève, but could not make any lasting gains; the US forces refused to panic at the approach of the German mobile troops. Peiper's men were guilty of one of the most shameful acts of World War II – the massacre of US prisoners at Malmedy.

Right: US M4 Shermans of the 40th Tank Battalion outside St Vith. The defence of St Vith was one of the crucial episodes of the 'Battle of the Bulge'. It seriously affected the German timetable and allowed the US and British forces to the north of the German penetration to prepare themselves for any further advances by the German forces.

The attack was carried out by the 6th SS Panzerarmee of Colonel-General Sepp Dietrich, the 5th Panzerarmee of General Hasso von Manteuffel and the Seventh Army of General Erich Brandenburger. It went in on 16 December, just before dawn, on a lightly held sector which Eisenhower had left sparsely garrisoned because of the need for troops elsewhere. A mere 83,000 Americans had to bear the brunt of an assault by over 200,000 German troops. At first, General Courtney Hodges (commander of the First Army) and his Army Group commander General Bradley thought that it was a local

attack, but it was soon clear that much more was at stake.

Bad weather (which lasted until 23 December) helped the Germans by grounding the Allied air forces, but, as at Arnhem, the determination and resourcefulness of the forces under attack stopped the classic Blitzkrieg exploitation of an initial break-through. In the north, where Dietrich's men were to lead the push for the Meuse, the US 2nd Division did not give way, and, with support from the less experienced 99th Division, held up the advance before the Elsenborn Ridge, while the area around the key town of St Vith was occupied by the US 7th Armored Division and some supporting units. On the German timetable, St Vith should have fallen two days after the first attacks, but in fact, it did not come into their possession for five days. Between St Vith and the Elsenborn Ridge, the Germans tried, in classic Blitzkrieg fashion, to push through into weaker rear areas, but the infiltration of Jochen Peiper's Kampfgruppe into the valley of the Amblève River was held up by the support units that happened to be there, and it was finally forced back by the arrival of the 82nd Airborne Division near Werbomont.

It was the same in the south. The town of Bastogne was resolutely held by the US 10th Armored and 101st Airborne Divisions, and although German tanks had managed to slip through between St Vith and Bastogne on 20 December, the shortage of fuel was such that they could not restart their advance until the 22nd. By then, the battle was almost decided, for on the 23rd the skies cleared, and the Allied fighter-bombers began taking a ter-

rible toll of the German armoured forces. Bastogne was finally relieved on 26 December, and the last serious attempt to reach the Meuse, by the 2nd Panzer Division, was counter-attacked by the US 2nd Armored Division on Christmas Day and thrown back. On 3 January 1945 major Allied counter-attacks began, and by the beginning of February the front line was back where it had been in mid-December.

A RESOLUTE DEFENCE

The Battle of the Bulge had involved 600,000 US troops and was the largest set-piece battle in which US forces had ever been engaged. US casualties were 77,000 to the Germans' 82,000; the Allies lost 733 tanks, and the Germans 324. When the battle began, Eisenhower had fewer mobile reserves at his disposal than were available to the French commander-in-chief, General Maurice Gamelin in 1940. Yet the offensive had, in the end, been contained within a very short time. This was partly because a few days of clear weather allowed the Allies to assert their superiority in the air, but it was equally because the response to such an offensive had by now become standard. The command structure was quickly reorganized to deal with the breakthrough – with Montgomery being given command of all troops to the north of the 'Bulge' and Bradley taking over the south. Positions were held while they were a serious block to the advance – as with St Vith and Bastogne – but not merely for the sake of holding ground. St Vith was abandoned before it became a death trap. And

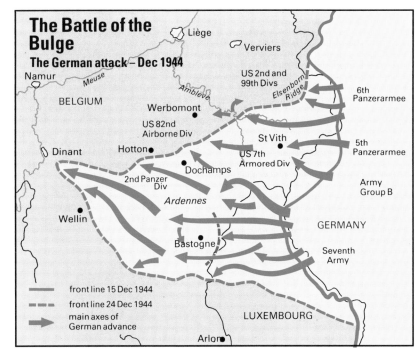

elsewhere US forces presented a resolute defence. They did not panic, and when Peiper's small thrust into the Amblève valley met rear-echelon units, these units did not break, but put up continued resistance. Montgomery was quite prepared to trade irrelevant space to allow the German advance time to run out of steam while he built up reserves ready to strike back at the over-extended Panzer columns.

Allied experience and expertise – as shown in the fighting qualities of the US 2nd Division and by Montgomery – won the Battle of the Bulge.

Below: US troops man a mortar emplacement. The US Army conducted a spirited defence at both St Vith and Bastogne.

THE CAMPAIGNS IN BURMA

The Burmese theatre was one of the most isolated of World War II. The fighting there was affected by events in China, but the conflicts in Europe, the Mediterranean and the Pacific were remote, apart from where the allocation of resources was concerned. Those fighting in Burma, therefore, felt they came far down the list of priorities and that they were consigned to wage a war in inhospitable terrain with few of the advantages enjoyed by Allied troops elsewhere. Indeed, the commander of the British Fourteenth Army, Lieutenant-General (later Field Marshal) William Slim, reflected the mood of his forces when he described them as the 'Forgotten Army'.

Burma was, however, one of the most interesting theatres of the war, partly *because* of this relative isolation. There, the problems of waging war on the modern scale were shown at their starkest. Both the Brit-

ish and the Japanese found that the jungles, mountains and rivers of north Burma made the simplest military operations difficult, and making the most of the advantages that each side enjoyed – the fighting abilities of the Japanese soldier and the technical qualities of the British infantry – was a tough task.

In addition to the problems presented by the terrain, Burma was the one theatre of war where the differences between the Allies proved a serious check on operations. The Chinese, under Chiang Kai-shek, had their own ideas of how the fight against the Japanese should be carried out, and were not prepared to subordinate their views to the requests of the Anglo-American commanders. At the same time, the Western Allies were not prepared to put more resources into China than they felt were justified. In these conditions, personality clashes between Chiang and men like the abrasive Lieutenant-General 'Vinegar Joe' Stilwell had serious consequences for Allied operations.

By May 1942, the Japanese had achieved all the objectives set out in December 1941. They had pushed the British back to India,

Below: Two machine-gun teams of the 19th Indian Division during the attack on Fort Dufferin, at Mandalay, in March 1945. The Indian Army had had its work cut out to learn methods that would succeed against the brave and resourceful Japanese fighting man, but eventually the greater technical expertise of the Allied forces proved superior to sheer courage.

and were able to call the whole of Southeast Asia a 'Co-Prosperity Sphere'. The Japanese forces in Burma consisted of the Fifteenth Army under Lieutenant-General Shojiro Iida. The troops themselves were all veterans, but their intentions were essentially defensive. Having cut the 'Burma Road' taking supplies overland to China, they had no objective worth a major offensive, as an attack into the vast plains of India across the difficult Naga and Patkai mountains by such a small force was out of the question.

The British, however, were preparing to attack the Japanese, and in September 1942, General Wavell ordered Lieutenant-General Noel Irwin to prepare an attack down the west coast of Burma, into the area of the Arakan to secure the island and port of Akyab. In theory, Wavell had immense resources at his disposal, in the shape of the manpower and wealth of British India, but in fact, the British Empire was severely stretched in late 1942 providing troops for the Mediterranean theatre, and the internal state of India itself, rent by nationalist agitation, soaked up more troops than could be released for operations at the front. The attack on the Arakan was therefore a failure, in circumstances which did not augur well for any further offensives. A small force of two Japanese battalions held off 12 infantry and six artillery units until the Japanese 55th Division arrived as reinforcement, and threw the British back in disorder. By May 1943 the British had suffered 5000 casualties – and had achieved nothing.

This disaster was somewhat mitigated, from the British point of view, by the fact that another operation, begun in February 1943, had been rather more successful. This was the first of the Chindit raids ('Chindit' is an anglicization of Chinthe, the name of the mythical griffin protecting the Burmese pagodas). A force of 3000 men, commanded by Brigadier Orde Wingate, was dropped behind Japanese lines, supplied by air, and after causing some confusion in the Japanese rear areas was pulled back to British lines in April. The Chindit operation had resulted in heavy casualties – of the 3000 men about half were lost – but it had shown that something could be achieved against the battle-hardened Japanese.

During the remainder of 1943, Burma was

Above: Japanese infantry on the advance early in the war in Burma. The great strength of the Japanese Army was its emphasis on the offensive, and its tactical doctrine of closing with the enemy at the earliest possible opportunity. Easy victories in China, however, had led the Japanese to neglect certain technical developments. Not only was the standard Type 38 'Arisaka' rifle very old-fashioned, but the armoured vehicles of the Japanese Army were hopelessly outdated. Left: Orde Wingate (at centre in topee) during the second Chindit operation. Wingate's vision of groups of well-trained men operating far behind enemy lines, and the implementation of some of his proposals, helped to lift Allied morale by demonstrating that the Japanese were not unbeatable.

relatively quiet. The Japanese completed the building of the 'Burma Railroad' that was to give them the opportunity to initiate operations by providing a more secure supply line, while the Allies concentrated upon reorganizing and retraining their forces. A new command, South East Asia Command, or SEAC, was created, and placed under Lord Louis Mountbatten, with the US representative in China, Joseph Stilwell, as his deputy. Wavell became Viceroy of India, and the British Eastern Army was renamed the Fourteenth Army, under Lieutenant-General Slim. In addition, to make their infantry brigades more effective against the Japanese, the British undertook a reorganization that placed one British, one Indian and one Gurkha battalion together as the basis of each brigade. The fighting qualities of the Gurkhas had been somewhat neglected previously, and they became a useful stiffening component in the infantry. Air supply was also improved, in the knowledge that it had been essential in the Chindit operation, and the huge distances to be covered and the difficult terrain made aerial communication an invaluable logistic aid. Finally, great efforts were made to combat the debilitating diseases that were as much an enemy as Japanese bullets. In XXXIII Corps between June and November 1944, for example, there were 3289 battle casualties, but 47,089 men went down with diseases, including 20,430

with malaria. The gradual lowering of such statistics was crucial to the creation of an army able to fight successfully in the Burmese climate.

As well as these general measures, the British had been working on the best method of countering the Japanese infantry, whose ability to infiltrate behind positions and to attack across difficult country had disconcerted Allied forces time and time again. The British were clearly superior in certain

Above: Using mules to transport supplies across the River Chindwin. Logistics was a major problem for all the armies that fought in Burma.

Left: A Bren gunner of the British Fourteenth Army advances through the undergrowth. In general, the support weapons of the British were superior to those of the Japanese forces.

Chiang Kai-shek, leader of Nationalist China. fought Mao Tse-tung's communist army in the 1930s and then had to defend China against the Japanese invasion of 1937, forming de facto alliance with the communists against the foreign aggressor.

Joseph Stilwell, or 'Vinegar Joe' as he was sometimes known. He served as Chiang Kai-shek's chief of staff from 1942 onwards, and commanded US troops in the Chinese/Burmese theatre. Not being noted for his tact, he was replaced in 1944.

Field Marshal William 'Bill' Slim, commander of the British Fourteenth Army and one of the most successful generals of the war. Slim got to grips with the difficult logistics of fighting in Burma, and knew how to inspire his men, whom he nicknamed the 'Forgotten Army'.

Major-General D.D. Gracey, whose 20th Indian Division was part of the garrison at Imphal. The Allied troops were not panicked by the Japanese advance, and held firm until the enemy ran out of steam. Gracey later commanded the British troops who moved into French Indochina in 1945.

fields, in the use of artillery, for example; the problem was, how to make this superiority tell. Slim believed in a combination of stiff resistance in some areas, which should not panic if outflanked, together with a more flexible response in others. And the troops themselves were given intensive training in the conditions they could expect in battle, including simulated attacks using live ammunition.

On 15 January 1944, Mountbatten felt confident enough to order a general offensive. Stilwell was to lead in some of the Chinese forces he had been training from the north, the British IV Corps was to attack the Japanese positions across the Chindwin River, while XV Corps was to move against the Arakan. Chinese forces in Yunnan were also asked to take part, although the extent of their involvement was impossible to specify.

In the event, however, the Japanese took the initiative. They attacked on two fronts, firstly in the Arakan. Here, on 3 February, XV Corps found itself under threat from the Japanese 55th Division under Lieutenant-General Tadashi Hanaya. Once again, the momentum of the Japanese attack and the flexibility of their infantry threw the British off balance, to such an extent that the British commander, Lieutenant-General Sir Philip Christison, wanted to withdraw at one point. But Slim had determined that the Japanese

would be held. A self-contained 'box' known as the 'Admin Box' formed itself at Sinzweya, and stopped the Japanese advance. The box was supplied from the air, with 2750 tonnes of supplies being dropped, and the Japanese, unable to remove the threat to their communications, withdrew on 23 February, after the Ngakyedauk Pass to the box had been reopened.

Stiff though the British resistance had been, the Japanese had achieved one of their

Below: Two members of the 1st Punjab Regiment in forward positions overlooking the 'Admin Box' in the Arakan. The British forces refused to retreat despite being enveloped by the advancing Japanese troops.

main objectives, for eight of their battalions had tied down 27 Indian, 18 British, seven West African and five Gurkha infantry battalions, not to mention 20 artillery regiments. Now the main Japanese attack could go in – the advance across the Chindwin towards the line Tiddim–Imphal–Kohima.

This attack was the brainchild of Lieutenant-General Renya Mutaguchi, who believed that he could forestall any British offensives, and might even create enough unrest in India (if he gained a rapid victory) to prevent the British gathering strength to push back into Burma for some time to come. In this he was encouraged by Subhas Chandra Bose, the commander of the Indian National Army that hoped to liberate the subcontinent from British rule.

Mutaguchi's attack was slightly delayed, because the Japanese 15th Division was slow in moving up from Thailand – an inauspicious start, but a prophetic one, for the great problem that the Japanese faced was the difficulty of moving troops and supplies. The attack finally got under way on 8 March. The plan was for three divisions, the 15th, 31st and 33rd, to drive towards Imphal from the centre, north and south, using a series of envelopments and moving in several columns. The first moves were successful; but they met a well-planned response from the British. Slim had decided to rest his defence on solid positions at Imphal and at Kohima in the northern sector, while withdrawing the 17th Indian Division from Tiddim in the south and pulling forward troops back to Imphal. The defensive plan depended upon good timing, good discipline from the troops who were withdrawing or required to hold fast, and the ability to ship in reinforcements and supplies from the air.

IMPHAL AND KOHIMA

The plan worked very well, right from the beginning, when the 17th Division withdrew in good order, pushing through road blocks set up by small groups of infiltrating Japanese – obstacles that had often caused panic in the past. Now, however, the British were prepared to fight an enemy which was more mobile, and they knew how to combat such tactics. The commander of IV Corps, Lieutenant-General Sir Geoffrey Scoones, assembled his men in boxes at Imphal to meet the attacks of the 15th and 33rd Japanese Divisions, and the efficient supply of these boxes enabled them to maintain a deadly artillery fire on the attacking Japanese, who were, in any case, unprepared for a long siege.

In the north, Lieutenant-General Naotake Sato had the job of taking Kohima, and rapidly realized that it was beyond the capacity of his 31st Division – not because he was unable to cope with the British Army, but because his men could not be supplied properly. He complained bitterly to Mutaguchi

Below: A Bren gun team of the RAF Regiment in position above an airfield in the Imphal valley. Airfield defence was of primary importance during the Imphal campaign, for without it the beseiged defenders could not have received the supplies needed for their 88-day defence.

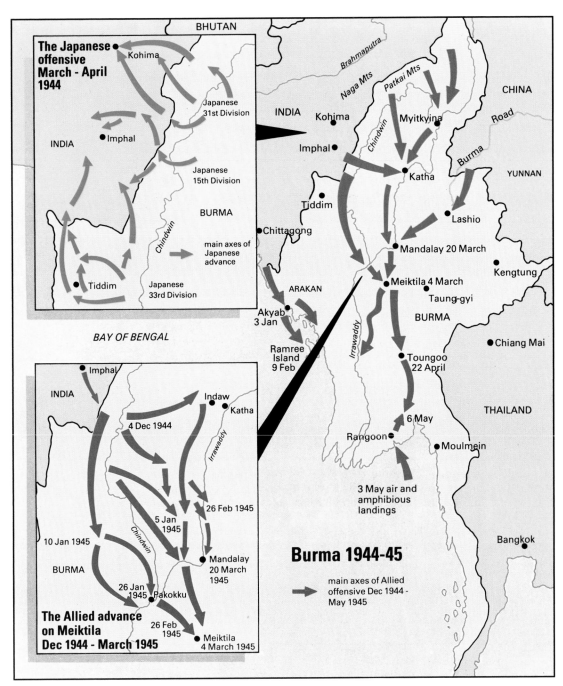

The Japanese offensive March - April 1944

BHUTAN

Kohima

Japanese 31st Division

INDIA

Imphal

Japanese 15th Division

BURMA

Chittagong

main axes of Japanese advance

Tiddim

Japanese 33rd Division

BAY OF BENGAL

Imphal

INDIA

Indaw

Katha

4 Dec 1944

Irrawaddy

26 Feb 1945

5 Jan 1945

10 Jan 1945

BURMA

Chindwin

Mandalay 20 March 1945

26 Jan 1945 Pakokku

The Allied advance on Meiktila Dec 1944 - March 1945

26 Feb 1945

Meiktila 4 March 1945

Brahmaputra

Naga Mts

Patkai Mts

CHINA

Kohima

Myitkyina

Road

INDIA

Chindwin

Imphal

Katha

Burma

YUNNAN

Tiddim

Lashio

Chittagong

Mandalay 20 March

Meiktila 4 March

Kengtung

ARAKAN

Akyab 3 Jan

Taung-gyi

BURMA

Irrawaddy

Ramree Island 9 Feb

Chiang Mai

Toungoo 22 April

THAILAND

6 May

Rangoon

Moulmein

3 May air and amphibious landings

Bangkok

Burma 1944-45

main axes of Allied offensive Dec 1944 - May 1945

Left: The Burmese theatre in World War II. The fighting took place over an enormous area, with wide rivers, jungle, mountains and tropical rainfall all combining to hamper operations. After the defeat of the Japanese offensive of spring 1944, it was not until December that the Allied forces could again go over to the attack; it took months to prepare for large-scale offensive action.

when the latter ordered him to press on with his attacks – for soon after crossing the Chindwin, Sato's men had been reduced to eating their mules, and within days of meeting the first British resistance his infantry were living on vegetable shoots they dug out of the ground. This was no way to conduct a modern war, and the Japanese fighting man paid the price. In addition, Japanese communications were harried by Chindits. On 5 February, a force of 9000 men and 1000 mules had been dropped behind Japanese lines, and although they did not create the havoc that had been hoped, they certainly caused some disruption to Japanese supply lines.

The result of all this was that the Japanese offensive against Imphal and Kohima had been decisively defeated by 21 April. Of

88,000 Japanese who had crossed the Chindwin, there had been 53,000 casualties by the time they finally pulled back across the river in October; and 30,000 of these had been from disease.

While the fighting across the Chindwin was being decided, the battles in the north and east of Burma had been growing in intensity. The objective of the Allies was Myitkyina, and Stilwell's Chinese and US forces were supported by the British Chindits and 36th Division in their attempt to take this crucial centre. The fighting here was hard, and not until the general Japanese retreat began could much headway be made. The Chindits in particular suffered heavy casualties. This offensive did, however, tie down large numbers of Japanese troops.

Myitkyina finally fell in August 1944, but by then, the Chinese war effort was being affected by other factors. In response to US air raids on Japan from bases in China, the Japanese had initiated a large-scale offensive in southeast China itself, and had taken vast areas of territory from the Chinese forces, who, in open battle, were no match for the battle-hardened Japanese. In this new crisis, Chiang Kai-shek saw an opportunity to rid himself of Stilwell (with whom he had always had bad relations) and also to withdraw his forces from Burma, which was peripheral to China's war aims, except for the land route to China, the Burma Road. The result was that Stilwell left the scene in October, and Chinese involvement in Burma was much reduced after the Burma Road was reopened in January 1945.

ON TO MANDALAY

Irrespective of the situation of the Chinese armies, the British were faced with severe problems after the defeat of the Japanese at Imphal and Kohima, in that the preparation of an offensive presented enormous logistics difficulties, of the kind that had proved so fatal to Mutaguchi's plans.

The first requirement for the British reconquest of Burma was that the number of troops at the front must be tailored precisely to the logistics capability of the support services. Thus it was that Slim was able to maintain seven divisions, with 260,000 men, up to the Irrawaddy River, but once he had passed it, he could only rely on supplies sufficient to maintain five divisions. To gain the necessary bases, especially for transport aircraft (of which there were 500 serving the British forces in Burma by May 1945), the coast of the Arakan and Ramree Island were retaken in a series of amphibious operations, although it was realized that no advance in this area could destroy the Japanese position in Burma by itself. Akyab, which had been the objective of the failed offensives of 1942 and 1943, was retaken in January 1945.

While the operations along the coast were helping to secure his communications, Slim was advancing towards Mandalay. His offensive began in December 1944, when the end of the monsoons permitted large-scale movement again. The plan, named 'Extended Capital' was for the remnants of the Japanese Fifteenth Army to be pinned down by an advance south between the Chindwin and the Irrawaddy while a sudden dash by IV Corps from the west would cross the Irrawaddy south of Mandalay and take Meiktila, effectively surrounding the Japanese forces in north Burma. The plan worked well. Meiktila fell in March 1945, and although the Japanese had fought hard to slow the advance of the forces from the north, they now had no hope of stopping the British advance further south – towards Rangoon.

The main problem in moving to take Rangoon was the distance involved – it was some 550km (330 miles) from Mandalay to Rangoon – and the logistics difficulties were now so acute that Slim had to reduce his forces to under five divisions. Complex plans for the supply of these troops from the air, however, enabled a swift rate of advance to be kept up. On 2 May, Pegu was occupied by the troops coming south after some fierce resistance; and the next day the prize of Rangoon was in British hands. It fell to an air and amphibious landing on 3 May, after the Japanese had evacuated the city shortly before on 29 April.

In these final offensives in Burma, the British lost just over 4000 killed and 13,700 wounded, while Japanese deaths are estimated at over 100,000. Japanese logistics weaknesses had been crippling for their troops, while Allied command of the air had been crucial. (In January 1945, the British had deployed 4464 aircraft, while the Japanese had had only 66, of which a mere 50 were serviceable by April.) The British Fourteenth Army had managed to solve the problems of waging war in very difficult conditions; and this had secured victory.

Above: The Union Flag flies again at Fort Dufferin after its recapture in March 1945.

Left: Two Japanese commanders – Lieutenant-General Takazo Numato (with glasses) and Rear-Admiral Keigye Chudo – arrive to surrender to the Allies in Burma.

VICTORY IN EUROPE

By the beginning of 1945, the armies of the Allied forces were massing for the final assaults against Hitler's 'Thousand-Year Reich' that had so far lasted, at the most generous estimate, a mere 12 years. These final battles saw enormous armies used by the Allies; but perhaps more impressive than the numbers of the forces involved was the weight of material – guns, tanks, aircraft – that made their ultimate success certain. The resources of the world's two largest states, the USA and the Soviet Union, were now operating at full stretch against Germany.

The German Army still retained many commanders of an extremely high calibre, and its weapons – the PzKpfw V Panther tank, or the new breed of jet fighters like the Messerschmitt Me-262 – were the equal of any possessed by the Allies. But the German Army had enormous weaknesses that had helped lead it into the position it now faced. The army as a whole had never taken a stand against Hitler, even in the most insane of his schemes, and at this critical point, early in 1945, there was still no possibility of the army informing him that Germany could not fight on without ruining itself. Individuals might have done so, but the high command as a body seemed incapable of taking such a step. The attempt to assassinate Hitler by a bomb placed in a room where he was attending a meeting in July 1944 had been supported by some senior officers, but most had been unwilling to stand against him. Of course, in a totalitarian dictatorship such as Nazi Germany, individuals who spoke out risked a great deal, and the question of the duty of an officer to obey orders from political authority is very complex. The fact remains that in the leadership of the German Army, there was a lack of both the broader view of civil–military relations and the political consequences of the use of armed force that men like MacArthur felt so acutely on the Allied side. This failure on the part of the army was responsible, in part, for Germany's final misfortunes.

The first sector in which the Germans admitted total defeat was in Italy. Here, the winter of 1944–5 had seen a lull in operations. Although the Allied advance from Rome to the Gothic Line just above Florence had been rapid, the Germans had reinforced this sector, and the Allied forces had been weakened by the allocation of seven of their divisions to Operation Dragoon, the invasion of southern France. The result was that although the line was penetrated at both the eastern and western sectors, there was no strategic break-

Left: A US soldier, M1 carbine in hand, surveys the ruins of Cologne. The twin spires of the cathedral, miraculously preserved amid the general destruction, are visible in the backround. By 1945, all German industrial centres had been bombed by the Allies, and the bomber forces were able to wreak havoc practically wherever they chose.

through. A counter-attack by fascist Italian forces in December had embarrassed the US Fifth Army, and although the British Eighth Army had gained ground along the Adriatic coast in January 1945, there was still no sign of a real collapse.

Spring saw the preparation of a major Allied assault, aiming to break through to Bologna, reach the northern Italian plains, and trap the German armies. The Allied 15th Army Group consisted of 17 divisions, in the Fifth and Eighth Armies. The Germans had 19 divisions in the line facing the enemy, and a further 10 in rear areas, guarding against partisans and possible amphibious landings. On 9 April 1945, after a diversionary feint had convinced the Germans that amphibious landings would be mounted, the British Eighth Army attacked along the Senio River, under cover of a massive aerial bombardment. Some 125,000 fragmentation bombs alone were dropped on the forward German positions, and when this offensive was combined with a thrust over the Santero River by the 78th Armoured Division and another by

Below: US troops cross the Rhine in 1945. They too are armed with the M1 carbine, a light but dependable weapon, all except for the leading soldier, who is carrying the standard M1 rifle.

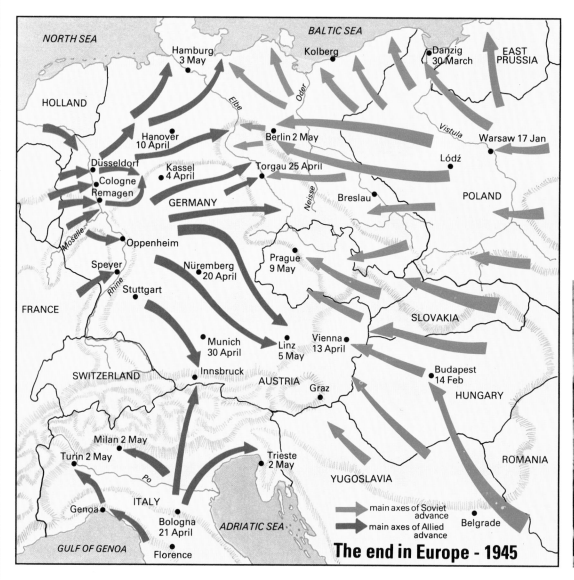

The end in Europe - 1945

main axes of Soviet advance
main axes of Allied advance

the Fifth Army along the Gulf of Genoa, the weakened German formations broke.

Bologna was taken on 21 April, and although the Germans tried to pull back across the Po, the bridges across that river had been so thoroughly destroyed by the Allied tactical air forces that the Axis formations were trapped. There were 65,000 German casualties and 35,000 prisoners, while Allied losses were just over 16,000 killed and wounded. Further resistance in Italy, although ordered by Hitler, was clearly impossible, and so General Heinrich von Vietinghoff negotiated the surrender of his Army Group C. The ceasefire came into operation on 2 May 1945, and over one million Axis troops were out of the war.

In northwest Europe, the fighting was harder than in Italy. The defeat of the German forces in the Battle of the Bulge was followed by the halting of a further offensive by the Wehrmacht on the southern sector of the line, in Alsace, an operation called 'Nordwind' that aimed to trap the US Seventh Army with a breakout from the German salient around Colmar. This attack

cost the Germans 25,000 men, while the Americans suffered 16,000 casualties. Eisenhower now decided that all his armies should move up to the Rhine together, and that only when this had been accomplished should the penetration of central Germany be attempted. The northern sector was still to have priority, and to this end, Montgomery was allowed to add the US Ninth Army to his British and Canadian forces.

To reach the Rhine, there were three basic areas that had to be conquered. The first was the Maas–Rhine corridor in the north. The Canadian First Army was given this task, which involved bloody fighting in the Reichswald forest as they forged their way south through the corridor. By 2 March, however, having begun this operation, codenamed 'Veritable', on 8 February, they were able to link up with the US Ninth Army near Dusseldorf. Meanwhile, in the centre, Bradley's 12th Army Group pushed forward to the Rhine; General Courtney H. Hodges's First Army had taken Cologne by 5 March (and two days later managed to capture a bridge across the river at Remagen intact), while

Top: The devastation of Germany in 1945 made some form of outside help essential to prevent starvation and epidemics during the following winter. Above: Soviet and US troops meet at Strakonice in Czechoslovakia, 11 May 1945. Above right: Soviet troops dash forward, covered by a soldier armed with a PPSh M1943 sub-machine gun, during the fighting for Budapest. The last German stronghold in the city fell on 13 February. Right: Colonel-General Jodl signs the final surrender document on 7 May at Rheims.

General Patton's Third Army carried out a whirlwind campaign in the Rhineland, first north and then south of the Moselle. Patton's and Hodges's victories claimed 250,000 German prisoners. Finally, in the south, the Colmar pocket was pinched out by the French First Army and the US Seventh Army advanced to Speyer.

All was now set for the thrust across the Rhine, with the northern sector, under Montgomery, leading the way. The crossing, code-named Operation Plunder, began on 23 March, after two days of intense preparation by the Allied air forces; over 16,000 sorties were flown in the 48 hours before the troops went over. Between Zanten and Rees, the British forces crossed with few casualties, to

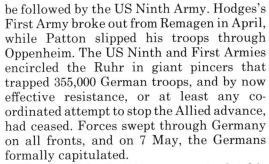

be followed by the US Ninth Army. Hodges's First Army broke out from Remagen in April, while Patton slipped his troops through Oppenheim. The US Ninth and First Armies encircled the Ruhr in giant pincers that trapped 355,000 German troops, and by now effective resistance, or at least any co-ordinated attempt to stop the Allied advance, had ceased. Forces swept through Germany on all fronts, and on 7 May, the Germans formally capitulated.

Eisenhower's decision not to to let his troops go further than the Elbe was largely due to the fact that this was part of the area that the Soviet forces were due to take over, under the terms of the Yalta agreement. (At the Black Sea resort of Yalta in February 1945, Roosevelt, Stalin and Churchill had come to basic agreement about the conduct of the final campaigns and the organization of the postwar world.). And, by April 1945, the Red Army was established deep in Germany.

THE FALL OF BERLIN

The Soviet drive that had carried the Red Army into Hungary late in 1944 continued in 1945 and the armies in this area continued their remorseless progress into Austria, occupying Vienna on 13 April. Impressive though these gains were, however, they were a sideshow to the main Soviet effort, in the north. Here, an enormous new offensive had opened on 12 January 1945, along the whole line from the East Prussian border down along the Vistula and the Narew Rivers. Soviet sources have given the relative strengths of the armies on the Eastern Front at this time as 6,000,000 Red Army troops versus 3,100,000 Germans, and, of course, the Red Army had the advantage of being able to concentrate its troops for the offensive. Punching a gap 290km (180 miles) wide in the German line, the Soviet forces took Warsaw on 17 January, swept into East Prussia and by 1 February had reached the Oder-Neisse line, 65km (40 miles) from Berlin. Here the advance stopped as the Red Army outran its supply system.

On 16 April, however, the Soviet forces were ready to attack again. Three 'fronts' under Marshals Georgi Zhukov, Ivan Konev and Konstantin Rokossovsky advanced under an enormous artillery barrage, and pushed west to the north and south of the German capital. By 21 April the Russians were fighting in Berlin itself. Hitler committed suicide on 30 April and Berlin was surrendered on 2 May. Already, on 25 April, Soviet and US troops had met at Torgau on the Elbe. The German Army had been smashed totally; since 12 January over a million Germans had been killed and wounded. The war in Europe was over.

VICTORY IN THE PACIFIC

The final battles of World War II in the Pacific theatre were waged using all the techniques of warfare that had been perfected during the previous six years. There were large-scale amphibious operations, enormous sea battles, mass bombing raids and heavy aerial combat; on the ground there were desperate hand-to-hand struggles in which suicidal bravery was met with the latest technology; and there was even an enormous Blitzkrieg-style campaign when the Soviet Army moved into Manchuria. There was, however, one element that was unlike anything the world had seen before. The dropping of the atomic bombs on Hiroshima and Nagasaki in August 1945 marked the culmination of total war by threatening the destruction of the whole enemy population. Although, in a sense, World War II had been leading up to such a point, the sheer power of the new weapon took warfare into a different dimension.

The first scene in the last act of the drama of World War II took place in the Philippines. It was as late as 12 March 1944 that Luzon, the main island in the group, had formally been made the target of both MacArthur's drive from the southwest Pacific and Nimitz's advance through the central Pacific area, and there were still arguments over whether Formosa would continue to be an objective. But for the moment, all energies were directed towards the archipelago to which MacArthur had promised to return.

The original plan had called for an attack on Mindanao, in the southern Philippines, to begin the campaign; but in August 1944, Vice-Admiral Halsey led his Third Fleet on a raid into the waters off Mindanao, Yap Island and the Palau Islands, and found the Japanese response very feeble. It seemed that after the battle of the Philippine Sea the previous June the Japanese might have been more weakened than had been surmised, and so the planned landing on Mindanao was replaced by one further north, on the central island of Leyte. The preparations were swiftly made. In September, Halsey established bases in the Palau Islands, 6900km (4250 miles) from Pearl Harbor, and 1600km (1000 miles) from the Philippine capital Manila, while Rear-Admiral Marc Mitscher's Fast Carrier Force, by now up to the phenomenal strength of 17 fleet carriers, plastered the airfields on Formosa, Luzon and the Ryukyu Islands – anywhere in fact that could send aircraft to help the defenders of Leyte. Over 500 Japanese aircraft were destroyed, for the loss of 110 US planes.

On 20 October, the US Seventh Fleet under Vice-Admiral Thomas Kinkaid sailed into Leyte Gulf. The Seventh Fleet was the naval force that accompanied MacArthur's Southwest Pacific Area, and although it was less strong than Nimitz's equivalent, the Third Fleet under Halsey, it was impressive enough, comprising 700 ships in all, including 18 escort carriers and the transport vessels carrying the force of 174,000 men that was to conquer Leyte. The whole operation was meanwhile covered by the looming presence of the Third Fleet, stationed off the east coast of the Philippines.

The Japanese had been expecting such an attack, although not on Leyte itself, and they had formed a contingency plan, codenamed 'SHO GO', to deal with it. This was a clever deception scheme, designed to draw off the carriers of the Third Fleet by offering them the bait of four carriers under Vice-Admiral Ozawa sailing down from the northeast, with, in fact, very few planes between them. Meanwhile three forces were to converge on Leyte from the west, one from the Ryukyus

Above: General Douglas MacArthur and members of his staff at Fort Stotensburg, Clark Field, on Luzon, the main Philippine island. Above right: A kamikaze *plane crashes onto the deck of the US carrier* Belleau Wood *during the battle of Leyte Gulf, October 1944. Right: US Marines go ashore on Iwo Jima, with Mount Suribachi looming in the background.*

under Vice-Admiral K. Shima and the larger (which itself would split into two parts) from bases near Singapore under Vice-Admiral Takeo Kurita. These naval units would destroy the landing ships and Kinkaid's Seventh Fleet, leaving the US troops landed on Leyte stranded.

Whatever the success or failure of the plan, the final result could only be the destruction of the Japanese forces involved (for as soon as Halsey had disposed of the aircraft carriers he would have crushed the Japanese ships near Leyte) but the Japanese Navy felt it had little choice. If the Philippines were taken, then the war was surely lost; and the ships of the navy would, in any case, soon be incapacitated by lack of fuel and by the raiding of Mitscher's Fast Carrier Force.

The battle of Leyte Gulf became the biggest naval battle of all time. More ships were in action at Jutland in 1916, but far more tonnage and far more fighting was on display at Leyte. In fact, the battle was a combination of four engagements. The first was in the Sibuyan Sea on 24 October, when US aircraft sank various of the vessels converging from the west. Halsey believed that he had no more to worry about from this quarter, and during the night turned north to meet the decoy force that had been spotted coming south. The same night, the second major engagement took place in the Surigao Strait, where a Japanese force coming up from the southwest was destroyed by a US force under Rear-Admiral Jesse Oldendorf.

The crucial battle took place the next day, when Kurita's main force, that had not been as badly damaged as Halsey believed, sailed through the San Bernadino Strait and

threatened to reach Leyte Gulf itself. During two hours of heavy fighting, known as the battle off Samar Island, Rear-Admiral Clifton Sprague's Task Group 77.4.3 fought off superior forces, losing two escort carriers and three other vessels in the process. Meanwhile, in the fourth engagement, Halsey had been wreaking havoc among the ships of the decoy force off Cape Engaño, but turned back when he heard of the Japanese attack on Clifton Sprague's force.

Leyte Gulf cost the Japanese fleet three battleships and four aircraft carriers; the Americans lost no fleet carriers, but two escort carriers. And whereas the Japanese lost 19 cruisers and destroyers, US losses of these smaller vessels were a mere three.

The destruction of the remnants of the Japanese surface fleet at the battle of Leyte Gulf practically doomed the Japanese garrisons on the Philippines. But the fighting was by no means over. The commander in the Philippines, Lieutenant-General Tomoyuki Yamashita, was a redoubtable warrior. The garrison on Leyte itself was built up from 15,000 to 60,000 men and put up a stiff resistance; and although US troops went ashore in Lingayen Gulf on the main island of Luzon on 9 January 1945, Yamashita conducted an adept defence. He refused to let

his forces be destroyed near the beach-heads, and withdrew major forces into the northern mountains, while Japanese Navy troops (who were not directly under his control) put up a fanatical struggle around Manila itself. There were still Japanese troops resisting on Luzon by the end of the war in September, although all large-scale opposition had been destroyed by June.

The final major battle in the Philippines was for the southern island of Mindanao, of

Above: Marines of the 2nd Battalion, 6th Marine Regiment, disembark onto Green Beach, Okinawa, during the landings of 1 April 1945. Green Beach 1 was the extreme northern flank of the landings. The troops are well equipped for close-quarters fighting, with a Thompson sub-machine gun and a flame-thrower.

Left: A Japanese Navy flyer prepares for a mission.

no military significance in itself, but an objective that MacArthur was determined to attain. Landings on Mindanao took place in March, but again there were still Japanese resisting there at the end of the war.

IWO JIMA

MacArthur had wished to use the Philippines as the springboard for the attack on Japan itself. Admirals King and Nimitz, however, had decided to move against two islands that would provide closer bases for the final assaults. These islands were Iwo Jima and Okinawa. Iwo Jima was a small islet barely 8km by 4km (5 miles by 2.5 miles), dominated by Mount Suribachi, an extinct volcano. Its main use would be for rescuing damaged aircraft on their way back from bombing Japan, and the Japanese themselves used it as an air base to intercept bombers attacking the home islands. The invasion of Iwo Jima went in on 19 February, after a bombardment by six battleships lasting three days, although there had been air strikes from heavy bombers throughout the previous year. The defenders numbered some 20,000 Japanese Army and Navy troops, dug into the volcanic rock that made up the island. Five kilometres (3 miles) of tunnels, and 80 pillboxes had been constructed, and the fighting was the most bitter of the Pacific war to date. It took over a month to force the last defenders out of their positions, and when, on

25 March, the island had been secured, there were 5931 US Marines dead, and 17,372 wounded. Only 216 Japanese were taken prisoner, but many had died a horrible death, incinerated in their bunkers by flame-throwers, by napalm or by phosphorus shells.

Operation Iceberg, the US descent on Okinawa, began on 1 April. The fighting on this island, which was so close to the main Japanese islands as to count as part of Japan proper and was an essential part of the inner island defences, was even more difficult than that on Iwo Jima. The forces were larger – the defenders numbering over 100,000 and the US sending in 154,000 men of the Marines and the army – and the defenders had created secure bastions in the south of the island, to

Above: A B-29 Superfortress takes off from Harmon Field on Guam. The bases in the Marianas were crucial for the US strategic bombing offensive on Japan.

Below: A plume of smoke rises from a stricken vessel while other US ships put up a heavy anti-aircraft barrage to beat off an attack by Japanese bombers.

Right: The mushroom cloud of the 'Fat Man' atomic bomb dropped on Nagasaki on 9 August 1945. Far right below: The ruins of Hiroshima after the 'Little Boy' bomb was exploded above the city on 6 August.

Far right: The Japanese surrender delegation aboard USS Missouri *in Tokyo Bay, 2 September 1945, where General MacArthur took the surrender on behalf of the Allies.*

The final campaigns in the Pacific 1944-45

→ main axes of US offensive
→ Soviet offensive in Manchuria

which they retreated when the first wave of US troops landed. The fighting did not cease until 21 June, and the cost was very high. There were 49,151 US casualties, and the Japanese must have lost about 110,000 soldiers and drafted civilian auxiliaries. Only 7400 prisoners were taken. Nor had the losses been confined to the ground troops. The *kamikaze* pilots had made determined attacks on the US naval vessels off Okinawa, and had succeeded in sinking 36 ships, although the price for this was a staggering 7800 Japanese aircraft shot down. Still, the prospects for assaulting Japan directly were not made more enticing by the fighting on Okinawa.

The home islands had been under intensive bombardment all through 1945 from US strategic bombers, mainly the B-29 Superfortresses. From March they had begun low-level incendiary raids, trying to destroy the homes and the morale of the Japanese civilian population, and these 'fire raids' had been very damaging. On the night of 9–10 March alone, there were over 83,000 casualties, and over a million civilians were made homeless as a result of a night-time raid on Tokyo. By July, it was estimated that over one quarter of all Japanese were homeless, and the bombers were beginning to run out of worthwhile targets. Yet even this did not dispose the Japanese high command to surrender.

THE ATOMIC SOLUTION

There were two ways of attacking the Japanese that the Americans were exploring. The first was a full-scale invasion of the Japanese archipelago itself, beginning with Operation Olympic in which 190,000 troops would invade Kyushu. It was estimated that this would cost 69,000 US casualties. Before this attack went in, however, it was important to weaken the Japanese as far as possible, and to this end the Soviet Union had been asked some time previously to declare war on Japan and to attack in Manchuria, where there were 1,000,000 men of the Japanese Kwantung Army. Once he had assured success in Europe, Stalin was quite happy to take such a step, and on 8 August 1945, after the Soviet declaration of war, 1,500,000 Red Army troops, with over 5500 armoured vehicles, took the offensive in Manchuria. In a whirlwind campaign they swept across the Gobi Desert and Great Hsingan Mountains in the last large-scale mobile advance of the war, which netted them almost 600,000 prisoners and gave them a commanding position in Manchuria and Korea within nine days.

In the weakening of the Japanese forces in the home islands, the US submarine offensive also played an important part. The Japanese had been steadily worn down by the

toll that US submarines had taken of their shipping, and the blockade they imposed might well have led to a complete collapse of the Japanese war economy before any attack had to go in. The Japanese had come round to the idea of the convoy system too late, and had been made to pay the price of having the raw materials they required being so far from the refining and industrial centres in the home islands. The US submarines, under the overall command of Vice-Admiral Charles Lockwood, sank 1178 Japanese merchantmen, totalling 5,405,000 tonnes, during the course of the war.

It was uncertain whether this gradual squeeze, from the Asian mainland and from the sea lanes, would actually force the Japanese to surrender unconditionally, however. So the other method of applying pressure was also used. This, of course, was the atomic bomb, the first of which was dropped on Hiroshima on 6 August 1945 and the second on Nagasaki on 9 August. The first bomb caused consternation in Japanese government circles and the second led to the decision to surrender, on condition that the Emperor was allowed to remain as the formal head of the nation. This was accepted, and on 15 August Emperor Hirohito himself broadcast to the Japanese people calling on them to accept defeat. The formal documents were signed on board the battleship USS *Missouri* in Tokyo Bay on 2 September, and World War II was over.

WORLD WAR II – THE AFTERMATH

In terms of extent, destruction and those killed, maimed and made homeless, World War II was the most terrible conflict that the world had ever seen. Some 50 million people perished as a direct result of its depredations – 20 million of them Russians. Four and a half million Germans died, two million Japanese, one million Yugoslavs, six million European Jews and four million non-Jewish eastern Europeans; while untold millions of Chinese (estimates range from three to 15 million) perished in the war against Japan that had begun in 1937. Western Europe got off relatively lightly: Italy, France and Great Britain all suffered about 500,000 dead (in addition, the British Empire and Commonwealth lost 120,000 dead) while of the major combatants the USA suffered least, with about 300,000 dead.

In addition to those who died as a direct result of the war, there were millions of others whose lives were probably curtailed by the diversion of resources from their needs by the exigencies of war – such as the 1,500,000 who died in the famine that afflicted Bengal in 1943. And further millions of those who survived the war were permanently affected, physically or psychologically, by the horrors and deprivations they had endured.

World War II is usually described as a 'total' war – total in the sense that the lives of all those in the societies involved were directly affected by the conflict, and the war was perceived as a direct contest between different societies, in which civilians were part and parcel of the struggle. This development had not been immediately apparent at the beginning of the war – indeed, Hitler had been determined at one stage to avoid the bombing of British cities, while Britain and France, in response to requests from President Roosevelt, had undertaken to attack only military targets within Germany. By 1945, however, the next US President, Harry Truman, was giving permission for the use of the atomic bomb against Japan, in what could not be disguised as other than an attempt to terrorize the Japanese government into surrender by promising that tens of millions of their civilian population would be wiped out if they did not give in. As early as January 1943 (at the Casablanca Conference) the USA and Great Britain had proclaimed that the Axis powers must surrender unconditionally, and by 1945 the total mobilization of society for war was accepted in all the major combatant nations.

In societies like that of Soviet Russia, where autocratic state control had long existed, the regulation of industrial and social life to prosecute the war was to be expected. Within Russia there were mass movements of the population (some 12 million people moved eastwards to new industrial complexes) and the nature of family

Above: A Jewish inmate of a German concentration camp. The existence of the concentration camps and the intentions of the men who set them up was the main justification for the trials of the Nazi leaders at Nuremberg after the war. Left: Soviet partisans. About 20 million Russians died in World War II. The massive involvement of civilians in the war foreshadowed the trend of postwar conflicts such as Korea and Vietnam. Right: Women too became involved in the war effort, often as workers in heavy industry – in this case in a steel works in the north of England.

and social life in the countryside changed, as about half the male peasantry were conscripted and the land was worked by women. But in nations such as Great Britain, where considerable personal liberty was traditional, the government stepped in also. The rationing of food, clothes and household goods; the complete control of the labour force (including the decision that all women between 18½ and 50 were liable to be directed to work unless they had young children or a husband living at home); and the control of prices – these were all part of unprecedented new powers that the British government adopted.

If conditions were new and frequently unpleasant and dangerous for the civilian populations in the countries fighting the war, these privations were as nothing compared to the conditions under which the inhabitants of the Axis-occupied areas had to live. The Germans (especially in eastern and central Europe) and the Japanese (especially in China) acted with a frightful disregard for what are normally considered human values in dealing with local populations. The massacre of whole villages in response to local resistance, and the belief that the occupied nations were peopled by sub-humans, were merely part of a period of history which for all the occupied nations was one of almost unrelieved horror. The single most abominable intention of the Axis powers was the German policy of genocide – the attempts to exterminate the Jews, and also the gypsies. It is as well to bear in mind, for example, when admiring the feats of Guderian

Above: Piles of skulls at Maidenek concentration camp. The Holocaust is a problematical subject. Was it a product of European anti-semitism, or a direct result of the Nazi totalitarian system? Below: Hermann Göring in the dock at Nuremberg. He remained defiant to the end, and cheated the gallows by taking poison in his cell.

and von Kleist in September 1941, when their armoured forces surrounded the Soviet formations at Kiev and took 600,000 prisoners, that of those 600,000 all probably died in the dreadful conditions in which they were made to work for the German war economy over the next three years, and that this same victory was followed by the usual massacre of Jews in the region by the SS *Einsatzgruppen*, whose sole task was to kill Jews, Communist Party officials, and the political commissars of the Red Army. In two days after the fall of Kiev the *Einsatzgruppen* had achieved their highest and most sickening tally to date by slaughtering 33,000 Jews.

Naturally, the harsh policies of the Axis occupying powers provoked resistance in the conquered nations – a resistance encouraged by the Allies. In some nations, the resistance could be little more than the gathering of information and the obstruction of economic help to the German war economy, but in others, it was on a large scale, especially after June 1941, when communist groups began actively working against the Germans. Partisans in German-occupied Russia were 150,000 strong by mid-1942 and soaking up 250,000 German security troops, while Eisenhower estimated the French Resistance as worth the equivalent of 15 divisions to the Allied advance in 1944.

Perhaps the most impressive achievement of the resistance forces was in Yugoslavia, where Josip Broz, known as Tito, led a communist partisan army that eventually numbered some 250,000 men and actually liberated the Yugoslav capital of Belgrade itself. In both 1943 and spring 1944, Tito's forces managed to survive in the face of sustained offensives by the Axis troops, and also to assert themselves over the rival resistance of the monarchist *četniks*. Partisan victory was part of a terrible price that Yugoslavia had to pay for its own internal and external problems during the war. At one stage Roman Catholic Croats (the *ustachi*) were massacring Greek Orthodox Serbs; then there was the conflict between the partisans and the *četniks*; and finally, at the end of the war, came the vengeance of the victors. Many *četniks* had fled into Austria at the end of the war and the British handed them back to the communist Yugoslav authorities, who

disposed of them as they saw fit.

This vengeance after the war was not confined to Yugoslavia. The disappearance of many prisoners who were shipped back to the Soviet Union has been well documented, and nor was the Soviet leadership prepared to give the smaller national groups within the Soviet empire any hint of autonomy. Ukrainians, Latvians, Lithuanians and Estonians were treated with utter ruthlessness in the last years of World War II and immediately afterwards.

A WAR TO BEGIN WARS

In spite of its wide range and the manifold horrors it had encompassed, and in spite of the fact that two governments which had aspired to dominate areas of the world had been destroyed, World War II had opened up as many possibilities for conflict as it had resolved existing tensions. It was true that the political and ideological clash between fascism on the one hand and communism on the other had been resolved in favour of communism in eastern and central Europe – but the ideological conflict between communism and liberal democracy, another of the tensions of the 1930s which had been veiled by the common cause of defeating Germany, was about to come to centre stage again in world politics. This conflict, enshrined in the opposed political systems of the two great giants that now bestrode the world – the Soviet Union and the USA – was to be of critical importance in underpinning warfare around the globe during the next four decades.

At the same time, although World War II had decisively checked Japanese efforts to create a new empire in East Asia and the Pacific, it had accelerated the decline of the existing colonial empires and given the subject peoples of Southeast Asia, India and (to a lesser extent) Africa a new impetus in their aspirations for nationhood. This was to be a second main background to conflict in the years after 1945: firstly in the wars against the colonial powers in Africa and Asia, and secondly in the wars between the states that emerged from the collapse of the colonial empires.

World War II had also set the scene for further warfare in a relatively restricted area of the world – in and around the region known as Palestine. Before 1939, Palestine was administered by Britain under mandate, and the British had, during the 1920s and 1930s, tried to maintain an even-handed policy. They had promised not to hinder Jewish aspirations for some kind of homeland in the area, but had an obligation to protect the rights of the Palestinian Arabs. After the slaughter of Jews in Europe the

determination of the Zionists to found a Jewish state was fiercer than ever, and attracted a great deal of sympathy worldwide. The resulting events were to provide one of the major causes of war in the following 40 years.

World War II had, then, ravaged many areas of the globe, and in some parts (notably Europe) it had imposed a settlement which endures to the present day. In other areas, however, it had merely prepared the ground for further conflicts. It is most convenient to divide these conflicts into three broad categories: firstly, the wars in which the superpowers or their proxies have been engaged, wars that form a part of the ideological conflict known as the Cold War; secondly, the struggles in the colonial empires of France, Great Britain, Portugal and Holland, in which a style of guerrilla warfare was developed that was to have profound consequences on all warfare in the 1960s and 1970s; and thirdly, the wars between states – largely wars between the new states of the Third World – where conventional weaponry and military tactics have been on constant display.

Above: Josip Broz (Tito) leads the way up a hill track during the final stages of the war. His communist partisans emerged victorious both over the occupying forces and over their rivals within Yugoslavia itself – notably the royalist četniks of Draza Mihailovic – to create a communist state which also managed to stay independent of Stalin's Soviet Union.

Part Six
The Cold War and its Conflicts

Below: Angry Soviet officers approach a Western cameraman at Budapest in 1956.

World War I had been called 'the war to end all wars', and the Armistice in 1918 had been hailed as marking the beginning of a prolonged period of peace. The end of World War II was accompanied by no such extravagant hopes, however. Partly, this was because the world had had such recent experience of how such hopes could be dashed. But there was another reason. World War II had been a war in which the rival ideologies of the 1930s – fascism, communism and democracy – had been fighting to survive and impose themselves. Fascism had been defeated, but the alliance between the Soviet Union and the Western Allies of Great Britain, the United States and France, had not removed the mutual hostility and suspicion between, on the one hand, a governing system based upon centrally controlled economics and strict regulation of political activity, and on the other, a system of liberal economics and greater personal freedom.

Even before the end of World War II, the British, in particular, were expressing concern over the ambitions of Stalin's Soviet Union. Stalin in his turn had never disguised his feelings that the Western Allies were delaying the opening of a second front in

Europe in order to weaken the Soviet Union by using it as a battering ram to destroy the German Army while the Western powers stayed relatively free from damage. The 'Cold War' (the phrase was originally used in 1947 by the financier Bernard Baruch) had its own momentum and its own background, which will be examined in the following chapter. But more than being a series of tensions in its own right, it set the scene for much of the warfare that was to follow, throughout the world, and even where it was not at the heart of events, its shadow lay over conflict everywhere.

The essential point about the Cold War was that in spite of the Soviet Union and the United States being in avowed ideological combat, and in spite of there being many incidents that increased tension, this never broke out into open hostilities. This was, of course, because of the power of atomic, and later nuclear, weapons, which threatened mutual destruction should fighting break out; but it was also because the two superpowers were sufficiently far from each other's vital concerns for neither to feel that it had to go to war over any particular incident. The nearest the world came to war was when the Soviet Union tried to place missiles in Cuba in 1962. Apart from this single episode, neither side has tried to detach those the other considers its closest allies. The Russians have never made any serious attempts to put pressure on western Europe, and the Americans have never openly tried to destabilize eastern Europe, even when, as in Hungary in 1956, the population there clearly expected the USA to intervene.

This respect for the vital interests of the other has not, of course, prevented a vitriolic war of words, nor has it seriously affected the various stages of an arms race that has been going on since the late 1940s. What it has done is introduce a new sense of the limits of what is possible in warfare. World War II had seen the level of warfare rise to an absolute peak; since 1945, nations have been involved in war at many levels, but it has been rare for the level to approach total war. Limited war

Above: Soviet delegates at the United Nations in urgent consultation during the Cuban missile crisis of 1962.

Below left: The awesome power of a nuclear explosion. Under the shadow of atomic and nuclear weapons, the Soviet Union and the United States, although ideologically antagonistic, have lived in peace since 1945. Below: In spite of the nuclear stalemate there have been many have been many conflicts in which the great powers have been engaged since the end of World War II. Here, American helicopters of the 1st Air Cavalry deliver troops into action during the Vietnam War.

has been the method of prosecuting conflicts.

This prevalence of limited war has not meant that warfare has become any less brutal or vicious. Indeed, the often artificial limits of conflict can throw into stark relief the violence of warfare, and especially the terrible nature of modern weapons. Nor has it meant that warfare itself has become less common. Both the Soviet Union and the USA have shown themselves willing to intervene in wars where they felt they could gain an advantage, or prevent the other side gaining an advantage. Because of their great influence, both the superpowers have had plenty of opportunities to involve themselves in conflicts. The USA, for example, had alliances with 26 states in 1961 (a figure which extends to well over 40 if the nations of the Organization of American States are included), and many of these were in unstable areas of the globe – Southeast Asia, the Middle East and southern Europe.

In all the conflicts that have taken place since 1945, therefore, one of the superpowers has normally been involved in some way; and if one is involved, then the chances are that the other will want to make its presence felt. The collapse of the great colonial empires of France and Great Britain and the resultant wars in the new nations have seen superpower entanglement; and so have most wars between states. The Falklands War, for example, was not merely a contest between Britain and Argentina. The USA gave Britain considerable help in the form of war supplies and intelligence information from satellites. Wherever a coup or change of power occurs in a sensitive area – in Iran in 1952, for example, or in Indonesia in 1965 – there is usually a suspicion of undercover involvement by one of the superpowers; and wherever civil war offers the chance of backing one side and obtaining a useful strategic advantage – as in Angola in 1975 – the temptation for a superpower to move in often proves irresistible.

In addition to this general tendency for the superpowers to become involved in the conflicts of other nations, there have been several wars since 1945 that appear as direct extensions of the Cold War itself, or where, whatever the primary causes, the most important aspect of the outcome has been in terms of the global ideological conflict. Normally, these have been wars where communist forces have taken on a regime backed by the USA. Five in particular stand out. First, there were the civil wars in Greece and China during the 1940s. In both these nations, communist insurgents tried to overthrow a regime that was closely linked to the USA. In the case of China, the armies of Mao Tse-tung succeeded in overcoming their Nationalist rivals under Chiang Kaishek, and imposed communism on the world's most populous nation, but in Greece the communists suffered defeat. It is interesting to note that in both cases the losers had been refused military help by the superpower to which they looked for aid.

The next important large-scale fighting of the Cold War took place in Korea, when the communist-run North invaded South Korea in 1950. This led to the direct involvement of US ground troops and the intervention of Chinese armies, while the Soviet Union supplied equipment to the communist side. Eventually a stalemate was reached and peace restored, roughly along the borders that had existed before the attack.

VIETNAM AND AFTER

The Vietnam War was an altogether different affair. Here, the USA took on the commitment to defend a small, vulnerable, badly governed state that was succumbing to communist insurgency, and rapidly found itself in trouble. Although hundreds of thousands of US troops, and vast amounts of material, were poured in, the very fact that this was a limited war, and that US commanders could not take the fight directly into North Vietnam, meant that the communists always retained the strategic initiative. Eventually, the US forces were brought home, and South Vietnam was taken over by the North in 1975.

The last of these ideological wars involving the direct intervention of a superpower began in Afghanistan late in 1979. Here, the boot was on the other foot. The Soviet Union, which had had great influence there since the 1950s, found itself in difficulties when a radical government initiated a series of reforms that provoked the conservative Muslim population to revolt. The Red Army was sent in to install a regime more acceptable to the mass of the people, but soon found itself entangled in a vicious guerrilla war that brought worldwide condemnation, demonstrating, as had Vietnam, the complexities of limited war within the Cold War context.

THE COLD WAR

Analysis of the Cold War is surprisingly difficult. The term describes, of course, the state of tension in relations between East and West that has underlain much of the political and military history of the modern world. But is the West to be taken as the USA and its NATO allies – or should it be extended to mean any states to which the USA is tied by treaty? And when did the Cold War actually begin – 1946, 1947, 1948? Has it ended, or rather, did it end in the late 1960s when détente became the fashionable term to describe a lessening of tension? All these questions are very difficult to answer precisely, for the very nature of the Cold War as a state of mutual hostility and tension means that it has many levels, and many phases, that do not always fit neatly together to form a unified pattern.

Perhaps, however, the most important aspect of the Cold War is also the most concrete: the arms race. The Soviet Union exploded its first atomic device in 1949. In 1957, it tested the first missile that gave it the capacity to strike directly at the USA. In 1972, an agreement on arms limitation was signed, but by the late 1970s, a second agreement was shelved because of increasing tension, and in the early 1980s the emplacement of new missiles in Europe – the Soviet SS-20s and the US Ground Launched Cruise Missiles (GLCMs) and Pershing IIs – was further confirmation that relations between the USA and the Soviet Union were strained.

The Cold War clearly originated in the ideological conflict between the Western democracies and the Soviet Union at the end of World War II; indeed, it is possible to argue that some tension was inevitable between states with such differing views of the organization of society and that it had its origins as early as 1917 and the Russian Revolution. This basic mistrust was reinforced by typical problems of alliances at the end of a victorious war – the apportioning of the spoils, and the need to organize a stable order for the postwar world. These factors formed the background against which a series of incidents took place.

From the Soviet point of view, control of the states of eastern Europe was essential for Russian security. The invasions of 1914 and 1941 had passed through Poland; as Stalin told Churchill at Yalta in February 1945: 'for Great Britain the question of Poland is a question of honour .... It is not only a question of honour but of life and death for the Soviet state.' This security might, of course, have been established under some

form of international agreement, but the Soviet leader, with memories of how the democracies of Britain and France had failed to stop the expansion of Nazi Germany, had failed to defend the Spanish Republic against a German-backed military revolt, and had made only the most feeble gestures when Japan invaded China and Italy took over Ethiopia in the 1930s, believed that only firm occupation could act as a guarantee.

The blatant imposition of Soviet-style regimes on the central and eastern European states and particularly the communist takeover in Czechoslovakia in 1948 seemed a chill warning to western Europe, however, particularly as the communist parties of nations such as Italy and France were very strong. Added to this was the revelation of Soviet spying networks in the USA and Great Britain – which had enabled the Soviets to acquire the secrets of the atomic bomb.

Yet if the West was feeling worried about Soviet intentions, the Soviet state itself still felt very vulnerable. The Soviet armed forces did not have any atomic weapons until 1949, and so, in spite of their enormous size, they

Above: Churchill, the ailing Roosevelt, and Stalin at the Yalta Conference of February 1945, when the shape of postwar Europe was decided. Above right: The resupply of Berlin during the airlift of 1948–9.

To many observers in the West, the fact that communism had expanded into China marked a significant increment in the threat from the Soviet Union, which was seen as dominating other communist parties in a great worldwide conspiracy. From this point of view, the communist insurrections in Malaya (1948–60), and the Philippines (1949–54) were both elements of the same global drive to power, and the invasion of South Korea by the communist North in the summer of 1950 was part of the same process.

The 1950s were, therefore, a period when the USA, under the Republican administration of President Eisenhower, thought of itself as in the front line of defence against a threat that Vice-President Richard Nixon described as 'universal, indivisible and total'. Secretary of State John Foster Dulles, too, was renowned as a 'Cold War Warrior'. The period was marked by the phenomenon in the USA known as 'McCarthyism', named after the US senator who initiated notorious 'witch hunts' against suspected communist sympathizers. The defensive strategy that the USA had worked out by 1954 in case of large-scale Soviet aggression in any part of the world was known as 'massive retaliation', by which was meant the application of nuclear force to smash the Russian homeland should fighting break out. The US nuclear arsenal began to expand, and tactical nuclear missiles and shells were brought into service in Europe. Alliances were set up in the Middle East (the Baghdad Pact of 1955 that later became the Central Treaty Organization – CENTO) and in Southeast Asia (the Southeast Asia Treaty Organization – SEATO – was created in 1954), while in 1957 the president announced the 'Eisenhower Doctrine' – the offer of armed help to any Middle Eastern state that felt itself in danger from communism.

Above: Joseph McCarthy, who instigated 'witch-hunts' against left-wingers in the USA. Left: Ethel and Julius Rosenberg, executed in 1953 for allegedly betraying US atomic secrets to the Soviet Union.

were no match for the forces of the USA. US President Harry Truman was quite clearly a determined anti-communist, while the Marshall Plan, an aid to economic recovery in western Europe, was interpreted by the Soviet Union as an attempt by the USA to assert dominance over that part of the continent. Nor were Soviet fears allayed when the Western states decided to end the payment of reparations from their zones of occupied Germany in May 1946, and began the process of setting up what eventually became the German Federal Republic.

Fear was common currency in Soviet life. The Russian people had been living in a society of purges and secret police for some time, and the climate of fear had permeated all levels, starting at the top with the mistrustful Stalin, whose behaviour was often classically paranoid. There was, therefore, a defensive mentality on both sides, which led to the confrontation of 1948. The Soviets imposed a blockade on Berlin from June 1948 to May 1949, and this blockade, during which Western aircraft kept the city supplied with food and other essentials, marked a point from which there was no going back. Confrontation between East and West was now to be the norm.

In 1949, four events between them set the seal on this confrontation. The first was in April, with the signing of the North Atlantic Treaty by the members of what soon became known as NATO (North Atlantic Treaty Organization). The second occurred in May, when the constitution of West Germany was approved, and a new German state was set up, to the chagrin of the Soviet Union. The third was the explosion of the first Soviet atomic weapon on 14 July. The fourth was the victory of the Chinese communists in their civil war against the Nationalists. They proclaimed the People's Republic of China in Peking in October.

BIRTH OF THE WARSAW PACT

If the perspective from Washington was that a world wide communist offensive had to be contained, then the men in Moscow had equally grave concerns. Stalin had died in 1953, and his successors had the difficult task of reforming the rigid and cumbersome structure through which he had ruled his empire, without risking the collapse of the whole communist edifice in eastern Europe. The Stalinist system was very unpopular in the eastern and central European satellite states. There were riots in East Berlin in 1953, while in 1956 there were serious disturbances in Poland, and a full-scale rising in Hungary. The Hungarians took to the streets of their capital, Budapest, and fought against the Red Army tanks that were brought in to re-impose Soviet control. As many as 25,000

Hungarians may have died in this tragic episode, which demonstrated beyond doubt that the defensive screen of satellite states was a liability rather than a shield to the Soviet Union. It was in response to the need to change the system in eastern Europe, and also in retaliation for the rearming of West Germany in 1955, that the Warsaw Pact, a military alliance of eight nations within the communist bloc, was set up in May 1955.

Although they had tested an atomic weapon in 1949, the Soviet armed forces lacked the means to strike directly at the USA until the mid-1950s, when the Tu-16, Tu-20 and M-4 bombers came into operation, and even this strategic bomber force was far inferior to the US fleets of heavy aircraft, many of which were now able to deliver their nuclear weapons from missiles before entering enemy airspace. In 1956, the Soviet Union possessed some 2000 atomic or nuclear warheads, whereas the USA had between 7000 and 10,000. This discrepancy soon began to be cut away, however, as the Soviet forces developed powerful new rockets, capable of intercontinental action. By 1959, they had deployed only 10 such missiles, but this stage of the arms race was the background to the intensification of the Cold War that took place over the next few years.

During the late 1950s, and especially during the election campaign of 1960, much was made in the United States of the so-called 'missile gap', the supposed superiority of the Soviet Union in intercontinental missiles. This 'gap' is now recognized to have been a misreading of figures, and an over-appreciation of the strength of the Soviet forces, but at the time it added greatly to US fears. The fact that the Russians had put an artificial satellite – Sputnik – into space in 1957 seemed to confirm fears of Soviet technical advantage. The result was that when John Kennedy became president in 1961, he began to stockpile strategic weapons, and showed a determination not to give in to communist expansion in any part of the world.

The Soviet leader of the period, Nikita Khrushchev, was equally determined to assert that the Soviet Union was in no way inferior to the USA, and must be treated as an equal on a global scale; and so the scene was

Nikita Khrushchev (top) and John F. Kennedy (above) led the USSR and the USA respectively through the confrontations of the early 1960s, the most dangerous period of the Cold War. Above right: A US Boeing B-52G with its complement of wing-mounted cruise missiles. Below: A US Minuteman III blasts skywards.

set for some dangerous confrontations. Relations between the USA and the Soviet Union were already worsening towards the end of Eisenhower's term of office in 1960, when the shooting down of a U-2 spy plane over the Soviet Union was used by Khrushchev as a weapon with which to berate the USA publicly. Then, in August 1961, came a more serious incident – the building of the Berlin Wall, cutting east Berlin off from the western sectors of the city. There was again sustained pressure on the Western presence in the city, and Kennedy, in a visit there, made a famous speech proclaiming his commitment to it.

Far more serious, however, was the Cuban missile crisis of October 1962. Cuba had fallen into the hands of the left-wing Fidel Castro after a guerrilla war that ended in 1959, and although Castro's actual political leanings were not initially communist, he had been forced into accepting help from the Soviet Union, especially after the US CIA (Central Intelligence Agency) had tried to unseat him by sponsoring an invasion by Cuban exiles at the Bay of Pigs in 1961. In 1962, Khrushchev believed that he could use his close relationship with Castro to place Medium Range Ballistic Missiles (MRBMs) on Cuba, thereby obtaining a strategically valuable base a mere 150km (90 miles) from the US mainland. In the event of an extreme US reaction, he probably hoped for a trade-off – removing missiles from Cuba if the USA removed its MRBMs from Turkey.

The events of the 15-day crisis (14–28 October 1962) were fraught with danger, as the two superpowers faced up to the prospect of nuclear conflagration. In the end, the Soviet Union backed down, because it realized that the US leaders had decided that the stationing of missiles on Cuba was an issue which threatened their vital interests. At the same time, the Soviet leadership was probably well aware that the Soviet Union was still, in spite of Khrushchev's boasts, inferior to the USA in strategic weaponry. The 63 US Intercontinental Ballistic

Missiles (ICBMs) probably just outnumbered similar Soviet rockets, while the 186 US MRBMs were positioned close enough to the Soviet Union to do great damage. In bomber forces the disparity was of the same order, with the USA deploying 600 long-range and 2200 medium-range aircraft, to the Soviet Union's 190 long-range and 1100 medium-range.

A MAD WORLD

In the aftermath of the events of 1962, the Cold War thawed somewhat. Each side was still very suspicious of the other, but relations had changed slightly. The Soviet Union realized that it could not, at that moment, match the USA in terms of sheer nuclear strength, and needed time to build up its arsenals, while the USA realized that Soviet nuclear strength was such that the old theory of 'massive retaliation' was becoming outdated, for 'massive retaliation' implied a clear US superiority and a Soviet response that could be withstood by the USA. In place of 'massive retaliation' a new approach was formulated under the inspiration of Robert McNamara, Secretary of Defense in the Kennedy administration. This new approach, known as graduated deterrence, led to the perception of a new situation in the strategic balance, which was called 'mutual assured destruction' (or MAD – an acronym some felt accurately reflected the thinking behind it).

MAD posited that for nuclear deterrence to work, both sides had to retain the ability to destroy the other, and even if one managed to put in a surprise attack, then the other must still have the capacity to inflict a crippling counter blow. There was, therefore, an emphasis on diversifying the nuclear forces, putting more resources into the development of submarine-launched missiles (the Polaris, Poseidon and later Trident range of weapons) while at the same time updating the land-based missile force, with the introduction of the Minuteman ICBM. The implication of all this was that the USA accepted

less responsible forces – witness, for example, the events of May 1968 in Paris and the attempts to liberalize Czechoslovakia in the same year.

The easing of tension, generally known as 'détente', was a slow one; but by 1972, when US President Richard Nixon visited China, inaugurating a new way of looking at super-power relationships, and the Strategic Arms Limitation Talks (SALT) bore fruit in a treaty that year, the atmosphere had definitely begun to change.

This thaw in relations between the USA and the Soviet Union was not to last for long, however. By the late 1970s, there was again confrontation, and both sides felt threatened. The causes of this were various, but the major one was the rise of the Soviet Union to parity with the USA in terms of armaments, and its activities in areas of the globe in which it had previously had little influence. This second 'Cold War' was unlike the first, in that Europe was no longer the centre of US concerns, and, indeed, many Europeans felt that US fears were exaggerated. Nor was the fear one of worldwide communist conspiracy, for the situation of China, the fighting between North Vietnam and China, and the wars between communists in Southeast Asia itself had scotched that particular worry. Now US statesmen were alarmed by the growing military might of the Soviet Union.

MISSILE-MATCHING

After the Cuban missile crisis, the Soviet leadership had determined to build up its strategic forces to a level at which they could match those of the USA. This had been very successful by 1980. In ICBMs, the Russians then outnumbered the US arsenal by 1398 to 1054, and in the warheads carried on those missiles by 4306 to 2154. Although the USA had more strategic bombers (338 to 156) these were now far less important than submarine fleets armed with nuclear missiles; and in this sphere, the Soviet Union had the advantage of 87 submarines to the US 41, and 1003 missiles to 656 (although the US missiles did have more warheads – 5120 to 1309). These weapons could have destroyed the world many times over, and, in a sense, the mere stockpiling of such killing potential was valueless, but the figures did show that the Russians had powerful strategic forces, that were in no way inferior to those of the USA.

In Europe too, the imbalance between the NATO forces and those of the Warsaw Pact had been steadily increasing. By 1980, although the NATO countries deployed 71 divisions opposite the Pact's 67, in tanks NATO was outnumbered by over two to one (26,200 to 11,000) and in aircraft 4170 NATO machines faced 5475 of the Pact. This im-

the fact of Soviet nuclear strength as a constant factor, and did not find the mere Soviet possession of such weapons a threat.

While MAD was at the basis of the new strategic thinking, it obviously required a more supple framework of possible military action around it, if any crisis was not to destroy the world. New emphasis was, therefore, put on strategies of 'containment' to stop communist guerrilla movements taking over in Third World countries, while in Europe, still the centre of Cold War confrontation, NATO adopted the 'flexible response'. Flexible response was designed to meet any attack at the level at which it could be contained. A purely conventional assault would, therefore, call forth a conventional response, and only if this was incapable of stopping the aggression would there be a resort to nuclear weapons. Even the resort to nuclear weapons might be graduated if the situation required it – tactical or battlefield warheads would be ready if the conflict could be maintained at this level, and distinctions drawn between 'counter-force' (attack on enemy military targets) and 'counter-value' (attacks on enemy populations and cities) responses.

Apart from the US acceptance of Soviet nuclear power, and the Soviet acceptance of the fact that the USA had several advantages in this area, the very shape of world politics was altering perceptions of the Cold War. By the mid-1960s, the colonial empires of Great Britain and France had all but dissolved, and the world order was changing, becoming more diversified. The Sino-Soviet split, and the fighting on the Amur River between Red Army and Chinese People's Liberation Army troops in 1969 made it clear that the Soviet Union was not the monolithic director of an indivisible communist bloc, while the emergence of independent states to the forefront of the world stage (India for example) was an indicator that previous Cold War stances were becoming outdated. There was even a feeling that both the USA and the Soviet Union were, in a sense, guardians of a conservative world system that was threatened by

Above: Practice manoeuvres on board the Soviet vessel Minsk. Aircrews scramble towards their Kamov KA-25 helicopters.

Opposite page above: The signing of the SALT I agreement in May 1972, during the process known as détente. Opposite page below: A Polaris A-3 submarine-launched missile being fired.

balance had always existed, however, and might not have been cause for great concern, had not other factors come into play.

The first of these factors was the growth of the Soviet Navy, which had been a small coastal defence force in the 1950s before it entered a great period of expansion under Admiral Sergei Gorshkov. He made it the second largest navy in the world, far outstripping the British and the French, and by 1980 had brought into service 344 submarines, three aircraft carriers, 75 destroyers and 173 frigates.

The other, and perhaps more important, factor was the involvement of the Soviet Union in conflicts over the whole globe. During the late 1970s, Soviet advisors and Cuban troops were used to defend the FNLA government in Angola from 1975, and to make their presence felt in the Horn of Africa from 1977, where the rivalry between Somalia and Ethiopia gave ample opportunity. Finally, US President Jimmy Carter (1977–81) was outraged when Soviet troops invaded Afghanistan in December 1979, and in response he organized a boycott of the 1980 Olympic Games in Moscow.

When President Ronald Reagan took office in 1981, therefore, there was already a strong swell of anti-Soviet feeling, which the new head of state did little to try to dispel. Convinced that the Soviet leadership was encouraging revolution in Nicaragua in Central America, and determined to wrest back some of the advantage in strategic nuclear weaponry that the USA had lost in the previous decade, Reagan's policies included an increase in aid to those South and Central American regimes that he saw as bulwarks against communism. He also began the deployment of GLCMs and Pershing II missiles in Europe.

This second phase of the Cold War is in many ways more difficult to describe than the events of the 1940s, 1950s and early 1960s. There is less perspective on US motives, while discussing Soviet intentions is even more complicated, because during most of the period the Soviet Leader, Leonid Brezhnev, was in poor health, while the man who succeeded him in 1982, Yuri Andropov, soon died, and his successor, Konstantin Chernenko, has still (in 1984) to make an impact. The intentions of the leaders of either side are therefore relatively obscure.

Both the USA and the Soviet Union obviously had, and still have, a picture of an ideal world that they would achieve if they could; and this may well involve the destruction by one of the governing system of the other. But in practice such vague fantasies are irrelevant. For the rest of the world, and for the peoples of the Soviet Union and the USA themselves, the maintenance of peace, albeit an armed peace, has been, and must be, the major objective.

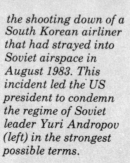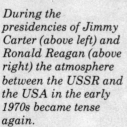

During the presidencies of Jimmy Carter (above left) and Ronald Reagan (above right) the atmosphere between the USSR and the USA in the early 1970s became tense again. For Reagan the Soviet Union's most provocative action was the shooting down of a South Korean airliner that had strayed into Soviet airspace in August 1983. This incident led the US president to condemn the regime of Soviet leader Yuri Andropov (left) in the strongest possible terms.

THE GREEK CIVIL WAR

The Greek Civil War (1946–9) was the first of the struggles to take place under the general shadow of the antagonism between the erstwhile Allies of World War II – the Western powers and the communist world. The outcome of the war was decided by the attitude of the great powers that were in ideological opposition; ultimately, US aid to the Greek government, coupled with Stalin's decision to abandon the Greek communist guerrillas, settled the issue.

The roots of the Greek Civil War lay in the closing stages of World War II. Greece had suffered a particularly brutal occupation by the German forces after the invasion by the Axis in 1941; in a mountainous countryside, made for guerrilla warfare, the resistance groups had begun their activities early, to be countered by the most atrocious repression. The most effective guerrilla forces were those of the communists, and their political organization, *Ethnikon Apeleftherotikon Metopon* or National Liberation Front (EAM), was in a position to start organizing regular units from its armed forces, *Ellinikos Laikos Apeleftherotikon* or National Liberation Army (ELAS), by the time the German withdrawal became inevitable. It had been decided between the Allied powers, however, that Greece should come within the British sphere of influence, and the British prime minister, Winston Churchill, had always seen Greece as having strategic importance.

By late 1944, the rumblings of the impending Cold War were already being felt, and Churchill was determined that the communist forces should not take over in Greece. British troops had entered the country in October 1944 in the wake of the retreating Germans, and they were able to prevent ELAS forces, estimated at 40,000 strong, from taking control of Piraeus and Athens in January 1945. In this fighting ELAS suffered heavy losses. A government more to the liking of the British was installed, and the communists agreed to take part in a democratic political process in the Varkiza Agreement.

During 1945 and 1946, however, there was very little real peace. Political tensions rose, especially over the March 1946 elections and the plebiscite in September of that year which decided that King George should return as head of state. In the mountainous countryside, militant communist groups were building up their supplies of arms, and right-wing terror bands (one of which was led by George Grivas, who was later to lead the armed resistance to British rule in Cyprus)

were active, delighting in various atrocities, such as decapitating their opponents. The national government was rent by internal feuds and conflicting local interests, and neither the police nor the army was reliable. By 1947, full-scale guerrilla warfare was once more under way.

Under the command of Markos Vaphiadis (usually known as 'General Markos') the communist forces (now known as the Democratic Army of Greece or DSE) established a pattern of hit-and-run raids against static government forces. The insurgents had secure bases across the borders in communist Yugoslavia, Albania and Bulgaria. By the end of 1947, there were as many as 23,000 guerrillas operating in the country, with an underground organization, known as YIAFAKA, of some 50,000 people giving them aid and information.

The situation deteriorated rapidly for the government. Its reliance on brutal paramilitary irregulars alienated many villagers and although the army was 180,000 strong, it had serious weaknesses in morale and train-

Below: The series of government operations that gradually cleared the communist guerrillas from Greece. In spite of the effort expended, however, the operations before 1948 had little long-term effect: it was only in that year that the government forces could begin to claim that they were winning.

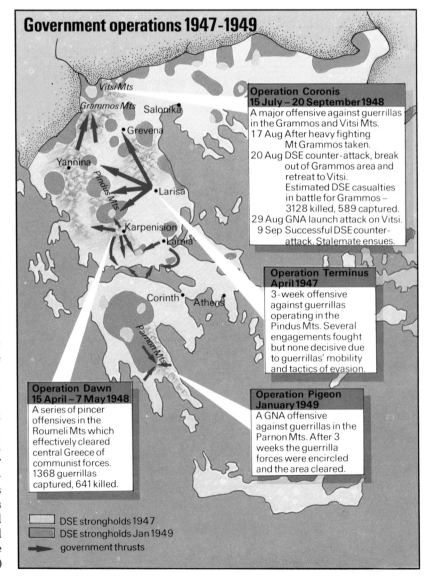

Government operations 1947-1949

Operation Coronis
15 July – 20 September 1948
A major offensive against guerrillas in the Grammos and Vitsi Mts.
17 Aug After heavy fighting Mt Grammos taken.
20 Aug DSE counter-attack, break out of Grammos area and retreat to Vitsi. Estimated DSE casualties in battle for Grammos – 3128 killed, 589 captured.
29 Aug GNA launch attack on Vitsi.
9 Sep Successful DSE counter-attack. Stalemate ensues.

Operation Terminus
April 1947
3-week offensive against guerrillas operating in the Pindus Mts. Several engagements fought but none decisive due to guerrillas' mobility and tactics of evasion.

Operation Dawn
15 April – 7 May 1948
A series of pincer offensives in the Roumeli Mts which effectively cleared central Greece of communist forces. 1368 guerrillas captured, 641 killed.

Operation Pigeon
January 1949
A GNA offensive against guerrillas in the Parnon Mts. After 3 weeks the guerrilla forces were encircled and the area cleared.

Vitsi Mts
Grammos Mts
Salonika
Grevena
Yannina
Pindus Mts
Larisa
Karpenision
Lamia
Corinth
Athens
Parnon Mts

DSE strongholds 1947
DSE strongholds Jan 1949
→ government thrusts

ing. Nevertheless, in spite of these problems, the government did manage to hold the largest-scale communist attacks – on the towns of Florina and Konitsa in the far north of the country late in 1948. Having managed to hang on, the Greek government then found international events coming to its help. The British government had given support and then US aid began to arrive in increasing quantities. As early as March 1947, President Truman had asked Congress for support for Greece and by 1949 some 170 million dollars' worth of military aid had arrived. The scale of US support increased as the Cold War with the Soviet Union grew in intensity, and the 8000 trucks, 50 Curtiss Helldiver ground attack aircraft and 4000 mules sent by 1949 made a substantial contribution to victory.

Meanwhile, events on the communist side were conspiring to weaken the guerrillas irretrievably. First, the growing split between Yugoslavia and the rest of the communist block led to the Yugoslavs closing the frontier to the essentially Stalinist Greek communists. Then the international communist body, the Cominform, decided that an independent Macedonian state would be established once the war was won. This lost the communists much support within Greece. The main wrong turning taken by the communists, however, was that, because they could no longer rely on the stability of their bases in the neighbouring communist states, they decided to fight a more static, set-piece, type of campaign. Markos was replaced by Nikos Zachariades in 1949 and a new policy was put into effect, in the creation of fortified mountain areas.

This establishment of static positions was just what the Greek government forces needed. Under the leadership of General Alexandros Papagos, who was appointed commander-in-chief with full powers in 1949, well-equipped regulars began a campaign to clear the whole country. Papagos wanted the peninsula swept from south to north, and he directed his efforts not only at the main guerrilla units, but also at the cells of supporters and sympathizers. The result was that by late summer 1949 the communists held only mountainous areas in the far north of the country. In August, the DSE bases in the Vitsi and then the Grammos mountain ranges were overrun; and, in effect, that was the decisive victory of the war, the few scattered guerrilla forces that remained presenting no threat. The DSE soon announced it had ceased operations 'in order to save Greece from destruction'. The government forces gave their losses as 12,777 dead, with 37,732 wounded, while it is estimated that 38,000 communists died.

Above: Villagers recruited into government employ choose their weapons, near Kalabaka in northern Greece. The use of irregular forces was partly forced on the Greek government because of the unreliability of the army, but it was also a reflection of the fact that in many areas of the country the civil war was an excuse for settling old feuds and prosecuting local vendettas.

Below: Captured communist guerrillas await their fate.

THE CHINESE CIVIL WAR

The Civil War in China during the late 1940s, that resulted in a decisive victory for the communist forces led by Mao Tse-tung, was the largest of the wars that have taken place since the end of World War II. The numbers of men involved were vast, with several hundred thousand being engaged in the enormous battles of envelopment that were conducted towards the end of the struggle. It is strange, then, perhaps, to find that the Chinese Civil War has had its greatest influence on small-scale military operations, on guerrilla warfare; for to many revolutionary and nationalist groups over the whole world, Mao's victory seemed above all a triumph for the guerrilla fighter over the regular soldier.

Mao has a good claim to be considered the most influential theorist of the period since 1945, because his methods have been employed in more modern wars than the ideas of any other military thinker. Yet Mao was not primarily a military man. He was a politician, who had to devise ways of fighting a war and gaining political power in China under the stress of threats from a number of quarters. His ideas were not strictly military, as neither strategy nor tactics was his forte.

Rather, he developed ideas of how the whole population could be mobilized as part of a revolutionary war that would change society.

In 1911, the last Manchu emperor of China had abdicated, and after a short experiment with parliamentary democracy, the country dissolved into chaos while warlords took control of much of the north of the country. By the early 1920s, however, a new unifying force in the shape of the Nationalist Party or Kuomintang (KMT), led by Dr Sun Yat-sen, had become a potent influence. Based in Canton and supported by the new revolution-

Above: Chinese communist peasant units on the march. It was Mao's ability to mobilize mass support in the peasantry that gave the communists eventual victory in the civil war. Below: A Communist Party poster celebrating the success of Mao – he is shown being hailed by his victorious army.

ary state of the Soviet Union and the Chinese Communist Party that had been founded in 1921, the KMT began to extend its control over all China. By 1928 it had taken Peking, warlord influence had been severely curtailed, and the leader of the Nationalists, Chiang Kai-shek (Sun Yat-sen had died in 1925) was installed as president of a national government at Nanking in October of that year.

This success had only been gained, however, at the cost of the alliance with the communists. Chiang had always been suspicious of communist motives, and he had purged communists in Canton in March 1926. The final rupture came in August 1927, when the communists in Shanghai, China's most populous city, were attacked by the Nationalists and thousands killed. Soviet advisors were asked to leave the country, and there were three abortive communist risings against the Nationalists: at Nanchang in Kiangsi province in August 1927, at Canton in December 1927, and, most importantly, in Hunan in September of that year.

The risings in Nanchang and Canton were urban-based, in accordance with classic Marxist-Leninist theories of the industrial proletariat being the revolutionary class, but that in Hunan, led by Mao Tse-tung, was rural, and depended on the peasantry for its success, as its very name, the 'autumn harvest rising', suggested. Its failure had not been catastrophic for the communists and they still maintained a large area between Hunan and Kiangsi provinces, in the Chingkiang mountains, as a viable base area. In this stronghold Mao and his political lieutenants began analysing the reasons for their defeat, and the methods they would have to use to turn the tables.

Apart from the basic error of having initially put themselves under KMT control, the conclusions the communist leadership came to were that they had not placed sufficient emphasis on the peasantry as part of the revolution, and that they had not been prepared for a long, uphill battle. The war would

Left: Chiang Kai-shek, leader of the Kuomintang, the party that dominated Chinese politics from the mid-1920s until the mid-1940s. In the 1920s, the Kuomintang (often known as the Chinese Nationalist Party) had been a dynamic, ruthless force, able to defeat local warlords and to resist the challenge of the small Communist Party. By the 1940s, however, a succession of defeats inflicted by Japanese armies, and rampant inflation had undermined its effectiveness when confronted with a new communist challenge.

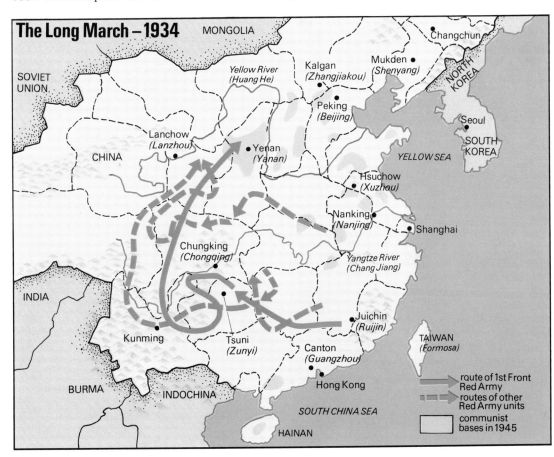

The Long March – 1934

Left: The Long March, one of the most important episodes of modern military history. This is because it was after the successful establishment of new base areas around Yenan that Mao Tse-tung was able to put into practice the theories of the political mobilization of the peasantry that have formed the basis of much of guerrilla warfare of the 20th century.

not be won quickly. It would have to be a long, hard struggle, in which their strategy must be to wear down gradually the better-armed and more numerous government forces. Thus, the Party would have to be geared to a prolonged war, not a short revolution, and this would have to be based on the solid support of the peasantry.

These conclusions could not be put to the test in Hunan, however, for in the early 1930s, the Nationalists, now with military advisors from Germany helping them, began a series of 'anti-bandit' drives against the communist areas. They had considerable success, and by 1934, final victory looked close for Chiang's troops. It was then that the single most dramatic episode of the Chinese Civil War took place, as a column of over 100,000 communists left Hunan in October 1934, heading west and then north for a safer refuge in the remote province of Shensi. Other communist forces joined in the 'Long March', and a 9660km (6000-mile) trek saw the communists installed in Shensi, centred around Yenan, by 1936, having outpaced the forces of the KMT.

The Long March had consolidated Mao's hold on the Chinese Communist Party. Some of his rivals had been killed, and he had, by his inspiring leadership during the hardships of the march (of the 100,000 who had set out, barely 20,000 fought through to Shensi), made himself a near-legendary figure to his followers. Mao at once set about putting his theories on the conduct of the long-term struggle against the Nationalist government into practice. All members of the Communist Party were thoroughly indoctrinated with

the precepts of the people's revolutionary war, and the part they would have to play in it, and the Party made sure that its influence throughout the countryside under its control was inescapable. An intense propaganda campaign in the villages, combined with literacy programmes, respect for peasant goods and possessions and the organization of various groups – of the young, of women, of farmers – began a process of social mobilization that identified the communists closely with the peasants.

Complementing this social mobilization of the peasantry was the actual conduct of the war. The key here was that Mao expected his troops, although outnumbered and out-gunned strategically, to seize the tactical initiative, by using superior mobility and the support of the populace to strike larger, conventional formations while they were on the move or from the rear. There would be no need to establish front lines or capture large cities; with the support of the population in 'safe base' areas, guerrillas would be able to harass an enemy and gradually extend their field of operations. It is interesting to specu-

Left: A Nationalist soldier stands guard at an outpost near Shanghai, just before the final communist assault of July 1949. He is armed with a US-made Thompson sub-machine gun. Below left: Communist troops on the move, carrying all their equipment with them. It was a central tenet of Mao's teaching that his forces should be more mobile than those of his enemy, able to harry the flanks and rear of any formations sent against the communist base areas.

late on what would have happened in China had not outside events taken a hand in the late 1930s. For before Chiang could begin to move sufficient forces up to threaten the communist stronghold in Shensi, China was attacked from the north by the armies of Imperial Japan, and this new war changed the complexion of the Chinese Civil War.

Under the threat of Japanese conquest, the Nationalists and the communists concluded a truce, to fight the common enemy. The agreement between Mao's forces and the KMT did not mean that the two rivals were able to work closely together, but it did enable the communists to consolidate their hold on Shensi relatively free from interference, for the Japanese were more interested in conquering the great cities of the eastern seaboard than in moving into the poorer western parts of China.

While the communists developed their hold on their areas of China during the Sino-Japanese War (1937–45), the new conflict proved catastrophic for Chiang's Nationalists, who lost prestige by having to abandon most of the east of the country to the invaders (a temporary capital was established at Chungking, now Chongqing). Inflation also raged in the Nationalist areas, cutting at the roots of the efficiency of the government apparatus and especially at the army, whose junior officers suffered severely.

The months after the Japanese surrender of 1945 saw the two opposing forces in China become far more evenly balanced than they had been in 1937. The communists spread their influence over much of the north of the country, especially into Manchuria, which

Soviet forces had overrun in the final days of the war, and Chiang was faced with having to reassert his authority over a country that had been devastated by the invaders. The communists were better armed than they had ever been, having been given access to large stores of captured Japanese equipment by the Soviet forces. But the Nationalists still far outnumbered Mao's men: there were probably one million communists under arms, but three million in Chiang's armies.

There was international pressure for the two great contending parties in China to reach an agreement after World War II. During the first six months of 1946, as hostilities escalated, especially in Manchuria, General George Marshall, former US Army Chief of Staff, tried to arrange various truces, but they all broke down under the mutual suspicion of both sides. By July 1946, full-scale fighting was going on, and the Civil War had entered its most intense, and final phase.

The two sides pursued different strategies, based on what they considered their respective needs and strengths to be. The communists aimed to consolidate their hold on the areas of the countryside that they held already, before gradually extending east from Shensi to cut China in two and take control of the north. The Nationalists, on the other hand, decided on a strategy of taking the great cities of the eastern seaboard and then pushing west. This was because Chiang believed that as ruler of China he should assert his authority over the main centres of population, and he was confident that with US aid and equipment he could hold the great cities

Below: Communist forces assaulting a walled city in Manchuria.

*Above: The public
execution of looters in
Shanghai during the
last months of
nationalist rule.*

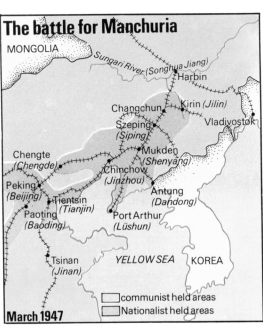

The battle for Manchuria

MONGOLIA

Sungari River (Songhua Jiang)

Harbin

Changchun · Kirin (Jilin)

Szeping
(Siping)

Vladivostok

Chengte
(Chengde)

Mukden
(Shenyang)

Chinchow
(Jinzhou)

Peking
(Beijing)

Tientsin
(Tianjin)

Antung
(Dandong)

Paoting
(Baoding)

Port Arthur
(Lüshun)

Tsinan
(Jinan)

YELLOW SEA   KOREA

☐ communist held areas
☐ Nationalist held areas

March 1947

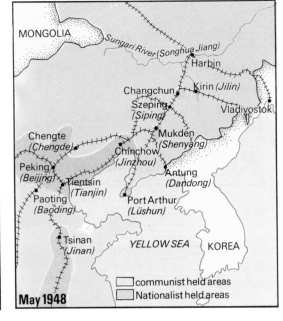

MONGOLIA

Sungari River (Songhua Jiang)

Harbin

Changchun · Kirin (Jilin)

Szeping
(Siping)

Vladivostok

Chengte
(Chengde)

Mukden
(Shenyang)

Chinchow
(Jinzhou)

Peking
(Beijing)

Tientsin
(Tianjin)

Antung
(Dandong)

Paoting
(Baoding)

Port Arthur
(Lüshun)

Tsinan
(Jinan)

YELLOW SEA   KOREA

☐ communist held areas
☐ Nationalist held areas

May 1948

against the advancing communist forces.

While it is true that Chiang was able to count on US aid and that the core of his army was a force of 39 divisions with US equipment, the Nationalist forces had glaring weaknesses. The defeats in the Japanese war, the inflation that had eroded the position of army officers and the inevitable corruption that came in the wake of large-scale aid from abroad all contributed to a lowering of morale, while the strategy of taking and holding large urban centres did not contribute towards the formation of an offensive spirit capable of matching the tactics of the enemy, and tied up large numbers of troops in static positions. The Nationalist regime was now far from the vigorous young party that had taken over China in the 1920s. It was old, with many vested interests, and showing all the outward signs of the vices – warlordism and the establishment of personal power in

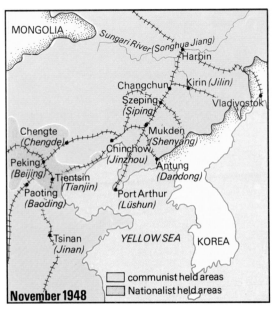

MONGOLIA

Sungari River (Songhua Jiang)

Harbin

Changchun · Kirin (Jilin)

Szeping
(Siping)

Vladivostok

Chengte
(Chengde)

Mukden
(Shenyang)

Chinchow
(Jinzhou)

Peking
(Beijing)

Tientsin
(Tianjin)

Antung
(Dandong)

Paoting
(Baoding)

Port Arthur
(Lüshun)

Tsinan
(Jinan)

YELLOW SEA   KOREA

☐ communist held areas
☐ Nationalist held areas

November 1948

areas where army generals were left for long periods – that it had once fought so hard to eradicate.

Finally, although Chiang Kai-shek himself was no military mastermind, he insisted on retaining control of operations that he was not fit to administer. It was he who made the most fateful decision of the war. For it was his wish to send Nationalist troops into Manchuria, against the advice of his US allies. Early in 1946, Nationalist forces began to occupy the major cities there, including Mukden and Changchun. These troops were dependent for supply on a very vulnerable railway system, and, being natives of the south and centre of China, often found it difficult to get on with the local inhabitants. With Mao's communist forces practising their revolutionary warfare in the villages, the large Nationalist garrisons soon found themselves isolated. During 1947, the net tightened, and by the end of the year rail links were cut. The Nationalists were forced to evacuate some strongholds, until by March 1948 a 200,000-strong garrison was besieged in Mukden with no way out, while its supporting forces at Changchun and Chinchow were gradually sliced away. In November Mukden surrendered, and the communists had won the battle for the north.

NATIONALIST DECLINE

As predicted in Mao's theories, the battle for Manchuria had been accompanied by a general deterioration of Nationalist forces all over China, as static garrisons had been unable to disperse or even effectively grapple with the communists. Nor was the Nationalist cause helped by the failure of the US to offer more help. The Americans, quite rightly, suspected that Chiang was not the person to administer a war, and did not wish to be dragged into an enormous struggle in mainland China. Yet their failure to give Chiang more aid should not necessarily have affected the outcome; the Nationalists still had great material superiority over the communists until late 1948.

The loss of Manchuria, however, had been a crushing blow to Nationalist morale, and even before the final moments of the campaign there, the communists had been moving towards the communications centre of Hsuchow on the north China plain, where victory would give them control over the north of the country. The battle of Hsuchow was an enormous set of engagements, with some reports putting the number of men committed at over one million on each side. But the Nationalists were doomed to defeat. Many of their commanders, conscious of how unlikely they were to succeed, were willing to come to an accommodation with their enemies; and one Nationalist general even

betrayed the basic operational plans to the communists. Fighting in the area began on 11 November 1948, and on 10 January 1949 the last of the Nationalist forces surrendered. Mao's generals claimed to have taken over 300,000 prisoners in this one campaign.

After Hsuchow, the Nationalists began to crumble. Chiang resigned the presidency on 20 January 1949; in April the Yangtze River was crossed; and on 1 October the People's Republic of China was proclaimed in Peking.

It is difficult to estimate the number of casualties in the Chinese Civil War. Certainly the total must run into millions on both sides. The results were decisive enough, however. The world's most populous nation was now part of the communist bloc, and a set of theories about revolutionary guerrilla warfare had been shown to have the utmost relevance to the modern age.

Below left: Nationalist artillery at the battle of Hsuchow, November 1948. Below: Mao announces the establishment of the new People's Republic of China, October 1949. Bottom: Nationalist positions just before the final communist victory.

HOLDING THE LINE IN KOREA

The Korean War (1950–53) was the first great confrontation after World War II between the forces of international communism and those of the USA. It was a war fought largely with weapons that had been developed during World War II, but the nature of the countryside and the shape of the peninsula combined to force the greater part of the fighting into static forms of positional warfare, not unlike the trench warfare of World War I.

Militarily, Korea was fascinating as a conflict between technically advanced Western forces, well equipped with support weapons, and the less well armed but in many ways more flexible armies on the communist side. In particular, the Chinese showed themselves masters of the arts of camouflage and deception, and had an enviable ability to launch surprise infantry attacks. But the most important aspect of the Korean War, as far as the history of warfare is concerned, is the fact that it did not escalate into World War III. Ignoring often vehement, and frequently popular, calls for the use of atomic weapons and the bombing of China, US political leaders managed to keep the conflict confined to the Korean peninsula itself, and demonstrated that such wars could be limited in extent.

Not that the US leaders were unwilling to use their possession of atomic weapons as a threat. Late in 1950, British Prime Minister Clement Attlee expressed grave concern at statements of US President Harry Truman which implied that the use of atomic weapons was being considered. And towards the end of the war, when negotiations were stalled, President Dwight D. Eisenhower made scarcely veiled threats that atomic bombs might be dropped if there was not more progress. Nevertheless, such public attempts to put pressure on the communists were the nearest that the US came to the employment of their most powerful weapons.

The war began when troops of the North Korean People's Army (NKPA) advanced

Above: South Korean troops advance to the front in July 1950.

Below: General Douglas MacArthur, whose military genius and political obstinacy were to prove important factors in the Korean War. Here he is shown observing the landings at Inchon, flanked by (left to right) Brigadier-General E.K. Wright, Rear-Admiral J.H. Doyle and Major-General E.M. Almond.

The invasion of South Korea
25 June – mid Sept 1950

CHINA

Hun River

Yalu River

MANCHURIA

NORTH KOREA

Taedong River

Pyongyang

Wonsan

Imjin River

SEA OF JAPAN

38°

Inchon

Seoul

Han River

Osan

Taebaek Mts

SOUTH KOREA

River Kum

Taejon

Naktong River

YELLOW SEA

Kunsan

Taegu

Pohang-dong

Pusan perimeter

Masan

Pusan

Straits of Tsushima

NKPA thrusts

(inset map)
SOVIET UNION

CHINA

SEA OF JAPAN

Peking (Beijing)

NORTH KOREA

Tokyo

SOUTH KOREA

JAPAN

YELLOW SEA

PACIFIC OCEAN

Above: The invasion from the North that took not only South Korea but also international observers by surprise. The attack initiated a period of fluid fighting which lasted until the summer of 1951. After that, the front lines solidified, and the war became a bloody attritional struggle.

Soviet-style state in the north of the country, while in the south a UN commission set up the Republic of Korea. In December 1948 Soviet troops withdrew from the North, to be followed by the US troops from the South in July 1949. The governments of both North and South claimed jurisdiction over the whole peninsula. The two new regimes were mutually hostile, and acts of sabotage and aggression were common.

THE ATTACK GOES IN

There was a great imbalance between the armies of the two states. That of the North was far stronger, consisting of 135,000 men, in eight full-strength infantry divisions, plus an armoured brigade and other supporting troops. The South, however, had only 95,000 men in four full-strength infantry divisions, with no tanks and little artillery. Both sides looked to greater powers – the North to the Soviet Union and the South to the USA – for aid and support in their claims; and what seems to have precipitated the attack is the impression gained by the Russians that the Americans would not come to the aid of South Korea if it was attacked. The USA had already abandoned mainland China to communist forces and in January 1950 Secretary of State Dean Acheson had stated that US defence commitments in the Pacific ran from the Aleutians, through Japan to the Philippines, to show a line excluding mainland Asia.

Plans for an attack were probably discussed between Northern leader Kim Il-sung and Stalin when Kim visited the Soviet Union in the winter of 1949–50; Stalin may well have looked favourably on the idea of a sudden invasion that would succeed before the US government could even consider intervening. So the Northern troops crossed the border on 25 June, sweeping the disorganized Southern units before them, the scale of their surprise having been increased by attacking on a Sunday, when many RoK soldiers were away on weekend leave.

There were three main prongs to the Northern attack: the crucial thrust was in the lower ground of the west of the peninsula, but there was also a subsidiary in the mountainous spine running down the centre of Korea, and in the east there was another attack, aided by an amphibious landing south of the 38th parallel.

In spite of Soviet and North Korean hopes that the attack would leave the USA confused and floundering for the few weeks necessary for total success, the US leadership reacted immediately, and with great decision. President Harry S. Truman instructed the commander of US forces in the Far East, that doughty warrior General Douglas MacArthur, to send supplies and

across the 38th parallel before dawn on 25 June 1950, catching the much smaller forces of the Republic of Korea (RoK) completely unprepared. Within four days they had taken Seoul, the capital of South Korea, and were rapidly advancing down the peninsula.

The reasons behind this surprise attack lay in the history of Korea since the end of World War II. Early in 1945, when the Western Allies were trying to persuade the Soviet Union to enter the war against Japan, it had been agreed that Soviet forces advancing from the north could take the surrender of Japanese troops in Korea (Korea having been incorporated into the Japanese empire before 1914) down to the 38th parallel. The Soviets did not actually declare war until 8 August 1945, but they then initiated a lightning campaign that took them down to the 38th parallel, and when the Japanese surrendered they set about establishing a

Above: US Vought F4U Corsairs of the Seventh Fleet prepare to go into action against the North Korean forces.

equipment at once to the RoK forces, and to report as soon as possible on what further measures were needed to defeat the assault. Truman also ordered the US Seventh Fleet to move into the area.

Truman's stand was considerably helped by the decision of the UN Security Council that North Korea was the aggressor. On 25 June itself, the council passed a resolution that NKPA forces should withdraw north of the 38th parallel, and this was followed by a resolution on 27 June that UN member states should give military aid to the RoK forces to help them withstand the attack. (The USSR, as a member of the Security Council, could have vetoed both these resolutions, but at the time was refusing to take part in UN activities because of the continued presence of Nationalist China in the body, regardless of communist victory in the country. This period of absence was presumably bitterly regretted by the Russians later.)

MacArthur reported back to Truman that RoK forces would be unable to hold the

PLATOON LEADER IN KOREA

John E. Jessup had just been commissioned as a 1st Lieutenant when the North Koreans invaded the South. He found his first weeks in action a harrowing experience, fighting in the Pusan perimeter.

'In mid-September my regiment was moved north to the vicinity of Waegwan to pass through the 1st Cavalry Division and break out of the perimeter in conjunction with the Inchon landings. My mission was to secure Hill 301 which intelligence said was held by only a handful of enemy troops. The handful turned out to be about a battalion

and we were in serious trouble from the very beginning. Nothing worked right. Ammunition we received at the height of the battle proved to be mislabelled and recoilless rifle rounds turned out to be 3.5in rockets when unpacked. Even more damaging was my inability to establish radio communications, as most of the channels were blocked by commanders complimenting each other on their great successes. I needed ammunition and fire support; we had been stopped dead in our tracks and were taking heavy casualties. We finally had to be withdrawn and the job of taking Hill 301 given to another battalion from the 1st

Cavalry. All of Company E had suffered because of the poor intelligence we had received.

'By dusk on 16 September 1950 more than three-quarters of my platoon were dead or seriously wounded, and more than half of the seriously wounded were dead by morning, primarily because the medical evacuation system was inefficient. When we withdrew, there were only seven of us who could still function, and all seven of us had been wounded, some several times. We were heavily mortared that night, however, and two of the seven were killed. For all intents and purposes, the second platoon had ceased to exist.'

Above: The moment of truth as US Marines go over the top at Inchon. The landing at Inchon was considered tricky not only because of the difficulties of the approach to the port and the wide tidal range; as far as the troops who had to carry out the landings were concerned, another major problem was that they would, in many cases, have to make an assault over sea walls. As the Dieppe raid of 1942 had demonstrated, this was an extremely dangerous proposition.

peninsula without direct US help, and so Truman authorized the commitment of US forces from Japan. Elements of the US 24th Infantry Division arrived in the south of Korea on 1 July, and by mid-July three US divisions had been committed, under the command of Lieutenant-General Walton Walker. These formations were relatively poorly equipped occupation troops, however, and were remorselessly driven back southwards, until by early August all that the RoK and US forces held was a block of land around the town of Pusan, where they established defences known as the Pusan perimeter. Here, they hoped to withstand the Northern onslaught, although the chances of doing so seemed slim, given the impetus of recent victories by the communists.

Walker handled his defences extremely ably, however; the North Koreans had, in any case, run close to the end of their rudimentary logistics, and the weight of US naval and air power helped the defenders.

THE INCHON LANDINGS

While Walker and his men held out in Pusan, MacArthur had been planning an attack on the rear of the NKPA forces. Indeed, as early as July MacArthur had tried to organize an amphibious landing at Inchon, the port nearest the South Korean capital of Seoul,

and had only been dissuaded by the impossibility of assembling sufficient troops and landing craft. But by early September, the US 1st Marine Division would have arrived in force in Japan, and the 7th Infantry Division there would have been brought up to strength; and this gave MacArthur the troops he needed.

Not that the idea of an amphibious landing was at all to the liking of many members of the US high command. Inchon was subject to a wide tidal range, there were very few days when a landing would be possible, the troops would not be going ashore on beaches but often directly against sea walls, while all possible landing sites (and the channel along which the invasion fleet would have to sail) were overlooked by hills surrounding the harbour. In spite of these difficulties, MacArthur forced his plan through at a conference in Tokyo on 23 August, and the landing took place on 15 September. Operation Chromite, as it was called, was a brilliant success. The planning had been meticulous and the landings at the three beaches ('Green', 'Red' and 'Blue') all attained their objectives. At the end of the first day, only 20 men had been killed and the port was in US hands. MacArthur had pulled off one of the greatest single feats of generalship since the end of World War II.

Seoul was entered on 22 September and the

North Korean forces in the south, vainly battering at Walker's Pusan perimeter, were suddenly in danger of being cut off. They soon had no recourse but to pull back as rapidly as possible, harried by US aircraft. While NKPA troops had resisted fiercely until Seoul fell, and the battle for the city had been intense, the advance north gradually became much easier, until by early October the 38th parallel was crossed, and the North Koreans offered little but sporadic resistance. The decision to advance further north was one that the US government was reluctant to take, but Syngman Rhee, the president of South Korea, was certainly not going to pass up the chance of inflicting a decisive defeat on his great rival Kim Il-sung, and MacArthur was fully prepared to back him up with the US troops at his command. As the allied forces moved north, however, China warned that she might have to intervene – the struggle was soon to enter a new phase.

The Soviet Union had warned that her air force would intervene if any air attacks were made on Chinese soil, and so it was only prudent for the US government to forbid MacArthur to bomb the bridges across the Yalu River, the border between China and Korea. MacArthur's motives for destroying the main means of communication between Manchuria and North Korea were quite clear; he wished to prevent the Chinese being able to send more troops than they already had assembled there. Early in November he had estimated that 60,000 Chinese were stationed in the country. The Chinese, moreover, were engaging in a rapid build-up. They had brought their strength up to 200,000 towards the end of November, and as

US and RoK forces began clearing the far north of the country, they struck.

The Chinese forces had entered Korea secretly, using night marches to avoid observation. They were usually veterans of the Chinese Civil War and often of World War II. They hit forces which were unprepared for the attack, and were even unprepared for the rigours of the Korean winter. Many US units had believed MacArthur's boast that they would be home by Christmas, and had no proper winter clothing. Chinese tactics were to attack as infantry units across high ground. The UN troops were handicapped by being tied to the roads, and the Chinese approach met with immediate success. In the

Above: A communist poster glorying in the successes of the Chinese forces that intervened in Korea late in 1950.

Below: UN infantry trudge through the barren Korean countryside during the bitter winter of 1950–51. The severe cold came as a great shock to many units, and drastically reduced their combat effectiveness.

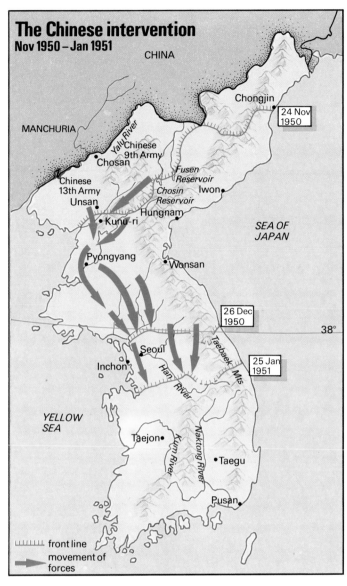

The Chinese intervention
Nov 1950 – Jan 1951

CHINA

MANCHURIA

Chongjin

24 Nov
1950

Yalu River

Chinese
9th Army

Chosan

Fusen
Reservoir

Chosin
Reservoir

Iwon

Chinese
13th Army

Unsan

Hungnam

Kunu-ri

Pyongyang

Wonsan

SEA OF
JAPAN

26 Dec
1950

38°

Seoul

25 Jan
1951

Inchon

Taebaek Mts

Han River

YELLOW
SEA

Taejon

Kun River

Naktong River

Taegu

Pusan

front line

movement of
forces

west of the country, Walker's Eighth Army was severely mauled, and forced to pull back; while in the northeast of Korea, X Corps, an independent formation composed of the troops that had landed at Inchon – the 1st Marine Division and the 7th Infantry Division – was hit hard. The Marines performed a heroic retreat from exposed positions near the Chosin Reservoir, and eventually X Corps was evacuated by sea. On 4 January 1951 Seoul was in communist hands again, and the great gains of September and October had all been lost.

In spite of their impressive fighting qualities, however, the Chinese were soon to run out of steam. Their infantry divisions only needed some 40 tonnes of supplies a day (as compared to 350 tonnes for a UN division) but their communications suffered a terrific pounding from US aircraft, and the long marches took their toll. By mid-January the front line had been stabilized south of Seoul and the UN ground forces, now under the command of General Matthew Ridgway (Walker had been killed in a road accident on

Christmas Eve), were planning to take the offensive.

Ridgway was determined to avoid the mistakes of the previous advance; he was not going to let his units push ahead too far and risk surprise counters. He devised a way of using UN technical superiority, especially in artillery and support weapons, which became known as 'the Meatgrinder'. Put most simply, Ridgway pinned down enemy forces along a stretch of front, and then destroyed them by the application of massive firepower. Communist casualties were enormous and they were forced to pull back, unable to withstand the pressure. By 15 March 1951 Seoul had been retaken yet again. Ridgway's men had reached the 38th parallel by the end of March, and then they halted, with the political decision whether to cross over into a full-scale invasion of the North once more posing a problem.

The UN forces now consisted of troops from some 15 nations. The most important contingent was from the USA, of course, and all the other national units were integrated

Above: A forward machine-gun post in front of the line established along the Imjin River, where the British Glosters were to make a heroic stand that blunted the Chinese offensive of April 1951.

into US divisions, but apart from the RoK forces themselves, there were significant contributions from Britain (which in all sent two infantry brigades, an armoured regiment and one and a half artillery regiments, ground support troops plus pilots and naval support), Turkey, Australia and Canada. It was British troops who were to bear the brunt of the next stage of the fighting.

That the Chinese had been planning a renewed drive south was clear to UN intelligence, but when they attacked on 22 April 1951 the effectiveness of their infantry attacks once more caused consternation. Under Peng Teh-huai, who had replaced the previous Chinese commander Lin Piao in March, the communists launched a three-pronged offensive, with the main assault going in in the west, towards Seoul. The British 29th Brigade on the Imjin River found itself isolated by the collapse of an RoK division on its flank, but barred the way against mass Chinese attacks from 22–5 April before withdrawing, and one of its battalions, the 1st Battalion, Gloucestershire Regiment, distinguished itself by a gallant stand before it was completely overrun. This block to the Chinese advance had given the UN forces valuable breathing space, and the new UN ground commander, General James Van Fleet, was able to construct defensive positions that stemmed the communist tide. Van Fleet then retook the offensive himself, using Ridgway's tactics of mass firepower, and once more his troops pushed north of the 38th parallel. Van Fleet wished to continue the advance, using amphibious landings, but the communists let it be known that they would be prepared to begin peace negotiations, and the advance was halted.

Van Fleet had replaced Ridgway because

Ridgway had replaced MacArthur. The great general had been sacked by US President Harry Truman because of his inflammatory statements on how the war should be extended. As early as December 1950, MacArthur had suggested to the US Joint Chiefs of Staff that the way to win in Korea was to attack China, and he was also a proponent of the deployment of Nationalist Chinese troops from Formosa (now Taiwan). Gradually, the dispute between MacArthur and those who favoured limiting the war grew; nor was the situation made any easier for Truman by the fact that MacArthur was so popular and that prominent Republican politicians eagerly picked up on his views. On 7 March 1951 MacArthur gave a press

Above left: US Marines during the retreat from the Chosin Reservoir, December 1950. Above: Australians of the UN forces. Above right: Vought F4U Corsairs on board the carrier USS Philippine Sea. Far right: 'The Meatgrinder' in action. US artillery was the key weapon in Korea, pounding the communist forces whenever they risked any offensive action.

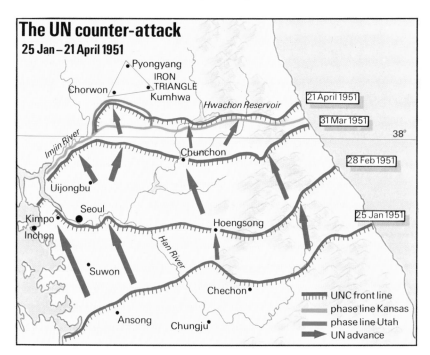

The UN counter-attack
25 Jan – 21 April 1951

conference at which he expressed doubts as to whether victory could be achieved in Korea without attacking China, and the final straw came in April. On the 5th, a Republican congressman read out a letter from MacArthur in which the general implied that opening a second front in Asia was the only way of dealing with the worldwide communist threat. On 11 April MacArthur heard that he was no longer in command of the UN forces.

STALLING AND STALEMATE

Truman's decision to confine the conflict to Korea had been sustained, but this gain from the point of view of world peace did not end the war in Korea. Although peace negotiations had begun on 10 July 1951, the final armistice did not come into effect until 27 July 1953. During these two years, the ding-dong advances and retreats of the first year of the war were replaced by static trench warfare during which there were bloody positional battles as attempts were made to inch the front lines forward.

The first period of large-scale action during this phase of the war was in the early autumn of 1951, when Van Fleet decided to push the communist forces further back in order to safeguard the Hwachon Reservoir which supplied Seoul with its water. This led to the struggles for Bloody Ridge and Heartbreak Ridge. There was a lull in the fighting from the end of November to the end of December, and the communists used this respite to construct a line of defences, 40km (25 miles) deep in some places. There were small battles for individual features – given memorable names such as 'Jane Russell Hill' and 'Luke the Gook's Castle' by the US

Above: South Korean troops man a 57mm anti-tank gun. Below: US front-line troops dig in during the long stalemate of 1952.

positions on the feature known as 'Old Baldy'. Although the UN troops held on to Pork Chop Hill, the effort was not considered worth the reward and the hill was abandoned two weeks before the ceasefire came into effect. The fighting for Pork Chop was a typical example of the bloody positional battles of the final two years of the war.

With the fighting on the ground stalemated, attention shifted to the air. Here, the nature of the conflict as an adjunct to the developing Cold War was clearly shown. The fiercest air battles of the war were those fought between the leading US and Soviet jet fighters – the F-86A Sabre on the UN side, and the MiG-15 on the communist side. The MiGs operated from airfields in Manchuria in areas out of bounds to UN aircraft, and took a heavy toll of the B-29 Superfortresses that were bombing communications until the introduction of the Sabres as escorts. The resulting dogfights showed that the Sabre had a clear superiority: 78 Sabres were lost in these struggles but they destroyed a total of 792 MiGs. The MiGs had better climbing performance and a higher ceiling, but US pilots adopted tactics that suited their heavier, faster-diving machines to wreak havoc on the Soviet planes.

troops – but in the autumn of 1952 there was a major series of communist attacks, probably designed to coincide with the US presidential elections. These attacks were successfully countered, but in the spring of 1953 came another wave. The most intense struggle was for the position known as 'Pork Chop Hill', which was overlooked by communist

Apart from the struggle for air supremacy, the air war revolved around sustained UN

interdiction bombing operations against the communications of the communist forces. There were very few worthwhile strategic targets in Korea, and targets in China were forbidden. The roads and railways of North Korea were, therefore, pounded day and night, by bombers such as the B-29 as well as by ground-attack planes. Whenever communist forces moved they were put under pressure: it was estimated that air attacks accounted for 40,000 casualties during the communist offensive of December 1950–January 1951 alone.

Another area in which the political and ideological aspects assumed great importance was the treatment of prisoners of war. The North Koreans and Chinese held in the South managed to organize themselves, to demand better treatment from their captors, and in fact riots were suppressed by US troops, while UN troops held in the North were subject to 'brainwashing' techniques to try to make them change political allegiance. A further, tragic aspect was that both sides wanted all their prisoners back; and many North Koreans would have preferred to stay in the South. But ideological considerations were paramount; this was as much a battle for men's minds as it was for territory.

The war ended, therefore, with the situation much as it had been before the start of

Left: A North Korean officer reports from the front by field telephone.

hostilities. Some 33,000 men of the UN command (including 30,000 Americans and 793 British) had died, with about 120,000 wounded and missing. A total of approximately 50,000 South Koreans were killed, with North Korean casualties some 520,000 and Chinese losses 900,000.

Below: General Mark Clark, as commander of the UK forces in Korea, signs the armistice agreement in Munsan on 27 July 1953.

SOUTHEAST ASIA IN FLAMES

Below: Armed with the standard-issue M16 assault rifle, a member of a Special Forces unit lies in wait for Viet Cong guerrillas on a jungle trail in the Central Highlands. By the mid-1960s, the US forces committed to South Vietnam had assumed a full-scale combat role and Special Forces units were deployed to fight the rising tide of communist insurgency in the countryside.

Like so many wars, the conflict in Vietnam (1959–75), that spread until it also engulfed both Laos and Cambodia, had its roots in the settlement of an earlier war. In this case it was the Indochina War of the 1940s and 1950s, during which a communist-dominated nationalist army, the Viet Minh, fought to force the French out of Vietnam. The result of this struggle, at its most intense in what was to become North Vietnam, was a resounding defeat for the French Army at the battle of Dien Bien Phu (see pp. 209–10), and in April 1954, when the stronghold of Dien Bien Phu was about to fall to Viet Minh forces, talks were begun in Geneva to discuss the future shape of what had been French Indochina.

The Geneva Conference reached a set of agreements in July 1954 that were not formally signed by any of the key parties concerned, but which became the basis for the restructuring of Indochina after the years of war. The independence of Laos and Cambodia (which in any case had been granted by the French some years before) was recognized, although Laos presented a bundle of problems in its own right, with a powerful communist movement, the Pathet Lao, controlling large stretches of the north of the country. Vietnam was divided into two supposedly temporary political bodies, split at the 17th parallel, the southern area under

The Geneva Accords

CHINA

Lao Kai

NORTH VIETNAM

Dien Bien Phu

Black River

Hanoi

Haiphong

LAOS

Luang Prabang

GULF OF TONKIN

HAINAN

Vientiane

Mekong River

Vinh

Thakhek

17th parallel

Quang Tri

THAILAND

Hue

Da Nang

Saravane

Pakse

Quang Ngai

Bangkok

Pleiku

Qui Nohn

CAMBODIA

Battambang

SOUTH VIETNAM

Kompong Cham

Da Lat

Nha Trang

Phnom Penh

Bien Hoa

GULF OF THAILAND

Long Xuyan

Saigon

Vinh Loi

Bao Dai, former emperor of Annam who had been installed as president of Vietnam, and the northern area under the control of the Viet Minh forces of Ho Chi Minh. Elections were to be held in July 1956 to decide the future of a united Vietnam.

The Americans, who had been largely paying for the French war effort in the early 1950s, had no intention of risking the South becoming another communist state. They strongly supported the installation of Ngo Dinh Diem, a staunch Vietnamese nationalist but also a strong anti-communist, as prime minister. During the two years after taking office, Diem set up a centralized regime, resisted efforts by local religious sects (the Hoa Hoa and Cao Dai) to remove him, broke the power of the Binh Xuyen, a gangster organization with its own private army, and crushed a coup attempt by his own chief of staff. Overcoming these attacks and in spite of damning reports from General Lawton Collins, Eisenhower's personal representative in Saigon, Diem survived, and put off the elections scheduled for 1956.

DIEM'S TROUBLED REGIME

Both North Vietnam and South Vietnam, as the two states in Vietnam came to be known, claimed sovereignty over the whole country. But whereas the North was an efficiently centralized state, run by a party that had built up disciplined obedient cadres during the long years of war against the French, the South was rent by internal problems.

First, there was the difficulty of imposing a centralized government on a rural society with long traditions of village autonomy. Then there was the religious question. The majority of the inhabitants of South Vietnam were Buddhists with a Confucian slant of ancestor worship. Diem, however, was a Catholic, and there was a large Catholic minority that had been swelled by the influx of some 900,000 Catholic refugees from the North after the Geneva agreements. It was widely believed in South Vietnam that Diem favoured Catholics for official posts, and this led to feelings of dissatisfaction and eventually to the wave of protest in the early 1960s, when Buddhist monks publicly burnt themselves to death.

Quite apart from the unpopularity of his religious prejudices, Diem was also hated because of the influential jobs he bestowed on his family. He gave his brothers Can and Nhu extensive powers, although they held no official posts, and another brother, Archbishop Thuc of Hue, became semi-official spokesman for the Catholic minority.

The Diem regime, then, was becoming increasingly autocratic and unpopular in the late 1950s. Not that this would have been so unusual in a small Southeast Asia country,

but, unfortunately for Diem, there was a force at hand ready and able to exploit the situation. This lay in the cadres of the Viet Minh, that had remained in being in the South after the partition of the country. Gradually, in response to the pressure that Diem was putting on them and also seeing an opportunity to capitalize on his unpopularity, they began to re-emerge as a guerrilla army, especially in the Mekong Delta region.

In 1959, the NLF (National Liberation Front) of South Vietnam was formed, with the Viet Cong as its military wing. There were then perhaps 5000 guerrillas active in the South, with a substantial layer of support from a rural population sickened by the excesses of the central government. The Viet

Above: During the 1960s, North Vietnamese society became totally geared for war and even the women and children were instructed in politics and the use of smallarms.

Below: Viet Cong guerrillas, equipped with Soviet AK47 assault rifles, rest up in a South Vietnamese village.

Above: Communist insurgency in South Vietnam depended heavily on the flow of supplies from the North, and peasant boats in the Mekong Delta were regularly searched for arms and ammunition. Above right: The flamboyant Marshal Ky, one of the main power brokers in South Vietnam's corrupt and ineffectual government. Below: US Marines under fire during the heavy fighting for Hue when the North Vietnamese launched their Tet Offensive in 1968.

Cong were certainly given encouragement and some military aid by the North Vietnamese government, but to what extent they were given more than this is unclear. The return of communists who had fled to the North after 1954 (it is estimated that about 80,000 had done so) was also set in motion.

The first reaction of Diem's government to the increasing level of insurgency was savage repression, with summary executions and arrests, but this had little or no effect upon the guerrilla activity. The South Vietnamese Army (known as the ARVN – Army of the Republic of Vietnam) was just not equipped to deal with a widespread internal crisis of the nature that it now faced. Using Korea as their yardstick, US advisors and aid administrators had given the government a force designed to combat a possible invasion across the 17th parallel, and not one that could cope with a guerrilla war raging in the densely populated areas in the far south of the country. By 1961 there were an es-

timated 10,000 Viet Cong guerrillas in action, and the ARVN could not claim to have secure control over more than 40 per cent of the country.

GROWING US SUPPORT

As the supporter of Diem and as the main nation to which South Vietnam looked for aid, the USA was already committed to the South by the early 1960s, when President Kennedy came to power. Kennedy faced a disturbing political scene all over Southeast Asia, for Laos too was disintegrating as military warlords and communists struggled with neutralist factions. Laos proved relatively easy to deal with, as international conferences managed to come to some agreement over the political future of the country; but Vietnam was an intractable issue. Gradually, more US aid and advisors were sent in until, by 1963, there were 16,000 US personnel in the South, an increase of 15,000 since 1961. This influx of US aid seemed to have little effect on the stability of the regime, however, and terrorism and military action by the Viet Cong grew. The government was proving incapable of implementing counter-insurgency policies such as the 'strategic hamlet' programme urged on it by US advisors, and the religious question was still unresolved, with Buddhist demonstrators being fired on by troops and Buddhist monks being arrested in their thousands.

In spite of Diem's promises to mend his administration's ways, the Americans, including the ambassador to Saigon Henry Cabot Lodge, were convinced by mid-1963 that Diem would never change his policies. On 1 November, high-ranking officers carried out a coup (probably with US consent). Diem and his brother Nhu were murdered, and a new regime took over. There was soon a new president in Washington, too, for Kennedy was assassinated shortly after Diem's mur-

Above: US troops cover an infantry advance with an M60 machine gun during heavy fighting for the northern provinces. Below: One of the most infamous scenes of the war was the summary execution of a suspected Viet Cong by the chief of police on the streets of Saigon during the Tet Offensive of 1968. The showing of such brutal incidents on US television raised questions for many Americans as to the morality of the continued US presence in Vietnam and served to fuel the growing anti-war campaign.

der, and Lyndon Johnson took over. Just before his death, Kennedy had wanted to reduce US force levels in Vietnam, but Secretary of Defense Robert McNamara persuaded Johnson that this was a mistaken policy, and so the levels stayed as they were.

1964 saw no improvement in Vietnam, with a gradual increase in US aid still making little impression. In August, there were clashes in the Gulf of Tonkin between US destroyers and North Vietnamese torpedo boats. The exact nature of these clashes is somewhat confused, and there have been varying interpretations of the incidents, but the main outcome was that Congress, in the Gulf of Tonkin Resolution, gave the president wide-ranging powers to deal with the situation in the Vietnam as he saw fit.

The problem for the president was, exactly how was he to deal with the situation? He resisted calls to bomb the North until February 1965, when in retaliation for attacks on US troops in South Vietnam he

agreed to the bombing of barracks in the North, and by March 1965 a sustained campaign of bombing the North, known as 'Rolling Thunder', was under way. The most important step of 1965, however, was that the troops guarding US installations gradually assumed a full-scale combat role. By the end of 1965 there were over 60,000 Americans in the country; by the end of 1966 this had grown to 270,000, and when US involvment was at its peak in 1969 the numbers had risen to about 540,000.

In charge of these US forces was General William C. Westmoreland, commander of Military Assistance Command Vietnam (MACV). His job was to find how the weight of US military power could be applied to the task of winning the war.

MOVING DOWN THE TRAIL

As the US build-up got under way, so the North Vietnamese Army (NVA) began to send in large units, using the so-called Ho Chi Minh Trail, a network of tracks and roads through Laos and Cambodia, to infiltrate forces into the sparsely populated Central Highlands of South Vietnam where there were few Vietnamese and Montagnard tribesmen subsisted on primitive agriculture.

The scene was now set for three years of bitter fighting, in which the Americans never lost a major engagement, but which ended with the communists staging the Tet Offensive, which took them into the centres of Hue and Saigon, and which seemed to show that US efforts over the previous three years had all been in vain. In the aftermath of Tet, there were bitter recriminations between politicians and generals over who was responsible for what appeared to be the failure of US forces in Vietnam, a debate intensified when South Vietnam fell to the North's attacks in 1975. Appointed in the wake of Tet, Secretary of Defense Clifford Clarke confessed himself

Above: General William Westmoreland, overall commander of MACV (Military Assistance Command Vietnam), with US President Lyndon Johnson. Westmoreland optimistically believed that the combination of superior US firepower and the interdiction of the flow of supplies from the North would bring the war to a swift conclusion. He had, however, seriously underestimated the North's determination and will to win and found himself fighting a long and incredibly costly war of attrition.

astonished that the US Joint Chiefs of Staff could give him no clear answers as to whether, in fact, US troops were winning the war, while the generals complained that they had not been given proper goals by the politicians. But the USA did have a strategy that it applied with a good deal of success in Vietnam; it was just that there were surrounding factors that ultimately doomed this strategy to defeat.

WESTMORELAND'S STRATEGY

The American political aim was to set up a peaceful, strong, anti-communist state, rather like South Korea. And Westmoreland had devised a military strategy that he believed would inevitably destroy the communist offensive. Put most simply, he intended to use the large, well-equipped US formations in Vietnam to attack the North Vietnamese concentrations, especially in the Central Highlands, while the task of pacifying the villages and populated areas would be left to South Vietnamese troops. In a war without front lines, he would not try merely to hold territory, but would attempt to destroy as many enemy soldiers as possible, with attrition his major aim, rather as the commanders of the UN forces in Korea had eventually decided that the application of firepower to kill large numbers of enemy troops was the optimum approach.

To carry out this strategy, Westmoreland not only had the enormous weight of US artillery and air power, he also had the support of the US Navy's guns off the coast, plus the vast technical resources of the world's most advanced nation. The US troops in Vietnam were, for example, given extreme mobility by the use of helicopters, and the 1st Cavalry Division was a totally airmobile formation. In their first large-scale encounters with the Viet Cong and the North Vietnamese at Chu Lai in August 1965, the

Americans shocked and routed the enemy by the combination of mobility and firepower open to them. By the end of 1965 Westmoreland's strategy seemed to be working, and the communist forces had been set a new series of problems.

Initially successful though it was, the US strategy had failed to take account of certain factors in Vietnam, or, rather, had optimistically imagined that they could be overcome by US technology and ingenuity. The first of these factors was the existence of the Ho Chi Minh Trail, or, to put it another way, the strategic vulnerability of South Vietnam. The country formed a huge crescent bordering Laos and Cambodia. The weak Laotian government could hardly prevent communist infiltration along the trail, and as long as the Viet Cong could use it for reinforcements, South Vietnam was vulnerable.

Bombing operations against the trail grew in intensity, but they never succeeded in cutting it. Westmoreland asked to be allowed to send ground troops over the border in 1967, but his request was turned down. (This may well have been a wise decision, for when

Vietnamese to abandon their aspirations in the South; and Westmoreland believed that he could force an unacceptably high level of casualties on the NVA. But the communists were able to sustain casualties of over 1,000,000, and still carry on the war, whereas US public opinion was unable to accept 47,000 dead – the eventual US total. It was only towards the end of the war that US officials involved in Vietnam began to comprehend the ferocious will to win of the men in Hanoi, a determination that the USA simply could not match, for all its technological superiority.

Finally, there was the problem of exactly how the ARVN was going to win its part of the war – the pacification of the villages. The Viet Cong had been firmly entrenched in much of rural South Vietnam for some time, and Westmoreland's battles of attrition against the NVA would have no long-term effect unless, under the umbrella provided by his US forces, the countryside could be cleared of communist influence.

Unfortunately, the ARVN was not suited to the task of sophisticated counter-insurgency. It had not been designed for such a role, and the attempt to make it operate schemes such as the 'strategic hamlet' programme (based on the British 'New Villages' in Malaya) had not been at all successful. Then, as the weight of US firepower began to come into play, and made communist operations in large-unit strength hazardous, so the Viet Cong began to make more use of the villages themselves as areas of operation and defence, putting yet more strain on the ARVN and drawing the US

ARVN forces tried to cut the trail in 1971, in Operation Lam Son 719, they soon found themselves bogged down, subject to fierce guerrilla attacks, and were forced to withdraw in disarray.) A sophisticated set of electronic sensors and non-stop reconnaissance was employed to guide the bombing of the trail, and US Special Forces carried out to no avail. The flow of supplies necessary to maintain communist insurgency at the level it had reached in 1965 was estimated at 60 truck-loads per day; and the trail never delivered less than this amount.

The second factor that was never properly taken into account was the will to fight of the communists. Late in 1964, US officials had believed that a short period of bombing would be sufficient to force the North

Above left: Supported by two comrades, a wounded US infantryman is helped to a medical evacuation area. The US lost over 56,000 men dead and 300,000 wounded during the war and as the so-called body count escalated, pressure at home for troop withdrawal increased. Above: The US campaign against the Ho Chi Minh Trail included the use of camouflaged seismic detection sensors, which were dropped from aircraft, and the extensive use of defoliants (left inset: a Fairchild C-123 Provider sprays jungle with Agent Orange) on the large areas of forest surrounding the Trail. Left: Communist supply trucks move through an area devastated by the US defoliation programme.

Left: A radio operator guides in heliborne supplies as troops establish a forward operations firebase. Using explosives to clear densely forested areas and helicopters to bring in artillery and heavy equipment, a firebase could be set up within 36 hours. While some bases such as Khe Sanh developed into large, heavily fortified positions, many bases were deployed for short periods of time to provide artillery support for search and destroy operations in particular areas, and then dismantled.

forces into operations in the populated areas. Sometimes the deployment of US troops in more populated zones was successful, as in the Mekong Delta where a large riverine force proved a considerable obstacle to the Viet Cong, but, more often, the fact that US firepower was being introduced into the villages had disastrous effects for the civilian inhabitants.

SEARCH AND DESTROY

The jargon of US tactics – 'Free Fire Zones', 'Search and Destroy' – was chillingly accurate in its reflection of the attitude adopted. Yet this was no way to win a war of small-scale counter-insurgency; merely a way of stemming the tide for a while. Gradually, US policy became one of deliberately creating refugees, of destroying those villages that were suspected of harbouring communist sympathizers rather than trying to win the 'hearts and minds' of the people. Westmoreland's neat division of the war into a largescale struggle between US forces and the NVA while the ARVN looked after the civilian population was eroded, and replaced with a much messier involvement.

Early in 1967, the US forces began making large-scale sweeps into populated areas that had been Viet Cong strongholds. The two biggest operations were 'Cedar Falls' (in January) and 'Junction City' (in February), aimed at clearing areas near Saigon that had always been troublesome. Junction City involved the largest drop of American paratroopers since the Korean War, while Cedar Falls saw the deployment of some 50,000 men. The problem was, however, that as soon as the large concentrations of troops had gone, Viet Cong cadres began infiltrating back into the supposedly cleared regions, while to assemble the amount of troops necessary to undertake the operations, other areas of Vietnam had been denuded of US forces.

Below: A flight of UH-1D helicopters comes in to land at a forward base. The UH-1D was mainly deployed as a first-wave troop transport for heliborne assaults and as a supply and equipment mover. It also served as a makeshift gunship until the arrival in Vietnam in 1967 of the AH-1G Huey Cobra gunship.

Above: Members of an immediate-response combat unit of the US Army leap from a Bell 'Huey' helicopter hovering a few metres above the ground to reinforce a hilltop position recently taken from the Viet Cong. Right: Helicopters were also used to provide close fire support for ground troops and to interdict daylight Viet Cong movements in the Mekong Delta.

Paradoxically, in spite of the large numbers of men committed, the US Army in Vietnam was very badly off for combat troops. The enormous logistics operation required to establish a modern army in a small, backward Asian nation soaked up personnel. Whereas in World War II, about 36 per cent of those in uniform were combat personnel, by the 1960s the percentage available for action had dropped to 22 per cent. This meant that although the US might send 500,000 men to Vietnam, only 100,000 of these would be available for direct combat with the communists. Westmoreland felt himself, therefore, always short of troops, and was constantly asking for more. By late 1967 this was beginning to worry the Johnson administration.

Although US methods may not have been

nists retained the priceless advantage of the strategic initiative, they were at something of a loss as to how to employ it. The decision was eventually taken in July 1967 (after much debate) to launch a major offensive early in 1968, during the Lunar New Year of Tet. The main offensive was preceded by a siege of the outpost of Khe Sanh, in the far northwest of South Vietnam, which was held by US Marines. From early January 1968 two NVA divisions were deployed against the 6000 Marines there, but the garrison held out under furious bombardment, with the US political establishment anxiously praying that the base would not become another Dien Bien Phu. In April the NVA raised the siege, but by then the whole complexion of the war had been changed by the Tet Offensive.

The Americans had been aware that there would be large-scale attacks on other positions and cities at or around Tet, but they were surprised by the ferocity and success of the initial assaults on 30 January 1968, as small groups of men managed to get into the centres of many of the largest towns all over the country, including Hue and Saigon. In Saigon, there was even a spirited attack on the US Embassy, while in Hue the attackers took the old citadel, and fought ferociously for a month before they were cleared out.

Tet resulted in enormous losses for the Viet Cong, who had carried out the main attacks, and of the estimated 70,000 men who took part, well over 30,000 were casualties.

Carrier-based US Navy Phantoms (above and below) provided air support in Vietnam, while 105mm artillery (opposite below right) arranged in fire support bases, enhanced the weight of US firepower.

bringing success, they were certainly posing problems for the communists. North Vietnam's General Vo Nguyen Giap had decided not to risk too much open confrontation with the US forces in 1966, but was finding it difficult to formulate a strategy that would bring victory. Whenever his men tried to stand up to US firepower they suffered enormous losses and although the commu-

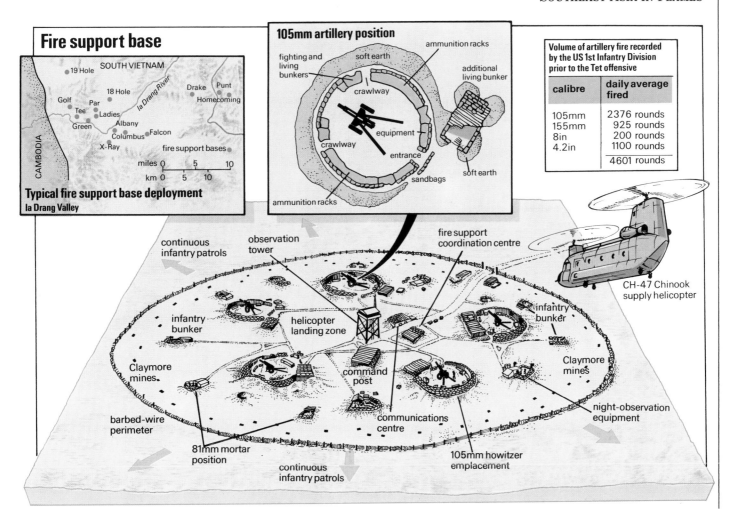

Fire support base

Typical fire support base deployment
la Drang Valley

SOUTH VIETNAM
19 Hole
18 Hole
Golf   Par   Drake   Punt
Tee   Ladies   Homecoming
Green   Albany
Columbus   Falcon
X-Ray   fire support bases
CAMBODIA
la Drang River

miles 0   5   10
km 0   5   10

105mm artillery position

ammunition racks
fighting and living bunkers
soft earth
additional living bunker
crawlway
equipment
crawlway
entrance
sandbags
soft earth
ammunition racks

Volume of artillery fire recorded by the US 1st Infantry Division prior to the Tet offensive

calibre	daily average fired
105mm	2376 rounds
155mm	925 rounds
8in	200 rounds
4.2in	1100 rounds
	4601 rounds

continuous infantry patrols
observation tower
fire support coordination centre
CH-47 Chinook supply helicopter
infantry bunker
helicopter landing zone
infantry bunker
Claymore mines
command post
Claymore mines
barbed-wire perimeter
communications centre
night-observation equipment
81mm mortar position
105mm howitzer emplacement
continuous infantry patrols

The Viet Cong was never as effective again. There was no mass uprising all over South Vietnam as the communists had hoped, and the ARVN performed very well, holding fast even though it suffered over 11,000 casualties. But the offensive had finally shaken the faith of the US political establishment in the ability of the USA to sustain the war – and this was the most important result.

HAWKS AND DOVES

Already, late in 1967, Secretary of Defense McNamara had wanted to resign, convinced that the war could not be won. Johnson was exhausted by the strain of a war that had caused him to abandon his programme of ambitious domestic reform. And soon after Tet, the new Secretary of Defense Clark Clifford, who had been well known as a 'hawk', reported that the Joint Chiefs of Staff seemed to have no plan that they could guarantee would bring success whether more troops were sent in or not. Wherever he turned, Johnson seemed to find a negative response, and he could not, therefore, agree with Westmoreland's claim that Tet had shattered communist strength, and that now was the time to send in even more troops to

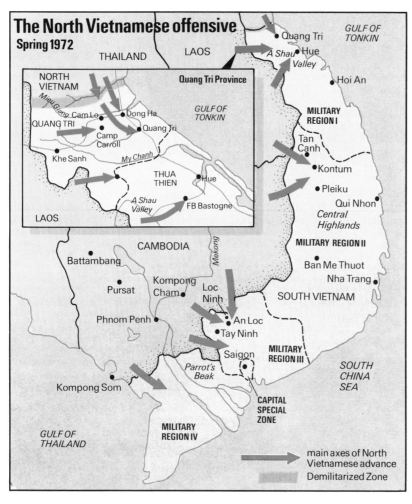

The North Vietnamese offensive
Spring 1972

Above right: Rough justice – a South Vietnamese Ranger punishes a farmer for allegedly supplying government troops with false information on Viet Cong whereabouts. Such behaviour did little to endear the government to the populace of South Vietnam, whose support was vital if ARVN and US counter-insurgency operations were to succeed. Right: An A-7 Corsair drops its load of high-drag bombs on communist positions in South Vietnam.

defeated enemy. Indeed, during the summer of 1968 there were renewed communist offensives in many areas. Johnson stopped the bombing of the North from 1 November 1968, and Hanoi accepted his offer of talks, which were under way by the end of the year. By

then there was another US President ready to take office: Johnson had decided not to run in the 1968 election, and Richard Nixon had been elected his successor.

From his inauguration in January 1969 to the agreement with North Vietnam that led to the final US troop withdrawals in January 1973, Nixon pursued a policy of the steady disengagement of US combat troops, while attempting to ensure that South Vietnam was able to defend itself against the communists. This dual process became known as 'Vietnamization' and 'pacification'. 'Vietnamization' involved the steady handing over of ground combat duties to the ARVN, which was expanded in order to cope with its new responsibilites. Eventually, South Vietnam had over a million men under arms,

Above: Lieutenant James Calley, whose men perpetrated the infamous My Lai massacre (March 1968). Below: South Vietnamese troops cover a street corner during the Tet Offensive.

including regional and militia forces. They were given support from the panoply of US air and sea power, and were generously supplied with equipment.

'Pacification' was a concerted effort to destroy Viet Cong control of the villages in the most populous areas of South Vietnam, while containing the communists in the vulnerable border provinces. As the Viet Cong had already been severely damaged by the loss of its best troops in the Tet Offensive, pacification proved easier than it had in the mid-1960s. By 1971 only 10 of the country's 45 provinces were seriously affected by communist activity. The methods used to achieve this end were often brutal and arbitrary, with selective assassination of Viet Cong sympathizers a common weapon, but they were undeniably effective against a weakened insurgent movement.

Nixon was ruthless in pursuit of his ends.

He was prepared to use whatever means he thought necessary to keep the North Vietnamese negotiating, and also to make the South Vietnamese, who naturally felt that they were being abandoned, follow the US line. The crisis in the whole process came in 1972, when the North launched a heavy attack on the South, hoping to catch the Americans unsure in an election year and to sweep away the still unproven ARVN. The new offensive, which began on 30 March 1972, had initial success, but the three main prongs of the offensive (towards Hue in the north, through Kontum in the centre and – from Cambodia – towards Saigon in the south) were too far apart to coordinate fully. The three key cities of Hue, An Loc and Kontum held out, and after a period of bad weather had lifted, US aircraft took a grim toll of the NVA. Nixon also authorized bombing the North again – Operation Linebacker

Right: US President Richard Nixon, elected in November 1968, adopted a hard-line policy towards the North which included the extension of the bombing campaign and the mining of harbours in 1972. Below: As Nixon began to withdraw US troops from Vietnam, so the responsibility for continuing the war fell on the South Vietnamese. Under the policy of Vietnamization their armed forces were fully equipped with American weapons, including M16s, M-26 hand grenades and radio equipment. But US kit alone could not make up for poor leadership, sagging morale and lack of technical expertise.

– including such measures as the mining of Haiphong harbour in May as part of the new policy.

In October, with the Northern offensive completely stalled, Nixon called a halt, but from 18 December 1972, to try to force the North Vietnamese to make concessions at the peace talks, US planes (including, for the first time, B-52 bombers) hit Hanoi and Haiphong, with devastating effect, in an 11-day assault known as 'Linebacker II'. The scene was now set for the successful negotiations that would end US involvement. Nixon had demonstrated to the US public that he was still a tough politician, willing to hit the communists hard, while for their part the communists had achieved many of their aims, in that NVA troops were now well established on South Vietnamese soil, giving them a useful springboard for any future offensives. The South Vietnamese government of President Nguyen Van Thieu was unhappy at the agreement that was signed in

Paris in January 1973; but he was forced to accept it, and US troops were finally withdrawn from the country.

Nixon's ruthless approach to Vietnam had extended to its neighbours, Laos and Cambodia. Both these nations were to bear the full brunt of war during the early 1970s, in spite of the fact that they had done their best to keep out of the war and remain neutral during the 1960s. Laos had long been an area of US interest. The tangled politics of the country had been deemed important enough to engage the attraction of a 14-nation international commission in the early 1960s, and in 1962 the neutralist Prince Souvannaphouma was installed as prime minister of a loose coalition, a position he was to occupy until 1975. Most of the important elements in Laotian public life were in favour of neutrality, but in the north of the country a strong communist grouping, the Pathet Lao, was a constant threat, while the army and the warlords of the south were always susceptible to US pressure. US influence also made itself felt in the shape of the Central Intelligence Agency (CIA), which began a clandestine war against the Pathet Lao using Meo hill tribesmen in the north, well supplied by the CIA's own 'proprietary' airline, Air America.

THE BOMBING OF LAOS AND CAMBODIA

By the late 1960s, Laos was in the grip of a full-scale war, with regular US bombing raids over much of the east and north of the country (more tonnage of bombs was dropped on the Ho Chi Minh Trail in Laos than the USA had dropped on Japan in World War II) as Nixon's administration strove to strike at the communists with whatever means it could. But US involvement in the country ended in disaster for the US allies. Even before the US withdrawal the Meo tribesmen were driven back by the Pathet Lao with NVA support, and when the Americans withdrew completely, Souvannaphouma was forced to negotiate a compromise with the Pathet Lao. Even this was not enough to halt the fighting, however; and as communist forces took over in Vietnam in 1975, so the Laotian capital of Vientiane also fell to the Pathet Lao.

In Cambodia US intervention also had disastrous consequences for the inhabitants, and here the ultimate results of cynical, ruthless US policies were, if anything, worse. During the 1960s Cambodia was ruled by Prince Norodom Sihanouk, an autocratic but relatively popular head of state who tried to keep his country out of the fighting. Indeed,

Above: A South Vietnamese patrol looks on from a safe distance as NVA artillery bombards a village just north of Saigon during the 1972 spring offensive. Below: Camouflaged against US aerial observation, an NVA advance unit moves into a South Vietnamese town.

Top: Communist Pathet Lao guerrillas in Laos in the 1960s. While US ground forces were engaged in Vietnam, US efforts to cut the Ho Chi Minh Trail which ran through Laos inevitably led to confrontation with the Laotian communists. Above: An NVA soldier keeps an eye open for ARVN sniper movements during the final phase of the war.

Cambodia was seen as a haven of peace in war-torn Southeast Asia. Sihanouk was forced to accept the use of his country by the communists, but did his best to limit their encroachments. From 1968 onwards, there was a series of US air raids on suspected communist assembly zones in the country – raids carried out with the utmost secrecy. In March 1970 Sihanouk went to Moscow, apparently to ask the Russians to persuade the North Vietnamese to make less use of Cambodia, and during his absence there was a US-sponsored coup, which installed General Lon Nol as prime minister. The Cambodian Army was rapidly expanded from 40,000 to 200,000 men, and in April and May 1970 the ARVN, with US close support, launched assaults into two salients of Cambodian soil jutting into South Vietnam, the so-called 'Parrot's Beak' and 'Fish Hook'.

The new regime was quite unable to control the country, however, and the communist Khmer Rouge rapidly built up control of the countryside. By January 1974 they had begun to besiege the capital, Phnom Penh, and Lon Nol looked in vain to his US sponsors for the massive aid that would have been necessary to drive them back. In April 1975 the city fell to the communist forces, which inaugurated a regime of awesome terror after their takeover. Here, as in Laos, US policy had failed utterly.

Whatever the unfortunate consequences of his policy for South Vietnam's neighbours, by 1973 President Nixon had managed to extricate his troops from South Vietnam, had brought US prisoners home, and had done so without surrendering South Vietnam to the communists. The agreements of January 1973 had, however, provided for the forces within South Vietnam to maintain the positions they held at the time of the truce. This placed substantial NVA units within South Vietnam, conveniently located for any future offensive. Of course, the USA had guaranteed the South Vietnamese government that any communist attacks would at once be met, as they had been in 1972, by the full might of US air power, but the South Vietnamese, and the communists, had good reason to suspect that this would not be the case. The Vietnam War had been the single most divisive issue in US politics since 1945, and any president who risked recommitting US forces to the country would be taking a grave chance with his political future. After 1974, also, the Watergate scandal, and the revelations about the true nature of the last years of the war (the bombing of Cambodia for example), made Vietnam an even more difficult subject for any administration to deal with. In 1974, Congress summarily cut military aid to South Vietnam from 1.6 billion to 700 million dollars. It began to look as if South Vietnam would have to stand alone.

Unfortunately, South Vietnam was in a very weak position. Her armed forces had been dependent on US close support, and were unreliable without such help, and as US aid was cut, stockpiles fell. Some ammunition dumps were at less than 20 per cent of their 1972 levels by the beginning of 1975. Desertion from the ARVN was estimated at 120,000 men a year, while the mass of US aid in the 1960s and early 1970s had helped to encourage corruption, which rapidly became endemic in the armed forces.

Above: A US Boeing B-52 unleashes its massive bombload. During the war the US dropped some 6.3 million tonnes of bombs over Indochina, more than three times the total amount dropped during the whole of World War II.

The NVA struck again in March 1975, attacking in the north and through the Central Highlands at Ban Me Thuot. The fall of Ban Me Thuot convinced South Vietnam's President Thieu that he needed to regroup his forces to avoid the country being split in two, but the retreat dissolved into chaos in the Central Highlands, while in the north the ARVN collapsed. The communists at once took the opportunity to apply maximum force. Troops poured through the Central Highlands towards Saigon, which fell on 30 April. Amid scenes of anguish and chaos, the Americans evacuated the city, in a fitting end to a disastrous military and political involvement.

AND THE WAR DRAGS ON

The success of the communist armies in Southeast Asia in 1975 (in April the capitals of South Vietnam and Cambodia fell to communist forces, and by December Laos had a communist government) did not end the fighting in the region. Indeed, conflict has carried on almost unabated to the present day.

Initially, this continuing conflict was internal. Hill tribesmen in Laos and Vietnam proved as unsusceptible to communist rule as they had to that of the previous regimes, while within newly conquered South Vietnam and also in Cambodia (renamed Kampuchea), there was considerable resentment at the way that the new regimes were imposing themselves. In Vietnam, hundreds of thousands were placed in re-education camps, and discrimination against the large Chinese minority (and also against religious sects such as the Cao Dai and Hoa Hoa) led to many refugees fleeing the country; it is estimated that by 1979 675,000 people had gone.

In Kampuchea the problems that followed the Khmer Rouge takeover were even worse. Almost four million Cambodians were forcibly resettled, many being moved out of the towns into the countryside, and this led directly to the disruption of the harvests upon which the country's economy was based. By January 1977, an estimated 1,400,000 had died, either through starvation or through brutal government attempts to change the nature of Cambodian society.

These internal tensions rapidly spilled over into international conflict. The Vietnamese minority in Kampuchea was particularly badly treated and relations between Kampuchea and Vietnam rapidly deteriorated. Cambodia's ruler Pol Pot initiated incursions into Vietnam, but by December 1978 the Vietnamese had begun a full-scale invasion of their neighbour. In January 1979 the capital, Phnom Penh, fell, and they installed a client regime. Guerrilla war continued in the countryside, however, and although the guerrillas have never looked like defeating the Vietnamese Army, they have caused it severe problems. Acting from near the Thai border they have also created another international problem that has occasionally threatened to pit Vietnamese forces against the Thai Army, as Vietnam has claimed the right of 'hot pursuit' over the border. This unresolved war has so far cost probably over 30,000 casualties to the armed forces of each side.

The war in Kampuchea was instrumental in bringing China into the fray. The Chinese had been very unhappy at Vietnamese treatment of the Chinese minority in Vietnam, and from the summer of 1978 had stopped aid to the government there. This had made the Vietnamese even more dependent upon Soviet help, further cooling relations between Hanoi and Peking. In February 1979, in order to deliver a short sharp shock to the Vietnamese communists, who had just invaded Kampuchea, the Chinese mounted a punitive assault across the northern border of Vietnam, took the town of Lang Son, and withdrew in March. The Vietnamese had proved a difficult foe, however, and the Chinese found the going hard. Vietnamese and Chinese casualties were around 20,000 each.

In the 1980s there is, therefore, a seemingly unending guerrilla war in Kampuchea, while the Chinese and the Vietnamese confront each other across a fortified border. The prospects for long-term peace in the region do not look promising.

THE SOVIET INTERVENTION IN AFGHANISTAN

On Christmas Eve 1979, the Soviet Union sent its forces into the Afghan capital of Kabul. An airborne division began securing Bagram military airport, and Soviet advisors disarmed many Afghan units, telling them that they would be re-equipped with new Soviet weapons. Within three days, the prime minister of Afghanistan had been assassinated and a Soviet protégé installed in his place; Soviet divisions were moving over the borders, while Soviet armoured personnel carriers and tanks were rumbling through the capital.

The commitment of Soviet forces to Afghanistan is the only time that the Soviet Union has used its troops outside the communist bloc since World War II. It called down a torrent of international condemnation and an extensive boycott (organized by US President Jimmy Carter) of the 1980 Olympic Games held in Moscow. It also landed the Russians with a bitter guerrilla war against hill people who had centuries of experience at fighting off unwelcome central authority.

The Soviet decision to intervene was probably not taken lightly, but the Russians felt they had to do something about a difficult situation in this primitive country on their southern border. Ever since 1953, when Mohammed Daoud Khan, a cousin of the king, had taken over effective authority, Afghanistan had been in receipt of considerable Soviet aid. In 1978, two left-wing parties, the Khalq and Parcham (named after their respective newspapers) had taken over, and moved the country even closer to the Soviet orbit. The new president, Mohammed Takriti, introduced a series of sweeping reforms, including the emancipation of women and the redistribution of land. The programme was accelerated after March 1979 when Hafizullah Amin became prime

Below: A Soviet Mil Mi-24 Hind gunship patrols the skies over Afghanistan. While armoured units (below left) have been confined to the sparse road network, helicopters have proved invaluable in anti-guerrilla operations.

Above: Proud and defiant, a group of Afghan mujahidin display their weapons for the benefit of a Western photographer. Although the Afghanis are known to use copies of the Lee Enfield rifle turned out in primitive local workshops, by far the most reliable weapons at their disposal are those captured from the Soviet occupation forces or the Afghan regular army. The guerrilla on the left is carrying a folding-stock AKM while the other two are equipped with the veteran AK47.

minister. The results of the reform programme in a deeply conservative, religious society were perhaps predictable. Revolt broke out, and the government replied with wide-scale repression. The situation soon threatened to get out of hand, and the Soviet Union tried to persuade the regime to slow down, to temporize. Takriti himself may have agreed to put the brakes on the process of modernization, but Amin did not, and in September 1979 Takriti was murdered in a coup.

By now the Soviet Union was thoroughly alarmed. The religious ferment in Iran under the Ayatollah Khomeini, coupled with an Islamic revolt in a regime to which the Russians were closely tied, was creating a band of instability along the borders of the three Soviet Islamic republics (Khazakstan, Uzbekhistan and Turkestan) and the dangerous religious fundamentalism might spread. Nor could the Russians afford to have a regime closely associated with them collapse in Afghanistan. So the decision was taken to introduce Soviet troops to Kabul, to force a change of policy.

The invasion came as a surprise. The troops used were not first-line divisions, but ones from the Central Asian Republics themselves, so that little shuffling of formations was necessary. The Soviet advisors in Afghanistan (an estimated 4000 in 1979) were able to give precise information concerning the best timing and targets of the intervention, and they were able, because of their influence within the Afghan Army, to prevent any coordinated opposition to the move emerging. The only problem was that although the 105th Guards Airborne Division was able to take over Kabul with little difficulty, the prime minister, Amin, refused to cooperate. He was killed, and Babrak Kamal installed in his place. All chance of presenting the invasion as 'aid' to a friendly regime had now vanished.

The takeover continued smoothly enough in January 1980, as four motor rifle divisions (soon followed by two more) crossed the frontier, one column moving through Herat in the west of the country and the other coming down from Termez; Kamal released political prisoners and tried to create a

Above: A Soviet encampment on the outskirts of Kabul. Although the Soviets have committed a great deal of manpower and hardware to the war, the mujahidin's *classic guerrilla hit-and-run tactics have made them impossible to defeat. Below: A monument to the Afghans' fighting skill and determination – a downed Soviet helicopter.*

climate in which tranquillity could be restored. An estimated 80,000 Soviet troops were in the country, and although the Afghan Army had all but dissolved (some authorities put desertion as about 50 per cent during January 1980), the Russians seemed in control. But in the main towns, there was still resistance, in the form of the *shabnama* (night leaflets) that called for action, and in the hills, the tribes were still unreconciled to an atheistic Marxist regime. In February there was a general strike in Kabul. Crowds were fired on by Soviet and Afghan government troops, and demonstrations carried on until the summer.

Meanwhile, guerrilla activity in the mountains began to increase. The *mujahidin* (warriors of God) were soon sniping at Soviet convoys, raiding into the towns, and generally making life unpleasant for the Russians. The occupiers concentrated on securing the main towns and the most important roads, from which they made sweeps using armour (where possible) and helicopters, especially the Mil Mi-24 Hind gunship, against hostile villages. The main areas of insurgency were the provinces of Paktia, Nangahar and Nuristan in the east, Hazarajat in the centre of the country, and around Herat in the west.

AMBUSHES AND AIRLIFTS

The Soviet forces gradually began to realize that the tactics and training they had developed to deal with large-scale conventional operations in Europe, or along the border with China, were not applicable to the kind of war they were fighting in Afghanistan, and they soon found that over-reliance on roads made them very vulnerable to ambush. A convoy of 120 vehicles, for example, was destroyed in the Panjshir region in 1981 – many of its personnel were airlifted out, but the hardware was abandoned.

The answers that the Soviet commanders came up with were increased use of helicopters, especially in the deployment of heliborne air assault brigades, and concen-

tration on making life unpleasant for the civilian population in areas of guerrilla activity, notably by the use of chemical weapons and almost indiscriminate raids on villages. In this deployment of their resources, their activities bore some resemblance to the US methods in Vietnam. Instead of pushing blindly into rebel areas, convoys would be guarded by units air-lifted onto the heights controlling the roads, and attempts were made to deploy infantry more flexibly, without the cover of the heavy armament of their transport vehicles.

In their turn, the guerrillas managed to improve their tactics, and to establish a more settled organization, notably in the Panjshir valley, where a regional group under Ahmad Massoud had a relatively well-trained force of some 3000 men by 1982. US sources have estimated that there were 90,000 guerrillas able to go into action – the Afghans themselves claimed 120,000. Their main problem was the lack of anti-aircraft weapons. The supply of SAM-7s dried up when the Afghan regular army was deprived of these systems and few have come from foreign sources.

Neither side has the resources to bring what has become a vicious guerrilla war to a definite conclusion. The Russians have so far not deployed sufficient troops to make a thoroughgoing attempt to defeat the *mujahidin* in their mountain strongholds (the

Soviet spring offensive of 1984 in the Panjshir valley had few lasting effects, for example), while the guerrillas do not have the weapons or a sufficiently strong backer to make the country too hot for the Soviet forces to hold. But the war soon developed all the ugly characteristics of such struggles. The Russians attack civilian villages; the guerillas use terror and mutilate their prisoners. For Soviet soldiers Afghanistan must be a most unwelcome posting, while for the Afghans the Russians are a most unwelcome presence. Casualties are difficult to estimate for the Soviet Army; they probably run at over 5000 per year, while the guerrillas must suffer at least as many.

Above: A small unit of Afghani guerrillas prepares to ambush a passing Soviet convoy. Below: Making up for their deficiencies of equipment by their intimate knowledge of the mountains and valleys of their Afghan homeland, the guerrillas proved to be far more resourceful opponents than the Russians had bargained for.

Part Seven
Guerrilla Wars

Guerrilla warfare has been by far the most prevalent form of armed conflict since 1945, and, indeed, might well be taken as characterizing the period. For if the typical fighting of World War II was undertaken by a massive army, with heavy aerial or armoured support, then the typical warrior since 1945 has been the lightly armed insurgent, freedom fighter, or terrorist (such descriptions depend upon one's political persuasion and which side the guerrilla is on) opposed by a regular army or police force whose job is to contain the guerrillas, using the minimum force necessary.

The word 'guerrilla' is the Spanish for 'little war', and describes perfectly the small-scale raids and ambushes Spanish irregulars carried out against the armies of the French in the period 1808–14; it also describes the activities of the Boer 'commandos' against the British during the last years of the Boer War (1899–1902). What these insurgents had in common was that they were part of the general population, and could return to civilian occupations as soon as they had carried out their raids, or relied on the civilian population to shelter them and provide supplies. Similar activities were carried out by the Resistance groups in World War II. They too relied on a large network of civilian sympathizers to underpin the actions of small bands of armed men, who, with their intimate knowledge of local conditions, made things difficult for occupying forces.

Since 1945, this method of warfare has become the common currency of revolutionary political groups, struggling to change a system of government or throw off foreign domination. This proliferation had been quite unforeseen by conventional military authorities in 1945, but was the result of three separate factors that came together in the late 1940s. The first of these was the success of Mao Tse-tung in China. Mao's success (examined on pp. 152–7) was largely achieved by the application of a set of theories about how the peasantry could be mobilized as the basis of a revolution. Mao envisaged three stages: first the establish-ment of 'safe base areas' where the revolutionary army and party (for the two were indivisible) could develop and establish a close relationship with the local population; second, the harassment of government forces while the revolutionary army was built up; and third, when the government forces had been sufficiently weakened, the change to a more open, conventional war by the carefully trained revolutionary main forces. This was, of course, only a very schematic guide, but the success of Mao in China by 1949 seemed to show that it was a useful starting point.

The second background factor was that there were many groups of individuals throughout the world who were looking for a way to use force to unseat an apparently all-powerful opponent. These groups were led by the nationalist politicians in the great colonial empires – the men who found the rule of the French in Indochina, the British in Malaya, the Dutch in the East Indies, the Portuguese in Africa intolerable, and wished to shake it off, but were unable to do so in the face of the armed forces and wealth of the European powers. For them, the concepts of guerrilla warfare as propounded by Mao were irresistibly attractive. For they showed how a weaker force could use its political advantages – the mass support of the people, or the determination of its cadres – to defeat far superior armed might.

The third factor lay in the aftermath of World War II. First of all, there were many resistance groups that had experience of fighting occupying powers – attacking the Germans in Greece, making life difficult for the Japanese in Malaya and the Philippines – and these groups were able to form the core of many of the guerrilla armies that prosecuted the earliest campaigns. Then, the ideological confrontation that emerged at the end of World War II, and which in global terms became the Cold War, was a further aid to these guerrilla groups. For most of the earliest revolutions (in Greece, Malaya, the Philippines and Vietnam) were communist in inspiration, and the Soviet Union and later China were very happy to give help, in the

Above: Vo Nguyen Giap, probably the single most successful practitioner of guerrilla warfare since World War II. Giap commanded communist forces in Vietnam from 1945 onwards, and directed his troops in wars that broke the will to continue of the establishments of both France and the USA. Giap always had a flexible, pragmatic approach to guerrilla forces; he suffered defeats at various times, but always retained sufficient 'balance' in his forces to recover to win the war.

crush a form of arms and encouragement, to any groups opposed to the Western powers. Once guerrilla warfare was shown to be effective (as it proved against the French and the Americans in Vietnam) the concepts of revolutionary guerrilla warfare began to be expanded. In South America in the 1960s, Fidel Castro and Che Guevara disseminated the concept of the *foco insurreccional* a small group of men as the core of a revolution rather than being the expression of a mass movement, and the Brazilian Carlos Mari-ghela published ideas on urban guerrilla warfare, in which the revolutionaries would use the anonymity of large cities as their 'safe base' while exposing the contradictions of modern industrial society by forcing the government to take unpopular repressive measures. This theory of urban guerrilla warfare was given further importance in the 1970s when it formed the basis of the activities of many terrorist groups in Europe, and influenced the activities of, for example, the Provisional Irish Republican Army (IRA) in Northern Ireland.

SUPPRESSING GUERRILLA FORCES

Modern armed forces are designed to manipulate devastating weapons on a battlefield where the enemy can be clearly identified. The guerrilla undercuts this totally, and yet he is not susceptible to a mere police action either, for by their very nature guerrilla groups tend to be stronger than police units, and are only tangentially involved in normal criminal activities.

A major part of the training and theorizing in modern armies, especially in western Europe, has therefore had to be concerned with the problems presented by the insurgent. The French and British armies in particular, because of their long colonial campaigns, have had to formulate sophisticated strategies which in Britain are grouped under the general heading COIN (COunter-INsurgency). There are normally three aspects to COIN, and all three must work together for the formula to succeed. These are good intelligence – finding out who the guerrillas are and how they are organized, pinpointing their leaders and disrupting their communications – then, the application of strong military force to crucial areas, to show that the government cannot be intimidated and to act as both a shield against guerrilla action and a sword to be used to attack identified guerrilla bands; and finally, and perhaps most importantly, the winning over of the civilian population. For without the support of large segments of the population, the guerrilla is powerless.

The 'winning of hearts and minds' (WHAM) can be done in various ways – by the application of a series of reforms, or by the actual physical control of the population who are then shown the way in which their life can be bettered – and is normally accompanied by vigorous security measures to prevent the guerrillas terrorizing those who have given their allegiance to the government.

In itself, this has two dangers. The first is that such measures automatically involve the army in politics, for the reforms and the decisions about the treatment of civilians are intrinsically political. This can lead to serious civil–military problems – as the French found during the counter-insurgency campaign in Algeria (1954–62). The second, related, danger is that the decision to control the civilian population may actually become the beginning of a reign of terror. In several South American countries, for example – Argentina, Guatemala, Brazil and Uruguay are the most notorious cases – right-wing 'death squads' worked within the armed forces and police, and state-sponsored terrorism in the form of wholesale torture and killing.

Specific factors limit or help the guerrilla in his campaign. In totalitarian or highly regimented societies, the restrictions on personal freedom that security forces may wish to impose are easy to apply. Nations like the Soviet Union (which has actually dealt with small guerrilla wars in the Ukraine and the Baltic states) and the military dictatorships of Latin America have an advantage over more libertarian societies in this regard. Where the guerrilla has a secure base outside the country in which he is operating, or can regularly be supplied from outside, then he has a great asset. The Portuguese forces in Africa, for example, were always fighting a losing battle because the guerrillas in Angola, Mozambique and Portuguese Guinea had the support of most of black Africa.

Modern guerrilla warfare is a combination of warfare and politics, and although the actual tactics used by the guerrilla and his opponents are very different from those applied during World War II by the major armies, in a sense they are a development of that conflict. For just as in World War II the civilian became a regular target of attack, so the guerrilla draws the civilian into the very heart of the military process. This almost automatically means that insurgency is a long-drawn-out process; and by its nature – assassination, bombing, ambush – it invites retaliation and atrocity. Guerrilla warfare is the most difficult of tasks facing a conventional army, and the most difficult to approach objectively for the observer. To substantial sectors of US society, the men of the Provisional IRA are nationalist heroes; to the British they are terrorist murderers. Who is to arbitrate?

Above: Young Palestinians being instructed in arms drill. The Palestinians, forced from their homeland by Israeli victories in successive wars, have become one of the major sources of international terrorism.

Below: A guerrilla in South American hill country, in the type of terrain which favours small-scale insurgency.

THE BRITISH WARS

The British Army is probably the most experienced of all modern armed forces in dealing with guerrilla warfare, having been engaged in such campaigns from the mid-1940s to the present day. Indeed, the history of British involvement in irregular warfare goes back even further – to the 'small wars' of the 19th century, the Boer War (1899–1902) and the defence of the Northwest Frontier in India up to 1947. In most of its post-World War II campaigns the British Army has enjoyed a good deal of success, by applying methods in which the collection of intelligence and the establishment of good relations with the local population have been of utmost importance. The creation of an anti-insurgent organization in which the duties of police forces and the army itself have been carefully delineated has been crucial; and in the actual conduct of operations, procedures – cordons, searches, crowd control – have been developed that have stood the armed forces in good stead.

Just as important as the actual conduct of specific campaigns, however, has been the political context in which the campaigns have taken place. In India, for example, the British relinquished control in 1947, realizing that they could not retain the subcontinent in the face of a determined nationalist movement. This granting of independence to what had always been seen as the cornerstone of the Empire showed a realistic approach to the possibilities of maintaining imperial possessions in a changing world. The British have used the promise of ultimate independence as a potent weapon to cut the ground from under the feet of many insurgent movements, and, in general, have not been prepared to hang on to a hopeless cause. In this they contrasted strongly with the French in Algeria and the Portuguese in their African possessions, where the decisions to withdraw were only taken after political traumas in the home country.

The first of the guerrilla wars that the British had to fight had begun even before the end of World War II. This was the struggle against Jewish nationalists and terrorists in Palestine, described on pp. 244–6. The British forces found it impossible to nail an elusive foe that had the support of the vast majority of the Jewish population, and the problems were compounded by the vacillations of government policy. The British government found itself in a difficult moral dilemma. In the aftermath of the Holocaust, the sympathies of much of the world naturally lay with Jewish aspirations to create

their own homeland. On the other hand it was undeniable that the Arabs comprised the vast majority of the population of Palestine (there were 1,300,000 Arabs as opposed to about 700,000 Jews in 1946) and that their interests would have to be disregarded if the Zionists, especially the more extreme groups, had their way. In the end, the British decision to hand the problem over to the United Nations in 1947 was welcomed with relief by the British armed forces, who had been dealing with an almost impossible task. Nevertheless, Palestine had been important in that the British Army had had to learn the hard way that anti-terrorist operations needed a new set of attitudes, and a new approach.

In their next campaign, the British were far more successful. During the fight against the communist guerrillas in Malaya, both government policy and military expertise worked together well, to bring victory in a campaign that had at one stage, in 1950–51, looked as if it would get out of control.

THE MALAYAN EMERGENCY

A state of emergency was declared in Malaya in 1948; communist insurgents had begun a campaign against the government and were enjoying considerable success. The communists had been the most important resistance group in action against the Japanese during World War II, had obtained many weapons

Above: A British jungle patrol fords a river in Malaya while on an anti-terrorist sweep. In order to destroy the MRLA bases, the security forces found it necessary to push deep into the treacherous jungle regions, which covered most of the Malayan peninsula, in search of its elusive enemy. Opposite above: After the surrender of the Japanese in 1945, the British found the communist forces already well established in Malaya. Here the 4th Regiment of guerrillas parades with M1 carbines and Mk II Sten sub-machine guns in 1945.

on the Japanese surrender and would have taken over in Malaya as a whole had not British forces acted promptly on their return to the country. The communists then decided, after two years of extending their control of trades union movements and making themselves a dominant force in the Chinese community of Malaya (the Chinese comprised some 40 per cent of the Malayan population), that they would only be able to take power if they used force. Following the example of Mao in China, they set about establishing an armed force, the Malayan Races Liberation Army (MRLA).

The initial British response was to try to find insurgents in the jungle, and to bring them to battle. This approach had some success during 1948 and 1949, but although it seemed to be cutting away at the guerrillas, it was not touching the Min Yuen, a political organization at the root of the MRLA that kept the fighting men supplied with food and intelligence. During 1949, the Min Yuen was built up to a high pitch of efficiency, notably by Chin Peng, Secretary-General of the Malayan Communist Party, and in 1950 there was a whole string of terrorist incidents. At one stage there were 400 attacks a month, and in October 1951 the communists scored their greatest single success when they as-

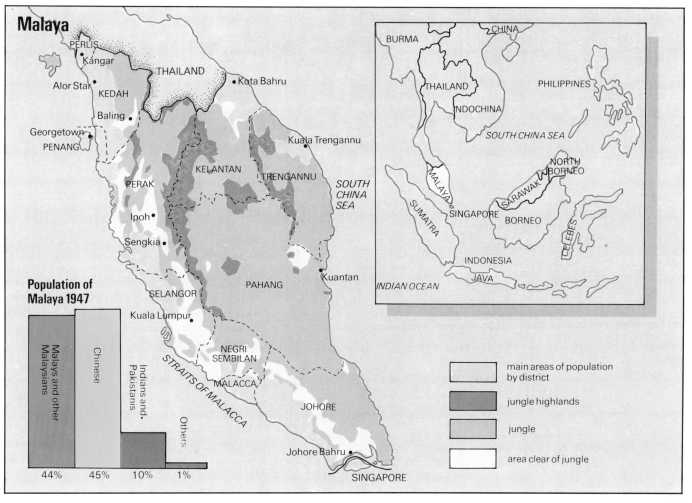

Malaya

Population of Malaya 1947

Malays and other Malaysians 44% | Chinese 45% | Indians and Pakistans 10% | Others 1%

main areas of population by district

jungle highlands

jungle

area clear of jungle

ON THE TRACK OF THE TERRORISTS

Arthur Hayward was a platoon commander in Malaya and was awarded the Military Cross after his tour of duty. Here he recalls an incident that occurred during the Emergency.

'I decided to go forward into the open to get a better view. Almost immediately I noticed footprints in the soft soil, clearly made by the rubber soles of bandit boots. I moved a little further and realized that the scattered footmarks tended to come together to form a rough pathway which led out of the clearing at the far end. Another step or two and, to my amazement,

I saw water from a puddle trickling down into what was obviously a very recently made footprint.

'We moved ahead, slithering under and crawling round broken palm fronds and dead wood and vegetation, fearful of making the slightest noise. As we advanced, the outline of the hut became clearer. I could see two men sitting inside. One was cleaning his teeth using an enamel mug, and the other was oiling his rifle. A Sten Gun was lying across the knees of the former. A little closer and I discerned, just below the hut, a third man crouched on his haunches, fully dressed and equipped and nursing a Mark V rifle. He was positioned to look

back along the track towards the clearing and was obviously a sentry.

'Slowly I raised myself to my feet, put my carbine to my shoulder and took aim at the sentry. I opened fire and the others instantly followed. There was a deafening roar as the jungle echoed back the firing of our weapons. Two of the guerrillas slumped down lifeless immediately but the sentry, my target, was thrown forward by the impact of the shots and started to crawl into the undergrowth. We lunged forward to make sure there were no others and my leading scout crashed into the undergrowth and returned to report that the sentry was also dead.'

Below: British troops in Malaya with a 25-pounder gun-howitzer. The density of the Malayan jungle was a great hindrance to the success of infantry anti-terrorist operations, and reconnaissance planes were of little help as the jungle canopy obscured any direct observation of guerrilla units on the ground. In these conditions artillery units would often lay down saturation fire on areas of jungle believed to be occupied by terrorists.

sassinated the British High Commissioner, Sir Henry Gurney.

This was also the period of communist attacks in Korea, and the great Viet Minh victories against the French along the Cao Bang ridge in Indochina, and followed hard on the heels of Mao Tse-tung's takeover in China. The Malayan communists were therefore very confident, and expected victory. They were foiled, however, by a number of factors, of which the tactics adopted by the British were an important part. For the British administration managed to find just the right mix of measures – controlling the population while still continuing to attack the guerrillas – that is at the heart of a successful counter-insurgency campaign.

The British did enjoy some basic advantages, on which they were able to

capitalize. The MRLA, for example, could expect no help from outside Malaya (unlike the Viet Minh, who received aid from China) and, in spite of its title, the MRLA was very much based upon one racial group, the Chinese, who were generally disliked by the Malays, who comprised the largest racial group in the population.

The man to capitalize on these advantages, and who worked out the scheme which was the core of the successful British response, was Sir Harold Briggs, who served as Director of Operations from April 1950 to December 1951. Briggs's theory was that the guerrilla bands in the jungle would 'wither on the vine' if they could be cut off from supplies and recruits provided by the Min Yuen, and he correctly identified the main operating ground of the Min Yuen as the half million or so Chinese squatters who lived in makeshift settlements throughout Malaya. His solution was to resettle these squatters in 'New Villages', where they could be brought under direct supervision, forbidden to leave at night, and also provided with the benefits of medical care and education that would persuade them to give a degree of allegiance to the administration. This was only half the answer, however; the security forces themselves also had to have a more effective way of striking at the communists than the rather hopeful sweeps of areas of jungle that they were using when Briggs arrived. He decided that it was essential for the functions of police and army to be more rigidly defined. The police would concentrate on gathering intelligence while the army would act on the intelligence so gained. This did not imply the separation of police and army, however; indeed, Briggs wanted personnel of both forces to share offices where possible.

The concentration on intelligence gathering and the policy of establishing the New Villages bore fruit under General Sir Gerald

Templer, who replaced Gurney as High Commissioner and combined this post with that of Director of Operations. Templer was an energetic and forceful director of the anti-communist drive. When he arrived in Malaya, morale was at a low ebb following the assassination of Gurney; when he left in 1954, Briggs's plans were all working well and the communist forces were in no condition to succeed. They were steadily hunted down and although the Emergency was not officially ended until 1960, the work of clearing the insurgents from jungle strongholds (impressive though it was) was no more than mopping-up. The real victory had been won in the early 1950s, in destroying the Min Yuen as an organization capable of supporting an insurgency, by a combination of controlling the Chinese population and concentrating on intelligence as the basis of security force operations.

MAU MAU

British methods of counter-insurgency had similar successes in Kenya, during the Emergency there from 1952 to 1960. The Emergency was proclaimed as a result of the activities of the Mau Mau, an underground organization among the Kikuyu, the dominant tribe in the country who inhabited the area just north of the capital, Nairobi. The roots of Mau Mau are not hard to discern. There was growing disaffection among the Kikuyu with labour they had to perform on the large white-owned farms; in the Kikuyu area itself, population growth had created enormous pressure on the land, and standards of living were declining rapidly (while the white settlers were becoming ever more prosperous); and the return of black soldiers who had fought in World War II provided a reservoir of individuals with wider aspirations than had previously existed among the Kikuyu.

The actual organization and aims of Mau Mau are, however, difficult to describe, even with hindsight. In many ways, the events of the period seemed more like a civil war among the Kikuyu than a full-scale nationalist revolt, and the oathing ceremonies that new recruits had to undergo together with the revolting mutilation of bodies of Mau Mau victims seemed a perversion of certain Kikuyu customs rather than politically orientated tactics. Indeed, the father of Kenyan nationalism, Jomo Kenyatta, always denied that he and the other leading nationalists were directly connected with Mau Mau.

Even so, the early disturbances among the Kikuyu were met by imprisoning Kenyatta and other leaders of the main nationalist body, the Kenya African Union, but this did not seem to have a significant effect on the troubles. In 1953, the two biggest incidents of

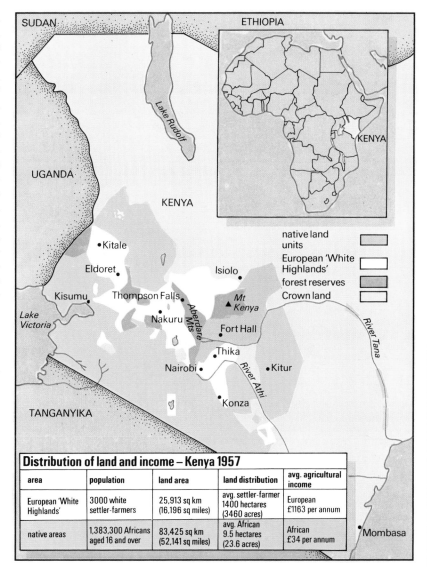

Distribution of land and income – Kenya 1957				
area	population	land area	land distribution	avg. agricultural income
European 'White Highlands'	3000 white settler-farmers	25,913 sq km (16,196 sq miles)	avg. settler-farmer 1400 hectares (3460 acres)	European £1163 per annum
native areas	1,383,300 Africans aged 16 and over	83,425 sq km (52,141 sq miles)	avg. African 9.5 hectares (23.6 acres)	African £34 per annum

the Emergency took place, when terrorists attacked the police station at Naivasha on 26 March, and massacred 100 Kikuyu at Lari on the same day.

In June 1953, General Sir George Erskine arrived to take up his appointment as commander of the security forces, including the army and the police. The main problem he faced was that whereas in Malaya the police had rapidly become a very effective force, working closely with the army, in Kenya this proved harder to achieve. As the Emergency had assumed the nature of civil war among the Kikuyu, attempts to use the Kikuyu Home Guard as a source of security and intelligence were fraught with difficulties, and complaints that the Home Guard abused its powers were frequent. In addition, the white settlers, who ran the existing civil police, generally wanted a harder line taken with the insurgents, and were not always easy to work with.

As in Malaya, the British realized that the key to defeating the armed gangs who operated in the forests of the Aberdares and Mount Kenya was to destroy their support

Above: Jomo Kenyatta, an early leader of the Kenyan nationalist movement who later became president. His involvement in, or responsibility for, Mau Mau atrocities has never been effectively investigated.

network in the Kikuyu reserves and in Nairobi. In April 1954 an enormous cordon was set up round the African section of Nairobi, and, in Operation Anvil, the army and the police combed the area thoroughly. Over 16,000 individuals were detained. From then on the active members of Mau Mau found their main source of supplies closed to them while careful questioning of the detainees yielded valuable information. Meanwhile, in the Kikuyu reserve a policy of concentrating the population in villages was beginning to bear fruit. Large numbers of potential Mau Mau members were detained; almost 80,000 individuals were held in captivity during the Emergency.

Once the groundwork had been laid, the security forces could begin the task of attacking the guerrillas themselves, in the mountain strongholds of the Aberdares and the White Highlands. Operations here – 'Hammer' and 'First Flute' – began in earnest early in 1955. The first sweeps were not very successful, but by 1956 the number of active terrorists had been reduced to 2000, whereas in 1953 there were probably 12,000 operating. To catch these elusive smaller groups, much use was made of 'pseudo-gangs', former Mau Mau members or loyal Kikuyu led by British officers or NCOs who posed as real terrorists and tried to trap the guerrillas in the jungle. In an encounter with one such group, in October 1956, the main surviving leader of the movement, Dedan Kimathi, was wounded, and later killed by a tribal policeman. This in effect ended any possibility that Mau Mau could recover lost ground, and in November the army was removed from oper-

ations. The Emergency was kept in force until 1960, mainly to allow for continued control of the Kikuyu population.

Over 10,000 members of Mau Mau were killed during the episode, and over 600 members of the security forces. Approximately 2000 civilians (of whom only 32 were Europeans) had been murdered by the insurgents.

CYPRUS

Cyprus presented the British security forces with a set of problems very different from those of Kenya and Malaya, and although the activities of terrorists were seriously

Above left: A member of the Kenyan security forces examines a suspect's armpit for the secret tell-tale markings of the Mau-Mau initiation ceremony.

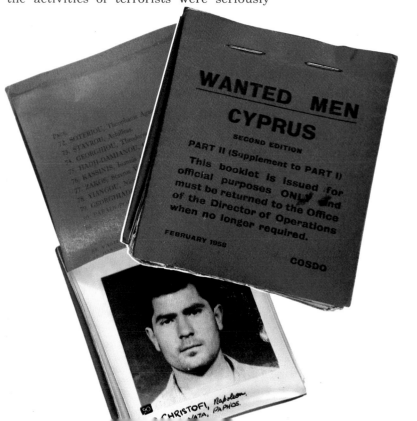

enosis, and ever since the early 1950s, the head of the Greek Orthodox church in Cyprus, Archbishop Makarios, had been leading a movement devoted to this end. He had discussed plans for a military campaign (if necessary) with a former Greek army officer, George Grivas, who had led right-wing irregulars in Greece during the mid-1940s. On a visit to Cyprus in 1953, Grivas had helped set up EOKA (*Ethniki Organosis Kuprion Agoniston* – National Organization of Cypriot Fighters).

In 1954, Britain and the USA persuaded the United Nations not to pass a resolution on the Cyprus question – Britain wished to retain her bases there. This made the Greek nationalists even more determined to undertake military action, and on 31 March 1955 a series of bombs exploded in the island. Over the next four years, despite a short-lived ceasefire in March 1957, there was a constant terrorist offensive against the British.

EOKA was always a very small organization, numbering no more than 300 full-time fighters in 1956, and British methods of countering the guerrillas in the Troodos mountains of the island were often very successful – Operations Pepperpot and Lucky Alphonse in May and June of 1956 respectively were very damaging to Grivas's force. But the basic British problem was that they could never secure the good intelligence necessary to cut through to the movement in the towns. Field Marshal Sir John Harding, who took over as Director of Operations and Governor from October 1955, implemented an organization that linked the police and the army, rather as Templer had done in Malaya, but the value of intelligence gained from the Greek Cypriot community was not high. Selective assassination of policemen by Grivas's ruthless terror squads kept morale low, and although great attempts were made to improve results, notably under Geoffrey White, Commissioner of Police from 1956, the fine edge of intelligence work that had been notable in Malaya was lacking.

Not that the British neglected to apply other lessons that they had learnt in previous insurgencies. Grivas and his men were kept constantly on the run, and by the ceasefire of 1957 the most important leaders of the revolt, with the exception of Grivas himself, had been captured or killed. The terrorists made extensive use of bombs in their campaign – some 1750 were activated during the Emergency – but were unable to undertake any large-scale actions. Nevertheless, by 1959 the British had realized that holding on to Cyprus was not possible, and the agreement in February of that year established an independent state – although not *enosis,* which was fiercely resisted by the Turkish Cypriots, backed by the formidable threat of military action by the Turkish government.

Above: British troops patrol the streets of Nicosia following the imposition of a curfew on the town in October 1956. Below: Suspects are searched for bombs and concealed weapons. To aid the security forces in their task of catching the Cypriot terrorists, photo identification booklets (below left) were issued to troops on patrol.

curtailed, the basic hold of the insurgents over large parts of the population was never broken – nor seemed likely to be. An Emergency was proclaimed in Cyprus in November 1955, and from then until agreement was reached in February 1959, there was an active anti-British guerrilla force, EOKA, in existence on the island.

The population of Cyprus in 1955 was 520,000, of whom 80 per cent were of Greek origin, and 18 per cent Turkish. Between the two communities there was always a latent hostility, which on occasion broke out into rioting in the tense years of the Emergency. The Greeks favoured a union with Greece,

Britain maintained its base areas, but 100 members of the security forces had been killed, together with over 50 terrorists.

THE FIGHT FOR ADEN

In December 1963 a grenade was thrown at the High Commissioner to the South Arabian Federation, Sir Kennedy Trevaskis, as he was boarding an aircraft. Sir Kennedy was wounded, and two people, including his assistant George Henderson, were killed. Thus began a series of terrorist attacks that only ended in November 1967, when British troops withdrew from Aden.

Aden is not a campaign that the British Army remembers with any affection. For although the troops acquitted themselves well, they were in an almost impossible situation, and the balance of power lay on the side of their opponents, radical Arab nationalists, the two most important groups being the Marxist NLF (National Liberation Front) and FLOSY (Front for the Liberation of Occupied South Yemen). The fact that these two groups, in spite of having worked together in 1966, detested each other (in 1967 they took to the streets in a naked battle for power) should have made the British task easier; but in fact, it was a measure of British weakness that even this advantage made no difference to their ability to re-establish control.

The Federation of South Arabia that the British had tried to create in the 1950s, and to which Aden was joined in 1963, was an

anomalous political body, consisting as it did of the small sheikhdoms of the poor hinterland yoked to the far more advanced and prosperous port of Aden itself. The Adenis disliked the union, and many of them were in any case swayed by the ideas of radical Arab nationalism that were sweeping the Middle East in the 1960s. There was, therefore, a basic level of hostility to the British presence even before any other factors intervened.

In 1962, there was a coup in the Yemen, the state to the northwest of the Federation, where radical army officers took over from the conservative regime of the Imams (religious leaders) who had ruled there for centuries. Civil war broke out, and Egypt, the fount of Arab nationalism, sent in troops to

Above: Moving in single file, a British Army unit patrols the arid countryside of Aden. Although most of the insurgency was centred on the town of Aden itself, the operations in the Radfan were some of the most gruelling experienced by the British Army in the postwar period.

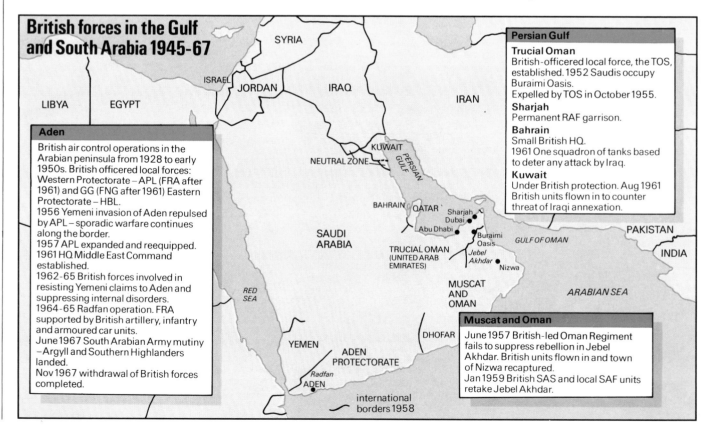

British forces in the Gulf and South Arabia 1945-67

Aden

British air control operations in the Arabian peninsula from 1928 to early 1950s. British officered local forces: Western Protectorate – APL (FRA after 1961) and GG (FNG after 1961) Eastern Protectorate – HBL.
1956 Yemeni invasion of Aden repulsed by APL – sporadic warfare continues along the border.
1957 APL expanded and reequipped.
1961 HQ Middle East Command established.
1962-65 British forces involved in resisting Yemeni claims to Aden and suppressing internal disorders.
1964-65 Radfan operation. FRA supported by British artillery, infantry and armoured car units.
June 1967 South Arabian Army mutiny –Argyll and Southern Highlanders landed.
Nov 1967 withdrawal of British forces completed.

Persian Gulf

Trucial Oman
British-officered local force, the TOS, established. 1952 Saudis occupy Buraimi Oasis.
Expelled by TOS in October 1955.
Sharjah
Permanent RAF garrison.
Bahrain
Small British HQ.
1961 One squadron of tanks based to deter any attack by Iraq.
Kuwait
Under British protection. Aug 1961 British units flown in to counter threat of Iraqi annexation.

Muscat and Oman

June 1957 British-led Oman Regiment fails to suppress rebellion in Jebel Akhdar. British units flown in and town of Nizwa recaptured.
Jan 1959 British SAS and local SAF units retake Jebel Akhdar.

international borders 1958

Above: Accompanied by a Ferret armoured car a patrol of Argyll and Sutherland Highlanders moves cautiously through the streets of the Crater district of Aden, keeping a careful eye on the rooftops in case of sniper attack. Right: 'Mad Mitch', Lieutenant-Colonel Colin Mitchell of the Argylls, takes the wheel of a Land Rover. Typical of Mitchell's tough and no-nonsense approach was his warning to the Arab chief of police in Crater that his command would be wiped out by the 'wild hillmen' of the Argylls unless his men surrendered at once.

aid the republicans. Yemen had always claimed control over the area of the Federation, and the Egyptians and Yemeni radicals were only too happy to encourage armed resistance to the British presence there. This encouragement, and the provision of arms and a safe refuge were of utmost importance in the development of insurgency around Aden.

To add to these factors, the policy of the British government itself dealt a bodyblow to the security forces. For in 1964, Conservative Prime Minister Alec Douglas Home announced that the British would grant independence to the Federation by 1968, only retaining forces in the base areas of Aden itself, and the harmful results of this were compounded in 1966 (as far as the army was concerned) by the decision of the Labour government of Harold Wilson that the base itself would be abandoned in 1968. The prospect of no continuing British military presence as protection against determined, well-armed terrorists with a powerful ally on the northwest border made the Federation's prospects of survival very slim indeed. Most important, from the army's point of view, it meant that very few Adenis were willing to provide the help and information that was required if the terrorists were to be eliminated.

The small change of the fighting in Aden was like that of all such small-scale counter-insurgencies. The guerrillas would attempt to snipe at British patrols, and would lay bombs to trap British servicemen and their families; a grenade was even thrown at a party of British schoolchildren. Sometimes, riots would be deliberately planned with the aim of drawing British troops within range of snipers. For their part, the British soldiers had to carry out an unending round of checks and cordons, hoping to glean some useful information that would lead to insurgent cells; for the basic intelligence-gathering machine of the police was ineffective. Until 1965, there were ten agencies whose tasks

included the collating and gathering of intelligence, and though they were then united under a single head, terrorist pressure, the knowledge of impending British withdrawal and the basic unpopularity of the British presence all told against the army.

The hopelessness of the army's task is perhaps best illustrated by the fact that the Chief Minister of Aden under the Federation, Abdul Mackawee, was certainly in sympathy with the essential aims of the guerrillas, and, with the support of the majority of the members of the Legislative Council, he obstructed many of the measures designed to improve security, until his dismissal in September 1965. In June 1967, during the aftermath of the Six-Day War between Israel and her Arab neighbours, when feelings were running very high, various of the forces of the Federation, both police and army units, mutinied and killed British troops before they were brought under control.

With no popular support, no effective help from the existing police and security forces, and the certain knowledge that withdrawal was inevitable, the British Army could do no more than hold the ring. There were some notable feats of arms: in 1964, forces moved against dissident tribesmen (armed and encouraged by the Yemenis) in the mountains of the Radfan area and established some form of control after hard fighting, while the actions of the Argyll and Sutherland Highlanders in retaking the Crater area of Aden after a mutiny by the Aden Armed Police there in the summer of 1967 were marked by

great skill and efficiency. But as all the soldiers knew, the cause was a lost one. The Federation was doomed, and even before the last British soldier left on 29 November 1967, the NLF had defeated its rival FLOSY and was preparing to take over. A total of 57 British soldiers had died (with 651 wounded), while the insurgents had suffered casualties of 290 dead and 922 wounded, the majority in the bitter internecine fighting which took place in 1967.

CONFRONTATION WITH INDONESIA

The period of 'Confrontation' in Southeast Asia saw the British Army in a war that was never declared, or even officially admitted to exist. 'Confrontation' was the attempt by Indonesia to prevent the formation of the Federation of Malaysia, comprising Malaya, Singapore, Sarawak and Sabah, that the British had enthusiastically promoted in the early 1960s. The Indonesian President Sukarno had ambitions to extend Indonesian influence over the area, nor was the concept of federation looked on with favour by all those involved. The Sultan of Brunei, for example, the head of a small, rich state lying between Sarawak and Sabah on the island of Borneo, eventually decided that his people would remain aloof, while Prime Minister Lee Kuan Yew took Singapore out of the Federation in 1964, just one year after it was set up.

When, in 1962, the British government announced the plan to set up the Federation, there was immediate hostility from Indonesia, and Sukarno gave support to political opponents of the Sultan of Brunei (at the time it was believed that the Sultan would take his state into the Federation). In December 1962 there was a revolt in Brunei, which was put down by the prompt action of British troops flown in from Malaya. This was merely the prelude, however, to a much longer conflict.

As plans for the Federation went ahead, those opposed to it in Sarawak and Sabah were encouraged by the Indonesians. There was a large Chinese minority in Sarawak which sustained a Communist Party opposed to the scheme, while in Sabah a colony of immigrant Indonesians was also a source of opposition. In April 1963, a police station at Tebedu in Sarawak was attacked by raiders from across the border in Kalimantan (as the Indonesian part of the island of Borneo was named), and it soon became clear that Indonesia was sponsoring a policy of cross-border raids to destabilize Sarawak and Sabah, using the local inhabitants when they were prepared to help, but equally happy to send over Indonesian forces.

To meet this threat, the authorities had to rely on the five battalions of the 17th Gurkha

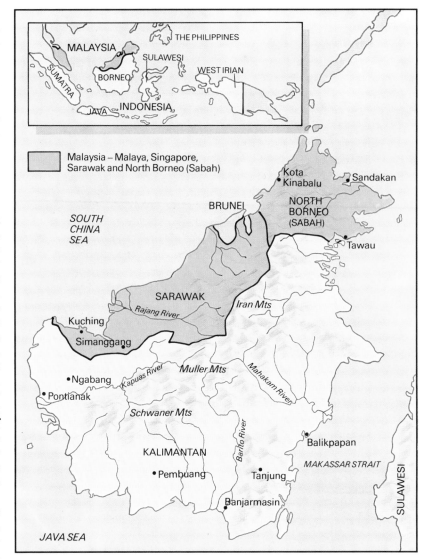

Malaysia – Malaya, Singapore, Sarawak and North Borneo (Sabah)

Division under Major-General Walter Walker. Walker's task was to defend 1560km (970 miles) of frontier which was mostly heavy jungle, against an enemy that could strike when and where it chose. Using techniques of ambush and helicopter-borne forces to give himself maximum mobility, Walker inflicted some severe blows on those groups that did infiltrate across the border; and a team of UN observers reported that a majority of the inhabitants of Sarawak and Sabah were prepared to accept the Federation, which was finally established in September 1963 – provoking further outcry from the Indonesian government and leading to the sacking of the British Embassy in Djakarta by demonstrators.

Despite the excellence of Walker's troops, the fact that the Indonesians retained the initiative was a considerable handicap to his forces. And neither the government of the Federation nor that of Britain was willing to admit that large-scale hostilities were taking place, which put Walker's troops under more pressure. In August 1964, however, the Indonesians themselves escalated the war by

Above: President Sukarno of Indonesia, who bitterly opposed the idea of a Malaysian federation and sanctioned the actions of insurgents against the British military presence in Sabah, Sarawak and Brunei. Sukarno's eventual fall from power in 1965 brought an end to the 'Confrontation'.

Above: A British artillery unit pounds enemy positions in the jungle with 105mm Model 56 Pack howitzers. Below: Police use strong measures against demonstrators in Sarawak protesting against the Federation of Malaysia.

dropping some guerrillas by parachute into the south of Malaya itself, near Singapore. Hitherto, the Confrontation had been confined to Borneo, but now it threatened to become much wider in scope. The unfortunates dropped into Malaya were soon rounded up, but their arrival persuaded the British and Malaysian governments to agree to a more aggressive attitude by their forces in Borneo. They were now allowed to operate across the border, going into Indonesian territory to a depth of 4500m (5000yd), a limit which was eventually extended to 18,000m (20,000yd) for some special operations. All actions carried out over the border were strictly controlled, and permission had to be given by the Director of Operations. Such raids were known by the codename 'Claret'; they were controlled by a separate operations room, and all were carried out in strict secrecy.

By the end of 1964, with 14,000 British, Malay, Gurkha and Commonwealth troops in operation, the Indonesians found that they were now on the receiving end. Their logistics system in the trackless wilderness of

Borneo had never been good, and the operations against their base camps sliced away at their capacity for offensive action. During 1965, their activities declined in scope, and the final blow came in October of that year, when a confused coup in Djakarta led to the army taking power and slaughtering hundreds of thousands of communists. In August 1966, a new, more pro-Western government under General Suharto signed an agreement with the Federation of Malaysia, and the Confrontation was over. It had cost the British and Commonwealth forces 114 dead, while an estimated 600 Indonesian guerrillas were killed in the fighting.

THE WAR IN DHOFAR

In Borneo the British had been defending a recently independent colony against small-scale aggression from an outside power. In the Sultanate of Muscat and Oman during the late 1960s and early 1970s they were involved in defending a friendly, dependent state against internal insurgency that was being given considerable external support.

Above: A patrol of the Trucial Oman Scouts, a unit first raised in the 1950s. British involvement in the affairs of Oman had a long history, beginning with the need to protect the sea route to India, and continuing until the exploitation of the oil of the Arabian (Persian) Gulf after World War II made the region of paramount importance. Many units of the Sultan's army were raised by the British, and commanded by British officers.

The Sultanate of Muscat and Oman (which dropped the 'Muscat' from its title after 1970), on the southeast corner of the Arabian peninsula, had always enjoyed good relations with · Britain. The importance of shoring up a friendly state was emphasized for the British because the Sultanate included the vital Musandam Peninsula, controlling the southern shores of the Strait of Hormuz, the narrow entrance to the Arabian Gulf, through which so much of the oil of the Western world has to pass. The Sultan's Armed Forces (SAF) had traditionally been equipped and partly commanded by the British, and in the late 1950s a revolt in Oman had been put down with the aid of two squadrons of the British Special Air Service (SAS). This particular British intervention had seen an epic assault on the mountain stronghold of the Jebel Akhdar in January 1959.

By the mid-1960s, trouble was brewing once more in the Sultan's domains, this time in the region of Dhofar, in the west of the Sultan's possessions, and over 1000km (600 miles) by road from Muscat. The Dhofaris were dissatisfied in particular with the extreme reactionary policies of Sultan Said bin Taimur. He had banned all aspects of modern civilization – including bicycles and spectacles – but many Dhofaris who had taken work abroad, in the northern Gulf states, had come back with some idea of the benefits that they were being denied. They had also come into contact with the radical ideas of Arab nationalism that were current in the Middle East, and formed a Dhofar Liberation Front (DLF) in 1962.

From 1965, the DLF was engaged in a small guerrilla war, in which there were a few casualties on each side. The terrain of Dhofar is ideal for guerrilla war: the craggy mountains of the interior slow the movement of conventional forces, while the coastal monsoon lasts four months in every year, encouraging the growth of tall scrub which inhibits aerial reconnaissance. The small and rather badly equipped SAF was unable to halt the revolt. But the guerrillas could hardly threaten the Sultan's rule. In November 1967, however, the British were forced out of the Federation of South Arabia, on the Sultanate's western border, and the radical Marxist regime that came into power there (calling the country the People's Democratic Republic of Yemen) was only too happy to encourage the Dhofar rebels. In 1968 the Dhofaris adopted a communist ideology and became the Popular Front for the Liberation of the Occupied Arabian Gulf (PFLOAG).

The insurgents now began to enjoy more success, having access to safe base areas and unlimited supplies of weapons from the communist bloc. In August 1969 they took the administrative centre of Rakhyut in western Dhofar, and the SAF was reduced to hanging on to its enclaves near the coast. One officer described the fighting: 'the Sultan's mud forts in the coastal villages were frequently attacked, camps were mortared almost every evening. . . . Water was very scarce, resupply became tremendously difficult, casualty evacuation was often by donkey, and apart from containing the enemy, we were certainly not winning the war.'

In 1970, however, the tide turned. Just as had happened in Malaya 20 years before, a new strategy began to be applied. In large measure this was due to the fact that the old Sultan was replaced by his son, Qaboos bin Said, who had been educated at Sandhurst and had served in the British Army. He was sympathetic to the concepts of winning over the allegiance of the Dhofaris by a policy of improving their lives rather than applying the savage vengeance that the old Sultan had meted out to the rebels. Qaboos took over after a bloodless coup in which Britain always denied any complicity, although it is clear that the new policies were those which the British advisors were keen to pursue.

The new measures were on various levels. First of all, the SAF was expanded, from 2500 men to 12,000 by the end of 1973. Specialized units of the SAS then moved into the country (officially they were described as engaged in training). There were soon 600 seconded or contract British officers effectively running the war, and they used many of the procedures which had stood the British Army in good stead in Malaya and Kenya. Desertion from the *adoo* (as the guerrillas were called) was encouraged by an amnesty for all who came over, and such deserters were organized in units of *firqat*. Although not always the most determined of fighters, the *firqat* were a useful link with the local population. A series of development projects for Dhofar was also announced, and a fortified barrier, the 'Hornbeam Line', built inland from the

coast and intended to inhibit *adoo* movement, was completed by June 1974.

The guerrillas could still mount large raids – in July 1972, for example, the government stronghold of Mirbat, held by just 10 SAS men and 100 *firqat*, was successfully defended against an assault by some 250 insurgents – but the SAF was regaining the initiative. The problem then was how to take over the guerrilla strongholds in the west of Dhofar, where the *adoo* were closest to their bases. The SAF established a base at Sarfait near the border with the People's Democratic Republic of Yemen, but this came under regular fire from across the border, and was of little use as a centre for offensive operations. Support from other states was gradually coming into the Sultanate, however. Jordan contributed troops and significant reinforcements came from Iran – from 1972 onwards the Shah sent both troops and support weapons, including helicopter gunships.

Under this mounting pressure the guerrillas gradually began to wilt. Their support among the population as a whole was declining as the development programmes began to take effect, while the Marxist ideology they espoused was not to the taste of the majority

Above: Members of the Popular Front for the Liberation of the Occupied Arabian Gulf, armed with typical weapons from the Eastern bloc (AK series assault rifles).

Below: A patrol of firqat in the hinterland. Although there were question marks against the military efficiency of these 'turned' terrorists, they represented an important strand of the counter-insurgency campaign in Dhofar.

of the population. There was now a general offensive by government forces. The SAF won important victories in November and December 1974 and Iranian forces, supported by gunships, retook Rakhyut. Government forces were now well on top. By December 1975 the Sultan had announced that the war was over, and in 1976, the last SAS personnel left. The British lost 35 dead in all.

NORTHERN IRELAND: THE CONTINUING CONFLICT

In Borneo and Dhofar, the British Army had been acting on behalf of friendly states. But its longest campaign since 1945, and one which shows no signs of being easily concluded, has taken place within the United Kingdom itself. This is the attempt to maintain peace in Northern Ireland, where both

The six counties

Map showing Northern Ireland and border regions, with locations including Ballycastle, Coleraine, Ballymoney, Limavady, Londonderry, Swatragh, Ballymena, Larne, Cookstown, Pomeroy, Lisburn, Belfast, Ballyclare, Antrim, Omagh, Dungannon, Lurgan, Portadown, Down, Enniskillen, Armagh, Banbridge, Downpatrick, Newry, and counties DONEGAL, ANTRIM, LONDONDERRY, TYRONE, FERMANAGH, LEITRIM, MONAGHAN, ARMAGH, DOWN; River Mourne, Lough Neagh, Newry Canal, IRISH SEA, REPUBLIC OF IRELAND.

and the other security forces in a constant round of debilitating controls and searches, always a target for gunmen. There have been substantial numbers of British troops there since 1970; normally well over 10,000, and reaching a maximum of 21,000 in 1972 during Operation Motorman.

The present 'troubles' in Northern Ireland really began in 1968, when the Catholic community, exasperated by the discrimination against them and the failure of the ruling body of Northern Ireland, the parliament at Stormont, to alleviate the political and social disadvantages under which they suffered, began giving mass support to NICRA (the Northern Ireland Civil Rights Association). A series of marches was organized, which were non-violent in themselves, but which drew the attention of violent Protestant groups. Early in 1969, marchers

Protestant ('Loyalist') and Catholic ('Republican') extremists, but especially the Catholic nationalists of the Provisional Irish Republican Army (IRA), have engaged in campaigns of terrorism within the province.

The conflict in Northern Ireland is the result of centuries of religious antagonism, coupled with the specific history of the modern period, especially the manner in which the separate province of Northern Ireland was established as part of the United Kingdom while the rest of Ireland became the independent state of Eire; following this partition in 1921, the Catholic minority in the North was deprived of many political and civil rights.

The scale of 'warfare' in Northern Ireland has always been small, but it has been a long campaign that has involved the British Army

Left: Armed with the standard British Army rifle, the SLR (Self-Loading Rifle, the Belgian Fabrique Nationale design), a corporal of the Parachute Regiment takes up position on a street corner in Northern Ireland. He has a light two-way radio, the earpiece of which can be seen here, and his flak jacket is constructed of several layers of the synthetic fibre material 'Kevlar'. Right: British troops come under bombardment from stones and bottles as they attempt to break up a crowd during the early 1970s.

Below left: A British officer falls to the ground as his squad comes under attack from rioters. Below: The 'H' blocks at Long Kesh, where internees were held during the early 1970s.

were attacked on the Burntollet Bridge, and the polarization of the community was demonstrated for all to see. That summer, there was widespread sectarian violence on the streets of Belfast and Londonderry, and the British Army was moved in to keep the peace. The Catholic population rejected completely the law enforcement agencies of Stormont, especially the notorious 'B'-Specials, a police auxiliary body composed totally of Protestants, and welcomed the army as a protective force.

During the next three years, however, the British Army's role gradually changed. From being a peace-keeping force between the two communities, its main task became protection against the terrorists of the Provisional IRA who had split away from the 'Official' IRA when that body (which had Marxist leanings) failed to take a lead in the defence of the Catholic community against Protestant pressure in 1969–70.

Quite apart from the activities of the Provisional IRA, there were various stages whereby the army began to lose support within the Catholic community. The Falls Road curfew in the summer of 1970, when the entire Catholic population of this area of Belfast was put under close surveillance, the introduction of internment without trial in 1971, and the events of 'Bloody Sunday' in January 1972, when British paratroops shot dead 13 Catholics in the aftermath of a march protesting against internment, were all important landmarks. By the time British troops entered the Catholic-controlled 'No Go' areas of Londonderry and Belfast during Operation Motorman in the summer of 1972, the rupture was complete.

Over the next few years, the security forces had to deal with IRA bombing campaigns against commercial targets in both Northern Ireland and the British mainland and selective attacks by the IRA on individuals prominent in public life or connected to the security forces. Meanwhile Protestant terrorist groups tried both to destroy the IRA and to scotch any attempts at a settlement that would change the status of Northern Ireland as an integral part of the United Kingdom.

By the late 1970s, the Protestant terrorists had been contained, but the problem of the IRA remained. Although the use of 'supergrasses' (members of terrorist groups who were given immunity from prosecution in return for information on the activities of other members of the organization) and more sophisticated methods of collating information on potential terrorists led to a reduction in the violence in the early 1980s, the problem

Above: An armoured demolition vehicle clears debris from the streets as British troops look on. Below: British soldiers move down a street after a car-bomb explosion.

of terrorism would not go away, and new groups, most importantly the Irish National Liberation Army (INLA), added their attacks to those of the IRA. The INLA's most notorious act was the murder of Earl Mountbatten of Burma in 1975.

The problem for the British Army has been that methods that were quite effective in other guerrilla wars are hardly applicable in Northern Ireland. In crowd-control, for example, the most telling way of dealing with rioters had always been held to be the use of marksmen to shoot the leaders of the riot. This was impossible within the British Isles – however well it may have worked in Aden. When the 13 Catholics were shot and killed on 'Bloody Sunday', there was public outrage and the effect on relations with the Catholic community was disastrous.

Nor had the army been brought in to take on a counter-insurgency role; it had gradually had to assume such a task, and there was initially little effective contact with the civil police. This led to a lack of the accurate intelligence that was essential for success – a failing highlighted by the internment fiasco. General Sir Harry Tuzo, in charge of British forces in Northern Ireland, had been unwilling to undertake the task of a sudden swoop on the Catholic community to arrest suspected members of the terrorist groups, but the decision was taken, and his men had to go in and do the job in August 1971. Not only did internment fail to deliver many of the ringleaders into the hands of the security forces, it also set the scene for a sudden escalation of the violence in the province (in 1971 before internment there had been 30 deaths in all in Northern Ireland; in the remainder of the year there were 143).

Nevertheless, in spite of the problems it has faced in Northern Ireland, it is undeniable that the British Army has adapted itself with a fair degree of success to yet another variant on the small-scale warfare that it has had to prosecute in the period since 1945. The violence has been contained within limits that permit normal life within most of the province; and this may be the farthest extent to which military means can guarantee victory. From 1970 to 1980 in Northern Ireland there were 1442 civilian deaths and 566 members of the security forces were killed. The yearly total has been declining sharply from a maximum of 467 deaths in 1972, and was only 26 in 1980. There has been less killing in the early 1980s, but the conflict goes on.

THE FRENCH WARS

The French Army was involved in two of the most savage colonial wars of the post-1945 period, those in Indochina (1946–54) and Algeria (1954–62), and suffered greatly in the process. In the case of the Algerian War the suffering was not only in terms of casualties and the human tragedy of all wars, but also in the fact that the French Army felt impelled to act politically against its own government in order to prosecute the war in the manner it thought necessary.

The French were far less ready to dismember their empire than the British. The fall of France in 1940 and the subsequent traumas of the conflicts between the Vichy regime and the Free French of de Gaulle meant that the retention of empire was seen as an essential part of the reconstruction of a strong French state after 1945. Quite apart from the bitter fighting in Indochina, there were other episodes in the 1940s that demonstrated the intentions of the French government. A revolt in Madagascar was put down with great loss of life in 1947, for example. In the 1940s, however, Africa was, in general, quiet. The main area of concern for the French lay in Asia – in the colonies that comprised French Indochina.

THE WAR AGAINST THE VIET MINH

In September 1945 Gurkha troops under the command of British Major-General Douglas Gracey repelled an attack by Vietnamese nationalists on Saigon's airport, Tan Son Nhut. This was the first fighting in a series of conflicts that have continued practically nonstop ever since, throughout what was then French Indochina, comprising the countries that are now Vietnam, Laos and Kampuchea (Cambodia).

The British troops were in Saigon to disarm Japanese prisoners and to ensure an orderly transfer of power to a new administration in the wake of World War II. During the war the Japanese had gradually taken over all Indochina, first by manipulating the French colonial administration (which after the fall of France to German forces in 1940 was in no condition to resist Japanese demands) and finally by disarming the French garrisons in the area during March 1945. At the Potsdam Conference between the Allied powers in July 1945, it had been agreed that British troops should take over in Saigon after the Japanese surrender, but that in the north of Vietnam (in the area known as Tonkin) Chinese Nationalist forces should move in to restore order.

Above: Viet Minh guerrillas man an anti-aircraft machine gun. The Viet Minh had been building up their strength in the mountains of the Viet Bac in northern Tonkin ever since 1944, and had been supplied with a certain amount of US equipment in order to help them in their campaign against the Japanese. In 1945, Vo Nguyen Giap, the military commander of the guerrillas in the Viet Bac, had taken over Hanoi hoping to establish an independent state. This set the scene for the warfare of the next 40 years, for the French were not prepared to hand over sovereignty. By the end of 1946 French troops had moved back into Hanoi, a move that was fiercely resisted by the Viet Minh, and Vietnam was plunged into war.

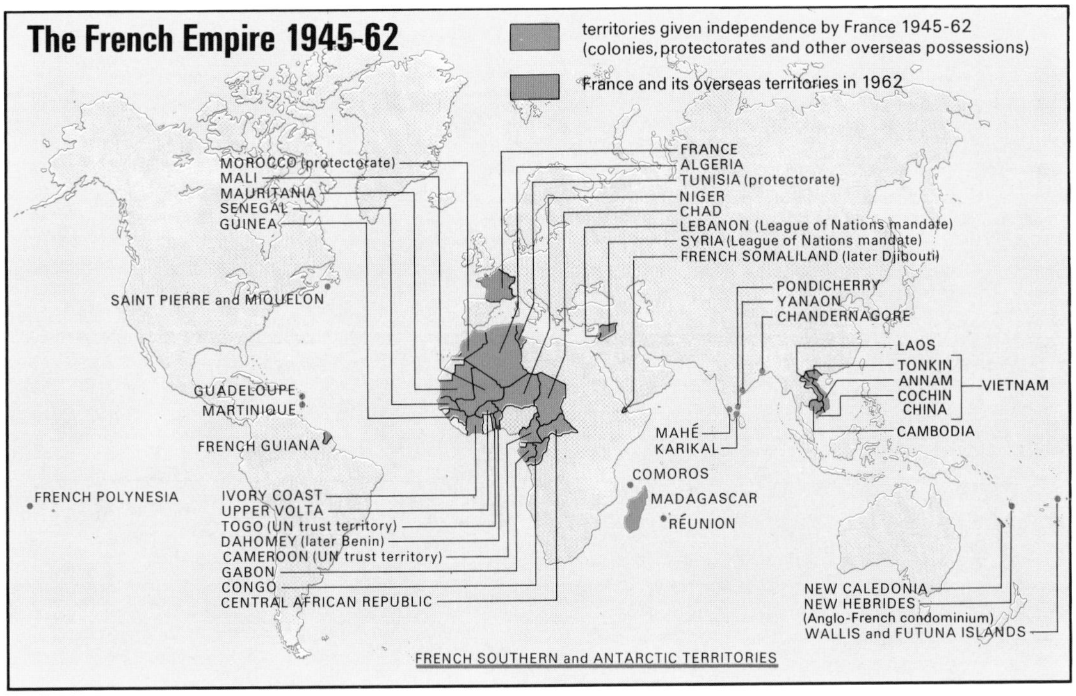

Above: Ho Chi Minh, the leader of the Viet Minh and the single most important individual in the success of the communist forces in Vietnam. Originally known as Nguyen Ai Quoc, he worked for the military governor of Kwangsi Province in southern China against the Japanese in northern Vietnam in 1943, and took the nom de guerre *Ho Chi Minh ('he who enlightens') in order to disguise the fact that he was a known communist agitator.*

The local Vietnamese nationalists had other ideas, however. Ever since 1944, there had been guerrilla groups operating in the north of Tonkin, ostensibly against the Japanese but in fact preparing to take control. The most important of these nationalist groups was the Viet Minh, a coalition of communists and other nationalists, which was soon to become dominated by the communists. Its leader was Ho Chi Minh, who had been an anti-French activist since the 1920s, and the commander of its armed forces was an ex-schoolteacher called Vo Nguyen Giap, who was an admirer of two very different military thinkers – Napoleon Bonaparte and Mao Tse-tung. From Mao, Giap had learnt the theory of revolutionary guerrilla warfare, and the stages by which a guerrilla army could defeat a seemingly superior conventional force, while from Napoleon he had taken in the basic principles of a military strategy founded upon always keeping the initiative, suddenly concentrating apparently dispersed units, and always having something in reserve. Over the next 30 years of warfare, he was never to lose sight of the precepts he had already thoroughly mastered by 1945.

RETURN OF THE FRENCH

When the Japanese surrendered in August 1945, the nationalists were ready to take over in Vietnam. Giap led his guerrilla forces into Hanoi in the north of the country, while in the south, in Saigon, a looser coalition of nationalists took over. It was these forces that the British and the Chinese had to deal with when they moved their forces in during September. The Chinese in the north were not inclined to disturb the Viet Minh's local power; they were more interested in loot, and although they had no love for the Vietnamese (there was a tradition of Sino-Vietnamese hostility stretching back 100 years) they had no particular love for the French either. In the south, however, the British actively helped the French back to power, and by January 1946 the British had handed Saigon over to them, in spite of often fierce resistance from the Viet Minh and their allies. The French also extended their control back over Cambodia and Laos, where the local royal houses, which had continued as the nominal rulers during World War II, were prepared to come to an accommodation with the colonial power.

In the north, things were very different. As the Chinese pulled out, the French were eager to replace them, while the Viet Minh were just as eager to assert total independence. Talks took place during 1946, but no real agreement was possible between parties with such divergent aims, and in December large-scale fighting broke out in Hanoi and

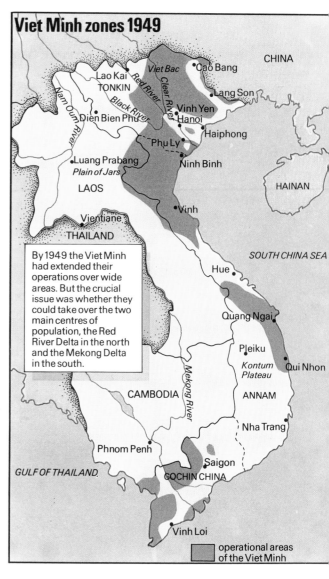

Viet Minh zones 1949

By 1949 the Viet Minh had extended their operations over wide areas. But the crucial issue was whether they could take over the two main centres of population, the Red River Delta in the north and the Mekong Delta in the south.

operational areas of the Viet Minh

the port of Haiphong as the Viet Minh attacked the returning French. The French were victorious, and drove out the communists; but this merely set the scene for eight years of war that ended in French humiliation.

The Viet Minh forces withdrew to the Viet Bac, the mountains of northern Tonkin. Here, where they had already established safe base areas in the guerrilla warfare against the Japanese, and where they enjoyed good relations with the local hill tribes, they began to put into practice Mao Tse-tung's theories of revolutionary war. The Viet Minh aimed to harass the French all over Vietnam, while building up their own regular force to a size capable of taking on the French in the open. There were three layers to Viet Minh organization. At the lowest level, all over Vietnam, and especially in the densely populated areas of the Mekong and Red River deltas they formed village militias, whose job was to undertake small-scale sabotage and intelligence work. Above this were the regional troops. They were better armed, but again their normal role was

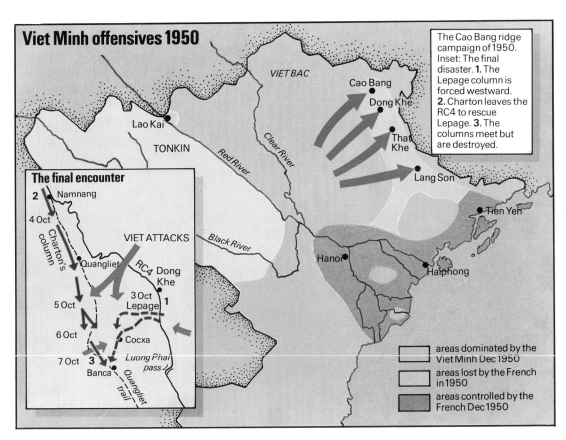

Viet Minh offensives 1950

VIET BAC

Cao Bang
Dong Khe
Lao Kai
TONKIN
Clear River
Red River
That Khe
Lang Son
Tien Yen
Black River
Hanoi
Haiphong

The Cao Bang ridge campaign of 1950. Inset: The final disaster. **1.** The Lepage column is forced westward. **2.** Charton leaves the RC4 to rescue Lepage. **3.** The columns meet but are destroyed.

The final encounter

2 Namnang
4 Oct
Charton's column
VIET ATTACKS
Quangliet
RC4 Dong Khe
5 Oct
3 Oct Lepage **1**
6 Oct
Cocxa
7 Oct **3**
Banca
Luong Phai pass
Quangliet trail

☐ areas dominated by the Viet Minh Dec 1950
☐ areas lost by the French in 1950
■ areas controlled by the French Dec 1950

limited to small-scale local action. Finally, there was the main force itself, known as the Chuc Luc. This was trained and built up in the northern mountains, far from French interference, until it was considered strong enough to go into action.

By 1948 the Viet Minh had divided Vietnam into eight regions, each controlled by a local committee responsible to the leadership in the Viet Bac, and these regions kept up a constant war of attrition against French forces. Holding territory was not the point of this war; but at night, bombs would be planted in towns, French posts would be attacked, and unsympathetic village headmen might be assassinated by the secret groups of Viet Minh terrorists.

The French found this form of action difficult to cope with. They tried to form an alternative to the Viet Minh by allying with local nationalists who resented communist power, and they were successful in using certain religious sects to control areas of Vietnam. There was also a large Catholic minority (about 1,700,000 strong out of a total population of 25 million) which was sympathetic to French offers of independence within some kind of Indochinese union. But the ruthless power of the Viet Minh was difficult to deal with.

Nor were French aspirations helped by the weakness of the government at home and the unpopularity of the war. The use of conscripts in Indochina was not permitted and although efforts were made to employ troops from the black African colonies (all known as

Above: A legionnaire prepares to fire a mortar from the fortress of Cao Bang. The French high command believed that the forts along the Cao Bang ridge could hold out against the heaviest weapons that the Viet Minh had to offer, but the provision of heavy equipment by the Chinese enabled the guerrillas to isolate and destroy these strongholds in 1950. Left: A Moroccan tirailleur armed with a 9mm MAT 49 sub-machine gun during a sweep through a village suspected of harbouring Viet Minh. The French Army made great use of colonial troops during the Indochinese War, partly because they were forbidden to use conscripts from metropolitan France and so had to rely on their regular armed forces, many of whom were recruited in the colonies.

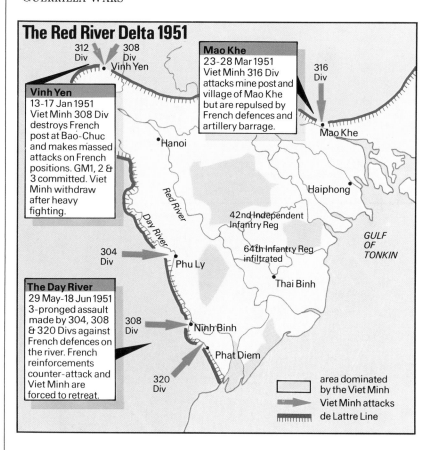

The Red River Delta 1951

312 Div   308 Div
Vinh Yen

316 Div

Mao Khe
23-28 Mar 1951
Viet Minh 316 Div
attacks mine post and
village of Mao Khe
but are repulsed by
French defences and
artillery barrage.

Mao Khe

Vinh Yen
13-17 Jan 1951
Viet Minh 308 Div
destroys French
post at Bao-Chuc
and makes massed
attacks on French
positions. GM1, 2 &
3 committed. Viet
Minh withdraw
after heavy
fighting.

Hanoi

Haiphong

Red River

Day River

42nd Independent
Infantry Reg

304 Div

64th Infantry Reg
infiltrated

Phu Ly

GULF OF TONKIN

The Day River
29 May-18 Jun 1951
3-pronged assault
made by 304, 308
& 320 Divs against
French defences on
the river. French
reinforcements
counter-attack and
Viet Minh are
forced to retreat.

Thai Binh

308 Div

Ninh Binh

Phat Diem

320 Div

☐ area dominated by the Viet Minh
➤ Viet Minh attacks
▥ de Lattre Line

Below: French troops count the dead after an unsuccessful Viet Minh attack on positions at Mao Khe in March 1951. This was part of the second series of attacks on the fortifications around the Red River Delta.

'Senegalese') and from North Africa (notably Morocco), the colonial forces, and the Vietnamese who were employed under French command, were not generally very effective, either as combat troops or as counter-insurgency forces able to protect and gain the confidence of the local population.

The key campaign in the Indochina War was in 1950. The previous year, Mao's forces had taken over in China, and the spectre of aid pouring across the border to the Vietnamese communists was very worrying for the French, who had made little headway in quelling insurgency. In order to cut losses and rationalize the areas that had to be held,

a scheme (the 'Revers Plan') was suggested, whereby all the garrisons in the north of Tonkin would be withdrawn, and French forces would be concentrated in the Red River Delta, to cut supplies of rice reaching the Viet Minh in the mountains. This plan was put into operation, but one string of forts in the north was left intact. These were along the Cao Bang ridge. The main garrisons there, at Lang Son, Cao Bang and Dong Khe, were well supplied, and, it was believed, impregnable to assault by lightly armed guerrillas. Their presence across the main route to the Viet Bac from China would, it was hoped, check Red Chinese war material reaching the Viet Minh.

SLAUGHTER ON THE RED RIVER

By 1950, however, war material, especially artillery, had already reached the Viet Minh in some quantity. Giap's men were able to launch an attack on the garrisons along the ridge with great success, and in spite of heroic last-ditch actions, especially by some French parachute units, the forces of the European power were driven off the ridge with great losses, numbering almost 6000 troops.

The following year, 1951, Giap made his major mistake of the war, when he launched a conventional attack on the French strongholds in the Red River Delta, mistakenly assuming that the stage of open warfare had now been reached. But the Viet Minh were in no condition to take on conventional forces. With effective artillery and air support (including the use of napalm), the French, under their new, energetic commander Jean de Lattre de Tassigny, stopped the attacks, although it was touch and go during the first series of assaults, around Vinh Yen in January 1951. After that, the separate attacks of March (towards Phu Ly, Ninh Binh and Mao Khe) and of May (at Phat Diem) were easier to cope with.

The seriousness of the French position in Indochina as a whole, however, now became apparent. De Lattre had hoped to regain the initiative by establishing solid defensive positions (around the Red River Delta these were known as the de Lattre Line) and creating a mobile reserve, of paratroop and other crack units, to carry the war to the Viet Minh. But as soon as de Lattre tried to take the war back to the enemy after their failure at the Red River Delta, he himself found that he could make no headway. A paradrop and the establishment of a garrison along the Black River at Hoa Binh was the prelude to a nightmare of resupply and eventually the battered garrison abandoned the position under de Lattre's successor, Raoul Salan, in February 1952.

The French, therefore, although they had

held the Delta, were confined to it, while Giap was able to keep the initiative, all the while building up his stocks of material. Late in 1952 the Viet Minh used their strong position in northern Tonkin to begin a drive towards Laos, swamping French garrisons on the Nglia Lo ridge as they did so. Salan's attempt to divert this move by driving forces up the Clear River valley in Operation Lorraine was a failure, and as at Hoa Binh resulted in a costly withdrawal.

In 1953 the French position all over Indochina steadily worsened, as guerrilla attacks on French positions and personnel drained the army of its enthusiasm. But by now, the USA was heavily involved in the war, providing the French with transport aircraft and considerable financial aid. It has been estimated that by the end of the war, 75 per cent of the war effort was paid for by the Americans. And although the French position was deteriorating generally, there were some bright spots. The establishment of certain garrisons designed to block the Viet Minh advance into Laos had been relatively successful, and one of them, at Na San, had been defended against intense communist attacks late in 1952. Resupply from the air had been the key to this victory.

Dien Bien Phu (on the border with Laos) was originally envisaged as a mooring point, from which to base mixed groups of hill tribesmen and French forces who would act

as a further block to the Viet Minh move on Laos, and the village was first occupied in order to distract attention from a beleaguered garrison further north. But in November 1953, the decision was taken to use Dien Bien Phu as a heavily garrisoned stronghold. Any arguments against this were countered by the example of Na San.

Two Viet Minh divisions began to con-

Above: French troops advance down a track in Tonkin, covered by a Sherman tank. In spite of their material superiority, the French found it impossible to take the strategic initiative during 1952 and 1953.

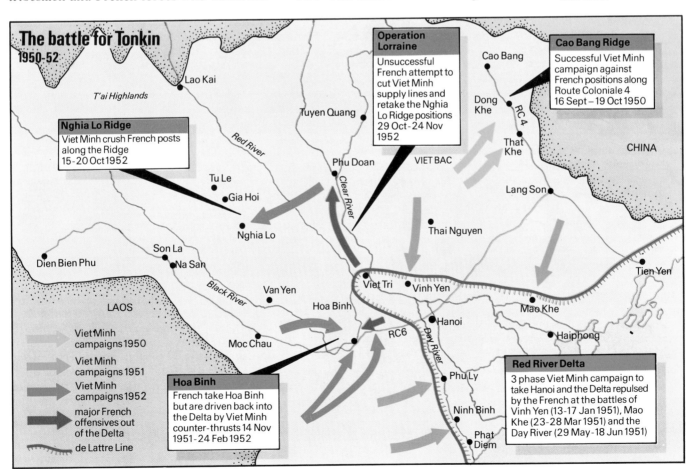

The battle for Tonkin
1950-52

Nghia Lo Ridge
Viet Minh crush French posts along the Ridge 15-20 Oct 1952

Operation Lorraine
Unsuccessful French attempt to cut Viet Minh supply lines and retake the Nghia Lo Ridge positions 29 Oct-24 Nov 1952

Cao Bang Ridge
Successful Viet Minh campaign against French positions along Route Coloniale 4 16 Sept-19 Oct 1950

T'ai Highlands

Lao Kai

Tuyen Quang

Cao Bang

Dong Khe

That Khe

Lang Son

CHINA

Red River

Phu Doan

VIET BAC

Tu Le

Gia Hoi

Clear River

Nghia Lo

Thai Nguyen

Son La

Na San

Dien Bien Phu

Black River

Van Yen

Viet Tri

Vinh Yen

Mao Khe

Tien Yen

LAOS

Hoa Binh

RC 6

Hanoi

Haiphong

Viet Minh campaigns 1950

Viet Minh campaigns 1951

Viet Minh campaigns 1952

major French offensives out of the Delta

de Lattre Line

Moc Chau

Hoa Binh
French take Hoa Binh but are driven back into the Delta by Viet Minh counter-thrusts 14 Nov 1951-24 Feb 1952

Phu Ly

Ninh Binh

Phat Diem

Day River

Red River Delta
3 phase Viet Minh campaign to take Hanoi and the Delta repulsed by the French at the battles of Vinh Yen (13-17 Jan 1951), Mao Khe (23-28 Mar 1951) and the Day River (29 May-18 Jun 1951)

centrate against Dien Bien Phu, and the French saw the opportunity to force a conventional battle that would shatter Giap's main force units. There was something of a confusion here in the French high command – the commander in Indochina, by now Henri Navarre, seems to have had ideas rather different from those of Brigadier René Cogny, the commander of the forces in Tonkin (differences that later caused public acrimony), but the flying-in of troops and men went on, the French confident that their firepower and air support were superior to anything the Viet Minh had to offer.

In this they were mistaken. The Viet Minh's superb logistics network, based upon human porters aided by bicycles, managed to supply the 50,000 men that Giap moved up to Dien Bien Phu; and, crucially, these porters brought along artillery, 75mm and 105mm field guns that matched anything the French had there. These guns were the more deadly because they were sited in the hills surrounding the valley where the set of strongpoints that composed the fortress were situated. The Viet Minh artillery was also almost invulnerable to air attack, being dug into the hillsides, and when Chinese 37mm anti-aicraft guns were received the besieged forces were in real trouble.

On the night of 13–14 March 1954, the French positions were swept by a devastating fire that took the defenders completely by surprise. The French artillery commander, Colonel Charles Piroth, who had boasted that his guns would rule the battlefield, took a hand grenade into his bunker and killed himself. By mid-March, the folly of committing the 16,000 French troops to the position was clear, but it was difficult to know how to recoup the situation. Dien Bien Phu was so far from the nearest French-held areas (270km/170 miles from Hanoi) that resupply or evacuation by land was impossible, while the airstrip, well within Viet Minh artillery range, was virtually unusable. Giap used a remorseless form of trench warfare, steadily closing in on the garrison, and, so he has stated, resisting the advice of Chinese advisors to go for a mass assault. On 7 May 1954, the garrison (now 11,000 strong) surrendered, and the French position in Indochina was in ruins.

Although the French Army formulated plans to hold on to certain key areas, there was now little hope. All over Vietnam, Viet Minh activity was increasing. As well as the disaster at Dien Bien Phu in the north, the French had to cope with the virtual destruction of a large mobile column in the Central

Below left: French troops captured during the ill-fated Operation Lorraine, the move up the Clear River in 1952 that ended in ignominious withdrawal. Bottom left: The planning for Dien Bien Phu. From left, Generals Gilles, Navarre and Cogny discuss the operation. Below: A French forward patrol in the hills around Dien Bien Phu (November 1953), soon after the original paradrop that established the isolated base.

Highlands. Nowhere was safe. An international conference at Geneva in April 1954 discussed the future of Indochina, and the eventual Geneva agreements were based on French withdrawal and the division of Vietnam into two political entities, that were eventually supposed to join up under a freely elected government. Probably over 150,000 Viet Minh had died, together with about 75,000 French troops.

Vietnam had been a traumatic experience for the French Army, which had previously prided itself on the expertise with which it had conducted colonial and pacification campaigns. In the wake of the debacle, the army began a period of analysis, centred around the correct method of dealing with the kind of revolutionary guerrilla warfare, based upon mobilization of the masses, that Vo Nguyen Giap and Ho Chi Minh had used. The conclusions, similar to those reached by the British in Malaya, are generally described as *guerre révolutionnaire,* a set of ideas about the political and military response necessary to cope with revolutionary nationalism. The core of *guerre révolutionnaire* was the recognition of the primacy of political action, and the need to establish a firm political base, both in the general direction of the war and in the relationships with the populations involved. If both these levels could be secured, then the military operations would have an excellent chance of succeeding. Without them, the tactics of counter-

insurgency would at best delay the victory of the insurgents.

The army was soon to have an opportunity to put its new theories to the test, in a theatre of war even more sensitive than Indochina. For in 1954 there was open revolt in Algeria, the oldest French possession in North Africa.

ALGERIA

The strength of Algerian nationalist feeling had been shown as early as May 1945, when there were demonstrations, followed by attacks on Europeans. These were met with savage retaliation on the part of the authorities and the white population of the country. It is estimated that over 100 Europeans and several thousand Muslims were killed in these encounters. The independence movement in Algeria was, however, weak and divided, with no clear strategy through which it could attain its goals. Indeed, even the goals themselves were cloudy, for some nationalist groups were happy to accept a form of autonomy while retaining close links with France, while others wanted complete independence.

The problem was that Algeria did not have the status of a colony; it was counted as part of metropolitan France, and although the Arabs were in a sense second-class citizens, there was a very large European element in the population, known as the *pieds noirs,* who were very much French citizens, and

Above: Last to leave. A unit of the Foreign Legion leaves the fort of Bac Ninh in Indochina during the general withdrawal following the Geneva agreements of 1954. The defeat in Indochina caused the French Army to rethink its attitude to counter-insurgency, and this rethink was especially important for the Legion and the crack parachute units that had had to bear the brunt of much of the fighting. When the army was employed in Algeria to combat the nationalist movement there, the fruits of this new approach were to have important political as well as military repercussions.

whose views counted for much in French political life. (In 1954 there were 800,000 *pied noirs* and nine million Muslims.) This was a situation that created the utmost difficulty when the French government did decide to withdraw from the country.

In April 1954, the leaders of the more extreme nationalist groups met and formed the FLN (*Front de Libération Nationale*). In October they set up six commands (or *Wilayas*) to run an insurrectionary war in Algeria, and in November began operations against the French in earnest. The *Wilaya* commanders were to have control over the armed forces, the ALN (*Armée de Libération Nationale*) which was based on the Viet Minh model, with some full-time forces supported by a much larger force of secret local troops.

MASSACRE AT PHILIPPEVILLE

The initial attacks by the ALN were not very successful, and resulted in the security forces taking steps against the insurgents that severely damaged the movement. But in August 1955, to show that they were still a force to be reckoned with, the ALN in *Wilaya II* carried out a massacre of *pieds noirs* and loyal Muslims at Philippeville. Over 100 men, women and children died in this attack, and thousands of Muslims died in the reprisals taken by the *pieds noirs* and a French parachute regiment stationed in the area immediately afterwards. The ALN now num-

bered over 15,000 effectives, and the international position of the FLN was improving; it was given support by the Egyptian government of Colonel Gamal Abdel Nasser and in April 1955 FLN leaders were asked to attend the meeting of non-aligned nations in Bandung.

Late in 1956, a new phase of the ALN campaign began, when the first wave of urban terrorism broke out in Algiers, under Saadi Yacef. Bombs were planted in the European quarter and policemen murdered. The French Army then began to take a more

prominent role in affairs. By mid-January 1957 the situation in Algiers was so out of control that power in the city was handed over to the 10th Colonial Parachute Division (many of whose officers were Vietnam veterans), under General Jacques Massu.

The paras had broken the power of the FLN in Algiers by the end of 1957, and Yacef himself had been arrested in September. The key French commanders were Colonels Godard and Bigeard. Godard was Massu's chief of staff and he collated a mass of information to establish a picture of the cellular organization of the ALN, gradually squeezing the life out of the insurgency. Bigeard was in charge of the paratroops who had to deal with the Muslim quarter, the *casbah*, and his ruthless pursuit of insurgents and constant patrolling provided the actual physical force that dealt with the rebels. There were serious questions asked about the methods the French Army had used, however. Torture had become commonplace to obtain information, suspects died in captivity or disappeared, and the spectre of military activities that were only too reminiscent of German actions in occupied France during World War II was very disturbing for many Frenchmen.

While the Battle of Algiers was taking

Above: General Jacques Massu, whose 10th Colonial Parachute Division contained many of the officers who had developed the new theories of counter-insurgency that the French Army put into operation during the Algerian War. In particular, Massu's men restored order in Algiers when they were given control of the city in 1957, and broke the power of the FLN nationalists. Left: The casbah, a warren of narrow streets and close-packed tenements that was the main Arab quarter of Algiers – and the stronghold of the FLN.

place, the French Army was undertaking the construction of a great barrier along the border with Tunisia. Tunisia and Morocco, France's two other possessions in North Africa, had been made independent by 1956, and it seemed clear that a major problem for the French Army would henceforth be in-filtration across the borders. On the Moroccan frontier, a variety of positions was established, but along the Tunisian border, which was adjacent to one of the main guerrilla areas (the Aurès mountains), the army constructed an enormous electrified fence and back-up defensive system, known as the 'Morice' Line. The line was extra-ordinarily effective, and cut off the insur-gents in Algeria from those outside.

After the French victory in Algiers, with the guerrillas in Algeria (the 'internals') cut off from those outside (the 'externals') and with their traditional differences creating constant difficulties for the FLN leadership, the nationalists were in some disarray by 1958. They could not see an easy road to victory; they could merely continue the struggle. Effective counter-insurgency had severely affected the two great advantages which the guerrilla movement had seemed to enjoy – internal cohesion and external support.

The French had very effectively addressed themselves to the military problems of fight-ing a guerrilla war, and although much of their counter-insurgency was on a far larger scale than that of the British in their wars, and the actual process of gathering inform-ation had been taken over largely by the army rather than being coordinated with the civil police, there were undeniable parallels between the strategies of the two European armies faced with radical nationalist insurgents.

Paradoxically, however, in spite of French

Above and top: French forces in action in the mountains of North Africa. In operations against guerrillas in the hinterland, the French were always militarily superior to their opponents – it was the general state of French politics that eventually gave Algeria its independence.

Above: Colonel Bigeard (seated), one of the most successful of the French commanders in Algeria. He commanded the paratroop battalion that controlled the casbah *during the Battle of Algiers in 1957. Like many French officers, Bigeard was dragged into politics when Charles de Gaulle, French head of state from 1958, decided that Algeria had to be allowed its independence. Right: Muslim troops serving with the French forces. The protection of such men from FLN vengeance was an important motive for many French Army officers who resisted independence.*

successes, 1958 saw a series of events that were eventually to lead to FLN victory. The French Army had, by 1958, been pursuing its theories of *guerre révolutionnaire* with considerable success. It had resettled large numbers of Muslims into areas protected by French troops, and was steadily isolating those sympathetic to the FLN. But the French government itself was a source of considerable concern to the military men. They did not want the ground cut from under their feet by a left-wing or liberal regime in Paris prepared to question their methods or negotiate over the status of Algeria; but in the unstable, shifting politics of the Fourth Republic, nothing could be guaranteed. Early in 1958, the government of Félix Gaillard agreed to international mediation after French aircraft had attacked the Tunisian village of Sakiet in reprisal for a cross-frontier raid by the ALN. There was confusion; the government fell on 15 April, and in the tense manoeuvrings that followed, General Jacques Massu and the commander-in-chief in Algeria, General Raoul Salan, involved themselves with *pied noir* groups, threatened incursions into mainland France if their wishes were not taken into account, and were instrumental in having Charles de Gaulle, whom they believed an immovable supporter of their cause, installed as prime minister. Within a few months, de Gaulle had established the Fifth Republic, with a new constitution, and had become president.

De Gaulle's rise to power, however, was to mark the beginning of the end for French Algeria. For he was prepared to follow whatever policy he thought necessary for the welfare of France itself, and if this included abandoning Algeria, then so be it.

THE CHALLE OFFENSIVE

The long-term implications of de Gaulle's accession to power were not at first apparent, however. To be sure, Salan was quietly moved away from Algeria to become military governor of Paris, but the man who took Salan's place, Air Force General Maurice Challe, instigated the most thoroughgoing set of offensives that the ALN had yet had to face. The so-called 'Challe Offensive' was a set of sweeps from west to east, designed to clear large areas of Algeria of insurgents and to push the guerrillas onto the Morice Line. It began in February 1959, and ended in November, but the key was Operation Jumelles, an attack on ALN strongholds in Little and Great Kabylia, the mountains near Algiers. So complete was the success of the Challe Offensive that Operation Trident, a final assault to destroy guerrilla activity in Algeria in an attack on the insurgents' bases in the Aurès mountains, was planned for January 1960 but never took place.

In September 1959, de Gaulle had spoken openly of 'self-determination' for Algeria, and had clearly decided upon a fundamental change in the status of the country. This led to widespread unrest in the army, and among the *pieds noirs*; in January 1960, Massu was recalled to Paris for having criticized de Gaulle in a newspaper interview, an order which precipitated rioting in Algiers, known as the 'week of barricades' (24–9 January). Challe was replaced as commander in Algeria, and Operation Trident cancelled, while in June, representatives of the French government met FLN negotiators for the first time.

THE GENERAL'S REVOLT

The French Army was now in a state of extreme tension. Challe had recruited thousands of Muslim troops, who had all been assured that France would never abandon them, and the 60,000 *harkas*, as these guides and scouts were known, were a great moral responsibility for their French commanders. The hundreds of thousands of resettled Muslims, too, were in great danger, for this had always been a vicious war of massacre and counter-massacre. The resettlement of civilians and the use of troops from the local population in close concert with European units – procedures which had proved so effective for the British in both Malaya and Kenya – were, therefore, now an added burden to the French Army in Algeria.

Late in April 1961, four generals who had been associated closely with Algeria – Challe, Salan, Edmond Jouhaud and André Zeller – made a bid for power in Algiers, backed by a parachute regiment of the Foreign Legion. After five tense days, during which de Gaulle made a successful appeal to the rest of the army to stay loyal, the revolt collapsed, and government authority was restored. But many army officers now went underground, formed the OAS (*Organisation Armée Secrète*) and carried out their own brand of urban terror, trying to

Above: Ben Bella casts a vote in elections following the French withdrawal. The FLN was always split between those who had gone abroad, the so-called 'externals', and those who had stayed in Algeria. The French tried to exploit this split, but never quite succeeded. Above left: The use of helicopters by the French was an innovation that produced results, especially during the offensives of 1959.

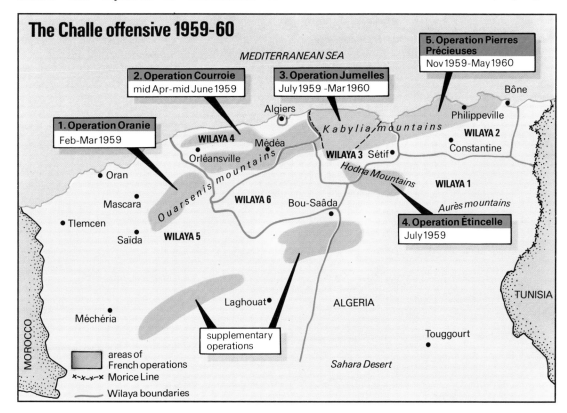

The Challe offensive 1959-60

MEDITERRANEAN SEA

5. Operation Pierres Précieuses
Nov 1959-May 1960

2. Operation Courroie
mid Apr-mid June 1959

3. Operation Jumelles
July 1959 -Mar 1960

Bône

Algiers

Philippeville

Kabylia mountains

1. Operation Oranie
Feb-Mar 1959

WILAYA 4 Médéa

Orléansville

WILAYA 3 Sétif

WILAYA 2

Constantine

Oran

Ouarsenis mountains

Hodna Mountains

WILAYA 6 Bou-Saâda

WILAYA 1

Mascara

Aurès mountains

Tlemcen

4. Operation Étincelle
July 1959

Saïda **WILAYA 5**

Laghouat

ALGERIA

TUNISIA

Méchéria

supplementary operations

Touggourt

Sahara Desert

MOROCCO

■ areas of French operations
×-×-×-× Morice Line
— Wilaya boundaries

Above: Maurice Challe, the air force general whose series of offensives in 1959–60 were the high point of French military action in Algeria.

Above: Members of the Foreign Legion on patrol around Kolwezi after the paradrop there in 1978. This operation demonstrated French determination to retain influence in Africa. Below: French troops in Chad in the late 1970s, during the fighting to maintain the government there against northern rebels.

European settlers also lost their lives.

While the French Army was being dragged so painfully out of Algeria, the government of Charles de Gaulle was striving to ensure that the independence of other colonies should go through smoothly, but that French influence in the new countries should be strong. De Gaulle attempted to form an equivalent to the British Commonwealth in the French Union, and although this and other attempts to forge formal links between the new nations and Paris came to naught, there were plenty of ties that were to be important for the future. France was, for example, prepared to offer help to those regimes that were in danger – and three times (in the late 1960s, the late 1970s and then in 1983) French forces intervened in Chad to give aid to the government of that country. The French have also retained forces able to intervene at any time in the affairs of African countries. In 1978 a dramatic operation saw French paratroops move into the town of Kolwezi in Zaire, ostensibly to rescue threatened European technicians, but also to shore up the threatened government of President Mobutu, a close friend of the French in black Africa.

The French colonial experience after 1945 was, then, very different from that of the British. The French Army faced more redoubtable foes, and was in strategic situations which were very difficult, both in Indochina and Algeria. Like the British forces, however, the French Army evolved a body of doctrine to deal with its problems. It was its tragedy that this doctrine, although effective on one level, led it inexorably into the murky corridors of military intervention in national politics, a labyrinth in which it perhaps inevitably lost its way.

assassinate de Gaulle and fighting both the FLN and the security forces in the towns of Algeria.

Agreement between the FLN (which had always maintained an unvarying hard line in the negotiations) and the French government was finally reached in March 1962, and the French abandoned the country. Most of the *pieds noirs* left at the same time; but the unfortunate *harkas* could not, and the majority were killed by the ALN. Over one million Muslims are said to have died in the fighting, although there are no reliable figures. The French Army lost 17,456 dead, and 2788

THE DUTCH AND PORTUGUESE WARS

The first of the European empires in the Third World to be destroyed by force was that of the Dutch; and the last was that of the Portuguese. Both these powers strove to retain their colonies because of the economic wealth involved and both found the struggle too exhausting to maintain. The tenacity of nationalist guerrillas meant that inferior armed forces won the day in both cases.

Within that basic history lies a fascinating contrast in the development of warfare. The French and the British had both, over the years that they had fought counter-insurgency campaigns, worked out methods of combating guerrilla armies. When the Dutch were fighting in Indonesia (1945–9), such methods were in their infancy, and they found it difficult to formulate an effective strategy. When the Portuguese were faced with revolt in their African colonies in the early 1960s, however, they were able to put into practice a set of established procedures and managed to achieve a military stalemate. Nor were the changes only on the side of counter-insurgency, for the nationalists themselves had developed their methods over the years. Those in the Portuguese colonies were prepared for a long hard struggle, and realized that they needed effective arms from the Eastern bloc if they were to prevail, whereas those in Indonesia had been improvising their military response as the situation developed.

INDEPENDENCE FOR INDONESIA

The main Dutch possessions were the so-called Dutch East Indies, which now make up the Republic of Indonesia. The minerals, oil and raw materials of this region had made it a prime target for the Japanese during World War II, and they had conquered it in 1942. Japanese conquest had resulted in the replacement of the Dutch administration by one composed of Indonesians, directed by the Japanese, and although Europeans might be horrified at collaborators, for the Indonesians themselves the experience of running their own country was such as to make it very difficult for the Dutch ever to come back. In August 1945, as the Japanese collapse seemed inevitable, nationalists began to plot to seize power before the Dutch could rein-stall themselves. On 17 August 1945 Ahmed Sukarno, the leading nationalist figure, proclaimed the independence of Indonesia, two days after the Japanese surrender. The nationalists began equipping themselves with Japanese arms.

Left: A Dutch soldier returns the fire of a nationalist sniper in Malang, East Java, in early 1946. He wears British personal equipment; at this stage the Dutch troops were largely equipped from British sources, and it was the British presence that had prevented the nationalists from taking over completely when the Japanese first surrendered in 1945.

The Dutch had no capacity to send forces back into Indonesia as their country had itself been occupied by the Germans for the greater part of World War II. But the British agreed to send in troops, to protect the large number of Dutch nationals who had been placed in internment camps during the war by the Japanese and who were still suffering very badly. The first British forces arrived in Indonesia in September 1945, and established themselves in the most important island, Java, after a hard-fought battle against na-

Below: Dutch troops advance into nationalist-held areas in 1948. They have been supplied from US sources, and wear US-pattern uniforms, carry M1 carbines and are supported by M4 Sherman tanks.

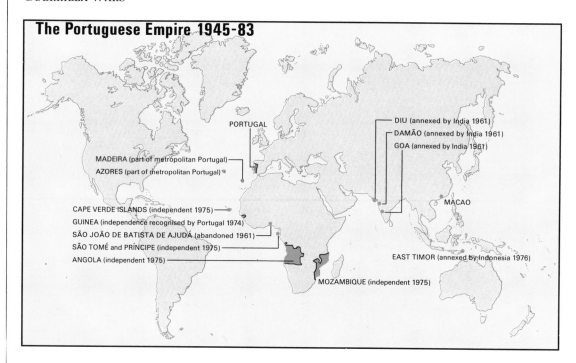

The Portuguese Empire 1945-83

PORTUGAL

DIU (annexed by India 1961)
DAMÃO (annexed by India 1961)
GOA (annexed by India 1961)

MADEIRA (part of metropolitan Portugal)
AZORES (part of metropolitan Portugal)

MACAO

CAPE VERDE ISLANDS (independent 1975)
GUINEA (independence recognised by Portugal 1974)
SÃO JOÃO DE BATISTA DE AJUDÁ (abandoned 1961)
SÃO TOMÉ and PRÍNCIPE (independent 1975)
ANGOLA (independent 1975)

EAST TIMOR (annexed by Indonesia 1976)

MOZAMBIQUE (independent 1975)

tionalists at Surabaya in November. Then Dutch troops began to come back, bringing a new colonial administration, although the British urged the Dutch to concentrate on negotiations with the nationalists, who obviously enjoyed strong local support and were relatively well armed.

The Dutch had recognized the nationalists as the *de facto* authority in Java, Madura and Sumatra, but elsewhere tried to reimpose their rule, being none too concerned about the methods used; it is estimated that about 40,000 Indonesians were killed, for example, during a notorious campaign to pacify part of the Celebes (now Sulawesi). In July 1947 the Dutch made an attempt to take control in Java, with a 'police action' that set out to capture the main towns on the island, including the capital of the nationalists, Yogyakarta. By the end of the year, however, they had made less progress than expected, and so accepted a ceasefire.

The Dutch problem was that they were fighting a new kind of war with outdated methods. This was not an old-style colonial campaign, in which a show of force would cow the local inhabitants into submission. Nor was it the kind of war where mere possession of a few major towns was the key to success. No serious attempts were made to win over popular support for the returning colonial power, and there was little enthusiasm for a thorough analysis of the motives, methods and weaknesses of their opponents. Brutality was no substitute for trying to gain the support of the inhabitants of the country.

During the ceasefire, there occurred an incident that made the Dutch situation even more precarious. The nationalists and their allies, the Indonesian Communist Party,

came into armed conflict, and after a short period of fighting the communists were routed. This served to weaken the nationalist movement to an extent, but it also convinced the USA that the nationalists were not a mere cover for a communist takeover in Indonesia, and deprived the Dutch of what might otherwise have been a major source of support.

In December 1948, the Dutch initiated another 'police action', which seemed initially very successful. All the major towns of Java (including Yogyakarta) fell to Dutch troops, but they now found that extending their area of control merely exposed them to more guerrilla attacks. The morale of the

Below: Portuguese government forces move through a devastated village in Angola. The civilian population in the war zones suffered severely during the long drawn-out war in Angola.

Dutch forces had fallen very low, and the USA threatened to cut off economic aid to the Netherlands unless negotiations with the nationalists were begun. So in the spring of 1949, talks started. By the end of the year, a complete Dutch withdrawal had been agreed, and the state of Indonesia was recognized by the world's governments.

PORTUGUESE AFRICA

Portugal had been the first European nation to establish a colony in black Africa, and was the last to accept the principle of decolonization, a decade after the other European nations had decided to abandon their possessions. Portuguese determination to hang on to its three colonies of Portuguese Guinea, Angola and Mozambique was based on the poverty and backwardness of Portugal itself, which its government (until 1974 an authoritarian right-wing regime, first under António de Salazar and then under Marcello Caetano) believed could be forced into economic growth only through the use of the mineral wealth of the colonies.

As early as 1961, however, Portuguese intransigence had resulted in considerable loss of face, when the Indian government had taken by force the enclaves of Goa, Daman and Diu on the coast of the sub-continent, and soon further problems were to arise, this time in Africa. In March 1961 there had been a savage uprising across northern Angola; by 1963 the *Partido Africano da Independência da Guiné e Cabo Verde* (PAIGC) had begun its guerilla campaign in Portuguese Guinea, and in 1964 the *Frente de Libertação de Moçambique* (FRELIMO) began raiding Mozambique from across the border with Tanzania. By 1965, the Portuguese Army was heavily engaged in all three colonies, trying to stem the tide of black nationalism.

While the revolts in the three colonies were carried out by quite distinct political groups, and while the conditions in each colony varied enormously, there were certain points that they had in common. The first was that the leaders of the insurgents had generally been educated under Portuguese rule, and were fighting the Portuguese Army, which tried to use the same counter-insurgency methods in each colony; this alone gave the three struggles a certain unity. And all three guerrilla movements came up against strong tribal problems.

In Portuguese Guinea, the PAIGC had been formed in 1956. It was predominantly composed of members of the Balante tribe, and the Fula and Mandinga peoples of the country never showed much enthusiasm for it. Led by the Cape Verdean Amilcar Cabral, the PAIGC began to gain momentum as a nationalist force after a strike at the docks of the port of Bissau on 3 August 1958 was harshly repressed by police, who fired on the

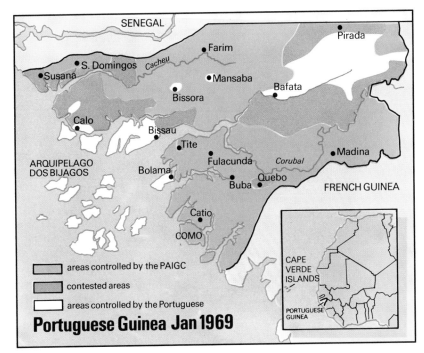

Portuguese Guinea Jan 1969

areas controlled by the PAIGC

contested areas

areas controlled by the Portuguese

strikers, killing 50. By the mid-1960s guerrilla activities had increased to an alarming extent, and the Portuguese Army could barely hold large stretches of the country. Indeed, the insurgents claimed to hold 60 per cent of the colony in 1970. Portuguese Guinea (now Guinea-Bissau) is a mass of rivers, and riverine warfare became very important there; it was also a relatively small colony, and outside aid from the sympathetic African states of Senegal and Guinea made a considerable contribution to the guerrilla movement.

Cabral himself was an inspiring leader, and although he was assassinated in January 1973 this hardly resulted in a slackening of

Below: Shelling nationalist positions in northern Angola. Material superiority enabled the Portuguese to maintain a military stalemate, but the very existence of the guerrilla armies imposed unacceptable costs on the desperately poor home country.

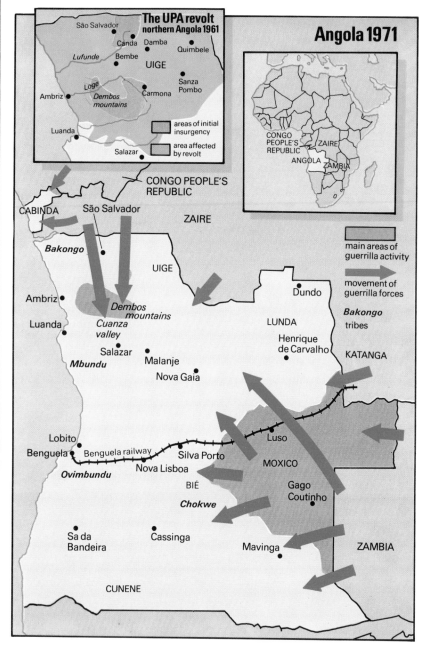

The UPA revolt
northern Angola 1961

São Salvador
Canda
Damba
Quimbele
Lufunde
Bembe
UIGE
Loge
Sanza
Pombo
Ambriz
Dembos
mountains
Carmona
Luanda
Salazar

areas of initial
insurgency

area affected
by revolt

Angola 1971

CONGO
PEOPLE'S
REPUBLIC
ZAIRE
ANGOLA
ZAMBIA

CONGO PEOPLE'S
REPUBLIC
CABINDA
São Salvador
ZAIRE
Bakongo
UIGE
Ambriz
Dembos
mountains
Dundo
Luanda
Cuanza
valley
LUNDA
Salazar
Malanje
Henrique
de Carvalho
Mbundu
Nova Gaia
KATANGA
Lobito
Luso
Benguela
Benguela railway
Silva Porto
MOXICO
Nova Lisboa
Ovimbundu
BIÉ
Gago
Chokwe
Coutinho
Sa da
Bandeira
Cassinga
Mavinga
ZAMBIA
CUNENE

main areas of
guerrilla activity

movement of
guerrilla forces

Bakongo
tribes

Above: The insurgency in Angola. Here, the nationalist movement was split into competing groups (that indulged in civil war once the Portuguese had decided to leave). The Portuguese were generally able to restrict the fighting against their regime to isolated areas.

the guerrilla effort. After 1968, however, the Portuguese did manage to bring more stability to the situation. Under General António de Spínola, who took over as commander in 1968, they managed to impose a stalemate, and by 1973, when Spínola was promoted to deputy chief of staff, the Portuguese hold was quite secure.

In Angola, the insurgents were rather less successful than those in Portuguese Guinea. This was mainly because they were divided into a number of mutually antagonistic factions. The *Movimento Popular de Libertação de Angola* (MPLA) had been founded in 1956, and drew most of its support from the Mbundu people around the capital, Luanda. The *Frente Nacional de Libertação de Angola* (FNLA) was based on the Bakongo people of the north, while the *União Nacional para a Independência Total de Angola* (UNITA) had been founded as a breakaway group from the

FNLA in 1966. Although these groups managed to tie down large numbers of Portuguese troops, they offered little military threat, and more Portuguese casualties were caused by mines than by direct guerrilla attacks. By 1970, the MPLA probably had over 5000 troops, but of these only 1500 would have been active inside Angola; the FNLA probably had rather fewer effectives, while UNITA was estimated to control less than 500 activists.

Finally, in Mozambique, FRELIMO was a coalition of various groups, but was mainly composed of members of the Makonde tribe, which made up less than five per cent of the population. FRELIMO was able to penetrate the Cabo Delgado and Niassa regions of Mozambique, but further progress south was hampered by the fact that the Macua people of central Mozambique were hostile to the Makonde; and although the guerrillas tried to stop work on the Cabora Bassa Dam project in the west of the country, they had no success. From 1969 to 1972 the Portuguese commander in Mozambique was General Kaulza de Arriaga who believed that the war was winnable; and, judging by the lack of progress of the guerrillas, there seemed to be some justification for his optimism.

A NEW APPROACH

The initial Portuguese strategy when confronted with guerrilla depredations had been based upon the unlimited use of force – in Angola, the first guerrilla attacks had been the signal for a reaction that killed an estimated 50,000 Africans in 1961 alone. Nor were the Portuguese troops skilled at taking the initiative outside safe base areas; they tended to remain within fortified areas where possible. But by the late 1960s, under the influence of commanders such as Spínola and Arriaga, a new approach was apparent. Well-tried techniques of counter-insurgency began to be applied (2000 Portuguese are said to have received instruction in counter-insurgency in the USA at this time).

There were three basic strands to the Portuguese strategy from the late 1960s on. Firstly, 'winning hearts and minds' (WHAM) policies were given prominence. In Portuguese Guinea, for example, 15,000 houses and 164 schools were constructed under Spínola, while in Mozambique, agricultural improvements (new farms, cattle dips and the like) were undertaken, and there were more roads built in Mozambique in 1972 than the British had built during the 12 years of the Malayan Emergency. Secondly, air power was used extensively, and a ruthless campaign, using herbicides, defoliants and napalm, was prosecuted against villages in guerrilla regions. Finally, small elite units, often including former guerrillas, were used

Above: Portuguese soldiers move warily through the outskirts of a village in Mozambique after a successful action against a guerrilla camp.

to penetrate guerrilla areas and to fight a small war of ambushes and raids that met the insurgents with their own tactics.

Although these methods could produce a military stalemate, the guerrillas always held the strategic initiative. They were not going to defeat the Portuguese in open battle in the near future, but by 1974 they were steadily building up their stocks and their reserves, and pushing the level of Portuguese commitment still higher in return. By 1973, anti-aircraft missiles were in use and the PAIGC claimed to have shot down over 20 aircraft by the end of the year. Exaggerated though these claims may have been, they were signs that even to maintain a stalemate would force more sacrifices from Portugal, which by 1970 had deployed 150,000 men.

Mere retention of territory was not victory for Portugal, especially as the guerrillas always had sanctuaries outside the colonies from which raids could be organized – from Senegal, Zaire, Tanzania and Zambia. Large numbers of Portuguese troops were tied down and the cost of protecting the Cabora Bassa Dam alone was enormous. In 1967, defence expenditure took over 40 per cent of the national budget. Nor could the army see how it could ever finally win the war. General Spínola, who had had such success in Portuguese Guinea, did not believe the government could carry on the struggle without radically altering its policy; and when he was dismissed from his post as deputy chief of staff for stating his views publicly, the 'Armed Forces Movement' carried out a coup which installed him as president and rapidly gave the colonies their freedom.

Portuguese Guinea became independent (as Guinea-Bissau) in September 1974, and Mozambique in June 1975. In November of that year, Angola too received its indepen-

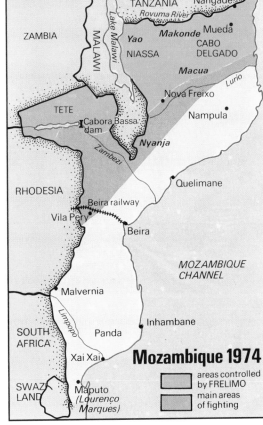

dence. In Angola, independence was only the prelude to a continuing conflict, however. The rival nationalist groups fought among themselves until the MPLA, with Cuban support, emerged triumphant in February 1976. Then, the linked problem of South West Africa (Namibia) reared its head. South African and Angolan forces clashed frequently (as described on p. 241) and there were years of fighting to come.

The Portuguese experience had demonstrated how isolated territories could not be held against a determined guerrilla movement that enjoyed substantial support from neighbouring states. It had also demonstrated that doctrines of counter-insurgency could be applied profitably by a determined army. In the end, however, the basic strategic problem was recognized as insuperable, and the army itself made the decision that withdrawal was the only practical course.

REVOLT AND REPRESSION IN LATIN AMERICA

Latin America presents a mass of contradictions as far as its politics and the wars that those politics have engendered are concerned. For although there is widespread political instability, and the coup has become one of the main ways of effecting a change of government, there have been very few radical changes in political systems. And although there have been guerrilla campaigns of various kinds in almost every state in Central and South America, only two – in Cuba in the late 1950s and in Nicaragua in the late 1970s – have had any lasting success. The essential stability of Latin American society has ensured that political instability has not led to radical change.

Ineffective though most of the guerrilla campaigns in Latin America have been, the region has been one of the most important arenas for the development of revolutionary warfare. The 'foco' theory, perfected by Ernesto 'Che' Guevara and Fidel Castro, was very important as representing an extension of the concepts of Mao and earlier theorists, while urban guerrilla warfare was underpinned by the writings of men like Carlos Marighela. In counter-insurgency, too, events in Latin America held very important lessons. US aid to beleaguered governments and the ruthless use of counter-terror, particularly in Brazil, Guatemala, Uruguay and Argentina, gave a new slant to the possibilities of aggressive government response.

Up to the late 1950s, Latin America was not considered a region with any possibilities for radical change. Under the overall eye of the USA, demagogues and military leaders succeeded each other with an almost monotonous regularity in many states (in Ecuador, José María Velasco Ibarra was five times president and four times deposed by military coups in a period of 30 years), while in those nations with a tradition of parliamentary

democracy, such as Chile and Uruguay, the institutions of state were steadily ossifying as much-needed reforms were neglected. By the early 1960s all this had changed, however. Suddenly, revolutionary change did seem possible – mainly because of the success of Fidel Castro's guerrilla campaign in Cuba.

REVOLUTION IN CUBA

Castro had been a prominent member of a group of Cuban revolutionaries who had made an unsuccessful attack on the Moncada Barracks in Cuba in July 1953. Captured in the wake of this failure, he had been exiled to Mexico, where he had concentrated on building up a group of like-minded exiles who could return to carry on the struggle. Thus the '26 July Movement' (named after the date of the attack on the Moncada Barracks) was set up. It was just one among many radical groups working towards the overthrow of the Cuban dictator, Fulgencio Batista, but its underground organization within Cuba was relatively well established, especially the parts under the control of Frank País.

Above: Fidel Castro (foreground) and his guerrillas in the mountains of southern Cuba in 1957. Castro's campaign set the pattern for the guerrilla warfare that engulfed much of Latin America during the 1960s and 1970s.

Below: Street-fighting in the latest guerrilla war in Latin America, in El Salvador in 1983. Here, as in Cuba 25 years before, the conflict is between a repressive, right-wing regime and a left-wing insurgent movement.

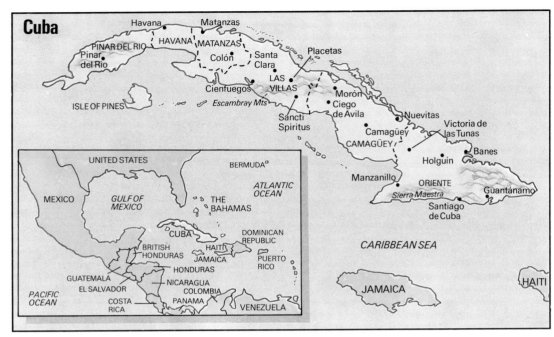

Cuba

UNITED STATES

BERMUDA

ATLANTIC OCEAN

MEXICO

GULF OF MEXICO

THE BAHAMAS

CUBA

DOMINICAN REPUBLIC

BRITISH HONDURAS

HAITI

JAMAICA

PUERTO RICO

GUATEMALA

HONDURAS

EL SALVADOR

NICARAGUA

COLOMBIA

PACIFIC OCEAN

COSTA RICA

PANAMA

VENEZUELA

Havana · Matanzas

PINAR DEL RIO HAVANA MATANZAS

Pinar del Rio

Colón

Santa Clara

Placetas

LAS VILLAS

Cienfuegos

ISLE OF PINES

Escambray Mts

Sancti Spiritus

Morón

Ciego de Avila

Nuevitas

Victoria de las Tunas

Camagüey

CAMAGÜEY

Banes

Holguín

Manzanillo

ORIENTE

Sierra Maestra

Guantánamo

Santiago de Cuba

CARIBBEAN SEA

JAMAICA

HAITI

Left: The initial guerrilla struggle in Cuba was concentrated in the Sierra Maestra in the south of the island. The rebel army there was able to set up a secure base, with little government interference, while the regime of Fulgencio Batista gradually weakened under the weight of its own contradictions.

In December 1956, Castro and 81 companions landed near Niquero, in the south of Cuba, after a number of attacks in Santiago by the 26 July Movement. Three days after landing, Castro and his men ran into an army patrol and were routed, and eventually only 22 of the original band met up again in the remote Sierra Maestra. Frank País and other members of the 26 July Movement kept the fugitives supplied, and funnelled more recruits to the mountains. In May 1957 the insurgents in the hills carried out their first large-scale assault when they attacked the army barracks at El Uvero.

Neither Castro nor the national directorate of the 26 July Movement had a clear idea of what strategy they should use to defeat Batista's forces. They had not bargained for a long guerrilla war, and, indeed, were not even recognized as the major revolutionary body. The most publicized attack on the regime in 1957 was the abortive assault on the Presidential Palace in March by a group calling itself the 'Revolutionary Directorate'. The connection between the guerrillas in Oriente Province in the Sierra Maestra and the urban underground (the *llano* or 'plain') was sometimes strained. The man who forged close links between the two – Frank País – was killed in July 1957.

By the end of 1957, however, Castro's guerrillas, although only about 200 strong, had established a strong presence in the Sierra Maestra and were able to move over large areas of the countryside at will. They built up good relations with the local peasantry (something that had been lacking during the early months of their operations) and the government forces that were supposed to deal with them were diverted by the general rise in unrest against the government that manifested itself all over Cuba.

In February 1958, the leaders of the 26 July Movement decided that the time was ripe to take the struggle on to a higher plane, and called a general strike. Unfortunately, there was little support for this move, and the strike ended in bloody disaster. The failure did, however, have the result of clearing up any problems in the relationship between the urban leadership and Castro's guerrillas. Castro was now definitely in charge, and his forces (from this period called the 'Rebel Army') became the core of the revolutionary movement. He began to extend his guerrilla activities, sending a column of men to the north coast under his brother Raúl, while the Revolutionary Directorate group imitated Castro's tactics by beginning operations in the Escambray mountains in central Cuba.

The forces of the insurgents were still much smaller than those of the government, however, and in May 1958 Batista decided to destroy the guerrillas in the Sierra Maestra. He ordered 11,000 troops into the region, against the few hundred men under Castro's command. Yet in spite of this enormous disparity in numbers, the guerrillas routed

Below: Guerrillas at one of their camps in the Sierra Maestra. Here they built up their numbers, until by the spring of 1958 they were perceived as a significant threat by the government. The result was an offensive by 11,000 government troops – an offensive that failed utterly.

CHE'S LAST CAMPAIGN

On 3 November 1966, disguised as a balding, middle-aged Uruguayan businessman, the Cuban revolutionary leader Ernesto 'Che' Guevara slipped through the immigration controls at the airport of La Paz, capital of Bolivia, and was whisked off by jeep to a distant jungle encampment where he was to begin his last campaign.

Che and Cuban leader Fidel Castro had decided upon Bolivia as an ideal place to initiate operations because it borders Argentina, Brazil, Chile, Peru and Paraguay, and revolution could, therefore, easily be exported to those countries if the insurrection succeeded in Bolivia itself. This was a very big 'if', however. In spite of revolutionary success in Cuba, no other Latin American countries had followed suit, and US backing for established regimes had made the export of revolution from Cuba a hazardous business. Nevertheless, in 1966 the USA was deeply embroiled in Vietnam, and there seemed mounting international sympathy for fundamental change in South America. Che, an inspirational leader and enthusiastic promoter of the 'foco' theory, seemed the ideal person to lead this new campaign.

In the event, however, the Cubans had gravely miscalculated. Land reform had blunted the edge of peasant grievance in Bolivia; none of Guevara's men even spoke the local dialect of the area in which they hoped to operate, and the army was relatively popular. After some early successes, the guerrillas began to be worn down by well-trained government troops who had been given intensive training by US advisors, and the local population gave information to the government forces but not to the guerrillas. In October 1967, the guerrillas under Che's command woke up to find themselves surrounded by soldiers. After a two-hour fight, the guerrillas were defeated; Guevara, wounded, was taken prisoner and shot dead the next day.

the regular units. The central engagement of the campaign came on 29 June, when 300 guerrillas took on the 1000 men of the government 11th Battalion, and put them to flight. By the middle of the summer, Castro was in secure control of eastern Cuba.

Batista's forces suffered severely from corruption. Officers saw the war as a means of getting rich by requisitioning for supplementary salaries and rations, and by accepting bribes from landowners in the expanded war areas, while the troops themselves were affected by the general dissatisfaction with a corrupt, incompetent regime. Nor had their training prepared them for the attacks of guerrilla forces; theories of 'counter-insurgency' were hardly considered necessary in Batista's army. The result was that the enthusiastic revolutionaries were superior when there was actual close-quarters fighting to be done. Even the technological advantages of the government forces were squandered – at one point, government planes napalmed their own side.

Above: Major Camilo Cienfuegos, who commanded one of the two columns that destroyed Batista's forces in Cuba in 1958, leads his cavalry through the streets of Matanzas.

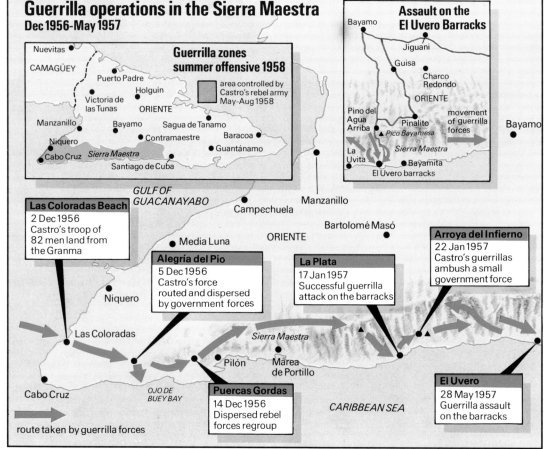

Guerrilla operations in the Sierra Maestra
Dec 1956–May 1957

Nuevitas
CAMAGÜEY
Puerto Padre
Holguín
Victoria de las Tunas
ORIENTE
Manzanillo
Bayamo
Sagua de Tanamo
Niquero
Contramaestre
Baracoa
Cabo Cruz *Sierra Maestra*
Guantánamo
Santiago de Cuba

Guerrilla zones summer offensive 1958
area controlled by Castro's rebel army May–Aug 1958

Assault on the El Uvero Barracks
Bayamo
Jiguaní
Guisa
Charco Redondo
ORIENTE
Pino del Agua Arriba
Pinalito
movement of guerrilla forces
Bayamo
Pico Bayamesa
La Uvita *Sierra Maestra*
Bayamita
El Uvero barracks

GULF OF GUACANAYABO
Campechuela
Manzanillo

Bartolomé Masó

Las Coloradas Beach
2 Dec 1956
Castro's troop of 82 men land from the Granma

Media Luna
ORIENTE

Alegría del Pío
5 Dec 1956
Castro's force routed and dispersed by government forces

La Plata
17 Jan 1957
Successful guerrilla attack on the barracks

Arroya del Infierno
22 Jan 1957
Castro's guerrillas ambush a small government force

Niquero

Las Coloradas
Sierra Maestra
Pilón
Marea de Portillo

Cabo Cruz
OJO DE BUEY BAY

Puercas Gordas
14 Dec 1956
Dispersed rebel forces regroup

CARIBBEAN SEA

El Uvero
28 May 1957
Guerrilla assault on the barracks

route taken by guerrilla forces

From within the government side, too, there was support for the insurgents, and the plans for the offensive of May 1958 were probably in Castro's hands before the campaign began. At this stage, Castro was not seen as a Marxist threatening to tear down the very fabric of society; indeed, the Cuban Communist Party was hardly represented in his 26 July Movement. Castro seemed to embody the ideals of liberal democratic socialism, and had the additional advantage of an acute military brain. For radicals and those opposed to Batista all over Cuba it was, therefore, natural to give him support.

The next phase of the Cuban Revolution saw the complete collapse of the government forces. Even during the final moments of the May–June offensive, Castro had been preparing a counter-stroke, and he put this into operation in August 1958, when two columns of guerrillas moved into the central provinces. Under Camilo Cienfuegos and Che Guevara, they were taking the fight to the demoralized government troops by mid-October, and had taken over the communist and Revolutionary Directorate forces that were operating in the region. In an audacious set of attacks, Guevara and Cienfuegos led small groups of men against vastly superior numbers, and won victories against seemingly impossible odds. At Guisa, for example, Guevara deployed 200 guerrillas in a raid on 5000 government troops, and won.

With its army and police force falling apart, the Batista regime could think of little but flight, and when the communications centre of Placetas fell to Guevara in December, there seemed no point in further resistance. Batista flew into exile on 1 January 1959, and that same night Guevara's men began to enter the capital. Castro himself entered Havana on 8 January.

EXPORTING REVOLUTION

In some ways, the victory of the Rebel Army is more astonishing in hindsight than it was at the time. In an unstable political world, the flight of a dictator and his replacement by a military leader was not unusual. Batista's rule had been inefficient and corrupt, while Castro represented the forces of liberalism and progress that were attractive to most of the elements of Cuban urban society. What made the victory of the Rebel Army so important was that after his success, Castro became the centre of Latin American revolution – real revolution, not merely a cosmetic change in the name of the ruler or ruling party. Partly by design (many of his associates, such as his brother Raúl, were genuinely interested in fundamental changes to Cuban society) and partly because he was under attack from the USA (the CIA organized the Bay of Pigs invasion

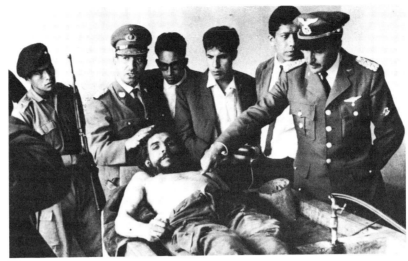

attempt in 1961 and the Cuban economy was put under great pressure, especially by the embargo put on its tobacco crop), Castro moved steadily left in the early 1960s, until he stood for revolutionary change in Latin American politics, the reordering of society and the rejection of US influence.

In the aftermath of Castro's success, there was a rash of insurrections across South and Central America, some directly instigated by the Cubans, but some that were local imitations. These, however, were not marked by great success. The three regimes of dictators that Castro had marked out as particularly worthy of overthrow – Anastasio Somoza in Nicaragua, Rafael Trujillo in the Dominican Republic and Alfredo Stroessner in Paraguay – were all able to cope without too much difficulty (although Trujillo himself was assassinated in 1961), and the bands of

Above: The Bolivian authorities exhibit the body of Ernesto 'Che' Guevara, whom they captured and killed in October 1967, after his attempt to export revolution to mainland South America.

Below: A poster celebrating the 24th anniversary of the Cuban revolution, featuring two of its heroes, Castro (right) and Cienfuegos.

guerrillas that moved into Panama and Haiti direct from Cuba had no success either. This did not prevent the Cuban leadership, and especially Che Guevara, from enthusiastically promoting its concept of guerrilla warfare. Broadly, this was called the 'foco' theory. Whereas in China and the Soviet Union, the revolutionary party had been seen as the vanguard of a peasant or working class movement, the 'foco' theory claimed that the guerrillas, rather than representing revolutionary aspirations, could actually go a long way towards creating revolutionary fervour among the peasantry (or urban working classes). In practice, this meant that small groups of guerrillas should be prepared to go into seemingly unfriendly territory, maintaining themselves by skilful use of small-scale warfare until they could establish a more general following.

There were two countries in which this first wave of revolutionaries posed a serious threat to the established order in the early to mid-1960s; but in both they were decisively defeated. The first was Venezuela, where Rómulo Betancourt and his reforming *Acción Democrática* party had taken power just before Castro had won his victory in Cuba. Betancourt, a lapsed communist, had refused to give Castro the aid the Cuban leader had hoped for, and by 1961 there was rioting in the capital, Caracas, while guerrilla bands were forming. By 1963, a full-scale guerrilla campaign was under way, aimed at stopping or at least disrupting the presidential elections set for December of that year. There were attacks on US property, oil installations were damaged and aircraft hijacked. Yet the government held out, and the elections took place on time and successfully. *Acción Democrática's* candidate (Raúl Leoni) was elected, and the guerrillas had failed. In spite of a resurgence of activity from 1965 to 1967, the government was henceforth secure.

The insurgency in Venezuela had been characterized by large-scale violence in the towns and cities, especially Caracas. In fact, no decisive actions had been fought in the countryside at all – a feature that was to be important in later guerrilla activity in South America.

The second country seriously threatened by insurgency in this period, Guatemala, also held lessons for the future. Guatemala had experienced important US intervention as early as 1954 when a CIA-backed coup had overthrown a left-wing regime. In 1960, in the aftermath of the Cuban revolution, a group of young army officers had tried to organize a reformist coup. Defeated, they took to the hills, and formed the 13 November Movement, or M.13. This split into various groups, the most important of which was the *Fuerzas Armadas Rebeldes* (FAR) which began a

selective campaign of assassination, often against US targets. One of their last successes was to assassinate the US ambassador in 1968.

The insurgents in Guatemala were defeated by a combination of heavy US aid – it has been estimated that about 1000 US Special Forces, the Green Berets, accompanied Guatemalan security forces during 1966–7 – and by the creation of right-wing death squads, which used techniques of terror against the guerrillas, and more importantly, those sectors of the population from which they hoped to draw support. The government (which was relatively moderate by 1966) did not necessarily have any control over these death squads, but they were often recruited from among the security forces and added a new, sinister dimension to army and police operations.

By 1967, the first wave of guerrilla activity against the governments of Latin America, inspired directly by Castro's example, had been shown to have failed. The most important symbol of this failure was the death of Che Guevara in October 1967 when attempting to stoke up the fires of revolution in Bolivia. Small guerrilla groups had been shown to have little hope of bringing down

governments that were strongly backed by the might of the USA.

INTO THE CITIES

The next wave of revolutionary activity, that began to gather momentum almost as soon as it became clear that the Cuban model was not working, gave the world a new slant on another form of insurgency – that of urban guerrilla warfare. It also saw the most widespread and horrific use of sheer terror as a weapon of counter-insurgency.

In their description of the events of the Cuban revolution, Fidel Castro and Che Guevara had always tended to play down the importance of the urban underground – partly because they had little control over it and partly because they had had occasion to disagree with it over various questions – and the urban wing's main attempt to assert its importance, the general strike of early 1958, had been a failure. But in fact the urban wing of the 26 July Movement had been very important in the survival and ultimate triumph of the Cuban revolutionaries. Latin America, with its mushrooming cities that housed not only underprivileged slum dwellers but also a middle class whose children were very susceptible to left-wing political ideas, was a continent in which the town was as ripe for revolt as the countryside. In Venezuela, the guerrillas had recognized this fact and had tailored their tactics accordingly. From the late 1960s there were important insurgent groups in three countries – Brazil, Uruguay and Argentina – that used the cities as the basis of their operations.

Theories underpinning urban guerrilla warfare came from Brazil, where Carlos Marighela codified the ideas of using the anonymity of urban life as the refuge of the guerrilla. He believed that a small number of fighters would be able to humiliate the authorities, undermining the sense of stability and legitimacy on which their power rested. In Brazil, the military rulers who had succeeded the democratic government in 1964 were extremely worried about the urban guerrillas who began operating from the mid-1960s, but the movement was so split into competing factions that the regime was never in real danger. Marighela himself was killed in 1969, and there was little threat to the military government in the 1970s.

In Uruguay, the so-called Tupamaros did present a serious threat, however. A group called the *Movimiento de Liberación Nacional* (MLN) had been founded in 1963 by Raúl Sendic Antanaccio and had naturally made Montevideo, where half the population of Uruguay lived, the focus of its activities. By 1965, the MLN was well organized and able to carry out raids that made the government seem unable to control the streets of its

capital. The Tupamaros (a name adopted in 1965 and taken from the last Inca king to be killed by the Spaniards – Tupat Amaru) were organized in small cells, and in fact had very little working-class support. But their raids (in which loss of life was kept to a minimum) and audacious propaganda exploits (including running their own radio station and capturing the British ambassador, Geoffrey Jackson) made them a considerable problem. The government was unable to curtail their activities until 1970, when the nature of the

Opposite page top: Rómulo Betancourt, who as president of Venezuela defeated the guerrilla movement of the early 1960s. Opposite page bottom: Bolivian troops with the body of one of their number, killed in a guerrilla ambush. Bolivian successes against guerrillas helped to persuade South American revolutionaries to take the struggle into the cities of the continent. The most important theorist of this new approach was the Brazilian Carlos Marighela (opposite page centre). The most effective practitioners were the Uruguyan Tupamaros, whose exploits included the capture of British ambassador Geoffrey Jackson in 1968 (left, photographed in captivity). In Argentina, urban guerrillas such as the Trotskyite group ERP (above) brought down an elected regime.

struggle began to change. Right-wing death squads were formed, and the Tupamaros could no longer avoid involvement in bloody terror. Unable to form a mass movement, they became increasingly vulnerable. In 1971 a hard-line conservative became president, and in 1972 a state of 'internal war' was declared against the guerrillas. Finally, in 1973, a military takeover allowed the army and police to use whatever methods they chose to break the movement.

TERROR IN ARGENTINA

An inability to make the transition from a small elite grouping to a mass political movement had doomed the Tupamaros to defeat in Uruguay at the hands of the increasingly unrestrained military. In Argentina the process of counter-insurgent violence was even more horrific. Economic hardship in what had traditionally been one of the more prosperous South American nations and the continuing agitation for the restoration of the charismatic Juan Perón, who had been deposed by a military coup in 1955, coupled with the example of neighbouring Uruguay, led to the gradual beginnings of Argentinian urban insurgency in the late 1960s. There were many guerrilla organizations, and a floundering military government that did not know how to cope. By 1973 the government had been forced to agree to elections, which resulted in the return of Perón. None of the guerrilla groups ceased their activities when Perón returned, however, and some of the pro-Perón insurgents stepped up their activities when he died in 1974 and his wife assumed the presidency. Order was quite clearly breaking down over much of the country; the guerrillas even shot down an aircraft carrying some members of the general staff and destroyed a frigate that was being built for the navy.

Far from being near success, however, the guerrillas were as split as ever between the various ideologies and goals that the different bands represented. They were in no position to take power, and the army moved in instead, when General Jorge Videla was installed as head of a military regime after a coup in March 1976. For about a year after this coup, the guerrillas were able to continue widespread insurgency; but they were now dealing with a very different regime from the uncertain military government of the late 1960s. Under Videla, a campaign of sustained terror was put into operation. The security forces aimed not merely to destroy the guerrilla movement, but to shatter its potential support in the population as a whole. Detention centres became notorious for torture and murder, and even the US government of Jimmy Carter professed itself outraged by the activities of the security

forces. The *Alianza Anticomunista Argentina*, a grouping of death squads that has always been assumed to have been composed of off-duty police and military personnel, took an indiscriminate toll of any suspected insurgents and their families, and this, combined with the concentrated wave of government terror, proved too much. By 1980, there was very little guerrilla activity.

By the late 1970s, then, revolutionaries all over Latin America had failed to impose either a Cuban model of rural insurgency or a successful urban guerrilla campaign on any country of the continent. A combination of lack of popular support, effective US aid to established regimes and the ruthless use of counter-terror by military regimes had blocked all guerrilla movements. Yet although the insurgents had been prevented from taking over, the military regimes could never feel entirely safe. The basic social conditions that had produced the initial dissatisfaction – extremes of wealth and poverty, lack of political opportunities – were ever-present, and many nations (such as Peru, for example) had undergone practically non-stop low-level violence throughout the two decades since 1960. The economic

Above: General Jorge Videla, who came to power in Argentina after it had become apparent that the government of Isabel Perón was incapable of coping with the various guerrilla groups in the country. Videla used every means at his disposal, including widespread use of torture and summary execution, to destroy the insurgents.

problems that authoritarian regimes had hoped to solve had refused to go away, so that balanced economic growth in nations such as Chile and Brazil was a remote dream.

In 1979, however, there was a guerrilla success, in the small Central American country of Nicaragua, whose ruling Somoza family had been one of the targets for revolt that Castro had set soon after his victory in Cuba. The Sandinista insurgents capitalized upon opposition to a corrupt regime, obtaining the popular support that had eluded other groups such as the Tupamaros, and overthrowing the government.

Events in Nicaragua seemed to open up new possibilities for revolution in Central America, with Nicaragua acting as a safe base for insurgents. As such Nicaragua was extremely worrying for the USA, and has since become the target for US attempts at 'destabilization' in retaliation for the help that the Sandinista government is claimed to have given to guerrillas in El Salvador, where an embattled right-wing regime has been struggling to maintain itself in power.

It is, indeed, somewhat ironical that, quite apart from the present situation in Central America, the most bloody single episode and the most impressive displays of armed force in modern Latin America and the Caribbean have all been closely associated with US attempts to maintain political equilibrium in these areas. In 1965, US Marines took over Santo Domingo, the capital of the Dominican Republic, to prevent left-wing political groups taking power. In 1973, the government of the Marxist Salvador Allende, the democratically elected president of Chile, was overthrown in a military coup sponsored by the USA; the coup was immediately followed by the widespread slaughter of left-wing elements. Finally, in 1984, the island of Grenada, part of the British Commonwealth, was invaded by US forces after a coup there had overthrown the radical regime under Maurice Bishop and replaced it with another.

The possibilities for continued warfare in Latin American are substantial. It seems that the revolutionary guerrilla will have an important role in the continent's history for some time to come, and that counter-insurgency will still be one of the main preoccupations of the armies of the region. Meanwhile the USA will continue to supervise developments, and will not hesitate to use armed force where it feels its interests are threatened.

Below: Belying its guerrilla origins, the post-revolutionary Nicaraguan Army is all drill and smartness on parade.

URBAN GUERRILLAS

Urban guerrillas of some kind have been a feature of much of the warfare since World War II. Even during World War II, there were numerous examples of Resistance movements operating in towns, and the Warsaw Uprising of 1944 was an attempt by the Polish Resistance to force the Germans out of the Polish capital. Fighting here lasted for ten weeks, and there were over 200,000 casualties. In the 1940s in Palestine, the Jewish resistance to British rule was concentrated in urban areas, while in Algeria and Cyprus in the late 1950s, nationalist opponents of the French and British respectively used the opportunities provided by the sympathetic populations of urban centres. In Uruguay and Argentina too, in the late 1960s and 1970s, the revolutionaries who had been unable to make any headway in the countryside became active in the towns.

Since the mid-1960s, groups of activists have also arisen in the prosperous industrialized world   western Europe, North America, Japan   and have taken to urban terrorism as a tactic. These groups fall into two main categories: those who wish to upset the existing social order, and those who act from a nationalist or separatist motive. They have undertaken acts of terror such as assassination, hijacking and sometimes indiscriminate attacks on civilian targets, and although the actual level of fighting may never have been high, they have proved one of the biggest problems for security forces in recent years, and a sophisticated response

Above: Ulrike Meinhof, who was one of the leading members of the notorious 'Baader-Meinhof' group that brought terror to German society. Left: A reward poster put out by the German government in an attempt to apprehend the terrorists.

has had to be developed to deal with them.

The social revolutionary groups included such organizations as the Baader–Meinhof group in Germany, the Red Brigades in Italy, the Red Army in Japan, the Weathermen in the United States, and the Angry Brigade in Britain. They largely grew out of the general student unrest of the 1960s, which resulted in very little long-term change, but politicized a whole generation and made the concepts of radical change common currency in many

Below: Paris 1968. Students dig up cobblestones by the light of burning barricades. It was the failure of the mass movements of 1968 that led many revolutionaries to consider going underground into urban terrorism.

Above: The crater left by the explosion in which the Spanish prime minister, Luís Carrero Blanco, was killed by the Basque terrorists of ETA in 1973. Below: Palestinians being trained. Many European terrorist groups relied on Palestinian support.

roots than the social revolutionaries, and traded on long-term feelings of grievance. The most important of these groups were the Provisional IRA (Irish Republican Army) in Northern Ireland, the Basque ETA (*Euskadi Ta Azkatasuna*, meaning Basque Land and Liberty) in Spain, and the FLQ (*Front de Libération du Québec*, or 'Front for the Liberation of Quebec') in Canada. Perhaps the Black Panthers, asserting themselves as a black power group in the USA, can be counted as part of this nationalist group; as also can the South Moluccan terrorists who demonstrated their concern for the situation in Indonesia by carrying out terrorist acts in Holland.

What gave these terrorist groups some kind of unity, and enabled them to play such a relatively important role from the late 1960s to the mid-1970s, was that they became part of an international network that provided equipment and support. Some, of course, like the IRA with its strong connections in the USA and a history of resistance to the British presence in Ireland, or the Basque nationalists who had enjoyed considerable support in France during the period of Franco's dictatorship in Spain, already had a strong position which they could exploit. But for the others, the opportunity to strike effectively was provided by the unrest in the Middle East. Here, the Israeli success in the Six-Day War of 1967 had been followed by a profound reorganization of the Palestine Liberation Organization (PLO), the major body linking the Palestinian groups, in which the leadership had come to Yasser Arafat, whose Fatah grouping believed in guerrilla warfare against Israel. More power also went to the extremist Popular Front for

circles. The failure of the mass demonstrations and student activity of the 1960s to bring about any significant changes in society led many individuals to consider that more violent steps were necessary. They found inspiration in the urban guerrillas of South America, especially the Tupamaros, and in Carlos Marighela's ideas of small groups humiliating governments.

The nationalist or separatist groups were rather different. They generally had stronger

THE LOD AIRPORT MASSACRE

At about 2200 hours on 30 May 1972, 116 passengers from Air France Flight 132 filed into the customs area at Lod Airport near Tel Aviv. Among them were three Japanese terrorists, Red Army supporters of the Popular Front for the Liberation of Palestine.

With passports checked and cleared, the passengers moved into the baggage area, where their luggage was arriving. The three terrorists suddenly seized their cases. In one smooth movement they unzipped them and extracted three stockless submachine guns, ammunition and grenades. Strangely calm in their manner, the gunmen opened fire on the roughly 300 passengers waiting in the baggage area. Panic filled the hall. One of the terrorists approached a floor-to-ceiling glass partition which separated the customs hall from the waiting area and emptied his magazine into the crowds beyond it. Then grenades were thrown wherever large groups of people had congregated, causing widespread casualties.

One terrorist fired out towards aircraft on the runway. As he did so he stumbled and dropped a grenade. There was a loud explosion and he was killed instantly. Another guerrilla raced out onto the runway shooting at everything in sight. As he passed an aircraft he threw a grenade between its wheels, discarded his weapon and ran off into the darkness, but an El Al mechanic caught him.

Among the blood-spattered pillars and chairs in the baggage area, the captured terrorist later identified the body of the third member of the gang. In a period of less than four minutes the attack had resulted in 24 dead and 78 seriously wounded.

Above: One of the Palestinian terrorists who held Israeli athletes hostage during the 1972 Olympics. Above right: Ilich Ramírez Sánchez, the notorious terrorist 'Carlos'. Below: One of the hostages looks for cover during the storming of the Iranian embassy in London by the SAS in 1980.

the Liberation of Palestine (PFLP) of George Habash, which was committed to international action. The Arab states were prepared to put money and arms behind this new approach, and within a short time an international terrorist network had been set up.

Exactly how connections between terrorist groups were made is still largely a matter of speculation. The links were presumably not very strong, nor particularly formal, but they certainly existed. Members of the Japanese Red Army, for example, undertook the attack on civilian passengers at Tel Aviv's Lod airport in May 1972 that left 24 dead; and in 1976, German and Palestinian terrorists together hijacked the aircraft whose Jewish passengers they held prisoner at Entebbe airport until a daring Israeli rescue operation released the hostages. Individuals such as the notorious 'Carlos' (the Venezuelan Ilich Ramírez Sánchez) were important in organizing raids all over Europe – including attacks on the representatives of conservative Arab states.

There was little or no contact between the groups in Europe or the Middle East and those in North America, however. The revolutionaries in the USA were dealt with relatively easily, while the FLQ in Canada,

in spite of some widely publicized actions such as the kidnapping and murder of a government minister in 1970, were suppressed by firm action from the administration of Pierre Trudeau. Things proved much more difficult for the authorities in Europe. Modern society proved vulnerable at various points aircraft hijacking, for example, was very difficult to deal with. The ability of small ruthless units to strike at a public figure or at a prominent industrialist could hardly be countered without abandonment of essential civil liberties, while the power of modern smallarms and explosives gave terrorists great hitting power.

The problem of how to react after a terrorist attack had captured hostages was also difficult. The temptation to give in to demands for the release of captured guerrillas or to pay a ransom that could fuel further outrages was strong, and any attempts to use force against hijackers or kidnappers could have disastrous results. The abduction of nine Israeli athletes by Palestinian terrorists during the Munich Olympic Games of 1972 ended in tragedy when the athletes and five terrorists were killed in a gun battle at Munich airport.

To combat these urban guerrillas, the first necessity for European states was to establish closer cooperation. Towards this end a series of bilateral agreements concerning extradition and a common policy towards terrorism was made between various countries between Great Britain and the Irish Republic, for example, and between West Germany and Austria. There were also larger international treaties, such as that signed by the nine members of the EEC in 1976 that sketched in the broad outlines of a common policy. There was also a great effort made to pool information on terrorist groups and their connections, in which computerized information was very important. In Northern Ireland, for example, the use of computers to identify all members of the population became an important part of security-force policy.

ANTI-TERRORIST SQUADS

These agreements and the pooling of information were implemented by specially created anti-terrorist units within security forces. The Germans, for example, created a 200-strong Federal force, which followed through contacts and worked on nothing else. But in addition to the creation of such forces, to carry out the collation of information and then to undertake traditional policing duties in relation to terrorist crime, the governments also began training special squads to combat terrorist tactics.

Inevitably, as in any military campaign, those involved began to work out how to combat the methods of their opponents. Although terrorists who had taken a set of hostages appeared to have a great advantage, security forces worked out how to isolate the terrorists with their victims, how to apply the maximum psychological pressure and how to strike suddenly and unexpectedly. At Mogadishu in October 1977, the German GSG9 counter-terrorist squad stormed a plane held by Palestinians and German terrorists, and the British SAS showed how such tactics could be used in May 1980 when they stormed the Iranian embassy in London, and freed the 26 hostages being held by six gunmen.

As the security forces began to work out more efficient means of dealing with the terrorists, so the terrorists were finding the struggle more and more difficult to maintain. They had been small groups in the first place, without much popular support, and gradual attrition over the years had its effect. In Britain, for example, the imprisonment of four people was sufficient to end the activities of the Angry Brigade in 1972, while the arrest, and subsequent death in prison in 1977, of four major figures in the Baader-Meinhof group severely curtailed its

Above and left: Palestinian guerrillas in training. The Palestinians were at the heart of much of the terrorism of the 1970s, feeling that they had no other way of bringing the plight of their people to the attention of the world. They were given much financial and practical support by certain of the established Arab regimes notably those of Colonel Gaddafi in Libya and of the Marxist rulers of South Yemen.

activities in Germany. Where there was a nationalist grievance that could be exploited, which normally meant that a substantial percentage of the population was on the side of the guerrillas, and where this was accompanied by help from outside as in Northern Ireland and in the Basque country in Spain then there was the potential for continued acts of terror. And, of course, the Palestinian organizations were still active up to the 1980s. But gradually, more efficient government response, and the weakening of the Palestinians and their absorption into the problems of Lebanon (where they were closely involved in the civil war that racked that unhappy country), had led to a slackening of international terrorism by the early 1980s.

THE WARS OF BLACK AFRICA

The wars that have afflicted the states of black Africa since they attained independence from the colonial powers have taken various forms. But they have all involved guerrilla warfare to a greater or a lesser degree, and the results have often largely depended upon one of the most important factors in such warfare: the provision of aid and sanctuary from outside sources.

Although there has been turbulence in many African countries, and coups have been as common as in Latin America, it is in some ways surprising that there has not been more outright warfare. For many of the states of sub-Saharan Africa are artificial creations, with borders that are lines drawn on a map by 19th-century colonialists. Problems of ethnic minorities and tribalism provide constant tensions in many nations, and the Organization of African Unity (OAU) has only been able to arbitrate on most of these problems by strict adherence to the rule that existing borders are sacrosanct – and even this ruling broke down over the problems of the Western Sahara and Morocco in the early 1980s.

Leaving aside the Nigerian Civil War, which manifested most of the features of a war between states and has been treated as such, the main wars of independent Africa have been those in the Congo, Chad, the attempts to break up the state of Ethiopia, the destruction of white domination in Rhodesia, and the linked conflicts in Angola and Namibia. There have, in addition, been long-running wars within certain states – the struggle for the autonomy of the southern Sudan from the early 1960s, or the attempt by the Polisario guerrillas to found a state of the Western Sahara from the early 1970s. In other areas, low-level violence has become commonplace – as it was in Uganda in the wake of the Tanzanian intervention there in 1979.

THE NIGHTMARE OF THE CONGO

The Congo was the largest, and the most confusing, of the wars of independent Africa; it was also the first, and set the tone for much of what was to follow. Few observers would have predicted that over five years of conflict were to follow the declaration of indepen-

Right: Katangese troops take cover during fighting in Elisabethville, the capital of the seceded province. Katanga seceded from the newly independent Congo in July 1960, but its revolt was ended in spring 1963, after UN forces had defeated Moise Tshombe's army.

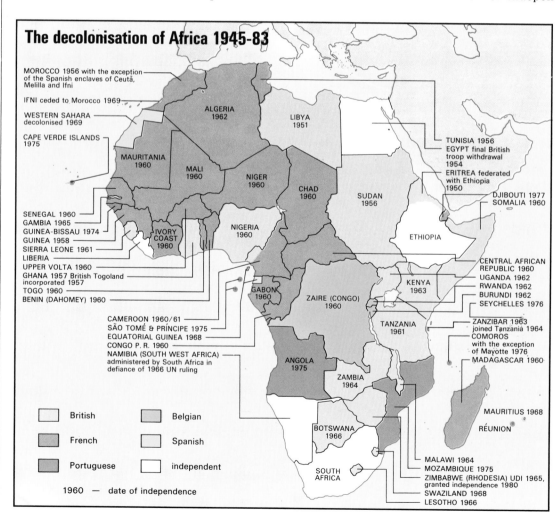

The decolonisation of Africa 1945-83

MOROCCO 1956 with the exception of the Spanish enclaves of Ceutā, Melilla and Ifni

IFNI ceded to Morocco 1969

WESTERN SAHARA decolonised 1969

CAPE VERDE ISLANDS 1975

SENEGAL 1960
GAMBIA 1965
GUINEA-BISSAU 1974
GUINEA 1958
SIERRA LEONE 1961
LIBERIA
UPPER VOLTA 1960
GHANA 1957 British Togoland incorporated 1957
TOGO 1960
BENIN (DAHOMEY) 1960

CAMEROON 1960/61
SÃO TOMÉ & PRÍNCIPE 1975
EQUATORIAL GUINEA 1968
CONGO P. R. 1960
NAMIBIA (SOUTH WEST AFRICA) administered by South Africa in defiance of 1966 UN ruling

ALGERIA 1962
LIBYA 1951
TUNISIA 1956
EGYPT final British troop withdrawal 1954
ERITREA federated with Ethiopia 1950
DJIBOUTI 1977
SOMALIA 1960

MAURITANIA 1960
MALI 1960
NIGER 1960
CHAD 1960
SUDAN 1956

IVORY COAST 1960
NIGERIA 1960
ETHIOPIA

CENTRAL AFRICAN REPUBLIC 1960
UGANDA 1962
RWANDA 1962
BURUNDI 1962
SEYCHELLES 1976

GABON 1960
ZAIRE (CONGO) 1960
KENYA 1963

ZANZIBAR 1963 joined Tanzania 1964
COMOROS with the exception of Mayotte 1976
MADAGASCAR 1960

TANZANIA 1961

ANGOLA 1975
ZAMBIA 1964

MAURITIUS 1968
RÉUNION

BOTSWANA 1966

MALAWI 1964
MOZAMBIQUE 1975
ZIMBABWE (RHODESIA) UDI 1965, granted independence 1980
SWAZILAND 1968
LESOTHO 1966

SOUTH AFRICA

British
French
Portuguese

Belgian
Spanish
independent

1960 — date of independence

Below: Katangan troops, well armed with Belgian FN FAL rifles.

dence on 30 June 1960 – although many had warned of the possible problems of independence in a country the size of western Europe, with mineral wealth that attracted many outside interests and a pitifully small educated elite to which the administration of the new nation was handed over by the departing Belgians.

In the Congo, the problems of regionalism, tribalism, outside interference and army intervention all coincided to produce a very blurred set of conflicts that overlapped each other. There were attempts at secession by provinces; external aid and intervention from the Soviet Union, international financial interests and the UN; personality clashes within a ruling elite; and armed forces that ranged from the Simbas who believed themselves invulnerable to bullets to the white mercenaries who fought for money and loot.

The Congo became independent on 30 June 1960, under the leadership of Patrice Lumumba. Lumumba himself was deposed in a military coup in September (and killed the following year), but by then the fabric of the country had been torn apart by army mutinies and the declaration of independence by the mineral-rich province of Katanga under the leadership of Moise Tshombe. Tshombe used white mercenaries to shore up his position, while the central government requested, and obtained, UN support in trying to end the secession.

These elements all came together over the next few years to provide a complex set of wars. First of all, there was the attempt to keep the state together. The UN troops that had begun arriving in the Congo in July 1960 managed eventually to bring the Katangese secession to an end by spring 1963, and Tshombe fled. But all through this period, the inheritors of Lumumba's radical, left-wing mantle had been consolidating their power in Stanleyville, in the east of the country. There were periodic outbreaks of violence there, and under Antoine Gizenga and later Pierre Mulele the east of the country could never be considered secure. Indeed, in July 1964, Tshombe was invited back to become prime minister of the whole nation, and had to deal

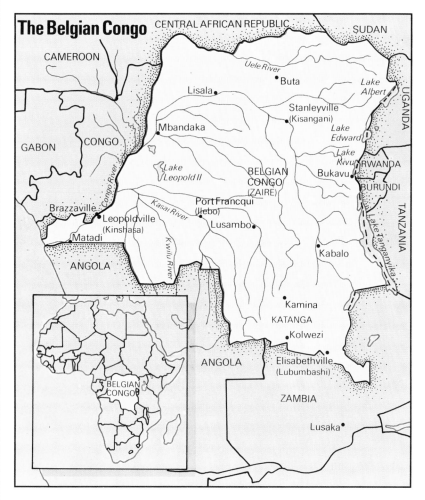

The Belgian Congo

himself fell from power in the summer of 1965. The new strong man in the country was the army chief of staff, Joseph Mobutu, and he faced a revolt among the mercenaries that Tshombe had hired. Not until 1967 could his government be said to have imposed itself on the whole country.

The fighting in the Congo consisted of small actions, in which a handful of good troops could decide the issue. For this reason, the experienced white mercenaries were very successful, even in resisting the UN troops who attacked them in Katanga. The national army was usually unreliable, and liable to indulge in frightful reprisals against the civilian population. Outside help was always essential – Soviet equipment was sent to Stanleyville, while Tshombe used US aid to good effect.

CIVIL WAR IN CHAD

The fighting that has taken place in Chad since its independence in 1958 has been almost as confusing as that in the Congo. Chad is an enormous country, of 1.28 million sq. km (495,700 sq. miles) but on independence its population was a mere 2.5 million people. There were internal divisions between the animist or Christian blacks in the south, and the Muslim Arabs of the north, while three of the nations that bordered the country were potential sources of trouble: the Sudan, which had its own civil war in the south from the 1960s onwards, Nigeria, which aspired to the leadership of black Africa, and Libya, which from 1969 has been under the control of the flamboyant revolutionary, Colonel Gaddafi.

Under President François Tombalbaye there was an attempt to integrate all parties in Chad into central government, but this broke down in the mid-1960s, when Arab ministers were expelled from the cabinet. Using Libya as a base, the Arab political groups formed the *Front de Libération Nationale du Tchad* (National Liberation Front of Chad), known as Frolinat, and by 1969 had managed to assert control over large areas of the north of the country. In the vast spaces of the southern Sahara, guerrilla bands could move around virtually at will, and took a heavy toll of government troops coming up from the south. Finally, the government invoked the Franco-Chadian treaty, and France sent in units of the Foreign Legion, which restored some kind of order. Acting in motorized columns and well trained in mobile warfare, the Legion was more than a match for Frolinat, and was able to claim victory when it left in 1971.

Tombalbaye had attempted to reach an agreement with Gaddafi, but this broke down, and Frolinat, now under the control of Hissène Habré and Goukouni Oueddi,

with a major rebellion in the east, in which the ferocious Simbas were the crack troops of the insurgents.

Tshombe was given support by a number of groups – notably the Belgians, who still maintained strong connections, especially financial, with the Congo and wished to install a stable regime favourable to their interests. Tshombe also used more white mercenaries, principally those under the command of 'Mad Mike' Hoare. This support proved insufficient, however, and Tshombe

Right: A paratrooper of Joseph Mobutu's forces in the streets of Stanleyville. Mobutu managed to bind significant elements of the Congolese Army to himself, and established an effective power base that stood him in good stead during the turmoils of the 1960s.

latest in modern weaponry, are encouraged by outside powers, it seems that Chad will never know peace.

ETHIOPIA, SOMALIA AND ERITREA

Outside intervention in Ethiopia and the Horn of Africa was of a different nature from that in Chad – but just as important in determining the nature of the fighting. Under the Emperor Haile Selassie, Ethiopia had made great territorial gains in the aftermath of World War II. She had been given control over the Ogaden, which had a majority of Somali speakers, and Eritrea to the north-east – the latter area had a semi-autonomous status until the emperor incorporated it into the state in 1960. Both these regions had potential for warfare; and indeed, the Eritrean nationalists had begun a guerrilla war as early as 1960.

The signal for larger-scale fighting to break out came in 1974. In September, Emperor Haile Selassie was overthrown, largely because his regime had proved incapable of dealing with the problems of the drought that was afflicting all the immediately sub-Saharan areas of Africa. In his place, a group of army officers known as the Dergue took over, and after some years of confusion in the capital, Major Mengistu Haile Mariam emerged as the most important figure. The years between 1974 and 1977 (when Mengistu asserted his control) were confused and bloody. There were major efforts to make radical changes to Ethiopia. Land was nationalized in 1975, and a People's Democratic Republic proclaimed in 1976. Attempts were made to form a people's army of the peasantry. In Addis Ababa itself there was street fighting between rival factions, and the central government was unable to assert control over many areas.

In this situation, separatists in both the Ogaden and Eritrea were able to take the

recommenced operations with such success that in 1975 Tombalbaye was overthrown in a military coup because of his inability to control the situation. Indeed, Habré came to an accommodation with the government in 1978 and was proclaimed prime minister. He sought, and was granted, more French aid against Oueddi's Frolinat. Once again, units of the Legion moved in and swept large areas of the north clear of rebels. Frolinat were now better armed than ever before, however; they were now getting modern smallarms and light support weapons from Libya.

The political confusion of the country soon deepened. Oueddi ousted Habré in a coup in 1980, but in 1982, Habré, at the head of a grouping called the *Forces Armées du Nord* took the capital of Chad, N'Djamena, and took power himself once again. In 1983, Libyan aid to Oueddi increased, and there was serious danger from the north; once again French troops were sent in to shore up the government forces. For as long as small groups of armed men, equipped with the

Left: A mobile anti-aircraft unit, with a Soviet-made KPVT 14.5mm heavy machine gun, patrolling the desert in Chad in 1983. Although the original fighting in Chad was largely between the Arabs of the north and the government forces from the southern areas of the country (mostly black Christians), by the mid-1970s both racial and ideological distinctions had become blurred.

Below: Frolinat rebels open fire with Soviet firearms on government troops. Help from outside – notably from Libya and France – has been very important in determining the direction of the civil war in Chad.

offensive. In the Ogaden, separatists had always been encouraged by the government of Somalia, which enshrined in its constitution the reunion of all Somalis (including those under Ethiopian and Kenyan rule) under one government. The Western Somali Liberation Front (WSLF) stepped up its activities, supported by the Somali government, which allowed regular officers to resign commissions in order to join WSLF forces. In 1977, the fighting escalated, and the WSLF troops moved steadily forward. By August they had laid siege to the towns of Harer and Dire Dawa, and threatened to cut

Ethiopia's main trade outlet, the rail link from Addis Ababa to Djibouti.

Further intervention from outside saved the Ethiopian troops. Under Haile Selassie, Ethiopia had been a firm friend of the West, while Somalia, with ambitions to upset the existing states structure in the Horn of Africa, had accepted Soviet aid, and given the Soviet Navy base facilities. But the radical changes in Ethiopia had brought to power men who had great sympathy for the Soviet model of government, and who were happy to accept Soviet aid. In April 1977, US personnel were asked to leave Ethiopia, and in May of that year, Mengistu signed a series of treaties with the Soviet Union. The Soviet leadership could see far more potential in the largest nation in the region than it could in relatively poor Somalia, and refused the Somalis help in their campaign to secure the Ogaden. The consequence was that Soviet personnel were forced to leave Somalia in November 1977. Soviet and Cuban aid was now given freely to the Ethiopians in their struggle in the Ogaden, and the provision of heavy support weapons and numerous advisors (some estimates have claimed that 11,000 Cubans were at work with the Ethiopian forces by 1978) was too much for the WSLF. By March 1978, the Ogaden was once more in Ethiopian hands, although the guerrilla war continued on a smaller scale.

In Eritrea, a similar infusion of Soviet aid was of crucial help to the Ethiopian government. Here, three main resistance groups had taken over large areas of the region by mid-1977, after attempts by the Ethiopians to use peasant levies in 1976 had been a failure. By the end of 1977, about 80,000 government troops were facing some 40,000 guerrillas who had strong local backing and had in-

Above: Members of the Ethiopian People's Militia on parade in Addis Ababa in 1977. The creation of a new mass army was one of the policies by which the revolutionary government hoped to stave off defeat in Eritrea and the Ogaden. Below: Eritrean guerrillas train with captured Soviet-made weapons.

Above: Eritrean guerrillas undergo rudimentary drill. In spite of the deployment of large amounts of Soviet-built weaponry against them, the guerrillas have maintained an effective resistance to the Ethiopian government forces. Below: Eritrean guerrillas manning an anti-aircraft gun.

300,000 Eritrean refugees had fled) provided a reservoir of manpower and the random bombing and casual brutality of the government's campaign had increased support for the insurgents. A further offensive of 1979, again heavily supported by Soviet equipment, was unable to make much headway against determined resistance. The war has, therefore, continued.

FROM RHODESIA TO ZIMBABWE

The war which the guerrillas of ZAPU (Zimbabwe African People's Union) and ZANU (Zimbabwe African National Union) fought against the white-dominated government of Southern Rhodesia from the late 1960s until the installation of ZANU's head, Robert Mugabe, as prime minister in 1980 is in some ways the last of the colonial wars rather than one of the wars of independent Africa. In other ways, it is merely a part of a larger struggle in southern Africa: the war between the white minorities and black majorities, of which the conflict in Namibia and Angola forms a part.

The basic causes of the war in Rhodesia were quite simple. The white-dominated government of that country declared UDI (Unilateral Declaration of Independence) from Great Britain in 1965, because it could not accept the British government's demand that independence must be accompanied by assurances that eventually there would be full political rights for the blacks who formed the vast majority of the population. The major African organizations, from the African National Congress in 1959 to ZAPU

stalled themselves in some towns. But in 1978 heavy Soviet equipment began to make itself felt. In July 1978, for example, 300 T-34 tanks were deployed in a major drive that took large sectors of the north, and eventually (in November) resulted in the fall of the stronghold of Keren. Increased bombing raids made it difficult for the guerrillas to move freely around areas under their control, and the threat that the Eritreans would be able to win a decisive military victory began to ease.

Just as in the Ogaden, however, guerrilla warfare was not stamped out. The massive refugee camps in the Sudan (where about

Right: A member of the Rhodesian Selous Scouts examines evidence of guerrilla presence. The Selous Scouts were an elite force, many of whom were black. They acted, as their name would suggest, as lightly armed small units, searching the bush for signs of the guerrillas sent in by ZAPU and ZANU, and trying to establish close contact with the local populace.

in 1962, had all been banned, and it seemed clear to many Africans that the right-wing Rhodesian Front Party which, under Ian Smith, ran the country, was determined to hang on to white privileges for as long as possible.

The earliest attempts by black guerrillas to unseat the white government were not particularly successful. The Rhodesian security forces were well trained, and contained many expert units, such as the Selous Scouts, while in spite of Britain's attempt to impose international sanctions, the white government managed to support itself relatively comfortably. Indeed, in spite of the emergence of black political groups within Rhodesia, and the importance of Bishop Abel Muzorewa in promoting black aspirations within the country, the guerrillas would probably have continued to enjoy little success were it not for changes in the international scene. The most important of these was the decision by Portugal in 1974 to abandon its African colonies. As soon as Mozambique became an independent black state, then the strategic position of the Rhodesian security forces was much more vulnerable, for the border with Mozambique was far longer than that with the other main refuge of the guerrillas (Zambia) and the border areas far more

rugged, making the detection of infiltration that much more difficult. ZANU, in the form of its military wing ZANLA (Zimbabwe African National Liberation Army) swiftly established itself in Mozambique, and its raids became very dangerous – a fact perhaps best evidenced by the ferocity of Rhodesian cross-border 'hot pursuit' raids as they struck at guerrilla bases across the border.

The independence of Mozambique also led the South Africans, hitherto one of the main supporters of the Rhodesians, to try to persuade Smith to reach an accommodation with black nationalists. The last thing the South Africans wanted was an enormous conflagration on their northern border in a conflict that white forces could not win, but which might lead to the creation of large, successful, well-armed and well-trained black guerrilla armies, probably closely supported by the Soviet Union. Smith, therefore, agreed to the principle of 'one man one vote', and in 1979 Muzorewa became the first black prime minister of the country.

Denouncing Muzorewa as a traitor, the guerrillas continued their attacks, however, and it became clear that an agreement would have to be reached with them. By 1980, agreement had been reached at Lancaster House in London and in March of that year, the leader of ZANU, Robert Mugabe, was elected prime minister. Once again, outside forces had been crucial in determining the outcome of an African guerrilla war.

ANGOLA IN TURMOIL

The Civil War in Angola, that has been raging since independence in 1975, has links with other struggles. From Angolan territory, the guerrillas of SWAPO (South West African People's Organization) have launched their raids into Namibia, while opponents of the ruling MPLA party in

Joshua Nkomo (left) is often referred to as the founding father of Zimbabwean nationalism. In the early 1960s, however, he was arrested, and his nationalist organization forced underground by the success of the Rhodesian Front Party led by Ian Smith (below left). The Rhodesian Front was determined to hang on to the privileges that the whites had hitherto enjoyed, and which would be ended were the black nationalists to take over the country after independence from Britain. This fear led Smith to announce the Unilateral Declaration of Independence (UDI) from Britain in 1965.

The history of the state of Angola since its independence has been one of civil war and outside intervention, as part of a larger conflict involving many of the states of southern Africa and centring round the position of South Africa as a self-consciously white and racially exclusive regime in a black continent. Above: South African troops in Namibia, the area of southwest Africa that they still control, in spite of the efforts of the Angolan-based guerrillas of SWAPO (South West Africa People's Organization) to force them out. Above right: Cuban troops, part of the 15,000-strong force that helped the Marxist government in Angola establish itself against threats in both the south and north of the country after independence.

Angola have received aid from South Africa; and the presence of Soviet advisors and Cuban combat troops on Angolan soil has given the struggle an international aspect and a link with the Cold War.

The MPLA and the FNLA had been the two most important of the insurgent groups fighting the Portuguese from 1961 (see pp. 219–21). In 1966, UNITA was formed; its main influence lay among the Ovimbundu people in the south of the country. There was always rivalry between these three groups, and a provisional government formed in 1974 to replace the Portuguese administration, in which all three participated, soon broke up. By the autumn of 1975, there was fighting all over the country. The MPLA had the strongest support, but in the north the FNLA under Holden Roberto had strong backing from the Zairean government of Joseph Mobutu (and recruited European mercenaries) while in the south, Jonas Savimbi's UNITA had the benefit of aid from South Africa.

The MPLA accepted help from the Soviet bloc, and also from Cuba, which sent in 15,000 troops. By the end of 1975, this help was making a considerable difference to the struggle. By February 1976, Zairean troops had been driven out of the north of Angola, and by March of that year most South African and UNITA forces had been pushed back in the south. Yet although the most intense phase of the war may have come to an end, the conflict as a whole did not. South Africa was very worried about the amount of aid being given to the guerrillas who, from Angola, were attempting to end South African occupation of Namibia (South West Africa), and were encouraging UNITA to continue its activities. There was, therefore, no real let-up in hostilities in the south of the country (although in the north, Angola's relations with Zaire improved so that the

FNLA found its main source of support considerably less helpful than in the mid-1970s). The presence of guerrilla bases from which the members of ZAPU and ZANU operated into Rhodesia was also a destabilizing factor – in fact, Rhodesian jets attacked such bases in 1978.

The situation in the 1980s developed into one in which UNITA gradually extended its control over an increasing area of the country, while the South African forces were always prepared to move into the south of Angola. But the South Africans could not hope to destabilize the MPLA while it had the backing of the Soviet Union and still deployed Cuban troops. There was, therefore, a kind of stalemate. The main prospect for a slackening of the fighting lay in an accommodation between South Africa and Angola. Just as South Africa had made an agreement with Mozambique that each nation would cease actively aiding the guerrillas that it encouraged against the government of the other, so the Angolan government, in desperate need of a respite in order to improve its economy, could see great advantages in a similar agreement with South Africa. For their part, the South Africans were trying (and continue to try) to come to a series of treaties with their black neighbours to the north in order to prevent what is potentially the most destructive of all Africa's wars – the fight to destroy white domination in South Africa.

Part Eight
Modern Conventional Wars

In addition to the wars that have been fought as part of the Cold War, and the numerous guerrilla campaigns that have taken place around the globe, there has been another category of conflict since 1945: wars between states. These may involve outside powers (indeed, in the age of the Cold War and with the superpowers concerned to keep control of events all around the globe, some form of outside intervention in any such war is probably inevitable) but the distinctive characteristic of such conflicts is that the states concerned have resorted to full-scale conventional war on their own initiative.

Some of the conflict between states has been small-scale - such as border clashes - or fought for reasons which are obscure - the Sino-Soviet clashes on the northern Chinese border in the late 1960s, for instance, or the short Chinese invasion of Vietnam in February 1979 - but most have been fought for specific objectives, and these form one of the most important trends of modern war.

An important element of these conventional wars between states is that they have taken place within certain limits. They have tended to be local in scope, and even in the most intense of them, the Arab-Israeli Wars, attacks on the civilian populations of the contending states have been rare. What is most noteworthy about these wars, however,

is that they show just how the battlefield of the post-1945 period has relied on the types of weapon that came to the fore in World War II. The tank and the close-support aircraft are still the critical weapons when they are allowed to get into action.

These weapons have changed since 1945, however. Not only are they much more destructive than their equivalents in World War II, but they also cost so much more that finding spare parts, or obtaining replacements, is an almost prohibitively expensive business. The cost of a Spitfire in 1940 was around £5000. By 1984, each new model of the US F-16 fighter that played such an important part in the Israeli invasion of the Lebanon in 1982 cost around $10 million. In real terms, this is 60 times as much. For a small country, such sums are hard to find, and even for a relatively wealthy nation like Britain the war in the Falklands could have been financially disastrous if, say, one of the two aircraft carriers had been sunk. As it was, the destroyer *Sheffield* that fell victim to an Exocet missile (which itself cost $400,000) meant the lost of a $150 million investment.

To justify this enormous cost, the latest weapons are much more efficient than their predecessors in World War II. The F-4 Phantom fighter/strike aircraft, for example, can carry 7258kg (16,000lb) of munitions with

Below: The AH-64 Apache helicopter, armed with 16 Hellfire anti-tank missiles. These descendants of the tank-busting planes of World War II have brought a new dimension to anti-tank warfare, and pack an awesome punch.

Right: One of the most fearsome modern warplanes, the US Fairchild A-10. Officially named the Thunderbolt, after the famous World War II aircraft, the A-10 is known to its pilots as the 'Warthog' because of its clumsy frame but deadly payload. The A-10 carries 7257kg (16,000lb) of weapons, and has the ability to absorb great punishment.

Above: NATO soldiers in NBC (Nuclear, Biological, Chemical) suits, man a TOW (Tube-launched, Optically-tracked, Wire-guided) missile launcher during exercises. All the armies in the European theatre have to be prepared to fight in conditions where nuclear fallout may be present.

which to support troops on the ground – a load comparable to that of a World War II heavy bomber (the British Lancaster generally handled about 8200kg (18,000lb) of bombs). Taking into account the accuracy of 'smart' bombs, and wire-guided munitions for use against aircraft and tanks, the hitting power of a modern weapons system is enormous.

These latest weapons are, then, very expensive and very destructive. This gives many wars between states a knife-edge quality – each side waiting for the enemy's most effective weaponry to come into play, while hoping that it does not have to use up too much of its own expensive equipment. Weapons that promise to undermine an opponent's systems – the Exocet, for example – are much sought-after. During the war in the Falklands, the revelation of the power of the Exocet saw the Argentinian government feverishly trying to obtain more from the arms dealers of Europe.

The arms trade has itself become an important component of modern warfare, the more so as the technology of weapons continues to spiral upwards. The main arms dealers are the two superpowers, who use their ability to equip entire armed forces as a lever in the manipulation of regional politics all over the globe. But there are also many private and state-owned armaments firms in the industrialized world that disseminate their products via an arms-trading network. The manufacture of arms has also spread, so that nations which aspire to supremacy in their region – Israel in the Middle East or India in South Asia – tend to institute their own armaments industry.

Finally, these wars between states show, in spite of the cost and efficiency of modern weapons, that one of the constants of warfare

through the ages has not lessened in importance. This constant lies in the ability and bravery of the individual soldier (or sailor, or airman) and the quality of the officers who direct him. In the wars between states where there is a marked disparity in these attributes – as in the early Arab-Israeli Wars (1948–72), or the land fighting in the Falklands (1982) – the side with the better men may effect a rapid victory, even though the enemy has weapons that are just as technically advanced. For the smaller the scope of the war, the more important these individual qualities become.

This theory is borne out by the outcome of wars where the military expertise has been low. In the Gulf War, which began in 1980, for example, the typically short and destructive modern battles have not taken place, largely because the men involved could not undertake the essentially expert tasks necessary to utilize the weaponry to advantage. An even more extreme case was the war in Biafra (1967–70). Here there was a lack of modern weaponry, and also a low level of expertise, with the result that the reduction of a small enclave took far longer than expected. The capital of Biafra fell on September 1967, but not until early 1970 could the war be said to have finished.

In this context, it is most interesting to observe the wars that the state of India has fought on her borders. For although the Indian armed forces in the early 1960s did not give the appearance of being able to prosecute an effective campaign, by the early 1970s they had improved greatly in their use of modern weapons, and in 1971 were able to undertake a large and complex operation against East Pakistan with great success. They had learnt how to wage modern war within the space of some ten years.

THE ARAB-ISRAELI WARS

The Arab-Israeli Wars have about them the feel of one long conflict. The guerrilla war against the British in the late 1940s, the war for the survival of Israel in 1948–9, the Israeli attack in Sinai in 1956, the Six-Day War of 1967, the Yom Kippur War of 1973 and the gradual Israeli involvement in and invasion of Lebanon during the late 1970s and 1980s are all susceptible to separate analysis, but they are all part of one process – the determination of the Israelis to establish an independent state, distinct from the Arab states that surround it. This objective has always been resisted by the Arabs, and has resulted in the creation of the enormous problem of the Palestinian Arab refugees who live in the surrounding states, and now threatens the peace of the whole world because of the involvement of the USA and the Soviet Union in the region.

The wars have seen a gradual increase in Israel's war-making capacity. From being a vulnerable new country, with no settled borders and hardly even a standing army worthy of the name, the Jewish state has developed into the prime military power in its region, able to mould the politics of its neighbours by the exercise of armed might. The Arab-Israeli Wars have seen the basic weapons of modern warfare – tanks and ground support aircraft – used at a more

advanced technical level than in any other conflict; and they have seen the weaponry of the USA and the Soviet Union tested in battle conditions which have often been stunning in their ferocity. To a certain extent the region has, therefore, been a testing ground for the technology of the superpowers, and certainly, wars such as that of October 1973, when new anti-tank and anti-aircraft missiles were employed, were held to have considerable relevance to any potential war in Europe. In the gradual evolution of the armed forces and the weaponry of the various states involved, these wars illustrate the extent to which modern warfare has

Left: The ruins of the southwest wing of Jerusalem's King David Hotel, the administrative centre of the British Protectorate of Palestine, destroyed by Jewish nationalists on 22 July 1946. Ninety-one people were killed and 45 injured in the blast.

Below: The might of Israeli armour crossing a ridge in Sinai in 1967. The thread running through all the wars fought around Israel since the late 1940s has been the success of the IDF (Israeli Defence Force) in maintaining military superiority over nations which have larger populations and greater natural resources. This has been achieved largely through the excellence of the Israeli fighting men, and the willingness of the high command to take the offensive before its strategic position could be made untenable.

Above: Members of the Haganah practise with a mortar. In the days of the struggle against the British, the Jewish organizations deployed very few heavy support weapons, and arms procurement was a major problem. Right: A religious student, a member of the Haganah, keeps watch in a strongpoint in Tel Aviv.

a considerable amount of sympathy for their cause in the Western world in consequence of the Holocaust of World War II. From the end of that war to the agreement for the British to relinquish the mandate in November 1947 the Jews pursued a highly effective guerrilla war against the British forces in the country.

The main armed force of the Jews was the Haganah, formed in 1920 as a defence organization against Arab attacks on Jewish settlements. There were also two small, extremist splinter groups that were a great embarrassment to the more official Jewish forces. These two groups were the Irgun – which never numbered more than 2500 members before independence but was, under the leadership of Menachem Begin, committed to armed revolt – and the LEHI (*Lohame Herut Israel*, meaning Fighters for the Freedom of Israel), better known as the Stern Gang, a group that had broken away from the Irgun in 1940.

There were frequently violent disagreements between the Haganah and the two smaller groups, and at one stage the Haganah cooperated with British security forces in trying to break the two terrorist bodies, but the LEHI and Irgun were merely the most extreme expressions of a well-nigh universal desire among the Jewish community to establish their own country. Begin always accepted that he was using terrorist methods to achieve his ends, and later boasted that he had invented the basic concepts of urban terrorism. British troops and officials were attacked and installations

developed; but they also show that the quality of the men who must fire the guns remains as important today as it ever was in the past.

All this must have been far from the mind of British Foreign Secretary Arthur Balfour when he signed the declaration of 2 November 1917 that agreed, in response to Zionist lobbying, that Great Britain would view 'with favour the establishment in Palestine of a national home for the Jewish people'. Having conquered Palestine during World War I, and having been given a mandate for this former part of the Ottoman empire by the League of Nations, Britain then found it very difficult to formulate a policy which took into account both the interests of the Palestinian Arabs and the wishes of the Zionists, the vocal Jewish settlers who were determined to found a Jewish state.

Between 1917 and the end of World War II there was a gradual build-up of Jewish immigration to Palestine (both legal and illegal) and a corresponding increase in the pressure for an independent Jewish state. By 1946, there were 700,000 Jews in Palestine, outnumbered by the 1,300,000 Arabs, but with

Above: After the massacre of Arabs at Deir Yassin and the success of the Jewish offensive to relieve the beleaguered Jewish community in Jerusalem in April 1948, the Palestinian Arabs began to move out of Jewish-controlled areas. The problem of the Palestinian refugees has bedevilled the Middle East to the present day.

Below: Jewish soldiers train a Vickers Mk 1 machine gun on Arab positions in Galilee in 1948.

bombed – the most notorious assault being the destruction of a wing of the King David Hotel in Jerusalem in July 1946, with the loss of 91 lives – and the British forces assigned to Palestine found they had a thankless task. With Jewish forces so well organized and supported, the main security operations against them could only be massive sweeps, which were speculative and hopeful rather than precise in their direction. The main civilian police body, the Palestine Police, was never able to provide a sufficient amount of information for the army to act effectively, and attempts to meet terror with terror by using small squads of counter-terrorists also failed.

By mid-1947, the British were unwilling to carry on the mandate any longer, but the question of who, or what, was to succeed them was a grave problem, especially as the Arabs were becoming increasingly militant in opposition to Zionist aspirations. The solution proposed by the United Nations in November 1947 was for the country of Palestine to be split between Arabs and Jews, as from May 1948. This plan was accepted by the British and the Jewish organizations, who

could at last see a possible state for themselves, but it also led to widespread fighting between the Arab and Jewish communities, with British forces trying to involve themselves as little as possible in the conflict but preventing the worst excesses. In communal bombing and small-scale attacks, 100 Arabs were killed in the first two weeks of December 1947, and one single bomb placed in the Jewish quarter of Jerusalem killed 52 people in February 1948.

These incidents, dreadful though many of them were, could not decide the struggle, however. The real question was whether the Arabs could cut off and destroy any of the Jewish communities, many of them isolated, that lay throughout Palestine. The biggest prize was Jerusalem, where the 100,000-strong Jewish community in the Old City was surrounded by Arab irregulars, and could only be supplied along one road from Tel Aviv. In March 1948 the Palestinian Arab forces, under the general control of the Grand Mufti of Jerusalem, stopped convoys getting to the city (and were happy to massacre and mutilate any Jewish prisoners that fell into their hands). In April, therefore, the leader of the Haganah, David Ben-Gurion, felt that he had no alternative but to order an offensive against the Arab positions, something he had wished to avoid before the British withdrawal. The offensive was successful, and the Old City was relieved; but during it occurred the massacre at Deir Yassin, where members of the Irgun and the LEHI slaughtered the inhabitants of an Arab village. The massacre was the signal for Palestinian Arabs in many of the areas that were to come under Jewish control by the terms of the UN agreement to abandon their homes, so creating the beginnings of the Palestinian refugee problem that has bedevilled the Middle East ever since. As the final arrangements were made for the British to pull out, further Jewish offensives took Jaffa and Acre while 60,000 Arabs were evacuated by sea from Haifa. On 14 May 1948, Ben-Gurion read the declaration of independence of the state of Israel in the museum of Tel Aviv; at the same time, the armies of the neighbouring Arab states began the invasion of the new country.

THE 1948–9 WAR

The Arab states had been waiting for the official British withdrawal before they made their assault. Now 37,000 troops from the armies of Syria, Iraq, Lebanon, Egypt and Transjordan, plus a force known as the Arab Liberation Army composed of Palestinians and equipped by the Arab states, aided by the irregulars already fighting the Jews within Palestine, struck into Israel. The Syrians, Lebanese and Iraqis attacked across the

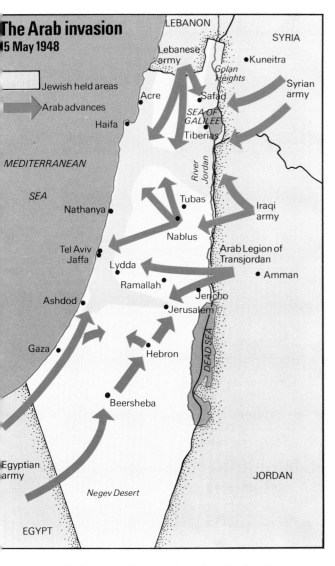

The Arab invasion 15 May 1948

Jewish held areas
Arab advances

LEBANON
SYRIA
Lebanese army
Kuneitra
Golan Heights
Acre
Safad
Syrian army
Haifa
SEA OF GALILEE
Tiberias
River Jordan
MEDITERRANEAN SEA
Tubas
Nathanya
Iraqi army
Nablus
Tel Aviv Jaffa
Arab Legion of Transjordan
Lydda
Ramallah
Amman
Ashdod
Jericho
Jerusalem
Gaza
DEAD SEA
Hebron
Beersheba
Egyptian army
JORDAN
Negev Desert
EGYPT

Force (IDF) to build up its meagre stocks of support weapons, however, and this included the purchase of aircraft. In October, when fighting restarted, the IDF was able to take the offensive, sweeping Syrian forces out of Galilee in the north by the end of the month, at the same time driving back the Egyptians in the south. Indeed, by December the Israelis were in a position to cross over into Egypt itself, where they took the town of Abu Aweigila.

A general ceasefire was arranged on 7 January 1949, with the state of Israel now secure from any immediate Arab threat. There had been about 6000 Israeli casualties, and probably more than this on the Arab side. There were mutual recriminations among the Arab states after the defeat of their superior forces; but this had been a war of small-scale encounters, between units that very often had few support weapons, and where the ability and determination of Jewish settlements to resist Arab forces had proved vital in slowing Arab offensives, especially on the southern front where the Egyptian Army was reduced to bypassing Jewish communities it was unable to subdue. The next round of fighting would be altogether different.

THE SINAI CAMPAIGN, 1956

The Israeli attack on the Egyptian positions in Sinai and in the Gaza Strip in 1956 was undertaken in collusion with the British and French, who launched their attack on the northern end of the Suez Canal, at Port Said, six days after the first Israeli assaults. All the

Above: David Ben-Gurion, who established the Jewish underground army, the Haganah. On 14 May 1948, after a long struggle, he read the declaration of independence and became the first prime minister of Israel.

plains in the north, the Jordanian Army came directly west, aiming to cut through near Jerusalem, while the Egyptians advanced through the Negev in the south. The Israelis had very few heavy support weapons, and no trained force that was the equal of the 4500-strong Arab Legion of King Abdullah of Transjordan.

What the Israelis did have, however, were interior lines of communication and a united command. Although the Arab forces were all in theory directed by King Abdullah, who clearly had the best army, the mutual jealousy of the various states, and especially the suspicions with which the other nations regarded the ambitions of Abdullah, meant that cooperation was rudimentary.

The first period of fighting, which lasted until 11 June when the United Nations managed to negotiate a ceasefire, saw the Israeli troops hold strong Arab offensives on all fronts, although Iraqi units almost split the country in two in southern Galilee and the Arab Legion took the Old City of Jerusalem. Then there was further fighting from 9–18 July, which ended inconclusively. The truces had enabled the 28,000-strong Israeli Defence

Left: Jewish troops snatch a break after taking the village of Kakoun in 1948. The fighting in 1948 was between small units, and mobile, highly motivated Jewish task forces were able to hold the offensives of better-equipped Arab armies.

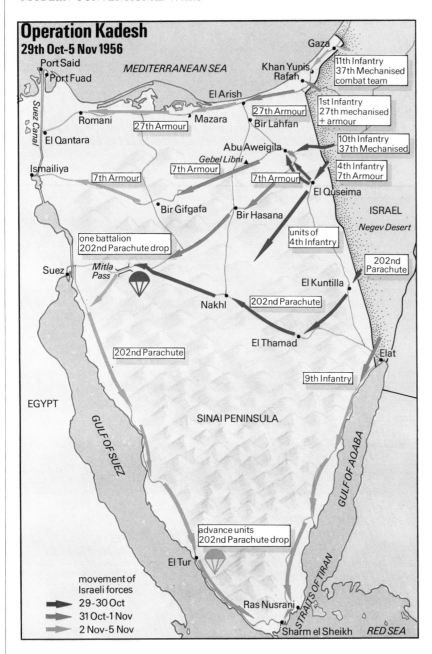

Operation Kadesh
29th Oct-5 Nov 1956

Port Said
Port Fuad
MEDITERRANEAN SEA
Gaza

Khan Yunis
Rafah

11th Infantry
37th Mechanised
combat team

El Arish

1st Infantry
27th mechanised
+ armour

Romani
Mazara
27th Armour
Bir Lahfan

Suez Canal

27th Armour

El Qantara

Abu Aweigila

10th Infantry
37th Mechanised

Gebel Libni

Ismailiya
7th Armour
7th Armour

4th Infantry
7th Armour

7th Armour

Bir Gifgafa
El Quseima

ISRAEL

Bir Hasana
Negev Desert

units of
4th Infantry

one battalion
202nd Parachute drop

Suez
Mitla Pass

El Kuntilla

202nd
Parachute

Nakhl
202nd Parachute

202nd Parachute

El Thamad

Elat

9th Infantry

EGYPT

GULF OF SUEZ

SINAI PENINSULA

GULF OF AQABA

advance units
202nd Parachute drop

El Tur

movement of
Israeli forces
➤ 29-30 Oct
➤ 31 Oct-1 Nov
➤ 2 Nov-5 Nov

STRAITS OF TIRAN

Ras Nusrani

Sharm el Sheikh   RED SEA

Above: The Israeli drive across the Sinai in 1956, Operation Kadesh, took place across three main axes. The crucial elements were the paradrop by the Mitla Pass and the fighting around the Abu Aweigila defensive complex.

partners in the attack on Egypt had their own motives; the British and French were upset by the nationalization of the Suez Canal Company in July 1956, the French were unhappy at Egyptian support for the Algerian FLN insurgents, while Israel had been the victim of attacks from Palestinian guerrillas based in the Gaza Strip. Israel had, in fact, taken punitive action against Egyptian positions in the Strip in February 1955 as a retaliation for such raids, and the opening moves of the assault in Sinai in 1956 were designed to look as though they could be another such small-scale retaliation. Israel also wished to preserve the freedom of movement of her shipping through the Straits of Tiran, dominated by the Egyptian port of Sharm el Sheikh.

These specific reasons for the secret alliance against Egypt were overlain by one major aim, shared by all three assailants:

they wished to see Egypt's President Gamal Abdel Nasser humiliated, and if possible removed from power. Nasser was at the centre of the radical politics that were sweeping the Middle East, and in 1955 he had concluded a deal with Czechoslovakia that gave him a large quantity of Soviet arms. He threatened traditional French and British interests in the region, and as a strong, popular Egyptian leader committed to the cause of Arab nationalism was a very real threat to the existence of the state of Israel.

Israeli-French negotiations had been going on since 1955, and in 1956 the Israeli government came under some pressure from its military establishment, notably from chief of staff Moshe Dayan, to take some positive action against Egypt. On 25 October, agreement was finally reached with Britain and France, and mobilization began. The plan, Operation Kadesh, was to be flexible, and in various phases. There were to be four main axes of advance, corresponding to the main routes across Sinai. In the north there would be a straightforward drive along the coast, isolating and then taking the Gaza Strip; in the centre, Israeli troops would assault the main Egyptian positions at Abu Aweigila; in the south, a parachute drop in front of the Mitla Pass would be followed up by a drive through Thamad and past Nakhl to support the paratroops, while in the east, units would push down the coast road towards Sharm el Sheikh.

On the afternoon of 29 October 1956, the paratroops dropped to the east of the Mitla Pass on schedule, and dug in, while other units of the 202nd Parachute Brigade under Colonel Ariel Sharon crossed the border, swiftly taking the frontier post of El Kuntilla. It had been Dayan's intention to wait after this initial attack, to test Egyptian reaction and also to leave his forces with the possibility of withdrawal should there be a hold-up in the Anglo-Egyptian descent on Suez. In the event, however, Major-General Assaf Simhoni sent his 7th Armoured Brigade towards Abu Aweigila in the morning of the 30th, and Dayan decided to continue this attack on the main Egyptian position in Sinai.

The Egyptian forces in Sinai were relatively light; ever since August, Nasser had kept his main concentrations west of the Suez Canal, to defend against a possible Anglo-French strike. The Egyptian Air Force, too, was directing its attention to the probability of action coming from across the Mediterranean, as the Anglo-French Task Force had now set out. On the night of 31 October, Egyptian airfields were bombed by the Europeans, and the Egyptians' main opponent was clearly going to be the invasion fleet.

This being the case, the Egyptians decided

SUEZ

The nationalization of the Suez Canal Company by Egyptian leader Gamal Abdel Nasser on 26 June 1956 was the crucial moment in a gradual breakdown of relations between the Egyptians and the two European powers, France and Britain, who claimed special authority over the vital waterway. The European powers devised a scheme for an attack on the Egyptians in collusion with the Israelis. The Israeli attack on the Egyptians in Sinai began on 29 October, and two days later the first Anglo-French aircraft began bombing Egyptian targets. On 5 November the first of the invading troops went in: British paratroops landed west of Port Said to secure the important airfield of Gamil, while French paras took Port Fuad to the east. On the 6th the seaborne assault got under way, and included a heliborne attack by men of the British 45 Commando.

Successful though these assaults were, the Suez operation had come far too late. World opinion, and especially US opinion had turned against the Anglo-French viewpoint during the months of tension and expectation since the nationalization of the Canal Company in June. Within Britain and France there was considerable opposition to the invasion. The crucial factor, however, was the disastrous run on British gold and currency reserves – 15 per cent left Britain during the crisis. Britain accepted a ceasefire on the evening of 6 November, and UN troops were swiftly brought in.

Suez was a humiliating climbdown for two powers that had once controlled large areas of the Middle East, and reflected their fast-waning influence.

---

that their units in Sinai should fight blocking actions, and disengage when they had bought a certain amount of time. The defence of the Abu Aweigila position, therefore, was kept up only until 1 November; in the Mitla Pass, the Egyptian forces also pulled back on 1 November (although not before they had inflicted severe losses on Sharon's men when, in defiance of instructions from Dayan, the Israelis had attempted to push through the defile) and when the Israelis moved along the northern coast, again on the 1st, Brigadier-General Jaffar al-Abd conducted a model withdrawal, even though he was under fire from French naval vessels in the Mediterranean.

Meanwhile, the prime Israeli target of the war, Sharm el Sheikh, was being approached by two columns – one down the east coast of the peninsula and the other composed of some of Sharon's 202nd Parachute Brigade, who had bypassed Mitla and were moving down the west coast. The defenders hung on grimly but after three days of air bombardment could not hold an Israeli armoured assault that breached the defences on the 5th.

The 5th was also the day that the Anglo-French invasion of Egypt (Operation Musketeer) finally got under way, as paratroops landed in Port Said, to be followed the next day by sea-borne troops. But already world pressure, and especially the disapproval of the USA, was making itself felt. On the evening of the 6th, a ceasefire was announced, and hostilities ceased at midnight. The Israelis had suffered 181 dead; the Egyptians in Sinai about 1500. After tortuous negotiations the Israelis handed back Sharm el Sheikh and the Gaza Strip in March 1957, with no guarantees about the activities of Palestinian guerrillas or the rights of passage through the Straits of Tiran.

What the Israelis had gained was a priceless lesson in the use of tanks on the battlefield. Before the war, they had seen armour as a close support for infantry, and little more; but after the experiences of some of the more hard-fought encounters, the value of independent mobile tank units was recognized. This was to be important in the future. But the main aim of the war, the humiliation of Nasser, was not achieved. He remained the great symbol of an Arab world dedicated to the destruction of a state whose very shape – Israel was only 29km (17 miles) wide at some points – made her constantly vulnerable to surprise attack. Israel's small population (less than two million in 1960) and insecure economy meant that she could not afford to maintain a large defensive army to defend these vulnerable frontiers. The solution arrived at was that of a highly trained conscript army which would be ready to strike into Arab territory whenever a threat emerged.

Above: Moshe Dayan, commander of the IDF in the Sinai Desert in 1956 and Minister of defence during the Six-Day War of 1967.

1967: THE SIX-DAY WAR

The war of June 1967, the Six-Day War, saw one of the most complete military victories of the modern period. In an astonishingly short space of time, the IDF broke the armed forces of three of its neighbours, conquered territory (Sinai, the West Bank and the Golan Heights) that gave it more security from attack, and secured a dominant military

Below: Young recruits to the Palestine Liberation Army practise weapons drill in Cairo.

Above: Israeli gunboats in the Straits of Tiran. The Arab decision to close the Straits was one of the major reasons for the Israeli attack in 1967. Below: When the Israelis did attack in 1967, the first move was a surprise air strike against the Egyptian airfields, which were devastated in Operation Dawn.

position in the region, which was only (temporarily threatened in 1973). The victory appeared the more amazing at the time because it seemed to the rest of the world that the Israelis were in imminent danger of being swamped by the powerful Arab armies surrounding them. In the event, however, poor coordination of Arab forces, the suddenness of the Israeli strike and the superiority of Israeli men and equipment won the day, in a campaign, especially in the Sinai, dominated by air power and armoured formations.

Throughout 1966 and 1967 there had been growing tension in the Middle East. The Arab world was still torn by the conflicts between radical and conservative states, but in November 1966 Egypt and Syria reached an agreement after years of quarrelling; and this accord between her most powerful neighbours was bound to cause disquiet in Israel. The Israelis showed they were not prepared to be a passive victim to the raids of Palestinian guerrillas, who were becoming more and more persistent in their forays from across the borders, when they attacked Palestinian positions near Sammu' in Jordan in November 1966 and killed 18 Jordanian soldiers, and the following April Israeli jets engaged Syrian MiGs, and shot six down.

In May, the Syrians were informed (probably by the Russians) that the Israelis were mobilizing against them, and so they requested Egyptian assistance. With great publicity, Nasser moved over 100,000 men into Sinai, and on the 16th requested that the UN remove the peacekeeping force that had been deployed as a buffer since 1956. There was a surge of enthusiasm for a united front against Israel throughout the Arab world, and, perhaps carried away by the rhetoric that he used so effectively, Nasser announced, on 22 May, that the Straits of Tiran would be closed to Israeli shipping. King Hussein of Jordan joined the Egyptians by agreeing to put his forces under Egyptian command. Israel now faced a crisis.

Premier Levy Eshkol tried to find international support, but neither Western Europe nor the USA seemed likely to offer any assistance. The closure of the Straits had always been seen by the Israelis as a *casus belli*, and to the inhabitants of a small vulnerable state, the build-up of force around it was very threatening – although it is doubtful if Nasser intended to attack. Certainly, the Arab states had no coordinated plan of response when the war began. On 1 June, however, the Army chief of staff, Moshe Dayan, became Israeli Minister of Defence,

Above: Israeli tanks and troop-carriers advance towards El Arish on 6 June 1967, at the start of the Six-Day War. Below: Israeli Centurions on the border with Syria. The heavy armament of the Centurion made it a very effective weapon in defensive positions, and superior to the Soviet-made T-54s of the Arab units.

and urged a preemptive strike, sooner rather than later. Eshkol and the cabinet agreed on 4 June, and the next day a set of prearranged plans was brilliantly executed.

The basis of Israeli victory was command of the air. Under Major-General Mordechai Hod, the Israeli Air Force (IAF) had worked out the best time to strike at the airfields of their main enemy, Egypt, and had developed special weapons, tactics and procedures to make the most of an initial surprise raid. The Egyptian Air Force was 450 aircraft strong, with 125 MiG-21 interceptors that were superior to the Israeli Mirages in aerial com-

bat, but Hod's strike on the morning of 5 June destroyed over 200 Egyptian machines, including 90 MiG-21s, for the loss of just 19 Israeli planes. The IAF struck at precisely 0845 Egyptian time, when the airfields had been stood down from their dawn alert. The first attacks came from the north, from the Mediterranean, to avoid the batteries of surface-to-air missiles (SAMs) along the Suez Canal, and special bombs were used to break up airfield surfaces and hamper repair work. To keep the momentum of attack going, the Israeli planes were refuelled and bombed up very quickly – sometimes in as little as eight minutes.

The IAF did not only destroy the Egyptian Air Force on this first day of the war. In mid-morning, the 22 Hawker Hunters of the Jordanian Air Force made a raid into Israel, but in one retaliatory attack the IAF destroyed or damaged them all as they refuelled. And in air raids against Syrian airfields the IAF put 57 planes, two-thirds of the effective Syrian aircraft, out of action. Finally, on 6 June, a strike against the only Iraqi airfield that could have been used as a base against the Israelis destroyed nine aircraft. Within a matter of hours, the Arab states had been put at a grave disadvantage.

While the Egyptian Air Force was being destroyed on the ground, the IDF was moving against the Egyptian ground forces in the Sinai, where it had to fight the first day without the benefit of much air cover. The

Above: Egyptian infantry in position in the Sinai Desert in 1967. Bereft of air cover after the Israeli surprise attack on their airfields, the Egyptians could only put up a brave resistance to the armoured forces of the IDF.

Below: An Egyptian SA-2 anti-aircraft missile, captured in 1967 by the Israelis after being abandoned in Sinai.

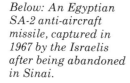

plan in Sinai had originally been to undertake a limited incursion, but Dayan changed this radically. He wanted to make a deep thrust, along the coast and in the centre, to break through the Egyptian defences, push on to the passes across the mountains in the centre of the peninsula, and there complete an encirclement of the Egyptian armies. The Egyptians had developed strong fortifications in the Gaza Strip and around Um Katef and Abu Aweigila in the centre; their infantry formations were well equipped with tanks and tank destroyers, while there were two armoured formations (Task Force Shazli along the border between El Quseima and El Kuntilla, and the 4th Armoured Division at Bir Gifgafa) that could be used to hit the Israelis when they got bogged down against the well-prepared defences.

The campaign was fought between two armies with radically different ideas on the conduct of war. The Israelis placed their trust in the firepower and mobility of their armoured formations, driving through de-

fences and striking into rear areas. To this end, there has been intense emphasis on the training of tank crews, and Major-General Israel Tal in particular had promoted the theories that accurate gunnery and the ability to move about the battlefield under fire were the keys to success. The Egyptians, on the other hand, wanted to force a more set-piece battle, where initiative and fluid front lines would have little place. In the event, Israeli control of the air and the superb performance of her armour won the day against the rather badly led and rapidly dispirited Egyptians.

ACROSS THE SINAI

The Israeli commander in Sinai was Major-General Yeshayahu Gavish. Under him were Major-Generals Tal, Avraham Yoffe and Ariel Sharon. The first attacks were in the north, by Tal's division. His heavy tanks, US M48s and British Centurions, moved against Rafah on 5 June; they took Khan Yunis and then moved along the coast towards El Arish. Although the supporting infantry and light tanks had difficulty keeping up with the spearhead, by 7 June the Gaza Strip had been cleared, in spite of its impressive defences, and the leading armoured units were well on their way to the Suez Canal.

In the centre, Sharon had been forced to abandon his first plan, for a surprise attack on the Abu Aweigila–Um Katef complex, but by feeling round the flanks of the position, he was able to launch a major assault in the night of the 5th, and had taken Um Katef by the 6th. Meanwhile, in the sector between Sharon and Tal, Yoffe had pushed an armoured brigade under Colonel Yiska Shadmi towards an important road junction south of Bir Lahfan. Here, on the night of 5–6 June, an Egyptian convoy of two brigades, one of them armoured, was ambushed (foolishly, the Egyptians had been driving with headlights on). The Egyptians were rapidly losing even the ability to regroup their forces.

The next day, the 6th, Gavish and his divisional commanders decided to concentrate on the move towards the passes, to cut off the large Egyptian forces on the border of the southern Negev and near Nakhl. By the 8th, this had achieved success of enormous proportions. Although Egyptian forces at Gebel Libni and Bir Gifgafa pulled back before they could be engulfed, Tal's armour had reached the Suez Canal at El Qantara (despite heavy fighting on the outskirts of the town) and had given Shadmi's brigade the support it needed to reach the Mitla Pass (albeit with only nine Centurions, four of them on tow). During the night of 7–8 June Shadmi's men held the Mitla Pass and on the 8th, as organized resistance disintegrated, Yoffe went through the Giddi and Mitla Passes. Vast quantities of Egyptian material were destroyed by the IAF in the approaches to the passes, particularly from the armoured units of Task Force Shazli, which had managed to avoid a drive by Sharon's forces that had destroyed the Egyptian 6th Mechanized Division near Nakhl. The destruction of the Egyptian forces in the south of Sinai left Sharm el Sheikh indefensible, and it surrendered to Israeli paratroops and gunboats. On the 9th, a United Nations ceasefire came into operation, but by then the IDF had completed its task. It controlled all the Sinai peninsula and had destroyed an entire army, with very little loss to itself.

While the main Israeli effort was concentrated against the Egyptians, the IDF had few forces with which to face the Jordanian and Syrian armies. Major-General Uri Narkiss commanded the three infantry brigades that were all the IDF could spare to face the Jordanians; and if the Arabs chose to

Operation Red Sheet
Thursday 8 June 1967

Israeli forces
→ Israeli advances 5-7 June
→ Israeli paras
→ Yoffe
→ Tal

attack, his task would be very difficult. The salient of land that led to the Israeli sector of Jerusalem was very vulnerable, and the Jordanian Army had available seven infantry and two armoured brigades. In the event, the Jordanians did attack, beginning their pre-

Above: The Israeli armoured advance westwards across the Sinai peninsula in June 1967 took the Egyptians by storm.

THE BATTLE FOR JERUSALEM

A young Israeli paratrooper describes his part in the fight for the Old City of Jerusalem on 6–7 June 1967.

'They told us to charge – we had a few tanks supporting us, but they couldn't touch those deep dugouts. In a charge it's every man for himself. You see people falling all round you, but you still don't believe it can happen to you. . . .

You just go on, running like hell. And a few metres in front is the officer. However fast you run, you can never catch up with him. That's why so many of them were killed.

'You find you've reached a dugout and you throw in hand grenades and hose it out with your Uzi. And that's it, till the next one. All the time you begin to get more and more scared and more and more angry. I remember when we rested I began to think what I'd done and I remember at one point –

I think it must have been then – hearing that my kibbutz had been shelled. So all at the same time, I was scared but I wanted to get at the bastards all the more.

'We went into the Old City and from then on it was hand-to-hand and house-to-house. That's the worst thing in the world. In the desert, you know, it's different. There are tanks and planes and the whole thing is at a longer range. Hand-to-hand fighting is different, it's terrible. I killed my first man there.'

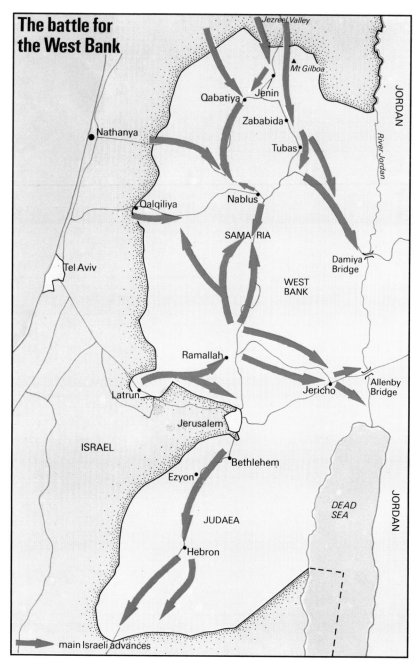

The battle for the West Bank

Jezreel Valley

JORDAN

River Jordan

Mt Gilboa

Jenin
Qabatiya

Zababida

Nathanya

Tubas

Qalqiliya

Nablus

SAMARIA

Damiya
Bridge

Tel Aviv

WEST
BANK

Ramallah

Latrun

Jericho

Allenby
Bridge

Jerusalem

ISRAEL

Bethlehem

Ezyon

DEAD
SEA

JORDAN

JUDAEA

Hebron

→ main Israeli advances

to match the flexibility of the Israeli formations. Peled's forces, for example, were stopped by fierce resistance at Kabatiya, but pushed tanks behind the Jordanian defences and took Nablus. The Jordanians found themselves gradually isolated, and without having given any ground themselves to frontal attacks, were forced to flee to the other side of the Jordan River. By the evening of 7 June, a ceasefire had come into effect as Hussein had been forced to accept the loss of the territories of the West Bank and the failure of his army to hold Israeli advances.

Having dealt with the Egyptians and the Jordanians, the rampant Israelis now felt able to take on the Syrians, who had so far not made any offensive moves but whose immensely strong positions on the Golan Heights were a threat to Galilee, giving them clear observation over northern Israel. In the northern sector the commander was Colonel David Elazar, and on the 9th he began attacks on the Golan defences. These were protected by 260 well-sited artillery pieces on steep escarpments that made armoured assault difficult, and over the years an interconnecting system of blockhouses and strongpoints had been constructed.

The advantages that Elazar had were the unlimited ability of the IAF to give him close support, the arrival of troops from the Sinai front, and the superb morale of his soldiers. His plan was to attack with infantry towards Mount Hermon in the north, while an armoured brigade would attempt to break through to Kuneitra and attacks on the Benot Ya'akov Bridge would draw in Syrian reserves away from the main attacks. The scheme succeeded totally. The infantry attack in the north outflanked and then took the key position of Tel Azaziat, in spite of heavy casualties; Avraham Mandler's armoured brigade smashed its way up steep

parations with an artillery barrage on the morning of the 5th. But Israeli infantry, particularly the reservists of the 16th Infantry Brigade, fought well, and made considerable headway around Jerusalem; Colonel Uri Ben Ari's reserve mechanized brigade was brought in and made a surprise attack which relieved pressure on the Jerusalem corridor; Mordechai Gur's 55th Parachute Brigade was hastily rushed up (its projected drop onto El Arish had been cancelled due to the rate of advance of Tal's armour in Sinai) and proved its ability in intense hand-to-hand fighting; while the main reserve armoured formation in Israel, Major-General Elad Peled's armoured division, moved down from the north towards Nablus.

With no hope of reinforcement because of total IAF air superiority, the Jordanians put up a brave fight, but found themselves unable

The initial fighting, which mainly consisted of artillery barrages, air raids and forays into opposing territory by commandos, died down in the winter of 1968, and the Israelis took the opportunity to build a set of defensive positions along their bank of the Canal, a series of strongpoints known as the Bar-Lev Line after the Israeli chief of staff. Fighting restarted in 1969 and again in 1970, but there were few engagements after late 1970 due to pressure from the USA, and because neither Israel nor Egypt could afford the drain on resources. In March, April and May 1970, for example, the Israelis lost over 200 casualties, and Egyptian losses were even more serious, in spite of rapid Soviet replacement of weaponry.

On 28 September 1970 Israel's great foe, Nasser, died. His successor, Anwar el-Sadat, at first seemed rather ineffectual (proclaiming 1972 as the year of decision and then

Below left: An Israeli Sherman, turret reversed, rolls forward in 1967. Left: Egyptian prisoners, with their uniforms removed, are taken back from the front while Israeli transports move IDF infantry forward.

escarpments to take Kuneitra by the 10th (although again losses were heavy and one battalion was down to two tanks after the first day's fighting); and the attack on the Benot Ya'akov Bridge succeeded in further confusing the Syrian defenders. By the 10th, the Syrians were in flight, abandoning their supposedly impregnable positions, and a UN ceasefire came into operation at 1830 hours.

COUNTING THE COST

Total Israeli losses during the Six-Day War were 689 killed and 2563 wounded; the Egyptians lost over 10,000 dead, the Jordanians about 1000 and the Syrians 2500. It had been a stunning display: the classic techniques of Blitzkrieg – armoured penetration with strong air support – had triumphed over the defensive. It had been a decisive victory for the Israelis in military terms; they had also extended their frontiers to make the state of Israel far more defensible, and they had proved without doubt that they were the prime military power in the region.

The war had solved nothing politically, however. The Arab states and Israel still regarded each other with barely disguised suspicion, to which were added acrimonious disputes in international forums such as the United Nations General Assembly over the fate of the territory that Israel had taken. After the war, in November 1967, the UN passed 'Resolution 242' which tried to lay down as the basis of negotiations an Israeli withdrawal from occupied territories while the Arabs were to recognize the existence of Israel as a sovereign power. Attempts to use this formula as the basis for a compromise all failed, however, and by 1968 there was fighting along the Suez Canal, which by 1969 had become known as the 'War of Attrition', as it was described by Nasser.

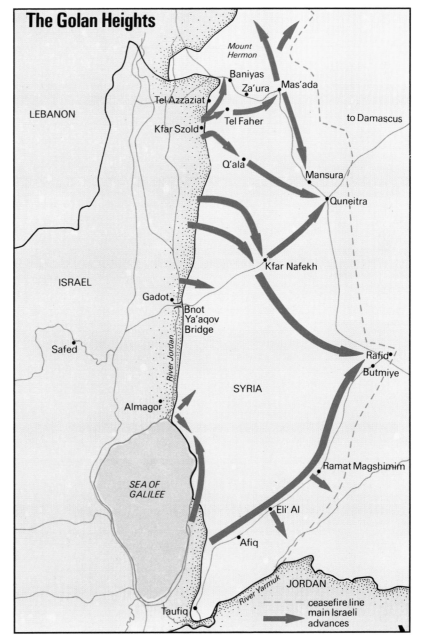

The Golan Heights

Above: Israeli tanks attack a SAM missile base while themselves being shelled by Egyptian forces during the Yom Kippur War.

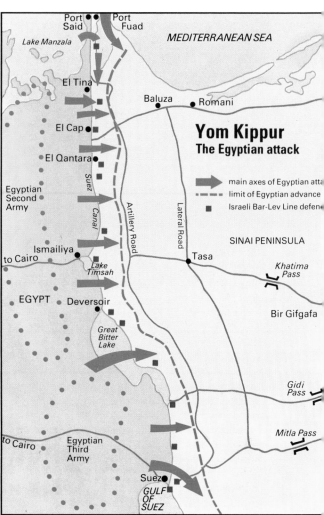

Yom Kippur
The Egyptian attack

→ main axes of Egyptian attack
- - - limit of Egyptian advance
■ Israeli Bar-Lev Line defence

appearing to do little), but he was to prove stronger than initially suspected. In July 1972, he expelled Soviet advisors from Egypt, and in November came to the secret agreements with Syria that paved the way for the Yom Kippur War. A joint planning command was established in January 1973.

1973: THE YOM KIPPUR WAR

The immediate Egyptian aims in 1973 were relatively modest. They may have hoped for the destruction of the Israeli state, but realized that this was probably beyond their military capacity. Instead, they decided to make a limited incursion into Israeli-held territory, as a bargaining counter to force more fruitful talks. Both the Egyptians and the Syrians faced great obstacles to these intended attacks. The Egyptians had to cross the Suez Canal, defended by the strongpoints of the Bar-Lev Line, and then to break through the Israeli armoured concentrations held back in Sinai between two newly built north–south roads designed to give the de-

Right: An M48 tank in an IDF armoured column prepares to pass its leader, which has just struck a mine. Together with the British Centurion, tanks of the US M48/60 series were the mainstay of Israel's armoured force in both the 1967 and 1973 wars.

fenders more mobility. The Syrians would have to assault defences in the Golan Heights that contained well-sited tanks and artillery pieces; and the front there was only 55km (35 miles) long, along the whole length of which was a 5m (16ft) wide anti-tank ditch.

The Egyptians worked out various schemes for crossing the Canal, using Soviet-supplied equipment, and devised plans for breaching the far bank with high-pressure hoses. The idea was to break through the Canal barrier, bypassing the strongpoints, and establish a line of defences a few kilometres inland, using a new range of anti-tank weapons and a screen of anti-aircraft missiles, Soviet SAMs, to blunt Israeli counters. Reluctantly, the Egyptian chief of staff, Saad el Din Shazli, who masterminded the planning, agreed to prepare plans for a possible advance to the three main passes in central Sinai. He believed such an advance would be disastrous, but the Syrians demanded proof that Egypt was prepared for a full-scale engagement in Sinai. The Syrians themselves planned a typically Soviet attack, pushing three mechanized divisions, supported by 200 tanks each, through the Israeli lines; when the breaches had been made, then two armoured divisions would pour through towards the Jordan River.

The Israeli intelligence services were aware of the build-up by both their neighbours, but refused to believe that it was more than a bluff, or normal autumn manoeuvres. Only at 0400 hours on 6 October 1973 did they suddenly realize that they were under direct threat. By then it was too late, for the attacks across the Suez Canal and onto the Golan Heights began at 1400 hours, before Israeli mobilization had begun to affect the fronts. In any case, Israel's concentration of her forces was somewhat hampered by the fact that it was the Yom Kippur religious holiday.

In charge of the Israeli forces in Sinai was Major-General Shmuel Gonen. Under him was a reserve infantry brigade along the Bar-Lev Line, and three armoured brigades under Major-General Avraham Mandler further back. Although the Israeli contingency plan called for the armoured brigades to advance to reinforce the Bar-Lev Line, Mandler refused to do this when the news of the impending attack came through early in the morning of the 6th, believing, probably correctly, that such a move would merely leave his tanks exposed to artillery fire. The upshot was that the troops on the Canal had little support when the first waves of Egyptian infantry came over, after a shattering barrage from 2000 guns (which fired 10,500 shells). Using the hoses to blast holes in the embankment to clear a way for their brigades and support vehicles, small groups of Egyptians, whose targets had been precisely planned and who knew their roles perfectly after months of training, pushed forward to engage Mandler's tanks as they advanced piecemeal during the afternoon. The Egyptians were using wire-guided anti-tank weapons (Soviet-supplied Saggers), and the Israeli armour fell prey to ambushes and the fire from well-sited Egyptian positions. Although the Egyptian assaults in the north were not successful, and the Third Army, which crossed south of the Great Bitter Lake, took some time to establish itself, in the crucial central area the Second Army had soon dug in, not pushing ahead of its anti-aircraft screen and taking a considerable toll of Mandler's tanks. By the early morning of 7 October, Mandler had only 110 tanks operational, compared to 277 on the morning of the 6th.

Mandler had, nevertheless, kept his force united and was able to manoeuvre. By the night of the 7th, reinforcement had arrived in the shape of two armoured divisions, one under Major-General Ariel Sharon and the other under Major-General Avraham ('Bren') Adan. At Gonen's headquarters there was a mood of over-optimism and it was decided to attack. But when the assaults went in, on the 8th, Adan's tanks ran into classic ambushes; there was too little co-ordination between infantry and armour,

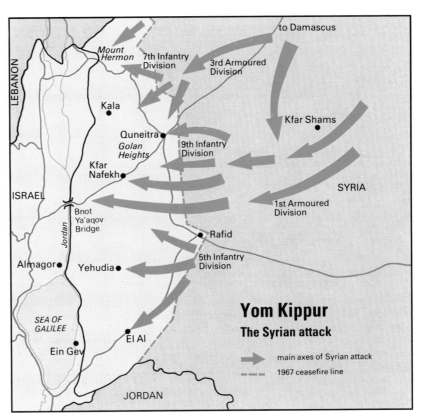

Yom Kippur
The Syrian attack

→ main axes of Syrian attack

--- 1967 ceasefire line

and Sharon's forces took little part in the fighting. Gonen then realized that he was facing an Egyptian Army very different from the one that had crumbled in 1967, and he chose to regroup, waiting for air support before committing himself again. Sharon disagreed with this policy and ordered an attack in flagrant disobedience to strict instructions from Gonen, who then asked for him to be recalled. Clearly, there were problems for the Israelis in Sinai.

The problems in Sinai were as nothing compared to those of Israeli troops on Golan, however. And the reason that Gonen was so short of close support from the IAF was that Israel's aircraft were fully employed backing up the hard-pressed ground troops in the heavy fighting on the plateau. The Israeli positions on Golan had been held by only one infantry and two armoured brigades (with a total of 177 tanks) when the massive Syrian

Below: An Egyptian T-55 burns fiercely after being hit by Israeli fire. Both Syrian and Egyptian tank crews showed great determination during the Yom Kippur War, but were ultimately unable to beat the better machines and better tactical expertise of the Israeli armoured forces.

Above: Looking out over the Syrian positions on the Golan from the Israeli side. The Israeli strongpoints gave the IDF a good field of fire, which they used to advantage in October 1973, taking a grim toll of the advancing Syrian forces.

Below: A MiG-17 makes an attack in Sinai. In spite of its relative age, the MiG-17 was still the principal close-support aircraft of the Egyptian forces in 1973.

assault went in on the afternoon of the 6th. Although only three of the 14 main defensive positions actually fell, the others were bypassed by the attackers, who pressed on to the edge of the plateau. In the southern part of the front, the 188th Armoured Brigade fought an unequal struggle against the Syrian 1st Armoured Division, and by the 7th the Syrians were only 10 minutes' drive from the Benot Ya'akov Bridge. Ninety per cent of the officers of the Israeli formation were casualties, including the commander and second-in-command. In the northern sector, too, the odds were formidable and by 7 October the Israeli 7th Armoured Brigade was down to 40 tanks facing 500 on the Syrian side.

The Israelis, however, were also taking a grim toll of the Syrians, who were advancing in a rather stereotyped manner and never showed the initiative that might have enabled them to push right through the thinly held Israeli positions. Well-sited tanks and excellent gunnery, plus last-ditch resistance, meant that the Syrians had been

held by the time night fell on the 9th. By then, too, newly mobilized formations, especially the armoured divisions of Major-Generals Dan Laner and Moshe Peled, had come into action. The only real territorial gain for the Syrians had been the taking of Mount Hermon on 6 October.

THE VALLEY OF TEARS

Nor had the IAF done anything less than its best in trying to slow the Syrian advance. Its pilots had suffered heavy losses (40 aircraft in the first two days) attacking forces protected by anti-aircraft guns and missiles, but had never let the Syrians feel secure.

Near Kuneitra, 260 Syrian tanks had been knocked out in the aptly-named 'Valley of Tears', and the Israeli 7th Armoured Brigade alone had destroyed about 500 tanks. Faced with these losses and a steady accretion of Israeli strength, the Syrians had to pull back. On the 10th, General Rafael Eitan, Israeli commander on the northern front, was given permission to continue the advance, off the Heights and deep into Syria. By the afternoon of the 11th, with Peled's and Laner's men in the van, they were over the pre-war ceasefire line. On the 12th Laner beat off an attack by an Iraqi tank division that had come to the aid of the Syrians (destroying 80 Iraqi tanks for the loss of none of his own), but by now the momentum of advance was slowing. Jordanian troops too came to the Syrians' aid, although coordination between Iraqis, Syrians and Jordanians was poor. The final Israeli success, just before the UN ceasefire came into operation on 24 October, was the recapture of Mount Hermon by paratroopers.

The Syrian reverses had serious consequences for the Egyptians. From the 9th to the 12th, both sides had been consolidating their positions in Sinai. Disputes within the

Israeli high command were still evident: Sharon was pressing for an all-out offensive as soon as possible and even the man sent to try to resolve the arguments, Lieutenant-General Chaim Bar-Lev, recommended Sharon's removal, twice. On the 12th, however, it became clear that the Egyptians were preparing a major set of attacks, and it was decided to wait for these before sanctioning a drive to and over the Canal. The Egyptian attacks were carried out against the advice of their own high command; but it was felt that something had to be done to relieve the Syrians who were, by the 12th, in full-scale retreat from the Golan Heights. The attacks were ordered for the 14th, and on that day there was a general advance along the routes towards the three passes and along the Mediterranean coast.

What followed was a large armoured confrontation, probably the largest since the battle of Kursk in 1943, and within hours the results predicted by the Egyptian high command had come to pass. The Israelis were well prepared and the superiority of their gunnery took its toll; they now also made sure that their tanks did not run unsupported against anti-tank missiles. Infantry support, with a liberal use of smallarms fire to distract missile operators, was a notable feature of the new Israeli tactics; and they too had been equipped with new wire-guided munitions – French SS-10 and SS-11 missiles and the US TOW (Tube-launched, Optically-tracked, Wire-guided) system – that had arrived barely 24 hours previously.

The main Egyptian thrust was in the centre, where the leading formation, the 21st Armoured Division, had lost 93 tanks by mid-morning, while the Israeli brigade that caused such havoc lost only three. The IAF,

by now relieved from its task of defending Golan, proved very effective as the Egyptians strayed beyond their missile screen, and by the end of the day the Egyptians were doomed to defeat.

Israeli plans for crossing the Canal to deal a decisive blow could now be put into operation, and by the evening of the 15th the first men of Sharon's division had crossed, near Deversoir. There were some problems in extending the bridgehead because of intense Egyptian resistance on the supply route from Tasa on the east bank, but by the 19th Adan's forces had pushed across and swung southwards, trying to trap the Egyptian Third Army near Suez. The outcome of the war was no longer in doubt, but each side was still intent on picking up or retaining the most valuable bargaining counters. To this end, Sadat insisted on retaining Egyptian forces

The crucial moves in the 1973 War in Sinai were the crossings of the Suez Canal, first by the Egyptian Army in its initial assaults (above) and secondly by the Israelis, from 15 October onwards (top, an IDF M48 moves across into Egypt).

Above: A Mirage IIICJ swoops low in preparation for an attack on Egyptian missile sites during the Yom Kippur War. The war severely shook the Israeli belief that the fighter-bomber and tank were the key to military success, and it became clear that a mix of arms and equipment would be necessary for continued Israeli superiority.

Below: Yasser Arafat (third from left) with President Nasser (second from right) shortly after Arafat was elected leader of the PLO in 1969. Arafat presided over the rise of the PLO to a prominent place in Middle Eastern politics.

to the east of the Canal. Meanwhile Adan, after a short break while the ceasefire negotiated by the UN on the 22nd came into operation and was then broken (probably by the Israelis), managed to reach the sea at the Gulf of Suez, completely isolating the Egyptian Third Army. He was, however, unable to take Suez itself, where well-laid defences caused considerable casualties, including the loss of 20 tanks when he began an attack there. Fighting gradually subsided from the 25th, and by the time UN observers arrived on the 28th, the fronts were quiet.

The losses in this war, by far the most intense and hard-fought in the Middle East since 1945, were about 8000 dead for both Egypt and Syria, and 2500 for Israel. Each of the nations involved had lost vast quantities of material: Egypt and Syria, for example, lost about 1000 tanks each (out of tank forces of 2200 and 2000 respectively), and Israel's armoured forces also lost about half of their strength of 1700 tanks (although many were recovered and repaired). Unlike the Six-Day War, the Yom Kippur War had seen the

defensive gain considerably at the expense of hasty or ill-prepared offensives, and it seemed that the new wire-guided missiles were the answer to the tank, while the ground-attack aircraft was vulnerable to the new SAMs.

In four major wars the armed forces of Egypt, Syria and Jordan had been defeated by the Israelis, who had also delivered severe blows to the armies of Iraq when they chose to enter the field of battle, but the real losers in the long story of the Arab-Israeli Wars have been the Arab population of Palestine and specifically those who became refugees after the 1948–49 and 1967 Wars. The Palestinian question is the single most vexed issue in Middle Eastern politics. The Israeli answer to the problem has not been marked by a great deal of sympathy, and although the original leaders of the Israeli state always realized that at some stage Israel would have to live in peace with the Arabs, the leadership of Israel during the 1970s became increasingly hard-line in its attitude to the Palestinians, the more so when Menachem Begin, the former leader of the Irgun, became prime minister in 1977.

The Palestinian leadership was always prepared to condone and encourage guerrilla raids on Israel to bring the question to the attention of the rest of the world, and throughout the 1950s, 1960s and 1970s, there were attacks and Israeli counters that added to the air of tension in the region. Nor were the Palestinians always welcome guests in the countries in which they took refuge: in September 1970, the Jordanian Army destroyed Palestinian power in their country. After 1974, however, when the Palestine Liberation Organization (PLO) led by Yasser Arafat was recognized by the assembled Arab nations in Rabat as the voice of the Palestinian people, and accorded 'observer status'

at the United Nations, Israeli opposition to the political organization of the Palestinians grew stronger.

It is the presence of the powerful Palestinian groupings, which after their defeat by the Jordanian Army transferred their bases northwest, and the intervention of the Israelis that have made Lebanon the seat of the most intense fighting around Israel since the end of the 1973 War.

THE ISRAELI INVASION OF LEBANON, 1982

For Israel the aftermath of the 1973 War was very favourable. Negotiations with Egypt were prolonged, but President Sadat was very interested in reaching a political accommodation that would enable his desperately poor country to devote its attention to is own internal problems, and after the Camp David talks of 1978, he claimed peace with honour, having secured the return of Sinai to Egypt and signed a treaty with Israel. The other Arab states did not see things this way and condemned Egypt, but Sadat had wrought a fundamental change in Middle Eastern politics.

The Israeli intervention in Lebanon in 1982 must be seen in the light of these two factors – fundamental Israeli hostility to the PLO, and the fact that after the mid-1970s the Israelis had nothing more to fear from the most populous and powerful Arab state, the one that bordered her on the south. Lebanon was in any case a divided and internally riven state. Disputes between Christians, the Muslim sects (in themselves the Christian and Muslims comprised a variety of different groupings) and the Druze (whose religion is based on the teachings of the 11th century Muslim heretic Ismail ad-Darazi) were accentuated by the fact that the Syrians had never reconciled themselves to Lebanon, once a part of Greater Syria, as an independent unit. The arrival of the PLO leadership was a final destabilizing factor.

By 1975 there was full-scale civil war in the country. The Palestinian strongholds were virtually independent states within the state, and Syria was heavily involved – after the ceasefire in 1976, Syrian forces became the main component of an Arab peacekeeping force that was set up. During the civil war, Israeli-backed Christian militias in the south of the country had taken control over areas along the border, the most powerful force being that of Saad Haddad, a cashiered major from the Lebanese Army. In 1978, the Israelis intervened directly in the country, following a further bout of civil war, and after some 20,000 troops had moved into southern Lebanon in Operation Litani, the Israelis got what they had ostensibly fought for, a 10km (6 mile) buffer zone to protect their northern

Above: Menachem Begin, prime minister of Israel in 1982, when the operation to 'cleanse southern Lebanon' of its PLO strongholds was authorized. Left: A Christian Phalangist militiaman (with Virgin Mary tracing on the stock of his Soviet-made AK47 rifle) keeps watch in Lebanon. The alliance of the Israelis with certain Christian groups in the Lebanon added a new complicating factor to the already tangled politics of this state during the 1970s.

settlements from rocket and guerrilla attacks. In 1980 there was a further Israeli incursion, and throughout the period PLO guerrilla attacks on Israeli territory were met by fierce retaliatory air raids on the refugee camps in Lebanon.

It was clear that Israel intended to break the power of the PLO, and this implied intervention in Lebanon and armed confrontation with the Syrian forces there. In June 1982, an opportunity for such a move presented itself when terrorists (not members of the PLO according to PLO leaders) tried to

Below: An Israeli F-15 Eagle climbs skyward, afterburners going at full blast. The F-15 proved a great success in 1982, when it was the spearhead of the Israeli Air Force that swept the Syrian Air Force from the skies.

over the Syrian aircraft that tried to oppose it. By the use of novel devices such as drone planes to fix the frequencies on which many of the SAM radars were operating and to provide reconnaissance information, Israeli aircraft, especially US-supplied F-15 Eagles and F-16 Fighting Falcons, were able to sweep aside Syrian air defences.

Along the coast, Israeli armoured columns took the port of Tyre and then continued their advance to link up with seaborne forces that had landed at Sidon. Their ultimate objective was Beirut and they moved on to Damour, on the outskirts of the Lebanese capital. Meanwhile, further inland, the second main thrust moved against PLO strongholds in the mountains – or rather, moved past many of the strongholds, content to let the infantry mop them up later, and concentrated on driving deep into what had previously been enemy territory. The most important defensive feature, Beaufort Castle, an old Crusader fortress, was overcome after fierce resistance on 8 June.

The final element in the advance was provided on 9 June, when the most dangerous phase of the operation began. This was a move to outflank and neutralize the Syrian forces in the Beqa'a Valley. Yet this too was a great success. Air superiority and the fine fighting qualities of the Israeli Army (aided by the performance of the new Israeli-built Merkava tank that proved superior to the Syrian T-62s and T-72s) gave the invaders a victory around Lake Qaraaoun on 11 June.

With the Syrians neutralized and the PLO forces in disarray, there was nothing to stop the Israelis moving on to the capital of Lebanon. Sweeping aside the final remnants of PLO resistance (and also those Shi'ite Muslim militiamen who tried to halt the advance) the IDF had encircled Beirut by 11 June, and, with the aid of Phalangist militia, bottled up at least 7000 Palestinian fighters and a similar number of Syrians in the city.

Eventually, after frantic international efforts, an agreement was reached (19 August) whereby the Palestinians and Syrians were to be evacuated, and a multi-

assassinate the Israeli ambassador in London, Shlomo Argov. Two days of intense Israeli bombardment of Palestinian camps and bases in Lebanon followed, and were met by PLO artillery and rocket attacks on targets within Israel. Then, on Sunday 6 June, the Israeli high command initiated Operation Peace for Galilee, an invasion of Lebanon that was, as soon became obvious, intended to destroy the PLO strongholds in that country. Although the Israelis claimed at first that they were interested only in southern Lebanon, the wider scope of their ambitions soon became clear as troops crossed the Litani River, linked up with Saad Haddad's forces and kept going north.

There were three main axes of Israeli advance and all were effectively covered by the IAF, which soon asserted air superiority

Top: Yasser Arafat, the head of the PLO, whose power in the Lebanon was one of the main targets of the Israeli invasion of 1982. Above: A PLO fighter surveys the burning tower blocks of Beirut. Above left: An Israeli tank commander directs operations during the IDF advance. Below left: An Israeli radio operator moves into Beirut. Below: PLO anti-aircraft artillery in Beirut, during the vain attempt to halt the Israeli advance.

Above: The bombardment of Beirut in 1982. The Israelis were unwilling to fight their way into the city, but were determined to force the PLO to move out.

Below: The bodies in Sabra refugee camp, after the massacres carried out by Christian militiamen in September 1982. These massacres, by troops under the overall control of the Israelis, created an international uproar.

national force supervised their exit from the city. Now, however, events took a twist that was as unsavoury as anything that had happened before in this unhappy country. The Israelis refused to leave until the Syrians too had consented to remove their troops from Lebanon, and in this highly charged atmosphere the newly elected Christian president of Lebanon, Bashir Gemayel, was assassinated on 14 September. The Israelis used this as an opportunity to move directly into Beirut, something that was much easier now that the PLO's main fighting force had departed, and during this advance Palestinians in the refugee camps of Sabra and Chatilla were massacred. It soon became clear that the massacres had actually been carried out by Christian Phalangist militiamen, but the Israeli government – which

should have been exercising control over such militiamen – was forced to convene a committee of enquiry and this recommended that Ariel Sharon be dismissed from his post as Defence Minister.

In the wake of world-wide condemnation, Israeli troops withdrew from Beirut and a Multinational Force (MNF – comprising troops from the USA, Britain, France and Italy) again moved into the city in October 1982. The IDF moved even further south, to the Awali Line, in September 1983.

THE MNF PULLS OUT

The withdrawal of Israeli troops further to the south did not end the fighting in Lebanon, however. Indeed, the government of the country (under Amin Gemayel, Bashir's brother) found itself more embattled than ever. The Syrians still had widespread influence, which they used to back up the forces opposed to the Christian-dominated Beirut regime; and these forces – notably the Shi'ite 'Amal' militias and the Druze in the Chouf mountains – pulled off some notable successes. In February 1984, for example, they forced the government's army to pull back, and made the position of the MNF almost untenable, for they wished to destroy the influence of the USA, which was both a major component of the force and the main supporter of the Gemayel regime. On 7 February, President Reagan announced the withdrawal of the US contingent to warships offshore, and the other nations involved inevitably had to follow suit. The French were the last to leave, late in March 1984.

Nor was the fighting confined to Beirut. In their quest for still more control, the Syrians supported a breakaway faction of the PLO that was opposed to Yasser Arafat's growing closeness to King Hussein of Jordan. Under Abu Mussa, this faction forced Arafat's supporters out of the northern Lebanese city of Tripoli in December 1983.

The latest round of fighting in the Arab-Israeli Wars had the effect, therefore, of letting loose many of the tensions within Israel's northern neighbour and accelerating a drift to civil war. The outcome is uncertain but will certainly have profound repercussions for the future of Israel – particularly if Syria comes to dominate the country.

The incursion into Lebanon had, indeed, seen all the features of the Arab-Israeli Wars at their most stark. First, there was the Israeli expertise in the manipulation of modern military equipment. Second, and perhaps more important, Operation Peace for Galilee highlighted the political impasse that exists around Israel: the intractable problem of the Palestinians, and the difficulty of achieving a lasting peace through military action, however skilled that action may be.

INDIA'S WARS

India has fought three wars against her neighbours since independence in 1947: in 1962 against China in the north, in 1965 against Pakistan in the west, and in 1971 against Pakistan again, this time in both east and west. These wars were all limited, in the sense that the protagonists had certain definite aims for which they were fighting and were not prepared (and to an extent were not able) to escalate hostilities beyond a certain point. The wars also demonstrated a steady improvement in the capability of the Indian armed forces, which were humiliated in 1962 by the Chinese and severely embarrassed by the Pakistanis in 1965, but which by 1971 had proved themselves far superior, at least to the Pakistani forces. This improvement lay partly in weaponry and armaments, but more in increasing expertise and better direction of the troops themselves, who became skilled in the coordination of techniques necessary for prosecuting a modern war.

The first war was on the northern border with China. At both the eastern and western ends of the frontier, in the areas of the Northeast Frontier Agency in the east and of the Aksai Chin mountains in the west, the Chinese had historical claims on territory that the Indians were determined to retain. During the early 1950s, both India and China played down the dispute, but in the early 1960s it became more important, partly because India was coming closer to an accord with the Soviet Union, but also because Indian governments, in the belief that the Chinese would not resort to force, had adopted a more forward policy in the areas in question. In the eastern sector, for example, India set up 40 new frontier posts, many inside the territory claimed by China.

In both sectors the Chinese lines of communication were far better than the Indian, and the Chinese deployed far larger numbers of troops. Nevertheless, the Indian government ordered action to be taken against the Chinese forces that had encroached over the old MacMahon Line (the border set up in 1914) in the east in October 1962, and this was the signal for a general outbreak of fighting in both regions. The Indian infantry and mountain units were forced back wherever the Chinese chose to attack, until by 20 November the Chinese had occupied their claim in both sectors. Declining to push the matter further by invading India itself, the Chinese announced a unilateral ceasefire and withdrew from all areas that they had not claimed. The Indian Army had lost 1383 men killed, and had been soundly beaten.

The defeat for the Indian Army was of

Above: General Ayub Khan, ruler of Pakistan during the 1965 war against India.

Below: Indian troops move up to the border with China in the Himalayas. The Indian Army was decisively worsted during the fighting along this border in 1962.

Right: An Indian soldier armed with a Mk V Sten Gun on watch in the Rann of Kutch in 1965. There were clashes between the forces of India and Pakistan in this region early in the year, but the main fighting took place later, and was linked with the situation further north, in Kashmir.

great interest to Pakistan, which had territorial claims of its own. The separate states of India and Pakistan had been born in 1947, when the British empire in the Indian subcontinent was split into these two new states, Pakistan largely Muslim and India Hindu. The process of partition was accompanied by much bloodshed, and several issues were left unsettled. Foremost among these problems was the fate of the state of Kashmir, in a strategically sensitive position in the northwest of the sub-continent, whose ruling maharajah was Hindu but whose population was largely Muslim. In confused fighting during 1947 and 1948, the Indians were able to assert authority over much of the state, while a rump area was held by the Pakistanis and known as Azad ('free') Kashmir. In spite of promises of a plebiscite on sovereignty, Kashmir was formally annexed by India in 1957.

Neither Pakistan nor India had particularly strong armed forces during the 1950s (and both were reliant on British equipment), although Pakistan decided to throw in her lot with the West, and joined the Central Treaty Organization; she was also in receipt of $1500 million of aid from the USA, which enabled her to equip five and a half divisions. By the early 1960s, however, India was receiving considerable amounts of weaponry from the Soviet Union, especially in the form of aircraft, although her armoured forces were still inferior to those of Pakistan – the Indians had only five armoured regiments armed with modern heavy tanks (Centurion Mk 5s) along the western border, while the Pakistanis had six equipped with the US M47 Patton.

A further area in which Pakistan and India had rival border claims was in the Rann of Kutch, a region of salt marsh and desert in the south of their common western frontier. In January 1965 there were armed clashes in the region, which finally ended in June, at a cost of 93 Indian dead. While these clashes were taking place, the Pakistanis had been training irregulars for use in Kashmir. They

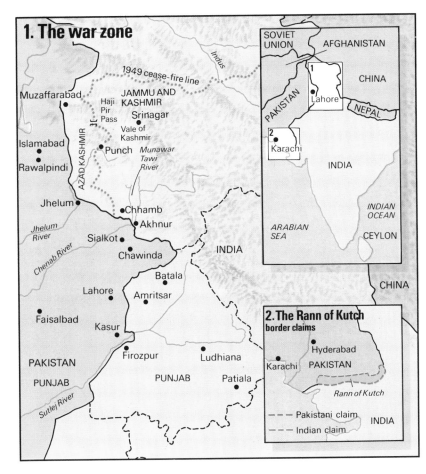

1. The war zone

1949 cease-fire line
Muzaffarabad
JAMMU AND KASHMIR
Haji Pir Pass
Srinagar
Vale of Kashmir
Islamabad
Punch
Munawar Tawi River
Rawalpindi
AZAD KASHMIR
Indus
Jhelum
Chhamb
Akhnur
Jhelum River
Sialkot
Chenab River
Chawinda
INDIA
Batala
Lahore
Amritsar
Faisalabad
Kasur
PAKISTAN
Firozpur
Ludhiana
PUNJAB
PUNJAB
Patiala
Sutlej River

SOVIET UNION
AFGHANISTAN
1
CHINA
PAKISTAN
Lahore
NEPAL
2
Karachi
INDIA
INDIAN OCEAN
ARABIAN SEA
CEYLON
CHINA

2. The Rann of Kutch
border claims
Hyderabad
Karachi PAKISTAN
Rann of Kutch
--- Pakistani claim
— Indian claim
INDIA

Above: Pakistani
infantry advance in
1965. Both the Indian
and Pakistani Armies
made use of British
personal equipment
and smallarms during
this period.

hoped the Muslims there would rise in a war of liberation if guerrilla groups could be inserted and kept supplied. In August these irregulars began to take on Indian troops in Kashmir. The Indians reinforced their garrisons, and Pakistani artillery began to come into play on the side of the irregulars. Indian units managed to secure the Haji Pir Pass, thereby threatening the Azad Kashmir capital of Muzaffarabad, and the Pakistanis decided to commit their ground forces in a diversionary operation towards the Chhamb salient. The commitment of these troops on 1 September 1965 marked the escalation to a full-scale war that did not end until the 23rd.

The fighting took place on the western frontier and there was very little activity around East Pakistan. There were four main actions in the war: the Pakistani advance to Chhamb, the Indian drive on Lahore, the Indian attack on the Chawinda salient, and the struggle in the air. In none of these was the standard of military expertise very high, and in all of them the Indians were shown to have serious deficiencies. The end result, however, was that the Pakistanis, whose main war aim was to force a rearrangement of the settlement in Kashmir, achieved very little.

The first assaults of the war proper were by the Pakistanis in the Chhamb salient. Although intended as a diversion from events further north, this was so successful, as seven Pakistani battalions overwhelmed four Indian battalions, that the Pakistani commander decided to push on to the town of Akhnur. Then the first major mistake of this war of errors was committed. The exploitation of this victory was left to a fresh formation that had not yet arrived. By the time it did so, the Indian defences had reformed and the fighting had become a stalemate by 7 September.

The second set of attacks took place further south, in the Punjab, where the Indians had a contingency plan for an advance from Amritsar to Lahore. The Indian overall commander, General Chaudhuri, was seriously worried about the capabilities of his army after the debacle of 1962, but the Prime Minister, Lal Badhur Shastri, insisted. Three divisions set off on the night of 5–6 September, two directly towards Lahore and one towards Kasur. Staff work was poor, and the support from artillery very inaccurate. The Indian forces barely managed to cross the Ichogil Canal before being driven back, almost losing Amritsar itself. But the Pakistanis in their turn found coordinating attacks very difficult. Resolute defence enabled the Indians to hold out until they were reinforced, and when support arrived heavy

Below: Indian infantry
man a jeep-mounted
recoilless rifle in 1971,
just before the outbreak
of hostilities in the war
of December of that
year.

losses were inflicted upon the Pakistani armoured forces.

The attack on the Chawinda salient, the other main ground action of the war, began on the night of 7–8 September, as three Indian divisions attacked from the north. Chawinda itself held out against Indian bombardments and clumsy frontal attacks, the last of which took place on the night of 18–19 September.

Meanwhile, in the air, the Indian Air Force (IAF), which outnumbered the Pakistani Air Force (PAF) by 775 aircraft to 141, had been unable to assert any kind of superiority, and, indeed, had caused serious problems to the Indian ground forces when some of its Vampires had the misfortune to bomb their own men. The fighting between aircraft revolved around dog-fights in which Pakistani Sabres took on Indian Foland Gnats, and the Pakistanis were able to assert a mastery of

all forward areas by 7 September.

By 23 September neither side had made the gains it had hoped for, and a ceasefire was accepted. In January 1966 formal peace talks took place at Tashkent under Soviet aegis, and a return to the prewar position was agreed. Both sides had lost some 6000 casualties, including about 1000 dead, while the Indians had lost 375 tanks and 35 aircraft. Pakistani losses in equipment totalled 350 tanks and 19 planes. The war of 1965 had revealed deficiencies in equipment and expertise on both sides. The losses in tanks especially were the result of poor handling and inadequate leadership. Things were to be very different in 1971, however, for in that conflict the Pakistani forces were to be outclassed by the Indians.

THE WAR OF 1971

The war of 1971 had its origins in the discontent of the people of East Pakistan, who, although they made up 75 per cent of the population and produced 75 per cent of the exports of Pakistan, were treated as a subordinate and inferior part of the state by the West Pakistanis who ran the country. Elections in December 1970 had given overwhelming support to Sheikh Mujibur Rahman's Awami League, which stood for more self-government for the East, but martial law was proclaimed in March 1971 and the West Pakistani forces stationed in the East went on a rampage of almost incredible brutality, seeking to quell East Pakistan's aspirations by sheer terror. Up to one million people may have died in the violence, and millions more fled the country, into the eastern provinces of India. These regions were poor enough in the first place, without the influx from East Pakistan, and the six million or so refugees put an intolerable strain on the Indian government. Appeals to the United Nations produced no worthwhile results, and it became clear that India would have to resort to armed force, at some point after the monsoon season ended in November 1971. Border clashes with Pakistani troops became more and more frequent, mainly because the Mukti Bahini guerrillas, fighting for the independence of East Pakistan, were increasing their activities within the country and using Indian territory as a refuge.

In spite of the fact that India was being forced into war, it was the Pakistanis who struck first, in what they hoped would be a devastating air strike on the western border and in Kashmir. But this was merely a useful *casus belli* for the Indians, who had already made their preparations.

In the period since 1965, the Indians had re-equipped with a great deal of Soviet weapon-

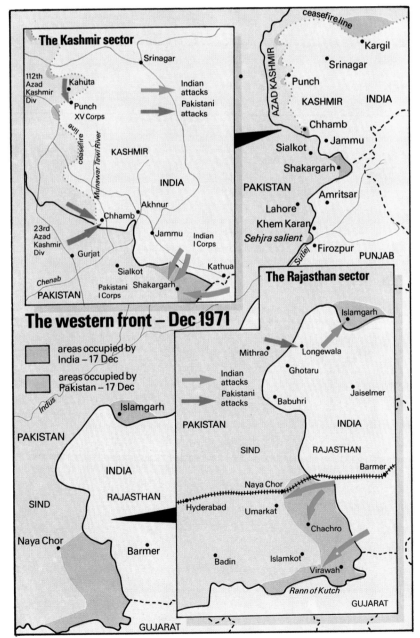

Right: Victorious Indian troops head towards Dacca in 1971 during the rapid advance that overwhelmed the Pakistani Army stationed in the area that was to become the state of Bangladesh.

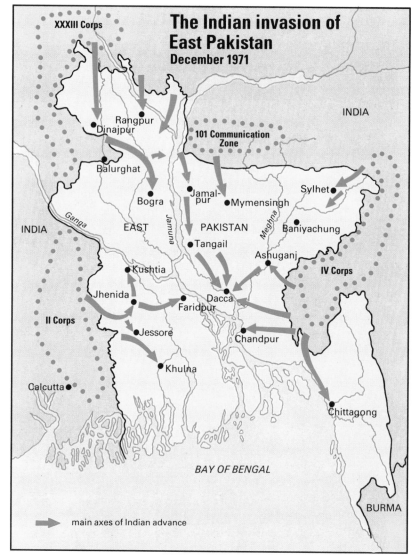

The Indian invasion of East Pakistan
December 1971

XXXIII Corps

INDIA

Rangpur
Dinajpur

101 Communication Zone

Balurghat

Bogra

Jamal-pur

Mymensingh

Sylhet

INDIA

EAST

PAKISTAN

Baniyachung

Ganga

Jamuna

Meghna

Tangail

Ashuganj

Kushtia

IV Corps

Jhenida

Dacca

Faridpur

II Corps

Jessore

Chandpur

Khulna

Calcutta

Chittagong

BAY OF BENGAL

BURMA

→ main axes of Indian advance

ry, and had learnt from their experiences in the earlier war. By 1971 there were 450 Russian T-54 and T-55 tanks in service with the Indian Army, while the Indian armaments industry had produced 300 models of the Vickers Vijayanta tank, basically a lightly armoured version of the Centurion. The core of the IAF lay in seven squadrons of MiG-21s, which quickly asserted superiority in the air, while the T-54s were quite capable of taking on the Pakistani M47 Pattons. The real difference between 1965 and 1971, however, was that the Indians had carefully examined the problems they would have to face, and had worked out effective solutions that were within the capabilities of their forces. Even when things did not go according to plan, the army was able to work out another option, to keep the momentum of advance going.

In the air, the PAF attack of 3 December 1971 was intended as a repeat of the Israeli air strike of June 1967, but the Indians were prepared for such an eventuality, dispersing their fighters on forward airfields and giving them good protection. The result was that the 100 or so Pakistani aircraft that tried to destroy the Indian planes on the ten most important airfields in the west had little success. The Pakistanis having failed, the Indians made sure that their numerical superiority (over 650 aircraft as opposed to under 300 for the PAF) was used to good advantage. The Indians are also said to have had the services of the Soviet Tu-126 Moss, which is a sophisticated AWACS (Airborne Warning and Control Systems) aircraft which is able to throw a blanket of electronic jamming over enemy radar screens and, at the same time, guide its own interceptors and ground-attack planes. Thereafter, apart from some activity in the Chhamb sector, the PAF made very little impression on the war.

Air superiority gave the Indian ground forces a priceless advantage, especially in the west where the nature of the terrain was often open and exposed. The Indians threw back Pakistani attacks near Punch, although they had to give ground in the Chhamb salient. Elsewhere, however, they made great gains. In the Punjab, there were fierce tank battles, especially around Shakargah, but the Indians came out on top, destroying 45 Pattons in this single engagement alone. Further to the south, in and just to the north of the Rann of Kutch, Indian gains were even greater, especially after a Pakistani armoured attack was destroyed by air assault at Ramgarh.

For the Indians, however, the war in the west was a sideshow. The real question was whether they could speedily destroy the Pakistani forces in East Pakistan. There, six Indian divisions and supporting units faced just over four Pakistani divisions. The nature of the terrain was such, however, as to place great obstacles in the path of an offensive. The land was criss-crossed with natural and man-made watercourses, and although the Pakistanis had a front of 2250km (1400 miles) to cover, if their forces managed to group themselves in the region of Dacca, they might have been able to hold out for some time – and also inflict frightful atrocities on the inhabitants, if their previous behaviour was anything to go by.

AMPHIBIOUS WARFARE

On the morning of 4 December, the Indians attacked from all sides, with three divisions moving in from Tripura, three from West Bengal, and a brigade coming down from Assam. The first assaults took place in 23 different places, with the intention of gaining some footholds and axes of advance to exploit. The Pakistani forces were deployed on the frontiers, to make the best use of the river barriers, but they were outflanked and forced back by these first attacks. The Indian problem was then how to get across the rivers quickly enough, and how to deal with any strongpoints. River-crossing equipment had been supplied by the Soviet Union and much of it worked very well, although it was found that the PT-76 amphibious tank tended to overheat after half an hour in the water. As many of the wider rivers took three hours to cross, where necessary these tanks were towed by boat. Very often, improvisation was necessary, and any available local transport was used – the troops coming from Tripura, for example, commandeered local steamers to cross the wide Meghra River on 10 December.

Extensive use was made of heliborne or parachute troops, and an Indian paradrop on the town of Tangail on 11 December prevented many Pakistani troops in the north, who had put up stiff resistance, from falling back on Dacca. Still, the going was hard, and it took the troops from West Bengal until 14 December to reach the line of the Ganges River. By then, however, the eastern thrust, from Tripura, was threatening Dacca itself, and the Pakistani Army asked for a ceasefire on 15 December. The troops in East Pakistan formally surrendered on 16 December, and amid ecstatic scenes, Bangladesh came into being. For the Indian Army, however, the creation of Bangladesh was probably less important than the fact that it had shown itself to be an effective modern fighting machine, and asserted decisive superiority over its rival in South Asia. The Pakistanis have never revealed their losses, but they must have been higher than those of the Indians, who suffered 1426 dead, 3611 wounded and 2149 missing.

Below: Jubilant Bangladeshis celebrate the victory of the Indian forces that brought independence to their country. The defeat of the Pakistani Army established Indian military supremacy on the subcontinent.

BIAFRA'S FIGHT FOR INDEPENDENCE

From 1967 to 1970 there was full-scale civil war in the state of Nigeria, the largest black African country in terms of population (about 50 million). Unlike most civil wars in the period since 1945, this conflict did not take the form of a guerrilla war. The breakaway Eastern Region (later Biafra) was more or less an established entity by the time fighting broke out, and even when it became clear that the troops of the Federal Government were superior in conventional terms, the leaders of Biafra did not choose to use guerrilla tactics. The war had, therefore, the character of a small-scale conventional war between two states.

The events leading up to the war really began in 1966, when there were two military coups. The first, in January, was a failure, but brought to power the commander of the army, Major-General Johnson Aguiyi Ironsi, ending a period of poorly functioning democracy. In his turn, Ironsi was deposed and killed in July, and this later coup was followed by widespread massacres of those members of the Ibo tribe, whose homeland was in the Eastern Region, who were living in the north of the country. There were

widespread tribal divisions in Nigeria, and the country had been established as a federation in which Muslim northerners, Anglican westerners and the Catholic Ibos of the east would, in theory, feel no fear of domination by another grouping. The coup of July, however, had revealed the extent to

Above: Federal troops man a 105mm Model 56 Pack Howitzer. In spite of Federal material superiority, the reduction of Biafra took three years.

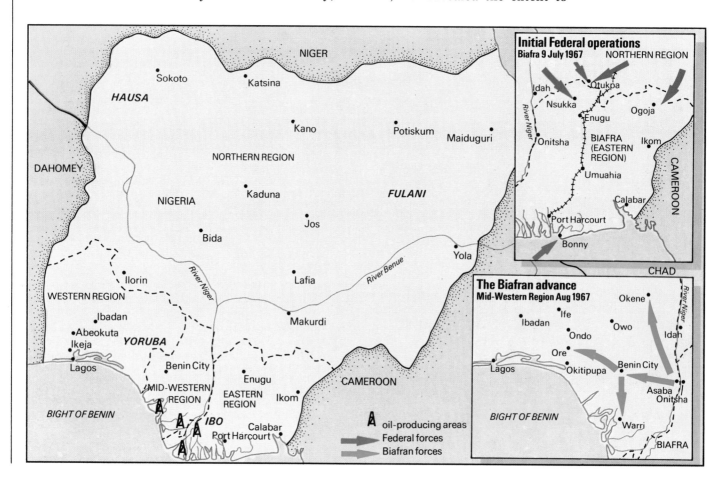

Right: Federal troops move cautiously forward, armed with NATO standard FN self-loading rifles (SLRs).

Below: A group of Biafran soldiers pose for the camera during a rest in a jungle clearing. The man in the foreground is armed with a Nato GPMG (General Purpose Machine Gun), while hanging round the neck of the soldier to his right is a Soviet AK47 assault rifle. Procuring adequate arms supplies was always the biggest problem for the rebels.

which the well-educated and thrustful Ibos were unpopular in the rest of the country, and it brought to power another army officer, Lieutenant-Colonel Yakubu Gowon, who in May of the following year announced a profound rearrangement of the structure in the country, which would leave the Ibos with much less power in the Eastern Region.

Ibo fears in the aftermath of the massacres of the July coup had not been allayed in the interim, and a powerful movement for independence had been gathering force. When Gowon announced the constitutional changes, the Ibo reaction was swift. On 30 May 1967, the state of Biafra, encompassing the old Eastern Region, was proclaimed under the leadership of Colonel Chukwu-emeka Odumeguo Ojukwu. The Federal Government condemned this move, and on 9 July began operations against the rebellious area.

The Biafrans had access to Nigeria's oil, and hoped for international support; the government's first move, therefore, was to try to secure the oil terminals. By August, Government forces had pushed well into the rebel area, and had taken the oil terminal of Bonny. These early successes helped persuade foreign governments and international oil companies to withhold support from Biafra, and without such support, it was difficult to see how the rebellion could survive.

Early Federal advances may have looked impressive, but a counter-stroke was in preparation. On 9 August, a Biafran column led by Lieutenant-Colonel Victor Banjo attacked across the Niger River, and within days had taken the capital of the Midwest Region, Benin City, and was threatening Lagos, the Federal capital. Meanwhile, the solitary warplane on the Biafran side (and indeed, the only one in all Nigeria), a B-26 bomber, also attacked Lagos. But in spite of a certain amount of panic in the government, the offensive soon stalled and was driven back by early September. Now it was the turn

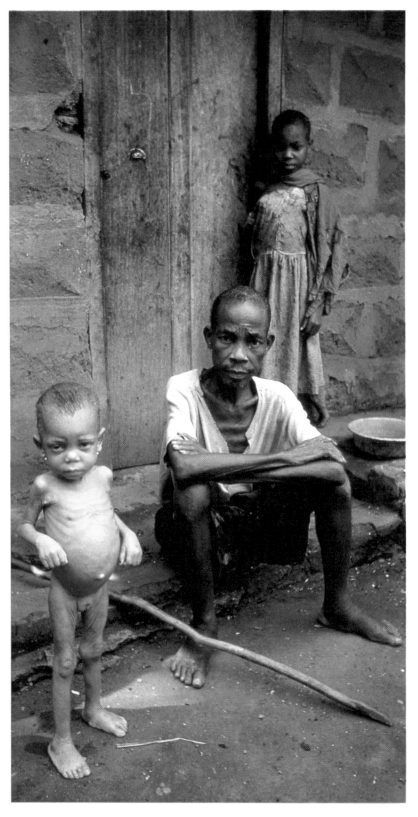

Above: The plight of the refugees in Biafra and the famine that struck the rebel province caught the attention of the whole world, and a mass airlift of food and medical supplies was organized.

this is surprising. The Biafran Army was heavily outnumbered (only 40,000 men compared to 120,000 in the Federal Army) and the Federal Navy, although small, was able to impose a blockade at sea. But in fact the Federal Army had the greatest difficulty in making its advantages tell. For a start, its forces were generally badly organized and led. The Federal Army had been only 9000 strong at the beginning of 1966, and half of the officers over the rank of major had been killed in the coups. When expansion for the war became a priority, there was, therefore, a serious lack of capable officers, and NCOs had to be promoted, leaving gaps at that level also. The most efficient formation on the Federal side was the 3rd Commando Division, under Colonel Benjamin Adekunle, and this carried out the most important operations. Adekunle himself, however, was dismissed in April 1969, as he was said to harbour dangerous political ambitions.

MERCENARIES AND MINICONS

On the Biafran side, a mercenary force, the 4th Commando Brigade, led by Rolf Steiner, was probably the best formation, but although the mercenaries managed a vigorous counter-attack late in 1968, again their commander was mistrusted, and Steiner had left the country by the beginning of 1969.

The weaponry that would have enabled either side to force a swift victory was lacking too. Both leaders, Gowon and Ojukwu, made strenuous efforts to find modern arms. The British and the Soviets were willing to give some to the Federal side; but in terms of wars that were contemporary with the Nigerian Civil War – say, Vietnam – the provision of 16 MiG fighters and three Il-28 bombers was not a cornucopia of armed might. These planes were, however, some improvement on the few trainers that the Federal government had pressed into service at the beginning of the war. A further mark of the poor quality of armaments was that the adventurer Count Carl Gustav von Rosen was able to make seven Swedish training aircraft (known as 'Minicons') into a Biafran air force that gave the Federal troops several frights. Lack of material was not the only problem, however. Neither side had men trained in the use of modern weapons. The pilots of the aircraft that the two sides obtained were, therefore, largely foreigners – Swedes flew the 'Minicons' and Egyptian pilots acted for the Federal side.

With neither the personnel nor the hardware typical of modern warfare, it is hardly surprising that the conflict dragged on. In May, the main Biafran outlet to the sea at Port Harcourt fell, and, by September, Biafra had been reduced to an area of only 160km by 80km (100 miles by 50 miles). A

of the Federal forces to push forward. They took the Biafran capital, Enugu, on 4 October, and by the end of the year had cut Biafra's land route to the Cameroon. On New Year's Day 1968, Gowon promised that the war would be over by 31 March.

It was to take two further years of fighting before the shrinking perimeter of Biafra was finally conquered, however. On the face of it,

Left: Rolf Steiner, head of the mercenary 4th Commando Brigade, with a young bodyguard. Fighting on the Biafran side, Steiner's force was very effective, but it was unable to turn the tide, and Steiner left Biafra after a quarrel with Ojukwu.

spirited rally late in 1968 saw the Federal forces pushed back again, and formal recognition by the French government enabled the rebels to obtain a regular source of weapons and ammunition. A converted road at Uli became the busiest airstrip in Africa, as munitions and foreign aid for the thousands of victims of the famine that was gripping the country were flown in.

Throughout 1969, however, the Federal forces were remorselessly closing in, now using ever-better equipment, including tracked vehicles (which had not previously been deployed in the conflict) and Soviet 122mm artillery pieces. In December 1969 a final offensive, spearheaded by the 3rd Commando Division, split what remained of Biafra in two. On 12 January 1970 the Biafrans capitulated and the war was over. The Nigerian Civil War had demonstrated many of the essential aspects of modern warfare by default. The lack of weaponry and the lack of efficient personnel had led to a long struggle, in which the rapid decision and great destruction of which modern armies are capable had largely been absent.

Below left: Nigerian Federal troops armed with British equipment. Arms supplies rapidly became of crucial importance to both sides in the Nigerian Civil War. Below: Colonel Benjamin Adekunle, head of the best Federal formation, the 3rd Commando Division.

THE GULF WAR

The Gulf War between Iraq and Iran, which began in September 1980, is one of the most perplexing of modern conflicts. The reasons behind the outbreak of hostilities are not difficult to describe, but what is more problematical is how the clash of two powerful armed forces, with very large armoured formations and strong air forces, can have produced a long stalemate, rather than, as happened in the Arab-Israeli Wars, a short, decisive struggle, with the destructiveness of modern weaponry given full rein.

The origins of the war lie in the long-lasting rivalry between Iran and Iraq for predominance in the north of the Arabian (Persian) Gulf, accentuated by racial and linguistic differences – the Iraqis are Arabs and the Iranians Persians. There were also various frontier disputes – such as the exact part of the Shatt al-Arab River (the southern border) through which the frontier line ran – and there had been Iraqi displeasure when Iran occupied three small islands in the mouth of the Gulf in 1971. These frontier disputes were not, however, as important as the ideological differences between the two nations. Since the bloody coup of 1958, Iraq had been a radical Arab state, committed to the cause of revolutionary nationalism in the Middle East. Iran, on the other hand, had been a bulwark of Western influence. The Shah was given arms and political support,

especially by the USA, and hoped to modernize his country by using oil revenues and Western expertise. In the mid-1970s, Iran was by far the most powerful state in the area, and its influence was felt throughout the Gulf – in the provision of troops and helicopter gunships to the ruler of Oman to help suppress Dhofari rebels, for example.

In 1979, this existing ideological conflict was given a new twist, for the Shah was overthrown in January, to be replaced by a regime in which the real power lay with Islamic fundamentalist religious leaders – notably the Ayatollah Khomeini. In Iraq, meanwhile, Saddam Hussein Takriti came to power. He was a determined Arab nationalist, with ambitions to restore Iraqi influence in the Gulf.

Further causes for conflict lay in the fact that the oil-rich province of Khuzestan in southwest Iran contained a large Arab popu-

Below: Iranian tanks near Shiraz. These are US-made M60s. The Iraqis calculated that the Iranian break with the West after the revolution that brought the Ayatollah Khomeini to power would leave the Iranian Army in a vulnerable state. Bottom: Jubilant Iraqi troops celebrate an early victory.

lation to which Iraq could claim to give some protection; in addition, the Ayatollah Khomeini's militant brand of religious fundamentalism was soon being used to stir up trouble within Iraq. The Islamic world is divided between Shi'ites and Sunn'ites, a split dating back to the very earliest days of the Islamic religion, and based on who should succeed the Prophet. The practical nature of this split had always been that Shi'ites believe religious leaders can play a far greater part in political affairs than do Sunn'ites. Most Islamic countries are ruled by Sunn'ites, but have substantial Shi'ite minorities. Iran, however, is mainly Shi'ite, and the Ayatollah was the incarnation of Shi'ite belief. Iraq was ruled by Sunn'ites, but over half the population were Shi'ite.

Iraq tried to stir up trouble among the Arabs of Khuzestan; Iran tried to create problems among the Shi'ites of Iraq. And a final twist to this explosive mixture was that Hussein and Khomeini personally detested each other; they had been enemies ever since Khomeini had spent 14 years' exile in Iraq. During the summer of 1980, tension increased. There were artillery exchanges, and attacks on border villages. Finally, on 12 September, Iraqi troops pushed across the border under an artillery barrage.

Hussein was hoping to catch Iran, in turmoil after the revolution, in a condition in which it could not resist a lightning incursion; he hoped to unseat the Ayatollah and establish the primacy of Iraq in both the Gulf and the Arab world. The Iraqi Army had been equipped by the Russians; it consisted of some 2500 T-54, T-62 and T-72 tanks, and probably 1000 field guns, while the air force had over 300 combat aircraft, most of which were MiG-21s and MiG-23s. The navy consisted of a few Soviet-supplied patrol boats. In normal times, this would not have been considered a match for the Iranian armed forces, for with almost 900 British Chieftain and 800 US M48 and M60 tanks, over 600 helicopters and an air force that had been provided with 188 F-4 Phantoms, 77 F-14 Tomcats and 166 F-5 Tigers, the Iranian forces were far higher in quality. Since the revolution, however, the new regime had cut off relations with the West, and especially with the USA, many of whose embassy personnel were held hostage from November 1979 to January 1981. The range of relatively sophisticated Iranian equipment was, therefore, lacking in spare parts and inadequately maintained.

Hussein's hope was that his attack would catch Iran unable to mobilize her resources. Indeed, his three divisions (about 40,000 men, – only a quarter of the Iraqi Army) made rapid headway. The main attacks were along the south of the border, into Khuzestan, while more limited incursions were made in

Right: The Ayatollah Khomeini, whose brand of Islamic fundamentalism proved popular in Iran after the fall of the Shah. Khomeini had spent years in exile before returning to his homeland to impose a theocratic regime that claimed to go back to the basic tenets of the Islamic faith.

the central sector, near Qasr-e-Shirin, and in the north, near Mahabad. The Iraqis rapidly reached Khorramshahr and isolated this important centre, while Abadan came under siege. Further north, Ahvaz and Dezful were bombarded, and the town of Susangerd was cut off. When the rains came in November, the Iraqis settled down to consolidate their gains.

The Iraqi calculations had gone awry, however. Rather than prompting a spontaneous revolt against the Ayatollah, the invasion united the country against the invaders, and although the Iraqis had been able to defeat those Iranian forces that had tried to engage them in open battle, the fighting for

Below: Despite the success of the initial Iraqi attacks, the Iranians hung on to force a stalemate, and then gradually to gain the upper hand.

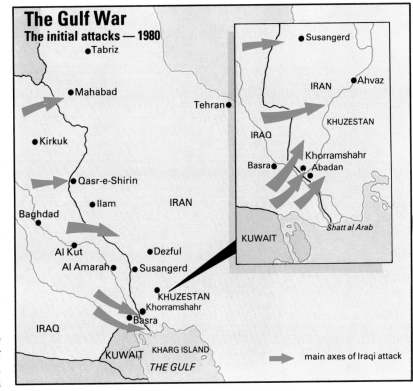

The Gulf War
The initial attacks — 1980

main axes of Iraqi attack

urban areas was different. In Khorramshahr especially, groups of Iranian Revolutionary Guards put up a bitter, last-ditch resistance that the Iraqis found difficult to deal with. Having crossed the border and suffered considerable losses, the Iraqis were unsure of what to do next. Their options were somewhat limited, for the difficulty in taking built-up areas meant that a drive on the capital, Tehran, was hardly possible, while the lack of any Iranian support for their adventure gave them few paths to explore in destabilizing the Iranian government.

1981 passed as a stalemate, with neither side making any effective gains. The Iranians managed to lift the siege of Abadan, and repulsed an Iraqi attack in the Qasr-e-Shirin sector, but Khorramshahr still remained in Iraqi hands. After initial air raids (including some on Baghdad and Tehran), there had been little activity by the air forces of either side, nor had there been any naval engagements of note. By 1982, both sides were

Above: Mortars in action near Kermanshah in Iran. Both Iran and Iraq had many modern weapons systems that they were able to deploy, but the largest battles of the war have tended to rely on the more traditional armaments – massed artillery and mortar barrages, for example. Left: Iraqi infantry deploy near the front line, armed with Soviet assault rifles and rocket-launcher. Right: Iranian troops on parade in Tehran, showing their devotion to the Ayatollah.

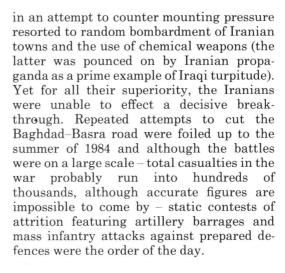

looking around for support. Jordan was enthusiastic in its help to Saddam Hussein, sending the 'Yarmuk' Brigade to fight alongside the Iraqis, while Iran received aid from Iraq's foes – including, paradoxically, both Israel and Libya. In March 1982 the Iranians felt strong enough to launch an offensive in the Dezful sector, and then into Khuzestan. On both fronts the Iraqis were driven back, with Khorramshahr being recaptured in September. Finally, in November the Iranians attacked again in the Dezful sector, this time moving into Iraqi territory and claiming to be within artillery range of the strategically vital Baghdad–Basra road. This success was once more followed by stalemate, however, and each side again began looking for new sources of arms.

The Iranians, with greater human and financial resources, were gradually asserting superiority during 1983 and 1984. The Iraqi government began to look for ways of ending the war with honour, but could find none, and

Above: The oil refineries at Abadan in Iran blaze fiercely after bombardment by the Iraqis.

in an attempt to counter mounting pressure resorted to random bombardment of Iranian towns and the use of chemical weapons (the latter was pounced on by Iranian propaganda as a prime example of Iraqi turpitude). Yet for all their superiority, the Iranians were unable to effect a decisive breakthrough. Repeated attempts to cut the Baghdad–Basra road were foiled up to the summer of 1984 and although the battles were on a large scale – total casualties in the war probably run into hundreds of thousands, although accurate figures are impossible to come by – static contests of attrition featuring artillery barrages and mass infantry attacks against prepared defences were the order of the day.

SECOND-CLASS STALEMATE

In some ways, the deadlock is very puzzling. Both sides possess the weapons that made the Arab-Israeli Wars such short, sharp conflicts; both are directed by leaders who have made clear their desire to bring down the governing system of the enemy; and the terrain over which much of the fighting has taken place is, in spite of the winter rains, perfectly adequate for mobile armoured warfare.

The problem seems to be that neither side is sufficiently adept at using the advanced weapons at its disposal and that the troops themselves lack the tactical acumen and expertise that would enable them to make decisive progress. Neither side, for example, has been able to use its well-equipped air force in an effective close-support role. The Iraqis showed a lamentable lack of energy when confronted with the task of assaulting the towns of Abadan and Khorramshahr, while the Iranian attempt to cut the Baghdad–Basra road in November 1982 was notable for the failure of the Iranian troops to exploit their initial breakthrough.

From the point of view of the West, the most important development has been the Iraqi attacks on shipping using the Iranian oil terminal on Kharg Island at the head of the Gulf. The Iranians have retaliated by attacking shipping on the Arab side of the Gulf, and their aircraft are reported to have entered Saudi Arabian air space on several occasions. The deployment of air-to-surface missiles (such as the Exocet) by the Iraqis has made these attacks on shipping very effective; and the possibility of other powers taking a hand cannot be ruled out.

By the summer of 1984 it seemed clear that the Iraqis were willing to accept a peace settlement on the basis of the prewar boundaries; but the Iranians were not disposed to agree to these terms. So the stalemate on the front line dragged on.

WAR IN THE FALKLANDS

From 2 April to 14 June 1982, Great Britain and Argentina were in armed dispute over the Falklands, a small and rather uninviting set of islands in the South Atlantic. Britain had long been in occupation of the islands, and the inhabitants, some 1800 people, were of British stock. The Argentinians had long claimed the territory as their own (under the name of the 'Malvinas') since Argentinian independence in the early 19th century, mainly on the grounds that Argentina was the nearest mainland – albeit some 770km (480 miles) away. Talks about the ultimate future of the islands and their inhabitants had been going on since the mid-1960s, but with little success. The Argentinians wanted recognition of their sovereignty, while the islanders were determined to stay under the British flag. The diplomatic exchanges had often been bitter, and in 1978 the British Labour government had felt compelled to send naval units to the area to guard against the possible use of force.

In 1982, the rulers of Argentina, a military junta headed by General Leopoldo Galtieri, decided that action must be taken. The junta may well have thought it could divert attention from the fact that the Argentinian economy was spiralling downwards, and could undercut the increasing public unrest over the brutal repression of left-wing groups from the late 1970s. The junta may also have felt that the British government (by now a Conservative administration led by Prime Minister Margaret Thatcher) was itself in trouble, with economic problems and defence cuts imminent, and would not seriously consider sending a fleet to the dangerous waters of the South Atlantic, some 12,900km (8000 miles) from the United Kingdom.

At 0430 hours on 2 April, therefore, the Argentinians sent in a force of about 2500 troops, who landed close to the Falklands capital, Port Stanley, and swiftly overpowered the garrison of 79 Royal Marines. By 0925 hours, the Governor of the Falklands, Mr (later Sir) Rex Hunt, had formally surrendered. Despite Argentinian hopes, however, the British government was certainly not disposed to accept this *fait accompli*. Rather as the Japanese attack on Pearl Harbor had galvanized the American people into action in 1941, so the occupation of the Falklands was followed by an intense wave of nationalism in Britain. The British government took measures to isolate Argentina internationally. She managed to persuade many of her partners in the EEC and NATO to sever trade links with the invading

power and to stop arms shipments. All this would have been of limited use, however, had not some kind of military action been initiated. On 5 April, two aircraft carriers, HMS *Hermes* and HMS *Invincible*, left Portsmouth as the core of a Task Force under Rear-Admiral J. F. ('Sandy') Woodward, to begin the long voyage south.

What followed the dispatch of the Task Force was the perfect example of a modern local war between two states. The fighting was almost all confined to the immediate area under dispute, or to the sea and air space surrounding it; each side wished to keep the fighting to as small a scale as possible, and was certainly unwilling to put its industry on a war footing. The war had to be fought with the weapons available (or ones that could be purchased quickly). Yet these weapons were of enormous destructive power, and were very expensive. The great concentrations of weaponry that had taken place during World War II had no parallel in this war. Given the small scale of the conflict and the sophisticated technology being used, the expertise of the forces on each side naturally became of paramount importance. Here, the tactical ability of British troops, and the bravery of Argentinian pilots, were proved beyond doubt in combat.

It was clear to all that the first battle would be to assert naval supremacy. The Royal Navy was clearly superior to the Argentinian fleet, although the Argentinians would have the benefit of support from shore-based aircraft (from the South American mainland itself; the airstrip at Port Stanley could not take modern fighters which did not have a vertical or short take-off capability). But the British put together a formidable array of warships, including two aircraft carriers, 11

Above: The Argentinian invasion of the Falklands met with rapid success. Here, British Marines are led away by an Argentinian soldier. Below: General Leopoldo Galtieri, the head of the ruling military junta in Argentina that decided on the invasion. Above right: The British aircraft carrier HMS Hermes en route for the Falklands. Below right: The sinking of the Argentinian cruiser General Belgrano, an incident that has since caused very great controversy.

destroyers, 16 frigates, two amphibious assault ships, and probably six submarines. The Argentinians had 17 major combat vessels, including an ageing aircraft carrier, two British-built destroyers, three French-built frigates, and the old cruiser, the *General Belgrano*.

THE TASK FORCE ARRIVES

On 7 April, the British government proclaimed a maritime exclusion zone around the Falklands, (to come into effect on 12 April), and on 30 April this was extended to include air space as well as the sea. Any ships or planes found in this area would be considered hostile. By mid-April, the Task Force had arrived in the South Atlantic, and on the 25th took the first of its objectives, the island of South Georgia, another British dependency 1300km (800 miles) to the southeast of the Falklands, that had also been invaded and taken over by the Argentinians. The next move was unquestionably for the British to land troops on the Falkland Islands themselves.

Woodward faced very difficult problems as he waited in the seas of the South Atlantic. Logistics were obviously very stretched. The first bombing raid on Port Stanley airstrip, for example, was by a Vulcan bomber that flew all the way from Ascension Island, the nearest British base, on 1 May. This involved an 11,300km (7000-mile) round trip, in which seven refuelling operations were necessary. Any munitions or supplies for the Task Force would take a great deal of time if sent by sea, and cost huge sums if sent by air. And Woodward's force was not only in difficulties over logistics. Its basic air cover was provided by the 40 Harrier jump-jets carried by

the two aircraft carriers between them. These were superb machines, but the Argentinian Air Force deployed nine Canberra bombers, 82 US A-4 Skyhawks, 47 French Mirages, and 10 French Super-Etendards. If the air war developed into a battle of attrition, the British would come off worse. It was fortunate that the seas off the Falklands were at the extreme operational range of the Argentinian aircraft, and, therefore, the air battles were brief, and fought at speeds at which the Harrier, normally far slower than the Mirage, was capable of beating its opponents.

There were two weapons that might have turned the war in favour of the Argentinians. The first was their aircraft carrier, the *Veinticinco de Mayo*, which carried 14 Skyhawks. If this had managed to escape the attention of the British screen of submarines observing

Above: Rear-Admiral J.F. Woodward, who commanded the British Task Force that won back the Falkland Islands.

'BOMB ALLEY'

Brian Hanrahan, a BBC journalist with the Falklands Task Force, describes being under attack by Argentinian planes in San Carlos Bay in May 1982.

'It was extraordinarily remote. The whole thing happens with such desperate speed. It's hard to believe that you're in the danger that you are in. When the planes come over the hillside they flash at enormous speed through the anchorage, which is a couple of miles long, they're going, it would seem, at something in the region of 400mph [640km/h], and dropping their bombs and firing their cannons as they go. The air fills with a kaleidoscope of different colours, as everybody in sight fires back at them. The noise is terrific. If you see the planes you're lucky. Normally they're through and gone and what you see are the trails of the missiles chasing after them. What seems to have happened is a foreshortening effect. Because of the missiles, because of the speed of the aircraft, everything happens in intensively short bursts, at very low level, because to go in and do it any other way would be sheer suicide for the pilots. So what happens is that you get these very intense bursts interspersed with enormously long periods in which nothing happens. But you know something might happen at any moment.'

the Argentinian coast, then one strike from the Skyhawks might have done sufficient damage to send the British home. It was probably this fear of Argentinian vessels escaping observation that led to the British decision, on 2 May, to sink the *General Belgrano*. The *Belgrano* had been easing its way round towards the south of the exclusion zone, and had just turned back into ostensibly safe waters outside the zone when it was torpedoed by the British submarine *Conqueror*. The *Belgrano* went down with the loss of 368 lives. The precise reasons for the sinking have never been given (and have since been the subject of some heated parliamentary debate), but it seems likely that it was intended as a warning that the infinitely more dangerous *Veinticinco de Mayo* would be considered fair game, whether it was encountered inside or outside the exclusion zone.

The second weapon that the Argentinians had was the Exocet missile. This could be launched either from the Super-Etendard planes, or from the British-built destroyers

Left: Men of the 2nd Battalion, The Parachute Regiment, snatch a quick meal in sheep pens at Fitzroy. Conditions were grim for the British land forces, and it took considerable expertise and sheer physical grit to maintain the advance against the Argentinian forces in Port Stanley.

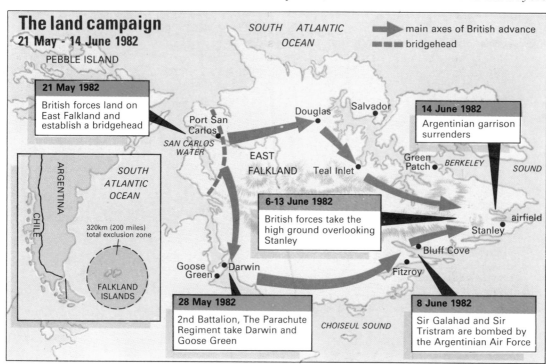

The land campaign
21 May - 14 June 1982

PEBBLE ISLAND

SOUTH ATLANTIC OCEAN

➡ main axes of British advance
▬▬▬ bridgehead

21 May 1982
British forces land on East Falkland and establish a bridgehead

Port San Carlos
SAN CARLOS WATER

Douglas   Salvador

14 June 1982
Argentinian garrison surrenders

EAST FALKLAND   Teal Inlet

Green Patch   BERKELEY SOUND

ARGENTINA
CHILE
SOUTH ATLANTIC OCEAN

320km (200 miles) total exclusion zone

FALKLAND ISLANDS

6-13 June 1982
British forces take the high ground overlooking Stanley

Stanley   airfield

Bluff Cove

Goose Green   Darwin   Fitzroy

28 May 1982
2nd Battalion, The Parachute Regiment take Darwin and Goose Green

CHOISEUL SOUND

8 June 1982
Sir Galahad and Sir Tristram are bombed by the Argentinian Air Force

and French-built frigates that the Argentinian Navy possessed. With a range of about 32km (20 miles), the Exocet possessed a deadly radar system that locked it on to its target when it got to within 9km (6 miles) of its prey. On 4 May, two Exocets were fired at the Task Force, and one seriously damaged the destroyer HMS *Sheffield*, killing 20 of her crew. The vessel had to be abandoned. The destruction of the *Belgrano* and the *Sheffield* had escalated the war, and made the conclusion of the campaign urgent for the British. The longer the Task Force had to wait, the more chance there was of it being crippled by air attack.

LANDING AT SAN CARLOS

On 12 May British reinforcements put to sea, in the form of the 5th Infantry Brigade, on board the requisitioned liner *Queen Elizabeth II*. And finally, on 21 May, the 3rd Commando Brigade landed on East Falkland, near San Carlos in the west of the island, after the way had been prepared by a raid on Pebble Island, in which some of the small close-support aircraft, Pucarás, that the Argentinians had brought in were destroyed. Landing on the west coast, whereas Port Stanley is on the east, surprised the Argentinian commander, General Mario Menéndez. He had concentrated his forces near the capital, partly because he was unsure of their fighting ability (many were conscripts) and partly because he expected a more direct attack.

Although a bridgehead was rapidly established, the Task Force now faced the most difficult period of the campaign, for many naval vessels were hemmed in to a small defined area (San Carlos Water), and the Argentinian Air Force could intensify its attacks. Two frigates, a destroyer and a supply vessel were lost to air attack in the first four days, and although the Argentinians were suffering crippling heavy losses in aircraft and pilots, they were making things very difficult for the Royal Navy. This was very much a battle between two forces with excellent equipment, and only relative

Above: Royal Marines land at San Carlos. Above left: An Argentinian unit prepares to report on British movements.

Below: The end of the frigate HMS Antelope, *hit in San Carlos Water. The vessels of the Task Force were far more vulnerable during the period of the landings on East Falkland, because the Argentinian air force had a definite location against which to launch its attacks.*

strengths and weaknesses. Destruction of expensive weapons and delivery systems was increasing.

The results of the air attacks directly affected the capability of the troops that had been landed, because of the severe logistics problems that the British faced. The loss of the container ship *Atlantic Conveyor* on 25 May was particularly serious, for when hit she was carrying four Chinook helicopters, capable of transporting 80 men each, that had been essential to any overland advance to Port Stanley from the bridgehead (one survived because it was airborne at the time of the attack). Other stores lost included tents for 4000 men and mobile landing strips that would have enabled the Harriers to operate from shore.

Notwithstanding the loss of the stores on the *Atlantic Conveyor,* the British forces began their drive to defeat the Argentinian land forces on 27 May, when the 2nd Battalion, The Parachute Regiment, moved out of the bridgehead and, on the following day, attacked the Argentinian garrison at Darwin and Goose Green to the south. British intelligence as to the strength of the enemy forces at Goose Green had been faulty – rather than facing an enemy roughly equal in numbers, the paras found they were taking on a vastly superior force: the 450 British troops were faced by 1600 Argentinians.

In spite of these odds, the British troops won the day at Goose Green, in a bloody fight, often at close quarters, during which the battalion commander, Lieutenant-Colonel Herbert ('H') Jones was killed. The man who replaced him, Major Christopher Keeble, later described the action as 'gutter fighting'. 'You have got to kill the enemy, you have got to destroy that machine-gun before he destroys you. When you fire an anti-tank rocket into a trench a lot of people die. If you have four people in a trench and a grenade

comes in, four people die. Every trench you attack, you destroy it. You jump in the trench and rake it with fire and if you see an Argie it's either him or you.'

The day after the victory at Goose Green, the 5th Infantry Brigade arrived at San Carlos with Major-General Jeremy Moore, who took over command of all the ground forces. While they were preparing for action, forward positions were being taken further to the east at Douglas and Teal Inlet and, on the south coast of East Falkland, Fitzroy and Bluff Cove. It was decided to ship the Guards of 5th Infantry Brigade to these footholds on the south coast which could then act as the base for the assault on Port Stanley, as it was quite clear that General Menéndez was going to remain in the capital. He was not going to

The single worst episode of the war for the British forces was the bombing of the Sir Galahad *on 8 June 1982, when landing troops of the 5th Infantry Brigade near Fitzroy. Fifty men died in this one incident. Below left:* Sir Galahad *on fire after the Argentinian air strike. Above: The survivors of the attack come ashore.*

come out and offer an open battle. While the troops of 5th Infantry Brigade were being landed at Fitzroy the single worst British loss of life during the war occurred, when the landing ship *Sir Galahad*, containing men of the Welsh Guards, was bombed by Argentinian planes. Fifty men died.

THE ASSAULT ON STANLEY

Nevertheless, the bulk of 5th Infantry Brigade had landed safely, and preparations began for the final assault. Mount Kent, which actually overlooked Stanley, had already fallen into British hands, but there were other well-garrisoned hills and ridges between the British and the Falklands capital. After discussion, it was agreed that the attack should be on a broad front, and in two waves. On the night of 11 12 June the first set of attacks went in, against Mount Longdon, Mount Harriet and Two Sisters. There were some unpleasant surprises for the British notably the effectiveness of Argentinian 'passive night goggles' which gave their snipers a valuable aid in darkness. But in savage fighting (the 3rd Battalion, The Parachute Regiment fought with fixed bayonets on Mount Longdon) and with effective artillery support, particularly from naval vessels offshore, the hills were eventually cleared.

The second wave of attacks went in on the night of 13–14 June. The first of this new series of assaults was directed at positions on the northern approaches to Stanley: Wireless Ridge (taken by paratroops) and Tumbledown Mountain (for which the Scots Guards had a tough fight). When these objectives had been taken, Argentinian resistance began to evaporate. Further south in the morning of 14 June Mount William and Sapper Hill fell without much of a fight (which the Gurkhas attacking Mount William may have found

somewhat disappointing). Under intense bombardment and having lost the advantage of the high ground, the Argentinians were clearly beaten but it took some time to organize the surrender, which was finally signed at 2100 hours that evening. The islands were now back in British hands.

The Falklands campaign had demonstrated that in spite of the excellence of modern weaponry, the expertise and bravery of individual soldiers was still crucial to the outcome of land warfare; and it had also shown how terribly vulnerable modern weapons systems could be to missiles such as the Exocet. Although it had been a very localized war, casualties were not light. The Argentinians lost over 1000 dead, and the British suffered 225 killed and 777 wounded.

Above: Argentinian troops near Port Stanley. One feature of the Falklands War was the fact that the two sides had certain weapons in common. The soldiers here, for example, have Belgian FN rifles, very similar to the standard British infantry weapon. Below: British troops enter Port Stanley. The campaign had demonstrated the enduring value of technical expertise and physical fitness in modern warfare.

Conclusion

After the shocking slaughter of World War I, there was a widespread revulsion at the idea of warfare, and the 1920s and 1930s saw pacifist movements achieve prominence in many European nations. This was not at all the case after World War II, however. The only important similar manifestations in Europe since 1945 have been those anti-nuclear groups that in the 1980s have found a new lease of life. In Great Britain these are now most commonly associated with the attempt to reduce or abolish the nuclear arsenal that is at present housed in this country – and in particular to remove the recently deployed 'cruise missiles' – a movement of which the women protesters at Greenham Common are the most obvious example.

Yet neither the CND movement in Britain nor the anti-nuclear groups in Europe are pacifist as such; rather, they are concerned to limit the destructive power of certain weapons. In the same way, the mass protests and the 'anti-war' movement in the USA during the US involvement in the Vietnam War were directed against US policy rather than the idea of war in itself. Many of the protesters would have found the decision of the North Vietnamese and the Viet Cong to take up arms for their political aims quite acceptable.

The ideal of progress and political change through non-violence, of which Gandhi was perhaps the most important symbol, has become outmoded and devalued in the modern world. Military success is accepted as the basic currency of political power, and armies have become the arbiters of the destinies of many, if not most, of the world's nations. War is not seen, as it was in the aftermath of the Great War, as a merely destructive force, which has no potential for positive decision; on the contrary, it is now seen as the way by which nations achieve statehood, as the way by which political systems can impose themselves, as the way to achieve lasting results.

Going to war to right a wrong, or to redress injustice, is increasingly considered quite justifiable. In the United Kingdom, for example, the opportunist invasion of Egypt during the Suez crisis of 1956 was widely condemned, but the political world was comparatively united over the British decision to retake the Falkland Islands when Argentinian forces annexed them in 1982.

War is, in fact, one of the most important factors, if not the key factor, in understanding the shaping of the contemporary world. And given the range of modern warfare, the level of technological innovation and the complex moral and political issues involved, it is hardly surprising that it should be a topic of abiding interest.

The importance of the study of modern warfare, however, lies neither in its intrinsic interest nor in the historical insights it offers. The very survival of the human race depends upon the careful management of the weapons of mass destruction that are in the hands of a few states, and which are likely to fall into the hands of many more by the end of the century. The possibility of future wars, the course that these wars might take, and how to limit their extent, are crucial questions for the future of humanity.

In assessing possible future scenarios for war, there are two main levels for concern. One is whether local, limited disputes (such as in Indochina, the Middle East or the Falkland Islands, for example) can draw in the superpowers, and provoke a global confrontation; the second is the nature of such a superpower clash – would it inevitably destroy civilization (and probably human life) on the planet, or could it be kept within limits?

SUPERPOWER SENSITIVITIES

So far as any possible conflict between the superpowers is concerned, it must be hoped, first of all, that neither the Soviet Union nor the USA tries to meddle too destructively in the 'backyard' of its fellow great power – that eastern Europe and Latin America (especially Central America) are viewed mutually as areas of vital concern. Although the inhabitants of both regions may well desire

Below: Anti-nuclear demonstrators in Britain in March 1973. This resurgence of the protest movement which originally grew up in the 1950s came about as a result of NATO's plans to deploy land-launched cruise and Pershing missiles in response to the USSR's deployment of SS-20s in Eastern Europe.

some fundamental change from the repressive and often brutal regimes under which they live and suffer at present, it is hard to see how such fundamental change can come about without the consent of the dominant superpower.

More disturbing from the point of view of world peace could be the situation in southern Africa, a region whose mineral wealth would be of benefit to the communist bloc, and much of whose population suffers under a racially discriminatory regime that the communist world is prepared to take the lead in opposing. Should the regime in South Africa ever seem in danger of collapse from Moscow-backed black guerrillas, then the situation could become serious for the rest of the world.

Another area where the line-up of opposing forces has the potential for upsetting world peace and where there is an inherent instability is northeast Asia, where three very different powers – the Soviet Union, China and Japan – encircle the divided Korean peninsula. Sino-Soviet hostility has been an accepted fact of international relations since the late 1960s, while the dynamics of economic change in China and the possible rearmament of Japan could have grave consequences.

Naturally enough, small conflicts between powers in any part of the globe are always capable of expanding. The activities of such ambitious despots as Colonel Gaddafi of Libya, for example, who threatens to destabilize large areas of northern Africa, and whose ambitions for Libya to become a nuclear power are quite obvious, can never be disregarded.

Far more important than any local conflicts, however, is the situation in the Middle East, where there are many interested parties in a fundamentally unstable region. The West has vital interests in a part of the world that provides so much of its oil; at the same time, the influential Jewish lobby in the USA maintains a fierce support for Israel. The Soviet Union, on the other hand, actually borders on many of the states of the Middle East and is concerned lest the religious fundamentalism that has recently assumed such importance infects her own large Islamic population. The two superpowers have found themselves, not altogether willingly, drawn closer and closer into the centre of the stage in the region, while their respective allies and clients have become enmeshed in increasingly complex and dangerous conflicts. Since the beginning of the Gulf War and the Israeli intervention in the Lebanon, the situation has become even more kaleidoscopic and unpredictable. Any hopes that the Camp David Accords of 1978 between Israel and Egypt would result in a less dangerous atmosphere have been dashed. Israel is more secure than she was in the 1960s, but the Middle East poses more of a threat to world peace now than it perhaps has ever done.

It is possible to point to some regions where tension has decreased over the past few years. In central Europe, for example, where NATO and Warsaw Pact forces face each other, and where the Cold War had its origins, the likelihood of a sudden attack by either side, unless motivated by events elsewhere, or, in the case of the Soviet Union, by severe difficulties within the Warsaw Pact, now seems remote. In southeast Asia, once a focus of world concern, the internecine conflicts within and between the communist powers have discredited the 'Domino theory' (which held that communism, germ-like, would quickly spread to neighbouring states), and the stability of Malaysia, for example, has hardly been threatened in the last two decades.

Identifying potential areas of conflict is one thing; predicting the shape of future wars is quite another. It can confidently be asserted however, that the long-running guerrilla wars that afflict so many of the states of the Third World will continue, and others will develop. In limited wars, too, such as in the Falklands or between Israel and her Arab neighbours, traditional military virtues and the weaponry that has dominated the battlefield since 1939 have been seen to be of continuing importance. But the big question concerns the use of nuclear weapons. No doubt both the USA and the Soviet Union have careful contingency plans for their use; but once they become operational, then we are in a new situation, of which no one has any experience – and, it is sincerely to be hoped, which no one will ever have to face.

Index